Quicken® 2011

THE OFFICIAL GUIDE

Quicken® 2011

THE OFFICIAL GUIDE

Bobbi SANDBERG

New York Chicago San Francisco
Lisbon London Madrid Mexico City Milan
New Delhi San Juan Seoul Singapore Sydney Toronto

The McGraw·Hill Companies

Cataloging-in-Publication Data is on file with the Library of Congress

McGraw-Hill books are available at special quantity discounts to use as premiums and sales promotions, or for use in corporate training programs. To contact a representative, please e-mail us at bulksales@mcgraw-hill.com.

Quicken® 2011 The Official Guide

1 2 3 4 5 6 7 8 9 0   QFR QFR   1 0 9 8 7 6 5 4 3 2 1 0

ISBN   978-0-07-174868-1
MHID   0-07-174868-7

Sponsoring Editor
Megg Morin

Proofreader
Teresa Barensfeld

Editorial Supervisor
Patty Mon

Indexer
Judy Davis

Project Manager
Patricia Wallenburg

Production Supervisor
George Anderson

Acquisitions Coordinator
Joya Anthony

Composition
TypeWriting

Technical Editor
Mary Higgins

Art Director, Cover
Jeff Weeks

Copy Editor
Lisa McCoy

To my kids and their kids—thank you for being the light in my world.
And, always, to Sandy.

Contents at a Glance

Contents

Part One   Quicken Setup and Basics

Part Three   Investing

Part Four   Net Worth

Part Five   Planning

Part Six   Tax

Acknowledgments

This book, like most others, is the end product of a lot of hard work by many people. Among them are:

- Megg Morin, acquisitions editor at McGraw-Hill, for her encouragement and support, always!
- The folks at Intuit, including Eddy Wu and Dale Knievel for their technical expertise, willingness to answer questions, and quick responses. Thanks also to Susan Oldham and Kristen Dillard.
- The editorial folks at McGraw-Hill, including Patty Mon, Patty Wallenburg, and Joya Anthony, three ladies whose expertise and superb craftsmanship make all editing tasks pleasant.
- The technical editor Mary Higgins, copyeditor Lisa McCoy, proofreader Teresa Barensfeld, and indexer Judy Davis for their wonderful skills!

Introduction

Choosing Quicken Personal Finance Software to organize your finances was a great decision. Quicken has all the tools you need to manage your personal finances. Its well-designed, intuitive interface makes it easy to use. And its online and automation features make entering transactions and paying bills a snap. But if that isn't enough, Quicken also offers features that can help you learn more about financial opportunities that can save you time and money—two things that often seem in short supply.

This introduction tells you a little about the book, so you know what to expect in the chapters to come.

About This Book

This book tells you how to get the most out of Quicken. It starts by explaining the basics—the common, everyday tasks that you need to know just to use the program. It then goes beyond the basics to show you how to use Quicken to save time, save money, and make smart financial decisions. Along the way, it shows you most of Quicken's features, including many that you probably didn't even know existed. You'll find yourself using Quicken far more than you ever dreamed you would.

Assumptions

This book makes a few assumptions about your knowledge of your computer, Windows, Quicken, and financial management. These assumptions give you a starting point, making it possible to skip over the things that are assumed you already know.

What You Should Know About Your Computer and Windows

To use this book (or Quicken 2011, for that matter), you should have a general understanding of how to use your computer and Windows. You don't need to be an expert. As you'll see, Quicken uses many standard and intuitive interface elements, making it easy to use—even if you're a complete computer novice.

At a bare minimum, you should know how to turn your computer on and off and how to use your mouse. You should also know how to perform basic Windows tasks, such as starting and exiting programs, using menus and dialog boxes (called just *dialogs* in this book), and entering and editing text.

If you're not sure how to do these things or would like to brush up on them, get *Windows 7 QuickSteps* from McGraw-Hill. This resource will provide all the information you need to get started.

What You Should Know About Quicken and Financial Management

You don't need to know much about either Quicken or financial management to get the most out of this book; it assumes that both are new to you.

This doesn't mean that this book is just for raw beginners. It provides plenty of useful information for seasoned Quicken users—especially those of you who have used previous versions of Quicken—and for people who have been managing their finances with other tools, such as Microsoft Money (welcome to Quicken!) or pencil and paper (welcome!).

Because the book assumes that all this is new to you, it makes a special effort to explain Quicken procedures as well as the financial concepts and terms on which they depend. New concepts and terms first appear in italic type. By understanding these things, not only can you better understand how to use Quicken, but you also can communicate more effectively with finance professionals such as bankers, stockbrokers, and financial advisors.

Organization

This book is logically organized into seven parts, each with at least two chapters. Each part covers either general Quicken setup information or one of Quicken's financial centers. Within each part, the chapters start with the most basic concepts and procedures, most of which involve specific Quicken tasks, and then work their way up to more advanced topics, many of which are based on finance-related concepts that Quicken makes easy to master.

It is not necessary to read this book from beginning to end. Skip around as desired. Although the book is organized for cover-to-cover reading, not all of its information may apply to you. For example, if you're not the least bit interested in investing, skip the chapters in the Investing Center part. It's as simple as that. When you're ready for the information that you skipped, it'll be waiting for you.

Here's a brief summary of the book's organization and contents.

Part One: Quicken Setup and Basics

This part of the book introduces Quicken's interface and features, and helps you set up Quicken for managing your finances. It also provides the information you need to test Quicken's online features. If you're new to Quicken, the first three chapters in this part of the book may prove helpful.

Part One has three chapters:

- **Chapter 1:** Getting to Know Quicken
- **Chapter 2:** Working with Accounts, Categories, and Tags
- **Chapter 3:** Going Online with Quicken

Part Two: Banking

This part of the book explains how to use Quicken to record financial transactions in bank and credit card accounts. One chapter concentrates on the basics, while another goes beyond the basics to discuss online features available within Quicken. This part of the book also explains how to automate many transaction entry tasks, reconcile accounts, and use Quicken's extensive reporting features.

There are five chapters in Part Two:

- **Chapter 4:** Recording Bank and Credit Card Transactions
- **Chapter 5:** Using Online Banking Features
- **Chapter 6:** Automating Transactions and Tasks
- **Chapter 7:** Reconciling Your Accounts
- **Chapter 8:** Examining Your Banking Activity

Part Three: Investing

This part of the book explains how you can use Quicken and Quicken.com to keep track of your investment portfolio and get information to help you make smart investment decisions. The first chapter covers the basics of Quicken's investment tracking features, while the other two chapters provide information about online investment tracking and research tools. You'll see how the features available at Quicken.com can help you evaluate your investment position.

There are three chapters in Part Three:

- **Chapter 9:** Entering Your Investment Transactions
- **Chapter 10:** Using Transaction Download and Research Tools
- **Chapter 11:** Evaluating Your Position

Part Four: Net Worth

This part of the book concentrates on assets and liabilities, including your home and car and related loans. It explains how you can track these items in Quicken and provides tips for minimizing related expenses.

There are two chapters in Part Four:

- **Chapter 12:** Monitoring Assets and Loans
- **Chapter 13:** Keeping Tabs on Your Net Worth

Part Five: Planning

This part of the book tells you how you can take advantage of Quicken's built-in planning tools to plan for your retirement and other major events in your life. As you'll learn in this part of the book, whether you want financial security in your retirement years or to save up for the down payment on a house or college education for your children, Quicken can help you. It includes information on using Quicken's financial calculators and provides a wealth of tips for saving money and reducing debt.

There are three chapters in Part Five:

- **Chapter 14:** Planning for the Future
- **Chapter 15:** Using Financial Calculators
- **Chapter 16:** Reducing Debt and Saving Money

Part Six: Tax

This part of the book explains how you can use Quicken's Tax features to simplify tax preparation, plan for tax time, and reduce your tax liability.

Part Six has two chapters:

- **Chapter 17:** Simplifying Tax Preparation
- **Chapter 18:** Planning for Tax Time

Part Seven: Appendixes

And, to help you even more, three appendixes offer additional information you might find useful when working with Quicken:

- **Appendix A:** Managing Quicken Files
- **Appendix B:** Customizing Quicken
- **Appendix C:** Converting from Microsoft Money

Conventions

All how-to books—especially computer books—have certain conventions for communicating information. Here's a brief summary of the conventions used throughout this book.

Menu Commands

Quicken, like most other Windows programs, makes commands accessible on the menu bar at the top of the application window. Throughout this book, you are told which menu commands to choose to open a window or dialog, or to complete a task. The following format is used to indicate menu commands: Menu | Submenu (if applicable) | Command.

Keystrokes

Keystrokes are the keys you must press to complete a task. There are two kinds of keystrokes.

- **Keyboard shortcuts** are combinations of keys you press to complete a task more quickly. For example, the shortcut for "clicking" a Cancel button may be to press the ESC key. When instructing you to press a key, the name of the key is in small caps, like this: ESC. If you must press two or more keys simultaneously, they are separated with a hyphen, like this: CTRL-P. Many of Quicken's keyboard shortcuts are explained in Chapter 1.
- **Literal text** is text that you must type in exactly as it appears in the book. Although this book doesn't contain many instances of literal text, there are a few. Literal text to be typed is in boldface type, like this: **Checking Acct**. If literal text includes a variable—text you must substitute when you type—the variable is included in bold-italic type, like this: ***Payee Name***.

Icons

Icons are used to flag specific types of information.

Sidebars

This book also includes "New to Quicken?" and "Experienced Quicken User" sidebars. These sidebars are meant to put a specific Quicken feature into perspective by either telling you how it is used or offering suggestions on how you can use it. You'll learn a lot from these sidebars, but like all sidebars, they're not required reading.

About the Author

Bobbi Sandberg has long been involved with computers, accounting, and writing. She is a retired accountant currently filling her time as a trainer, technical writer, and small-business consultant. As a Quicken user and teacher since its inception, she knows the questions users ask and gives easy-to-understand explanations of each step within the program. She teaches at several venues, offering step-by-step instruction in a variety of computer applications. Her extensive background, coupled with her ability to explain complex concepts in plain language, has made her a popular instructor, consultant, and speaker. She has authored and co-authored more than a dozen computer books including *Quicken Quicksteps 2010*.

About the Technical Editor

Mary Higgins is a long-time Quicken user, having used each version since 1999. She enjoys pushing the limits of what the software is intended to do—clicking every button, navigating every menu path, reading the help files, etc. She reads and posts on the Quicken forums and finds it interesting to see how others are using Quicken and the different approaches to resolving issues.

Quicken Setup and Basics

This part of the book introduces Quicken Personal Finance Software's interface and features. It begins by explaining how to install Quicken and showing you the elements of its user interface. It offers an entire chapter with instructions for setting up Quicken for the first time. Then it tells you all about Quicken's accounts, categories, and tags. Finally, it explains why you should be interested in online account services and how you can set up Quicken to access the Internet and download information from your financial institutions. The chapters are:

Part One

Getting to Know Quicken

Chapter 1

In This Chapter:

- *An overview of Quicken*
- *Installing Quicken*
- *Starting Quicken*
- *The Quicken interface*
- *Onscreen Help*

If you're brand new to Quicken Personal Finance Software, get your relationship with Quicken off to a good start by properly installing it and learning a little more about how you can interact with it.

This chapter provides a brief overview of Quicken, explains how to install and start it, takes you on a tour of its interface, and shows you how to use its extensive Onscreen Help features. Although the information provided in this chapter is especially useful to new Quicken users, some of it also applies to users who are upgrading. If you are a former Microsoft Money user, see Appendix C for some Microsoft Money–specific comparisons and explanations.

What Is Quicken?

On the surface, Quicken is a computerized checkbook. It enables you to balance your accounts and organize, manage, and generate reports for your finances. But as you explore Quicken, you'll learn that it's much more. It's a complete personal finance software package—a tool for taking control of your finances. Quicken makes it easy to know what you have, how you are doing financially, and what you should do to strengthen your financial situation.

What Quicken Can Help You Do

At the least, Quicken can help you manage your bank and credit card accounts. You can enter transactions and have Quicken generate reports and graphs that show where your money went and how much is left.

Quicken can help you manage investment accounts. You can enter transactions and have Quicken tell you the market value of your investments. Quicken can also help you organize other data, such as the purchase price of your possessions and the outstanding balances on your loans.

With all financial information stored in Quicken's data file, you can generate net worth reports to see where you stand today. You can also use a variety of financial planners to make financial decisions for the future. And Quicken's tax features, including export into TurboTax and the Deduction Finder, can make tax time easier on you and your bank accounts.

Quicken's online features can automate much of your data entry. Online banking enables you to keep track of bank account transactions and balances, and to pay bills without writing checks or sticking on stamps. Online investing enables you to download investment transactions. You can also read news and information about investment opportunities and advice offered by financial experts.

Quicken Versions

Intuit offers several versions of Quicken 2011 for Windows for managing personal finances: Starter, Deluxe, Premier, Home & Business, and Quicken Rental Property Manager.

Quicken Starter is an entry-level product designed for people who are new to personal finance software. As its name suggests, it includes basic features to track bank accounts and credit cards. It also enables you to use online account services and payments, shop for insurance and mortgages, and download investment information for a brokerage account. This version is sometimes included in computers you purchase from the manufacturer. You can also import your files from previous versions of Quicken Starter edition, but not from other versions.

Quicken Deluxe is more robust. Designed for people who want to take a more active role in financial management, investments, and planning, it includes all the features in Quicken Starter plus the financial alerts feature, money-saving features for tax time and debt reduction, and free access to investment information.

Quicken Premier has all the features of Quicken Deluxe, plus additional features for investing and tax planning and preparation.

This book covers Quicken Premier. Although much of its information also applies to Quicken Starter and Deluxe, this book covers many features that are not included in the Starter version and a handful of features that are not included in the Deluxe version. If you're a Quicken Starter or Deluxe user, consider upgrading to Quicken Premier so you can take advantage of the powerful features it has to offer. One more thing—Intuit also offers two special versions of Quicken. If you're a small-business owner, Quicken Home & Business can handle all of your personal and basic business financial needs, including the business expenses you need to track for your tax return's Schedule C. If you manage one or more rental properties, Quicken Rental Property Manager can handle transactions and other information for tenants, rental income, and related expenses that you need to track for your tax return's Schedule E. As you can see, Intuit has you covered with a Quicken product, no matter what activities are part of your financial life.

System Requirements

Quicken 2011 is designed to work with Windows 7, both 32- and 64-bit machines. It also works with Windows Vista and Windows XP – SP2 and later. You'll need at least 1GB of random access memory (RAM) and a minimum of 450MB of free space on your hard drive. You'll need a monitor that has a resolution of 1024 × 768 or higher as well as a CD/DVD drive. Internet access is needed for online work as well as program updates. You'll also need a printer if you want to print reports and graphs.

Getting Started

Ready to get started? This section explains how to install, start, and register Quicken.

The instructions in this section assume you're installing Quicken on a computer running Windows 7. Although Quicken will run under Windows XP or Windows Vista, the pathnames mentioned in this section may be different if you are installing Quicken on a computer running an operating system other than Windows 7.

Installing Quicken

Quicken uses a standard Windows setup program that should be familiar to you if you've installed other Windows programs.

Insert the Quicken 2011 CD into your CD or DVD drive. A dialog should appear, asking if you want to install the program to your hard drive. If so, click Yes to start the Quicken installer.

If this dialog does not appear automatically, you can start the installer by double-clicking the Computer icon on your desktop and then double-clicking the icon for your optical drive in the window that appears.

The installer displays a series of dialogs with information and options for installing Quicken. Read the information in the Welcome

screen, and click Next to continue. When asked to agree to a software license agreement, select the I Agree To The Terms Of The License Agreement And Acknowledge Receipt Of The Quicken Privacy Statement option. (If you select the other option, you cannot click Next and cannot install the software.) You can click the Quicken Privacy Statement link to open this important document in a Web browser window and read it; close the browser window when you're finished to return to the installer. You may clear the anonymous usage message check box if you choose. This option allows Quicken to collect information about how you use the program so that Intuit can make the program even more user-friendly. Click Next in the Install Wizard window.

In the Destination Folder screen, the installer tells you where Quicken will be installed—normally C:\Program Files(x86)\Quicken. You can click the Change button and use the screen that appears to change the installation location. To keep the recommended, default location, just click Next.

In the Ready To Install The Program screen, the installer displays a summary of what it will do. If this is a first-time Quicken installation, all it will do is install Quicken 2011 and any updates to the program. But if you're upgrading from a previous version, the installer will begin by uninstalling whatever version is currently installed. (You can have only one version of Quicken installed on your computer at a time.) Only the Quicken program files will be deleted; your data files will remain intact so you can use them with Quicken 2011. Click Install.

For upgraders, the data file you most recently used in the previous year's version will be converted to the Quicken 2011 format. A copy of the previous year's version data file will be placed in a folder Q*xx*Files, where *xx* is the previous year's version.

Wait while the installer uninstalls the previous version of Quicken (if necessary), copies the Quicken 2011 files, and downloads any updates to your hard disk.

As part of the installation process, the installer uses your Internet connection to check for and download Quicken updates. This ensures that you have the most up-to-date version of Quicken installed. When the update is complete, the Installer displays an Installation Complete screen as seen here. Click Done.

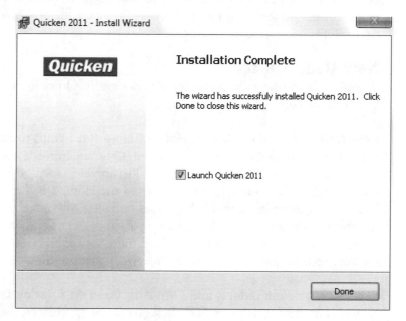

Quicken should start automatically. Skip ahead to the section titled "Preparing a Data File," later in this chapter, to start using Quicken. If Quicken does not start automatically, follow the instructions in the next section to start it.

Starting Quicken

You can start Quicken in several different ways. Here are the two most common methods.

Opening the Quicken Shortcut

The Quicken installer places a Quicken Premier 2011 shortcut icon on your Windows desktop, seen here. Double-clicking this shortcut opens Quicken Premier.

Opening Quicken from the Task Bar

You can also use the Start button on the Windows task bar to start Quicken and other Quicken components. Choose Start | All Programs | Quicken 2011 | Quicken 2011 to start Quicken.

Preparing a Data File

Quicken stores all of your financial information in a Quicken data file. Before you can use Quicken, you must either create a data file or convert an existing data file for use with Quicken 2011.

New User Startup

If you're a brand-new Quicken user, a Welcome To Quicken 2011 dialog appears. You have two options.

I Am A New User or I've Used Quicken Before But I Want to Start Over   When you select this option and click Get Started, Quicken creates a new data file called *yourname*'s Quicken Data in a Quicken folder in your Documents folder. It opens the file and displays the Main View screen of the Home tab. This screen includes information and buttons that help you set up your Quicken data file. If you're following along and would like to set up your data file now, skip ahead to Chapter 2 and follow the instructions there. Then, to learn more about how Quicken works, read the section titled "The Quicken Interface," later in this chapter.

I've Used Quicken Before, and I Want to Open an Existing Quicken File
When you select this option and click Get Started, Quicken displays the Select Your Data File dialog. Continue following instructions in the section titled "Existing User Startup," next.

I Want to Import My Data From Microsoft Money   Select this option if you want to convert and use the Money file saved on the computer you are using. Choose the first option if you want to start from scratch. For additional information about this option, see Appendix C.

Existing User Startup

If you upgraded from a previous version of Quicken, when you first start Quicken, the Select Your Existing Data File To Get Started window appears. It offers three options for getting started:

- **Open A File Located On This Computer** displays the Open Quicken File dialog, which you can use to select a file on your hard disk. After selecting and opening a file, continue following the instructions in the section titled "Converting a Data File as Part of an Upgrade."

- **Restore A Quicken Data File I've Backed Up To CD Or Disk** enables you to open a backup file for use with Quicken 2011. (This option works only with files you created using Quicken's Backup command, which is discussed in Appendix A.) When you select this option and click Next, Quicken displays the Restore From Backup File dialog so you can select the type of backup file, locate it on disk, and open it. Along the way, it prompts you for a location in which to save the file; normally this will be in the Quicken folder inside your Documents folder. If a dialog appears telling you that you have to convert the data file, continue following the instructions in the section titled "Converting a Data File as Part of an Upgrade." When restoration is complete, Quicken opens the data file.

- **Start Over And Create A New Data File** displays the Create Quicken File dialog, which you can use to enter a name for your new Quicken data file. It then opens the file and displays the Main View screen of the Home tab. This screen includes information and buttons that help you set up your Quicken data file. If you're following along and would like to set up your data file now, skip ahead to Chapter 2 and follow the instructions there.

Converting a Data File as Part of an Upgrade

The Convert Your Data File To Quicken 2011 dialog appears any time you indicate that you want to update an existing Quicken data file for use with Quicken 2011. Clicking the Convert File button converts the data file named in the dialog to the Quicken 2011 format and saves the original file in C:\Users*yourname*\Documents\Quicken\ Q*xx*Files. The path for the saved copy of the original file may vary depending on which previous version you are upgrading from.

Registering Quicken

Sooner or later Quicken's Product Registration dialog will appear. It tells you about the benefits of registering Quicken and displays two buttons:

- **Register Later** lets you put off the registration process. Use this option if you don't have the few minutes it takes to register or your computer is not connected to the Internet. Keep in mind, however, that certain Quicken features will not function until you register.

- **Register Now** begins the registration process. You'll need Internet access to complete this process.

To start the registration process, click the Register Now button. Then follow the instructions that appear on screen. When the registration process is complete, you can continue working with Quicken.

The Quicken Interface

Quicken's interface, which has been reworked for Quicken 2011, is designed to be intuitive and easy to use. If you are starting Quicken from scratch, after you have installed and registered your program, Quicken opens to the Quicken Home page as seen in Figure 1-1. This interface puts the information and tools you need to manage your finances right within mouse pointer reach. You never have to dig through multiple dialogs and menus to get to the commands you need most. You'll see how to get started using this Home page in Chapter 2.

Figure 1-1 • The Quicken Home page helps you get started quickly.

This section tells you about the components of the Quicken interface and explains how each feature can help you manage your financial life.

The Main Window

The main Quicken window gives you access to most of Quicken's features and your financial information, as seen in Figure 1-2.

Account Bar

The Account Bar lists each of your Quicken accounts on the left side of the main Quicken window (refer to Figure 1-2). In addition to the All Transactions register, there are three main sections to the Account Bar: Banking, Investing, and Property & Debt. If the Account Bar is not displayed (refer to Figure 1-2), you can display it by clicking the small arrow beside the Accounts button on the left end of the main window's tabs.

If you can't see all of the accounts in the Account Bar, you can use the scroll bar on the right side of the Account Bar to scroll through its contents. You can

Figure 1-2 • When you select an account in the Account Bar, Quicken displays the register for that account.

also click the downward or right-pointing arrow beside a section heading on the Account Bar to hide or display, respectively, the list of accounts beneath it.

By default, account balances appear in the panel; however, you can right-click the Account Bar to open a context menu. Choose Hide Amounts to hide amounts from view. (This also makes the Account Bar narrower so more information appears in the window beside it.) This contextual menu offers additional options for the display of the Account Bar, such as displaying cents in the amounts, as seen here. You can also change the width of the Account Bar by dragging its right border.

The account names in the Account Bar are links; click an account name to view its register. You can customize the Account Bar to move accounts from one section to another or to hide an account from the Account Bar totals; learn how in Chapter 2.

Go to Money Market
Edit account
Collapse all accounts
Expand all accounts
✓ Show amounts
Hide amounts
✓ Show cents in amounts
✓ Show Current Balance in bar
Show Ending Balance in bar
✓ Show Account Bar on left
Show Account Bar on right
Minimize Account Bar
Add new account
Add/remove accounts from bar
Rearrange accounts
Delete/hide accounts in Quicken

Tabs

Tabs occupy the main part of the Quicken program window. Some tabs, such as the Spending and Investing tabs, provide information about your financial status, as well as links and buttons for accessing Quicken features. Other tabs, such as the Home tab seen in Figure 1-3, enable you to view and customize Quicken settings for your financial situation. Use the Tabs to Show option from View in the Quicken menu to specify which tabs to display or hide from view. Chapter 2 explains how.

A tab exists for each major area of Quicken:

- **Home** displays customizable views of your Quicken data. Learn how to work with and customize the Home tab views in Chapter 8 and Appendix B.
- **Spending** provides information about your income and expenditures for all accounts or one of your choosing, for all dates, or for a custom date that you choose. You can use the drop-down lists to customize the information in both graphical and list formats. See Chapter 8 for more information about the Spending tab.

Figure 1-3 • The Main View in the Home tab helps you see what you have spent.

- **Bills** provides information about your upcoming bills and offers tools for working with bills and reminders. Chapter 6 discusses Bills tab options.
- **Planning** gives you access to Quicken's financial planners, as well as the assumptions you need to set up to use the planners effectively. Part Five

discusses Quicken's financial calculators and the Planning tab. In Quicken 2011, the Planning tab also includes tax-related options, such as projected taxes, a tax calendar, and your year-to-date income and tax-related expenses. Part Six covers Quicken's tax features.

- **Investing** provides information about your investment and retirement accounts and any stocks or mutual funds you've asked Quicken to watch for you. Part Three covers investing and the Investing tab.
- **Property & Debt** provides information about asset and debt accounts, including your home, car, related loans, and auto expenses. Part Four discusses the Property & Debt tab and its related features.
- **More From Quicken** displays information about additional Quicken services. Learn more about this tab in Chapter 2.

The button bar in each tab indicates the current view or other options within each tab section. If there's more than one button or a menu in either of these areas, you can click a button or choose a menu command to switch to another view or account.

Other Windows

Quicken uses other windows to display information, depending on what you want to see or what task you are trying to perform.

List Windows

A list window such as the one you see in Figure 1-4 shows a list of information about related things, such as accounts, categories, tags, or scheduled transactions. You can use a list window to perform tasks with items in the list.

Report Windows

Quicken's report windows (see Figure 1-5) enable you to create reports about your financial matters. You have the option to change date ranges, create comparisons, and customize reports. You can also use options and buttons at the top of the window to work with, customize, and save reports. Chapter 8 explains how to create and customize reports and graphs.

Features and Commands

Quicken offers a number of ways to access its features and commands, including standard Microsoft Windows elements, such as menus and dialogs, and Quicken elements, such as the Tool Bar, button bar, and links and buttons within Quicken windows.

Category	Hide	Type	Group	Tax Line Item	Action
Bonus	☐	Income	Persona...	W-2:Salary or wages, self	
Div Income	☐	Income	Persona...	Schedule B:Dividend income	
Gift Received	☐	Income	Persona...		
Income/Interest	☐	Income	Persona...		
Interest Inc	☐	Income	Persona...	Schedule B:Interest income	
Investment Inc...	☐	Income	Persona...		
Net Salary	☐	Income	Persona...		
Other Income	☐	Income	Persona...	Form 1040:Other income, misc.	
Child Support Rece...	☐	Income	Persona...		
Gifts Received	☐	Income	Persona...		
Loan Principal Rec...	☐	Income	Persona...		
Lotteries	☐	Income	Persona...	1099-MISC:Prizes and awards	
State & Local Tax ...	☐	Income	Persona...	1099-G:State and local tax refunds	
Unemployment Co...	☐	Income	Persona...	1099-G:Unemployment compensation	
Retirement Income	☐	Income	Persona...		
IRA Distributions	☐	Income	Persona...	1099-R:Total IRA taxable distrib.	
Pensions & Annuities	☐	Income	Persona...	1099-R:Total pension taxable dist.	

Figure 1-4 • The Category List window displays a list of categories you can use to identify your transactions.

Menus

Quicken displays six menus in a menu bar when you choose to display the recommended Standard menus as shown here. If you choose Classic menus, you have an additional seven from which to choose, as shown here. You can choose commands from the menus as follows:

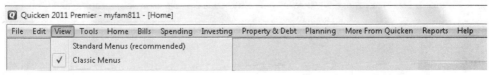

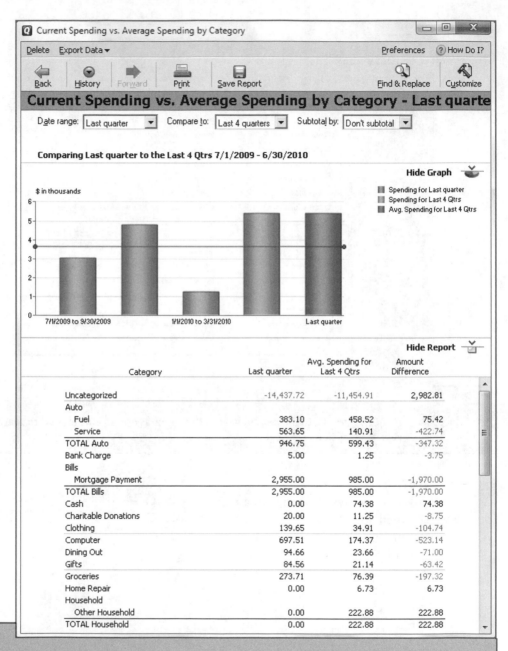

Figure 1-5 • The report window may include both a report and a graph.

EXPERIENCED QUICKEN USERS

Keyboard Shortcuts

In answer to a number of requests, Quicken 2011 now defaults to the standard Windows keyboard shortcuts instead of the Quicken shortcuts. For example:

Quicken 2011		Earlier Quicken Versions	
CTRL-C	Copy a transaction	CTRL-C	Opens Category List
CTRL-V	Paste a copied or cut transaction	CTRL-V	Voids a transaction
CTRL-X	Cut a transaction	CTRL-X	Goes to a transfer
SHIFT-CTRL-C	Category List		
SHIFT-CTRL-H	Loan Details	CTRL-H	Opens Loan Details

Table 1-1 • Quicken 2011 Keyboard Shortcuts

You'll also notice a few other changes in this version. For example:

- Inactive tabs are on a black background while the currently selected tab is highlighted.
- The Spending tab replaces the Banking tab. This tab displays all spending or all income transactions for a date range you choose.
- Quicken offers an All Transactions register on the Account Bar to display transactions from all of your accounts for a chosen date range.
- A new Category List that reflects more of "real life." See more information about categories in Chapter 2.

You can still opt to use the Quicken shortcuts in Preferences. See "Quicken Keyboard Shortcuts" later in this chapter for more shortcuts.

- Click the menu name to display the menu. If necessary, click the name of the submenu you want, and then click the name of the command you want.
- Press the shortcut key combination for the menu command that you want. A command's shortcut key, if it has one, is displayed to the right of the command name on the menu.
- If your Windows program is set up to have keyboard access keys underlined, you can press ALT to activate the menu bar and press the keyboard key for the underlined letter in the menu that you want to open. If necessary, press the key for the underlined letter in the submenu that you want to open, and then press the key for the underlined letter in the command that you want.

Shortcut Menus

Shortcut menus (which are sometimes referred to as context or context-sensitive menus) can be displayed throughout Quicken. Point to the item for which you want to display a shortcut menu and click the right mouse button. The menu, which includes only those commands applicable to the item, appears at the mouse pointer.

Quicken Keyboard Shortcuts

Quicken lets you access many of its features directly from the keyboard with one or a combination of keys. Table 1-2 lists some of these shortcuts, which are also mentioned throughout the book.

Dialogs

Like other Windows applications, Quicken uses dialogs to communicate with you. Some dialogs display a simple message, while others include text boxes, option buttons, check boxes, and drop-down lists you can use to enter information, similar to the one shown here. Many dialogs also include a Help button that you can use to get additional information about options. The Help button is often a small question mark inside a yellow circle. Note the button on the illustration here.

Tool Bar

The Tool Bar is a row of buttons along the top of the application window, just beneath the standard menu bar, shown next, that gives you access to other navigation techniques and features. The Quicken Tool Bar does not appear by default, but can be turned on and customized. Learn how to customize it in Appendix B. Here's a quick look at the default Quicken Tool Bar.

Quicken Keyboard Commands	Result
CTRL-A	Opens Account List
CTRL-B	Opens Quicken Backup dialog
CTRL-F	Opens Quicken Find dialog
CTRL-G	Opens Go To Date dialog
CTRL-H	Opens Find And Replace dialog
CTRL-J	Opens Bill And Income Reminders dialog
CTRL-K	Opens the Quicken Calendar
CTRL-L	Opens the Tag List
CTRL-M	Opens the Memorized dialog (from within a register transaction)
CTRL-N	Opens the Customize View dialog (from the Home tab)
CTRL-O	Opens the Open Quicken File dialog
CTRL-P	Opens the Print dialog
CTRL-S	Opens the Split dialog
CTRL-T	Opens the Memorized Payee dialog
CTRL-U	Opens the Investing tab
CTRL-W	Opens the Write Checks dialog
CTRL-Y	Opens the Security List
CTRL-SHIFT-A	Opens Account Attachments dialog
CTRL-SHIFT-C	Opens Category List
CTRL-SHIFT-E	Opens Account Details dialog (from the Account Bar)
CTRL-SHIFT-H	Opens View Loans dialog
CTRL-SHIFT-O	Opens Account Overview window (from account in the Account Bar)
CTRL-SHIFT-P	Opens Print Screen
ALT-SHIFT-F	Opens File menu
F1	Opens Quicken Help
F11	Displays a full-size screen

Table 1-2 • Quicken Keyboard Shortcuts

- **Back** (an arrow pointing left) displays the previously opened window.
- **Forward** (an arrow pointing right) displays the window you were looking at before you clicked the Back button. This button is only available if you clicked the Back button to view a previously viewed window.
- **One Step Update** opens the One Step Update menu, so with your Internet connection you can update all of your online information at once. Clicking the triangle that's part of this button displays a menu of commands related to the One Step Update feature, including Update Settings, Manage My Passwords, Update Summary, and Schedule Updates. Chapter 6 discusses One Step Update.
- **Search** is a global search feature you can use to search for transactions entered into Quicken. Just enter the search criteria in the field and press ENTER.

Button Bar

The button bar is a row of textual buttons and menus that appears just above the contents of many Quicken windows (refer to Figure 1-2). Most items on the button bar, which vary from window to window, are buttons; simply click one to access its options. The items with triangles beside their names are menus that work just like the menu bar menus.

Keep in mind that Quicken's Onscreen Help may refer to the button bar as the Tool Bar. Throughout this book it is called the button bar to differentiate between it and the Quicken Tool Bar.

Onscreen Help

In addition to the How Do I? menu in the button bar of many Quicken windows and the Help button in dialogs, Quicken includes an extensive Onscreen Help system to provide more information about using Quicken while you work. You can access most Help options from the Help menu, which is shown here.

Here's a brief summary of some of the components of Quicken's Onscreen Help system.

Quicken Help

Quicken's Onscreen Help uses a familiar Windows Help interface. You can use it to browse or search Help topics or display Help information about a specific window.

Getting Started Guide

The Getting Started Guide link and your Internet connection take you to the Quicken website where you can download a .pdf file that gives you information on getting started with your Quicken program.

Browsing or Searching Help

Start by choosing Help | Quicken Help or pressing the F1 key. A Quicken Help window appears. The left side of the window has two tabs for browsing Help topics:

- **Contents** (see Figure 1-6) lists Help topics. Clicking a topic link displays information and links for accessing additional information in the right side of the window.
- **Search Quicken Help** enables you to search for information about a topic. Enter a search word in the top of the tab, and then click the Ask button. Click the title of a topic in the search results list to display information about it in the right side of the window.

NEW TO QUICKEN?

Onscreen Help

These days, any decent software program offers on-screen help. So what's the big deal about Quicken's?

Quicken's Onscreen Help is especially ... well, helpful. It covers every program feature and provides step-by-step instructions for performing many tasks. Clickable links make it easy to jump right to a topic you want to learn more about. And as you'll discover while using Quicken, Help is available throughout the program—not just in the Quicken Help windows.

Onscreen Help also gives you, a Quicken user, the opportunity to help make Quicken a better software program. At the bottom of most Help windows, you'll find Yes and No buttons that you can use to tell Intuit whether the Help topic gave you the information you needed. Click the appropriate button as you use Onscreen Help to help the folks at Intuit make Onscreen Help more useful to you.

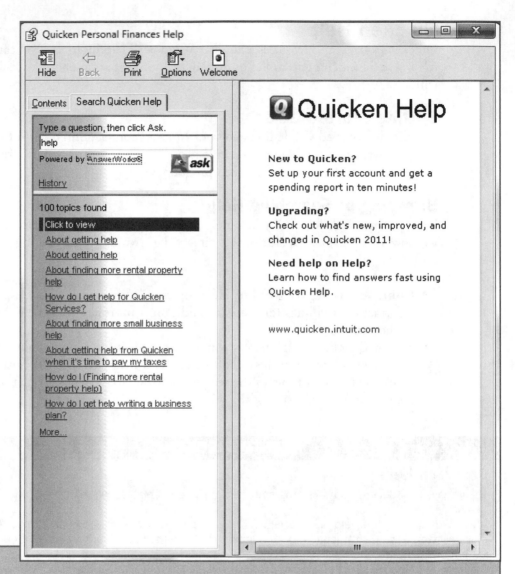

Figure 1-6 • The Contents tab of Quicken Help makes it easy to browse through Onscreen Help for specific information.

Quicken Live Community

The Quicken Live Community command takes you to Quicken's online user-to-user forum, where you can ask questions, get answers, and share information with other Quicken users. Click links or use the search feature to get the information you need to make the most of Quicken.

Quicken Support

Click Quicken Support on the Help menu to open the Quicken support site on the Internet. Here you can look through frequently asked questions as well as find links to other Quicken resources.

Submit Feedback on Quicken

This link opens a Quicken feedback page on the Internet. While you may think that your idea or concern is not "important," it is to Quicken. It is partly through this feedback that Intuit designs its products.

Join the Quicken Inner Circle

The Quicken Inner Circle is more than just a user feedback site. Intuit has created a collaborative community, one that works directly with product managers and others on the Quicken team.

Privacy Statement

Intuit takes the job of protecting your information very seriously. The policies and procedures taken by the company to protect all of your information is displayed in this message. The statement explains what information is collected by Quicken, how that information is used, and how you can find out more about Intuit's specific methods to ensure your information is safe at all times.

Log Files

This link contains other links to several files created in the "background" by Quicken. Should you ever need to contact Quicken Support, the helpful Quicken support person may ask you to refer to these files for troubleshooting. As shown here, there are several types of log files.

About Quicken

This tells you which version of Quicken you are using, as shown below. Along with the Privacy Statement menu option, this gives copyright information and credit to the many

people who have made the program possible. The Privacy Statement tells about Quicken's policies that ensure your privacy. Additional technical information about your Quicken file and system resources can be displayed by holding down CTRL and clicking Help | About Quicken, as seen on the top of the next page. This can be useful when troubleshooting or working with Quicken Support.

Upgrading Quicken

If you're wondering whether the version of Quicken installed on your computer is the best one for you, be sure to check out Help | Add Business Tools or Help | Add Rental Property Tools. With your Internet connection, these commands display a window that provides more information about features in Quicken Home & Business or Quicken Rental Properties. From this website, you can purchase either the Home & Business or Rental Property versions of Quicken.

If you have already purchased an unlock code for Quicken, choose Help | Unlock Again to enter it into Quicken and upgrade immediately.

Exiting Quicken

When you're finished using Quicken, choose File | Exit. This closes the Quicken application. You can also click the red X on the title bar to close the program.

Sometimes when you exit Quicken, you'll be asked whether you want to back up your Quicken data file. Learn how to back up data files in Appendix A.

Working with Accounts, Categories, and Tags

Chapter 2

In This Chapter:

- *Overview of data files and accounts*
- *Overview of setting up accounts*
- *Setting up your first accounts*
- *Working with the Account List window*
- *Setting up categories and subcategories*
- *Working with the Category List window*
- *Setting up tags*
- *Working with the Tag List window*

To use Quicken Personal Finance Software, you must set up your Quicken data file for your financial situation. This means creating accounts and entering starting balance information.

When you first set up your Quicken Personal Finance Software data file, it includes a number of default categories. Don't think you're stuck with just those categories. You can add and remove categories at any time. The same goes for accounts—you can add them as you see fit. Modifying the accounts and categories in your Quicken data file is a great way to customize Quicken to meet your needs.

In this chapter, you'll learn how to modify and work with the Quicken accounts and categories you'll use to organize your finances. This chapter also explains how to set up and use an optional categorization feature: tags.

Quicken opens to the Home tab's Main View, as seen in Figure 2-1, where you begin by entering your bank accounts.

Before You Begin

Before you start the setup process, it's a good idea to understand how data files and accounts work. You should also gather together a few documents to help you set up your accounts properly.

Figure 2-1 • Quicken's setup makes getting started easy and efficient.

Data Files

All of the transactions you record with Quicken are stored in a *data file* on your hard disk. This file includes all the information that makes up your Quicken accounting system.

Although it's possible to have more than one Quicken data file, it isn't usually necessary. One file can hold all of your transactions. In fact, it's difficult (if not downright impossible) to use more than one Quicken file to track a single account, such as a checking or credit card account. And splitting your financial records among multiple data files makes it impossible to generate reports that consolidate all of the information.

When would you want more than one data file? Well, you could use two data files if you wanted to use Quicken to organize your personal finances and the finances of your business which has entirely separate bank, credit, and asset accounts, or if you're using Quicken to track the separate finances of multiple individuals.

Appendix A covers a number of data file management tasks, including creating additional data files and backing up your data files.

Accounts

An *account* is a record of what you either own or owe. For example, your checking account is a record of cash on deposit in the bank that is available for writing checks. A credit card account is a record of money you owe to the credit card company or bank for the purchases on your credit card. All transactions either increase or decrease the balance in one or more accounts.

You create accounts within Quicken so you can track the activity and balances in your bank, credit card, investment, and other accounts.

What You Need

To set up accounts properly, you should have balance information for the accounts that you want to monitor with Quicken. You can get this information from your most recent bank, investment, and credit card statements. It's a good idea to gather these documents before you start the setup process so they're on hand when you need them. If you have online banking available with your financial institutions, make sure you include your passwords and PINs.

If you plan to use Quicken to replace an existing accounting system—whether it's paper-based or prepared with a different computer program—you may also find it helpful to have a *chart of accounts* (a list of account names) or recent financial statements. This way, when you set up Quicken accounts, you can use familiar names.

Accounts

To track your finances with Quicken, you must have created at least one account. While many of your expenditures may come from your checking account, you probably have more than one account that Quicken can track for you. By setting up all of your accounts in Quicken, you can keep track of balances and activity to get a complete picture of your financial situation.

This part of the chapter tells you a little more about Quicken's accounts and how you can use the Account List window to create and modify your accounts.

Types of Accounts

As discussed earlier, an *account* is a record of what you either own or owe. Quicken offers various kinds of accounts for different purposes. A link for each account you set up in Quicken appears in the Account Bar. You can choose to hide accounts from the Account Bar, as discussed later in this chapter. Table 2-1 summarizes the accounts and how they are organized within Quicken.

What You Own

In accounting jargon, what you own are *assets*. In Quicken, an asset is one type of account; several other types exist as well.

Account Type	Account Bar Section	Asset or Liability
Checking	Banking	Asset
Savings	Banking	Asset
Credit Card	Banking	Liability
Cash	Banking	Asset
Standard Brokerage	Investing	Asset
IRA or Keogh Plan	Investing	Asset
401(k) or 403(b)	Investing	Asset
529 Plan	Investing	Asset
House	Property & Debt	Asset
Vehicle	Property & Debt	Asset
Asset	Property & Debt	Asset
Debt	Property & Debt	Liability

Table 2-1 • Overview of Quicken Account Types

Spending   Spending accounts, which are displayed in the Banking section of the Account Bar, are used primarily for expenditures. Quicken distinguishes between two types of spending accounts: checking and cash.

Savings   Savings accounts, which are also displayed in the Banking section of the Account Bar, are used to record the transactions in savings accounts.

Investment   Investment accounts, displayed in the Account Bar's Investing section, are for tracking the stocks, bonds, and mutual funds in your portfolio that are not in retirement accounts. Quicken distinguishes among two types of investment accounts: Standard Brokerage (which may be used for one or more mutual funds) and 529 Plan.

Retirement   Retirement accounts, which are included in the Investing section, are for tracking investments in retirement accounts. Quicken distinguishes between two types of retirement accounts. One type includes individual retirement accounts (IRA) or Keogh Plans, and the other combines 401(k) or 403(b) accounts. Retirement accounts should fall into one of these two broad categories.

Asset   Asset accounts, which are displayed in the Property & Debt section of the Account Bar, are used for tracking items that you own. Quicken distinguishes among three different types of asset accounts: House, Vehicle, and Other Asset.

What You Owe

The accounting term for what you owe, or your debts, is *liabilities*. Quicken offers two kinds of accounts for amounts you owe.

Credit   Credit, which is displayed in the Banking section, is for tracking credit card transactions and balances.

Liability or Debt   Debt (Liabilities), which is displayed in the Property & Debt section, is for tracking loans and other liabilities.

Setting Up Quicken

After you have installed Quicken, its opening window offers easy access to features you can use to configure your Quicken data file. This Home tab's Main View includes several areas. This part of the chapter provides a tour of each area and explains how you can use it to set up a Quicken data file.

Use the "See Where Your Money Goes" Section

To begin using Quicken, you must tell the program what bank and credit cards you wish to track. Click the Get Started button to begin. If you are connected to the Internet, a message box appears indicating that Quicken is updating the latest list of financial institutions available, as shown here. As Quicken often adds new financial institutions to their services, this update occurs regularly.

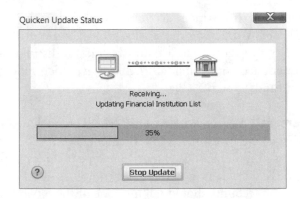

After the update is complete, the Add Your Primary Checking Account dialog box appears, as seen in Figure 2-2. Choose the name of your bank from the list displayed or type its name in the Enter The Name Of Your Bank field. See the section "Using Advanced Setup" later in this chapter if you want to set up your account manually or your financial institution offers more than one type of download services.

Click Next to continue. In the dialog that appears, as seen in Figure 2-3, you are prompted to enter your user name and password as provided by your bank. Should you want to save this password in the Quicken Password Vault, click Save This Password. See Chapter 6 for more information about the Password Vault.

You may be prompted for a branch, bank, or account type, depending on your institution. Click Connect to go online and download the information about your account. (If there are additional passwords or security phrases required by your bank, you are prompted to enter them. Do so and click OK.)

If you have more than one account that uses the user ID and password you entered, all of the accounts may be downloaded. Also, depending on the type of connection offered by your institution, Quicken may display a screen where you can change the account name as you add it. See "Using Advanced Setup" later in this chapter for more information on this method.

After the download is complete, your account (or accounts if you have more than one at that bank) is shown, as seen on the bottom of the next page. Click Finish to return to the Home tab's Main View. See "Setting Up Other Banking Accounts" next to add accounts.

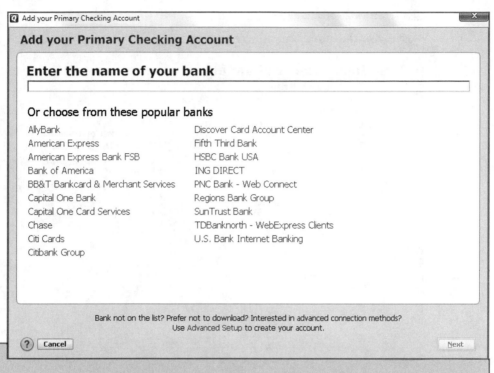

Figure 2-2 • Simply click or type to enter the name of your bank to set up your checking
account in Quicken.

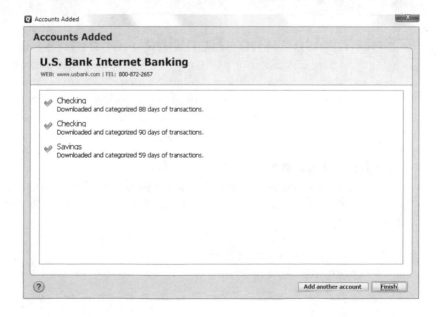

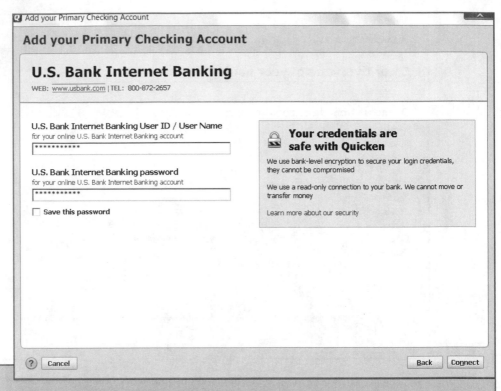

Figure 2-3 • **Use the ID and password provided by your financial institution to add your primary checking account.**

Setting Up Other Banking Accounts

After you have created your primary checking account, you can create additional new accounts with the Add An Account dialog. No matter what type of account you create, Quicken steps you through the creation process, prompting you to enter information about the account, such as its name and balance. In this section, you'll learn how to use the Add Account dialog to set up new accounts.

Adding New Accounts

Quicken calls its default method of adding accounts "Simple Setup." Begin by opening the Add Account dialog. There are several ways to do this; here are some of them:

- Click Add An Account from the bottom of the Account Bar, as seen here.

+ Add an Account

- Choose Tools | Add Account to display the Add Account dialog.
- Click CTRL-A to open the Account List. Click the Add An Account button at the bottom right of the Account List. Of course, you can also open the Account List by choosing Tools | Account List.
- Right-click anywhere in the Account Bar and choose Add New Account from the context menu.
- Select the Property & Debt tab, and choose the Account Overview subtab. Click Options | Add An Account in the

> **EXPERIENCED QUICKEN USERS**
>
> ### Changes in Adding New Accounts
>
> You should be comfortable adding new accounts in Quicken 2011, as most of the buttons are in the same location as in earlier versions of Quicken. However, adding new accounts has become more efficient and less confusing. The Add Account dialog calls your spending accounts the Primary Accounts and displays them in a separate section. The "Net Worth" accounts—that is, the Asset and Debt account types—are displayed below the Primary Accounts. You can still choose to add an account from the Account List in addition to using the Add An Account button at the bottom of the Account bar.
>
> To eliminate redundancy, the only tab from which you can enter a new account in Quicken 2011 is the Property & Debt tab.
>
> As in earlier versions, the account name with which you are working appears on the title bar as well as above the account's register.

Property and Debt Accounts section, or click Add A New Loan in the Loan Summary section.

As seen in Figure 2-4, the Add Account dialog begins by asking what type of account you want to create. From there, its options change, depending on the account type and whether you want to set it up for online account services, if available.

Using Advanced Setup

As mentioned earlier, the Advanced Setup option is used when you prefer to enter transactions manually, your institution does not offer download services, or you do not want to connect to the Internet at the time you are setting up the account. To use Advanced Setup:

1. Open the Add Account dialog as described in "Adding New Accounts" earlier in this chapter.
2. Choose the type of account you are entering (as seen in Figure 2-4), and click Next.

Add Account

Primary Accounts (for managing your finances)

Spending
- ☉ Checking
- ○ Savings
- ○ Credit Card
- ○ Cash

Investing
- ○ Brokerage
- ○ IRA or Keogh Plan
- ○ 401(k) or 403(b)
- ○ 529 Plan

Property & Debt (for net worth tracking)

Property
- ○ House
- ○ Vehicle
- ○ Other asset

Debt
- ○ Loan
- ○ Other liability (not a credit card)

(?) Cancel   Next

Figure 2-4 • Quicken 2011 makes adding your accounts an easy process.

3. From the Add (*type of account*) dialog, click Advanced Setup at the bottom of the dialog, as shown next.

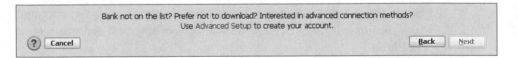

4. The Add (*type of account*) dialog appears, as seen in Figure 2-5. Choose either:
   a. **I Want To Select The Connection Method Used To Download My Transactions**   This option is used when your bank has several methods of online services and requires you to choose the method, or you just want to tell Quicken how to download your information. You may be prompted to choose the type of service, enter your user ID and password, and answer additional questions, depending on your bank.
   b. **I Want To Enter My Transactions Manually**   Use this option if your bank is not found by Quicken, you cannot connect to the Internet, or prefer to enter your information manually.

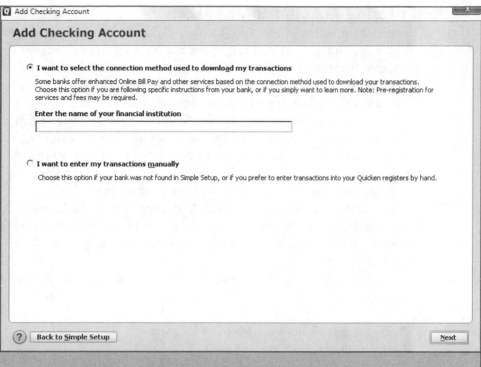

Figure 2-5 • Advanced Setup offers you choices when setting up your new accounts.

5. In both instances, you are prompted for an account name or nickname, and if setting up manually, a statement ending date and balance before you see the Account Added message, as shown here. Consider giving each account a name that uniquely identifies the account, such as Sam's Checking or Royce's Savings.

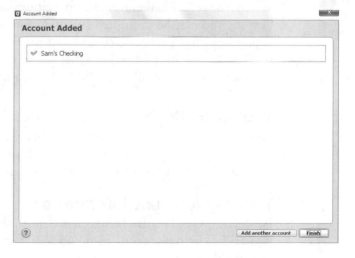

Entering Account Information

Follow the prompts in the Add Account dialogs to enter required information for the account you are creating. Click the Next button to progress from one dialog to the next. You can click Back at any time to go back and change information. You know you're finished when the Next button is replaced with a Done or a Finish button; click it to save the account information.

Account information includes the financial institution in which the account is held (if applicable), the account name, an optional description, the account balance, and the date of the account balance. Almost every type of Quicken account requires this information. If you don't know the balance of an account, you may set it to $0.00 and make adjustments later, either when you get a statement or when you reconcile the account. If the account can be accessed online by Quicken, Quicken automatically downloads the account balance information, as well as recent transactions, as part of the account creation process.

You can find details for creating specific types of accounts throughout this book:

- Banking accounts are covered in Chapter 4.
- Investing accounts are covered in Chapter 9.
- Property & Debt accounts are covered in Chapter 12.

Finishing Up

When you've finished entering information for a new account, click the Done button. You may be prompted to enter more information about the account, depending on the type of account and the financial institution you selected for it. The detailed instructions in Chapters 4, 9, and 12 for creating specific account types review all of the additional information you may have to enter.

Working with the Account List Window

You can view a list of all of your accounts at any time. Choose Tools | Account List or press CTRL-A. The Account List window appears (see Figure 2-6). This window displays a list of all accounts organized by type of account.

Viewing Account Information

By default, Quicken displays each account in the Account List window (refer to Figure 2-6) by the account name (grouped by account type), transaction download settings, and the current balance. If you have told Quicken to hide any of your accounts, you see an additional "Hidden" column. You can add

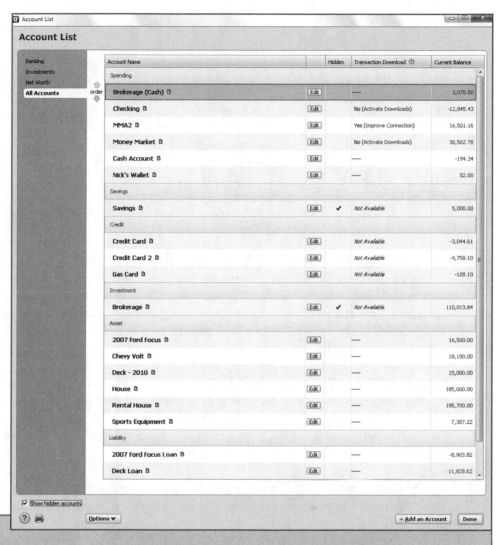

Figure 2-6 • The Account List displays information about all of your accounts.

columns of information to the list by choosing commands from the bottom of
the Options pop-up menu in the Account List window, shown on the next page.
Just select a command on the menu to toggle the display of some information
on or off. This makes it possible to fully customize the appearance of the list and
the information shown. See "Using Account List Options" later in this chapter
for more information.

Working with Accounts in the Account List

Select an account on the Account List, and press Edit to open the Account Details dialog seen in Figure 2-7. From this dialog you can enter additional account information, tell Quicken how to display the account, and modify the account's online services. Move between the tabs by clicking the tab with which you want to work.

General Tab   The General tab displays basic information about the account that you can view or edit, as shown in Figure 2-7. From this dialog you can enter information such as the interest rate you receive on this account, the account number, and create a link to the bank's home page. There are a number of options, of which only the account name is required.

- **Description**   This field is for additional information about this account.
- **Account Type**   This field cannot be changed. It is the type of account you established when you first created the account.
- **Tax Deferred**   Click Yes to tell Quicken this is a tax-deferred account; click No if it is not.
- **Interest Rate**   Enter the rate of interest, if any, for this account.
- **Set Up Alerts**   You can tell Quicken to alert you if this account reaches a maximum or minimum balance. See Chapter 8 for more information about setting alerts in Quicken.
- **Financial**   Enter the name of your bank or credit union in this field.
- **Account Number**   Type the account number issued by the bank for this account if the information has not been downloaded from your bank.
- **Contact Name**   Enter the name of the person with whom you normally work at your bank in this field.

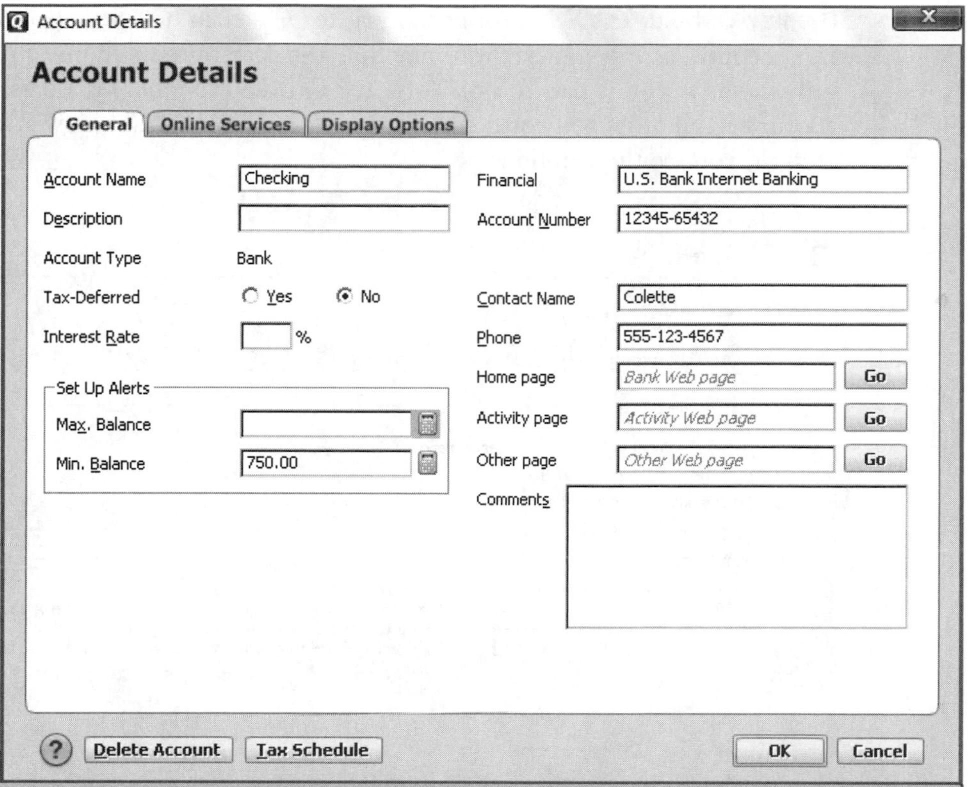

Figure 2-7 • Use the Account Details dialog to set account attributes.

- **Phone** Enter the local branch's phone number here so you won't have to look it up each time you call the bank.
- **Home/Activity/Other Page** Use these fields to enter the website(s) for your bank. Use the Go button to connect to these websites using your Internet connection.
- **Comments** Use this field for any additional information about this account.

Online Services Tab This tab allows you to modify the settings in each account for your institution's online services. If your bank offers One Step Update or Online Bill Pay, you can set those options here. See Chapter 5 for more information about the online services offered by many financial institutions.

Display Options Tab   From this tab you tell Quicken how you want to display this account, as shown next. You may hide the account entirely in Quicken or only in the Account Bar. You may also tell Quicken to ignore the balance of this account in all of its net worth computations. In the Hide Or Show Accounts section, you see these options:

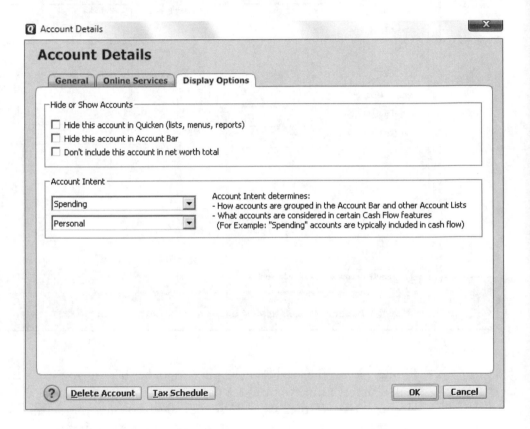

- **Hide This Account In Quicken**   This check box, when turned on, prevents the account from being displayed in lists, menus, and reports. This disables the two check boxes beneath it and removes the account from view in any list in which it would appear, except the Account List window. You may want to use this feature to remove accounts you no longer use or need to see—without removing the transactions they contain. Keep in mind that you cannot use a hidden account in a transaction; to do so, you must first unhide the account by turning off this check box for it. Just a side note: To truly hide an account in Quicken, select the Hide This Account In Quicken check box, and make sure the Show Hidden Accounts check box at the bottom-left corner of this Account List window is not selected.

You can use a hidden account in a transaction; you just have to type out the full name enclosed in square brackets, for example, a transfer to [Hidden].

- **Hide This Account In Account Bar**   To remove an account from the Account Bar, turn on this check box. Although the account remains visible in other lists and menus where it would normally appear, it no longer appears in the Account Bar. You may want to use this feature to keep the Account Bar short by excluding accounts you seldom access.
- **Don't Include This Account In Net Worth Total**   To exclude an account's balance from subtotal and total calculations, as well as the net worth displayed in the Account Bar, turn on this check box. This displays the balance for the account in gray in the Account Bar and omits the balance from any totals calculated in Quicken.

The Account Intent section lets you tell Quicken how you plan on using this account. For example, you might have a savings account that you actually are using as an additional retirement account. (However, you might want to check with your financial advisor to see if this is a wise use of your money.)

To let Quicken know how you intend this account to be used, choose a value from the drop-down list.

On the bottom of the Account Details dialog are several other option buttons.

Delete Account   The Delete Account button enables you to delete the account. It displays a dialog you can use to confirm that you want to delete the account. You must type yes into the dialog and click OK to delete the account, as shown here. If you have scheduled bills or deposits for this account, they must be removed before you can delete it.

Remember that when you delete an account, you permanently remove all of its transactions from your Quicken data file. To get the account out of sight without actually deleting it and its data, consider hiding it instead, as described earlier.

Tax Schedule Information   If the account has income tax implications, is tax exempt, or tax deferred, click the Tax Schedule button to use the Tax Schedule Information dialog shown here. As always, if you have any questions about the tax status of an account, check with your tax professional.

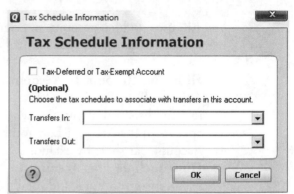

Once you have made all of the modifications to this account, click OK to close the Account Detail dialog and return to the Account List.

Working with Accounts

You can use options in the Account List window to reorganize accounts so they appear where you want them to in the Account Bar.

Changing the Order of Accounts   To change the order in which accounts appear in the Account List window and Account Bar, select an account and click the up or down Order button to move it. You can move an account to any position within its group.

Once you have changed the order of accounts from the default alphabetical sort, new accounts will be added at the bottom of the section. For example, if you add a new Apple Investments account and you already have a Zebra Investments account, Apple will appear below Zebra. So you will have to continue reordering accounts as you add them if you want to view them in alphabetical order.

Viewing Your Accounts   You can set your Account List to display only your Banking, Investments, or Net Worth (Property & Debt) accounts on the list. Click the group you choose to display on the left side of the Account List window.

Show Hidden Accounts   Click the Show Hidden Accounts check box at the lower left of your Account List window to display accounts you have marked as hidden. To hide them from the Account List, clear the check box.

Help Icon   Clicking the small question mark at the lower left of the Account List opens Quicken Help to the section on managing your accounts.

Printing the Account List   Click the Printer icon at the bottom of the Account List window to print your list. The Print dialog appears as shown here. Click Preview to see how your list will appear. Click Close to close the preview window. Click Print to print the list.

Using the Account List Options   The Options menu, as seen earlier, offers you several ways to display your Account List.

- **Include Additional Info When Printing**   This option, when chosen, includes bank name, account number, contact name, and other information when you print the Account List.
- **Show Net Worth/Ending Balance In Account Bar**   This option tells Quicken which balance to show in the Account Bar. For example, if you have sent information to your bank to pay your phone bill next Tuesday, opting to show the ending balance would include that payment in your account's total showing on the Account Bar. The Net Worth option displays that account's balance as of today, not what it will be next Tuesday after the phone bill is sent.
- **Show Current/Ending Balance**   This is similar to Show Net Worth/Ending Balance In Account Bar, but refers to what is displayed in the Account List.

All of the other menu options tell Quicken what to display in the Account List. When you have made any adjustments or are through with the Account List, click Done to close the dialog.

Categories

When you create a data file, Quicken automatically creates dozens of commonly used categories. Although these categories might completely meet your needs, at times you may want to add, remove, or modify a category to fine-tune Quicken for your use.

Types of Categories

There are basically two types of categories:

- **Income** is incoming money. It includes receipts such as your salary, commissions, interest income, dividend income, child support, gifts received, and tips.
- **Expense** is outgoing money. It includes insurance, groceries, rent, interest expense, bank fees, finance charges, charitable donations, and clothing.

Subcategories

A *subcategory* is a subset or part of a category. It must be the same type of category as its primary category. For example, you may use the Auto category to track expenses to operate your car. Within that category, however, you might use one of the subcategories to record specific expenses, such as auto insurance, fuel, and repairs. Subcategories make it easy to keep income and expenses organized

---

NEW TO QUICKEN?

Categories

Categories? Subcategories? Sound confusing? Like a lot of work? It is not a lot of work, and using categories is well worth the time you spend doing it.

Here's how it works. When you enter a transaction in Quicken, you'll categorize it using one of your predefined categories. (Sometimes Quicken can even guess the right category the first time you enter a transaction for a payee!) The next time you enter a transaction for the same payee, Quicken automatically assumes the transaction will use the same category, so Quicken enters it for you. Most of the time, Quicken's assumption is right. So it really isn't that much work.

And you don't have to type the entire category and subcategory, usually just the first few letters. Once the category is selected, type : and begin typing the subcategory. The subcategory should be selected after a few letters.

Worth the trouble? You bet! By properly categorizing transactions, you can get a true picture of where your money comes from and where it goes. You can create realistic budgets based on accurate spending patterns to help you save money. You can create tax reports that'll save you—or your tax preparer—time. You can even automate much of your tax preparation by exporting all those properly categorized transactions right into Intuit's TurboTax tax preparation software.

So don't leave category fields blank when you enter transactions. Take that extra step. It's worth it.

into manageable categories, while providing the transaction detail you might want or need.

Working with the Category List Window

You can view a list of all of your categories at any time. Choose Tools | Category List, or press CTRL-SHIFT-C. The Category List window appears (see Figure 2-8).

In this section, you'll learn how to use the Category List window to display, add, modify, delete, and perform other tasks with categories.

> ## EXPERIENCED QUICKEN USERS
>
> ### Category List Changes
>
> Quicken 2011 has made some changes to the default Category List. When you upgrade, your existing categories will be added to the new Category List, which has been streamlined. For example, in the new default Category List, Quicken has reduced the number of Tax category choices.
>
> The 2011 Category List has eliminated some of the extra category types found in earlier versions of Quicken. You now have only two default category types in most versions of Quicken, Income and Expense, as described in this chapter.
>
> Also, Quicken 2011 has restructured the way in which downloaded transactions are categorized. This automatic matching with your transactions will save you time.

Changing the Category Display

The Category List window lists all categories and transfer accounts within three broad headings: Personal Income, Personal Expenses, and Transfers. You can click a heading on the left side of the Category List window to display just those categories within it. Or, click All Categories to display all categories in your data file. You can also use the Show drop-down list at the top of the window to display categories that meet certain criteria, such as tax-related categories or unused categories.

In the main part of the window, category names appear in an outline view, with subcategories indented beneath them. You can turn on the Hide check box for a category to remove it from lists and menus without actually deleting it from your Quicken data file.

You can also choose commands from the Options menu at the bottom of the window to determine what information appears with the category names in the Category List window. Figure 2-8 includes category names, Hide status, types, and tax-line item information. When you click a specific category, the Action buttons appear as shown here. (Chapter 17 explains more about assigning tax lines to categories.)

	Category	Hide	Type	Tax Line Item		Action	
▯	Auto Payment	☐	Expense			Edit Delete Merge	▲

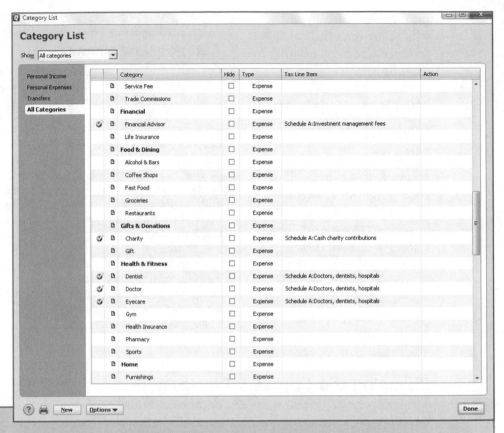

Figure 2-8 • The Category List window displays the categories in your Quicken data file and can include information about tax-line assignments.

Creating a New Category

To create a new category, click the New button at the bottom of the Category List window (refer to Figure 2-8). The Set Up Category dialog appears. Enter information about the category—this illustration at the top of the next page shows an example—and click OK.

Here's a quick summary of the kind of information you should provide for each category.

Category Information The basic category information, entered in the Details tab, includes the category name, which is required, and the description and the main category if this is a subcategory. You have the option of entering additional information in the Description field.

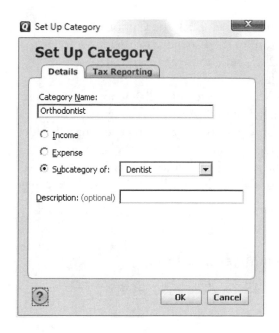

Tax Reporting

You can use the Tax Reporting options, seen here, to specify whether a category is tax-related and, if so, what tax form it appears on. This can be a real timesaver at tax time by enabling you to organize your income and expenditures as they appear on tax forms. You learn more about using Quicken at tax time in Chapter 17. You are not required to enter anything in this area.

Click OK to close the Set Up Category dialog and return to the Category List.

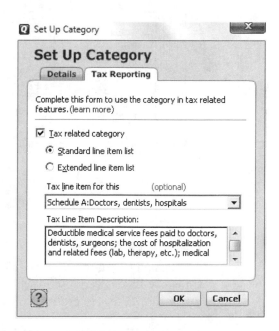

Adding Multiple Categories at Once

Quicken makes it easy to add multiple related categories at the same time. For example, suppose you just bought a rental house and want to add categories for that property to your

Quicken data file. Click the Options button at
the bottom of the Category List window (refer to
Figure 2-8) and choose Manage Categories as
shown here.

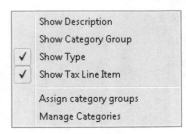

The Manage Categories dialog appears. Choose
a category from the Available Categories drop-
down list. Click to add a green check mark beside
each category you want to add. When you click
Add, the selected categories appear in the
Categories To Add list. Click OK to add the categories and close the dialog.

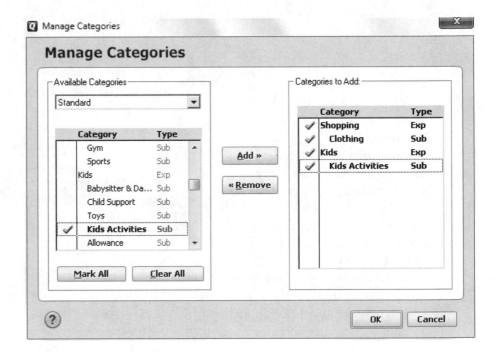

Category Groups

The Assign Category Groups dialog, opened from the Options menu on the
Category List, is very useful when creating a budget and grouping expense
categories. Category groups are explained in detail in Chapter 16.

Editing, Deleting, and Merging Categories

You can also use the Category List window (see Figure 2-8) to edit, delete, or
merge categories. Select the name of the category you want to work with, and

then click a button in the same row in the Action column on the right side of the window, as shown here. Consider backing up your data before you edit, delete, or merge categories. Refer to Appendix A for more information about backing up in Quicken.

ATM Fee	☐	Expense	Edit Delete Merge

Edit   Click a category to display the Action buttons. The Edit button displays the Set Up Category dialog (shown earlier) for the selected category. You can use this to make just about any change to a category. You can even "promote" a subcategory to a category by clearing the Subcategory of: field.

Delete   When you choose to eliminate a category, first select it to display the Delete button in the Action column. Clicking the Delete button displays different dialogs, depending on the category that is selected. Quicken begins by warning you that the category and any subcategories beneath it will be deleted. Then:

- If you selected a category without transactions, when you click OK, the category is deleted.
- If you selected a category or subcategory with transactions, a warning message appears that this category has been used in transactions. If you choose to delete the category, the Delete Category dialog, shown next, appears. You can use this dialog to replace the category with another category throughout your data file. Choose another category from the drop-down list, and click OK. If you click OK without choosing a replacement category, any transactions that referenced the category you deleted will be marked as uncategorized. If the category you deleted has subcategories, this dialog appears for each subcategory that has transactions.

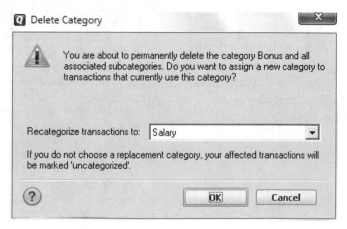

Merge   The Merge button lets you merge transactions using the currently selected category with transactions using another category. This, in effect, recategorizes all of the transactions for the selected category. Clicking Merge displays the Merge Category dialog. Choose another category from the drop-down list. If you want to delete the category you selected, turn on the check box—this makes the dialog work the same way as the Delete Category dialog shown earlier. Click OK to perform the merge. One thing to keep in mind: If the category you selected is not used in any transactions, a dialog will tell you that there's nothing to merge.

Tags

A *tag* is an optional identifier used to specify what a transaction applies to. For example, if you have two vehicles for which you track expenses, you can create a tag for each vehicle, such as "Jeep" and "Chevy Truck." Then, when you record a transaction for one of the vehicles, you can include the appropriate tag with the category for the transaction. Because Quicken can produce reports based on categories, tags, or both, tags offer an additional dimension for tracking and reporting information.

Using tags is completely optional. It's not necessary to set them up or use them at all. In fact, many Quicken users—including a few at Intuit—don't take advantage of this feature. It's your decision.

Displaying the Tag List Window

Quicken maintains a list of all the tags you create. You can display the Tag List window by choosing Tools | Tag List, or by pressing CTRL-L. This illustration on the next page shows an example with some tags.

NEW TO QUICKEN?

Tags

If you were doubtful about the benefit of using categories in transactions, tags will certainly be a hard sell. Fortunately, there'll be no sales pitch because you really don't have to use this feature at all.

That said, let me explain how some people use tags. Got kids? Try this. Create a separate tag for each child. Then, when you've got expenses for a specific family member, record the transaction with the appropriate tag name. (If you've got income related to a specific child, that's terrific; be sure to include the tag name with those transactions, too.) Then, when that partially grown bundle of joy asks for $257.49 to buy a new cell phone, you can show him a report of how much he's cost you so far when you say no.

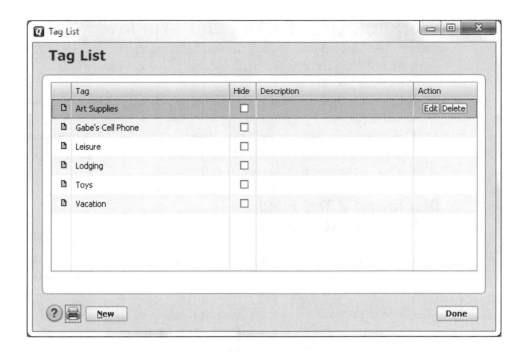

Creating a New Tag

Click the New button on the button bar in the Tag List window. The New Tag dialog, shown here, appears. Use it to enter information about the tag.

Only one piece of information is necessary: the tag name. You may want to make it short so it's easy to remember and enter. The description can be used to provide additional information on the tag's use. The copy number enables you to associate tags with different but similar activities. For example, if you have two separate businesses for which you report activity on two Schedule Cs, you can assign Copy 1 to one business's tags and Copy 2 to the other business's tags.

When you click OK, the tag is added to the list. You can create as many tags as you like.

Working with the Tag List Window

You can use buttons that appear beside a selected tag in the Tag List window to work with the tag list or a selected tag.

- **Edit** enables you to modify the currently selected tag name or other information.
- **Delete** enables you to delete the currently selected tag. When you delete a tag, the tag name is removed from all transactions in which it appeared, but the transaction remains properly categorized.

Displaying a Tag Field in an Account Register

By default, each account register displays a Tag field. You can easily turn off the display if you choose not to use tags.

1. Open the account register. Click the small "gear" icon found under the Account Actions button.
2. From the drop-down list, clear the Tag check box as shown here.

Other Setup Options

There are two additional sections in the Main View of the Home tab that you may use to help Quicken create your accurate financial picture. Both are discussed in detail in later chapters but are introduced here.

Stay on Top of Monthly Bills

This section gets you started working with your regular bills, such as your mortgage or rent, phone bills, and so on. If you have downloaded and categorized transactions from your bank, selecting the Get Started button will open the Stay On Top Of Monthly Bills dialog as shown next. Click Add A Bill to add a new bill. Click Next to open a dialog in which you can add regular income.

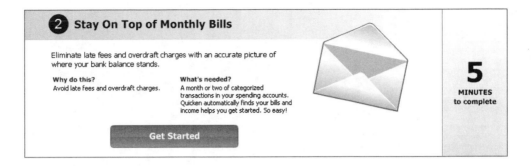

For a complete description of working with your bills in Quicken, see Chapter 6.

Track Spending Goals to Save Money

This section helps you track specific expenditures so that you can watch how much you spend. When you click the Get Started button, the Monthly Spending/Saving Plan dialog appears, as seen here. You can enter your goals for spending in each category. See Chapter 8 for an in-depth discussion about creating a spending plan.

Going Online
with Quicken

In This Chapter:

- *Benefits of going online with Quicken*
- *Testing and troubleshooting your connection*
- *An introduction to web surfing*
- *Accessing Quicken.com*
- *Quicken financial partners*

Many of the features of Quicken Personal Finance Software work seamlessly with the Internet. Thus, if you have access to the Internet, either through a connection to an Internet service provider (ISP) or through a connection to an online service such as America Online, you can take advantage of these online features to get up-to-date information, automate data entry, pay bills, and obtain Quicken maintenance updates automatically.

This chapter tells you why you might want to take advantage of Quicken's online features. You'll learn a little about surfing the Web and will be introduced to Quicken.com, a source of information and services for Quicken users.

Going Online

If you're already using your computer to access the features of the Internet, you probably already know a lot about the Internet's capabilities. This part of the chapter fills in any gaps in your knowledge by telling you about the benefits of going online with Quicken and addressing any security concerns you might have. Finally, for the folks who aren't already online, you will learn what you need to connect to the Internet to use Quicken's online features.

Why Go Online?

Remember, you don't *have* to go online to use Quicken. Quicken is a good financial management software package, even without its online features. But Quicken's online features make it a *great* financial management software package. As you'll see in this section and throughout this book, Quicken uses the Internet to help you make better financial decisions. How? By providing you with information and resources that are relevant to your personal financial situation.

The best way to explain the benefits of going online is to list a few of the features that online users use.

If You Have a Bank Account, You Can Benefit

Throughout the month, you write checks and mail them to individuals and organizations. You enter these transactions in your checking account register. At month's end, you reconcile the account. You can do all this without going online; learn how in Chapters 5 and 8.

When you register for Transaction Download with your bank, you can download all bank account activity on a regular basis, so you know exactly when the transactions hit your account—even the ATM and debit card transactions you may forget to enter. If you register for Online Payment, you can pay your bills without licking another envelope or pasting on another stamp. Chapter 5 explains how all this works.

If You Have Credit Cards, You Can Benefit

Do you have credit cards? If so, you can take advantage of Quicken's credit card tracking features, which are covered in Chapter 4, to keep track of your charges, payments, and balances. You don't need to go online, but if you sign up for Transaction Download, all your credit card charges can be downloaded directly into Quicken, eliminating the need for time-consuming data entry, while giving you an up-to-date summary of your debt and how you spent your money. Learn more about this in Chapter 5.

If You Invest, You Can Benefit

Quicken can keep track of your investments, whether they are 401(k) accounts, mutual funds, or stocks. You can enter share, price, and transaction information into Quicken, and it will summarize portfolio value, gains, and losses. It'll even keep track of securities by lot. Chapter 9 explains how.

Again, you don't need to go online to track your investments, but with online investment tracking features, Quicken can automatically obtain quotes on all the securities in your portfolio and update your portfolio's market value. Depending on your brokerage firm, you may also be able to download transactions, account balances, and holdings. Quicken can also alert you about news stories that affect your investments and automatically download the headlines, so you can learn more with just a click. You can also get valuable up-to-date research information about securities that interest you, so you can make informed investment decisions. Learn all about this in Chapter 10.

If You Want to Save Money, You Can Benefit

If you're like most people, you spend money every day on the things you need or want to make your life better. Quicken can help you keep track of your spending by summarizing expenditures by category. It can also help you save money by enabling you to create a budget and keep your expenditures under control.

Security Features

Perhaps you're already convinced that the online features can benefit you. Maybe you're worried about security, concerned that a stranger will be able to access your accounts or steal your credit card numbers.

You can stop worrying. Intuit and the participating banks, credit card companies, and brokerage firms have done all the worrying for you. They've come up with a secure system that protects your information and accounts.

PINs

A *PIN*, or *personal identification number*, is a secret password you must use to access your accounts online. If you have an ATM card or cash-advance capabilities through your credit card, you probably already have at least one PIN, so you may be familiar with the idea. The PIN simply prevents anyone from accessing the account for any reason without first entering the proper numbers.

An account's PIN is initially assigned by the bank, credit card company, or brokerage firm. Some companies require that your PIN consist of a mixture of letters and numbers for additional security. You can change your PINs to make them easier to remember—just don't use something obvious like your birthday or telephone number. And don't write any PIN or password on a sticky note attached to your computer's monitor!

If you think someone might have guessed your PIN, you can change it. In fact, it's a good idea to change all your PINs and passwords regularly—not just the ones you use in Quicken.

Encryption

Once you're online and you've correctly entered your PIN, the instructions that flow from your computer to the bank, credit card company, or brokerage firm are *encrypted*. This means they are encoded in such a way that anyone able to "tap in" to the transmission would "hear" only gibberish. Quicken uses Secure Sockets Layer (SSL), which is the industry-standard method for protecting and encrypting your data. Once the encrypted information reaches the computer at the bank, credit card company, or brokerage firm, it is unencrypted and then validated and processed.

Encryption makes it virtually impossible for any unauthorized party to "listen in" to your transmission. It also makes it impossible for someone to alter a transaction from the moment it leaves your computer to the moment it arrives at your bank, credit card company, or brokerage firm for processing.

Quicken also takes advantage of other security methods for online communications, such as digital signatures and digital certificates. Together, these security methods make online financial transactions secure—even more secure than telephone banking, which you may already use!

Getting Connected

To take advantage of Quicken's online features, you need a connection to the Internet. You get that through an ISP, an organization that provides access to the Internet, usually for a monthly fee. These days, literally thousands of ISPs, including local phone and cable television companies, can provide the access you need for Quicken's online features.

If you don't already have an account with an ISP, you must set one up before you can use Quicken's online features. Check your local phone book or newspaper to find an ISP near you. Your ISP can explain everything you need to get connected and help you set up your computer to go online.

Testing Your Connection with a Visit to Quicken.com

A good way to test your Internet connection is to visit Quicken.com, the official Quicken website. This site offers information about Intuit products, as well as special features for registered Quicken users. You'll learn more about Quicken.com later in this chapter and throughout this book. For now, connect to it to make sure your Internet connection works.

If the Quicken Tool Bar is not showing, click View | Show Tool Bar. If the text does not appear beneath each icon, hover your mouse over the icons to determine which one is the Quicken.com button. (It is the one with the Q in the cloud, as shown here.) When you click the Quicken.com button, Quicken attempts to connect to the Internet using the settings in your default Internet browser. You may have to customize the Quicken Tool Bar to see the Quicken.com button. To learn how, see Appendix B.

What you see during the connection process will vary depending on your connection type. If you have a modem or use an online service, access software may start automatically to make the connection. You may be prompted to enter a user name or password. Other dialogs may appear. It may be necessary to switch from connection software back to Quicken by clicking the Quicken button on the Windows task bar.

When the connection is complete, Quicken requests the Quicken.com home page. It appears in a Quicken Internet window. Figure 3-1 is an example of the Quicken.com page, however, what you see may be different as the page is updated regularly.

If you were already connected to the Internet when you accessed one of Quicken's online features, or if you have a direct connection to the Internet, you won't see the connection happening. Instead, the Quicken.com page simply appears in a Quicken Internet window (see Figure 3-1).

Troubleshooting Connection Problems

If you follow the instructions provided throughout this chapter, you shouldn't have any trouble connecting to the Internet with Quicken. But things aren't always as easy as they should be. Sometimes even the tiniest problems can prevent you from successfully connecting and exchanging data.

This section provides some troubleshooting advice to help you with any connection problems you may experience. Check this section before you start pulling out your hair and cursing the day computers were invented.

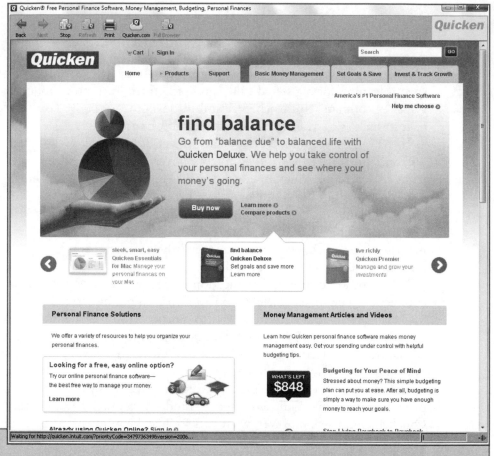

Figure 3-1 • The Quicken.com page provides articles and information about Quicken products and services, as well as useful money management information.

Setup Problems

If you have problems connecting to the Internet from within Quicken, exit Quicken and try connecting to the Internet from another program, such as your regular web browser or e-mail program.

- If you can connect to the Internet from another program but not from Quicken, the problem may be with Quicken's Internet connection setup. Try closing Quicken and reopening it. That may solve the problem.
- If you can't connect to the Internet from any other program or with dial-up networking (for dial-up connections), the problem is with your Internet

setup for Windows, your modem (for dial-up connections), your network (for direct connections), or your router (for direct connections). You must fix any problem you find before you can successfully set up and connect with Quicken. Consult Windows Help for assistance.

Modem Problems

Problems with a dial-up connection may be related to your modem. Try each of the following, attempting a connection after each one:

- Check all cables between your computer and your modem (if you have an external modem), and between your modem and the telephone outlet.
- Check the telephone line to make sure it has a dial tone and that it is not being used by someone else or another program.
- Turn off your modem and then turn it back on. Or, if you have an internal modem, restart your computer. This resets the modem and may resolve the problem.

If you can connect but have trouble staying connected, try the following:

- Make sure no one is picking up an extension of the phone line while you are online.
- Make sure call-waiting is disabled by entering the appropriate codes for the dial-up connection.
- Have the phone company check the line for noise. If noise is detected, ask the phone company to fix the problem. (It shouldn't cost you anything if the line noise is the result of a problem outside your premises.)

Network or Router Problems

Problems with a direct connection may be related to your network or router. Try these things, attempting a connection after each one:

- Check all cables between your computer and the network hub or router.
- Reset or turn your router off and then back on. This may clear the connection problems.
- Restart your computer. Sometimes resetting your computer's system software can clear network problems.
- Ask your system administrator to check your network setup.
- Consult your ISP for additional assistance.

Exploring Quicken's Web-Based Features

You access Quicken's web-based features from within Quicken software. In some cases, Quicken uses its built-in web browser to display information; in other cases, it opens the default browser on your computer. This section tells new Internet users a little more about using the Web and then explains how you can access Quicken's web-based features.

An Introduction to Web Surfing

Let's take a moment to explain exactly what you're doing when you connect to Quicken.com and the other Quicken features on the Web. If you're brand new to *web surfing*—that is, exploring websites—be sure to read this section. But if you're a seasoned surfer, you probably already know all this information and can skip the section.

One more thing: This section is not designed to explain everything you'll ever need to know about browsing the World Wide Web. It provides the basic information you need to use the Web to get the information you need.

Going Online

When you access Quicken's online features, you do so by connecting to the Internet through your ISP. It doesn't matter whether you connect via a modem or a network, or whether your ISP is America Online, your local cable company, or Gabe's Internet Service. The main thing is having a connection or a conduit for information.

Think of an Internet connection as some PVC piping running from your computer to your ISP's computer, with a valve to control the flow of information. Once the valve is open (you're connected), any information can flow through the pipe in either direction. You can even exchange information through that pipe in both directions at the same time. This makes it possible to download (or retrieve) a webpage with your web browser while you upload (or send) e-mail with your e-mail program.

Quicken's online features use the pipe (or connection) in two ways:

- The integrated web browser enables you to request and receive the information you want. It's live and interactive—click a link, and a moment later your information starts to appear. Quicken can display webpages in its built-in Internet window (see Figure 3-1) or your default browser's window.
- Transaction Download, Online Payment, and several other features work in the background to communicate with financial institutions with which you

have accounts. Quicken sends information you prepare in advance and retrieves the information the financial institution has waiting for you.

This chapter concentrates on web browsing with Quicken—using Quicken's integrated web browser to access interactive features on Quicken.com. But it also provides some information to help you find financial institutions that work with Quicken for the Transaction Download and Online Payment features.

Navigating   The main thing to remember about the Web is that it's interactive. Every time a webpage appears on your screen, it'll offer a number of options for viewing other information. This is known as navigating the Web.

Hyperlinks and Forms   You can move from page to page on the Web in two ways:

- **Hyperlinks** (or links) are text or graphics that, when clicked, display another page. Hypertext links are usually underlined, colored text. Graphic links sometimes have a colored border around them. You can always identify a link by pointing to it—your mouse pointer will turn into a hand with a pointing finger, and a screen tip may appear to describe the link.
- **Forms** offer options for going to another page or searching for information. Options can appear in pop-up menus, text boxes that you fill in, check boxes that you turn on, or option buttons that you select. Multiple options often appear. You enter or select the options you want and click a button to send your request to the website. The information you requested appears a moment later.

Other Navigation Techniques   Several of the buttons on the Quicken browser's toolbar, as seen here, are navigation buttons:

- **Back** displays the previously viewed page.
- **Next** displays the page you viewed after the current page. This button is available only after you have used the Back button.
- **Stop** stops the loading of the current page. This may result in incomplete pages or error messages on the page. You might use this button if you click a link and then realize that you don't really want to view the information you requested.

- **Refresh** loads a new copy of the webpage from the website's server. This button is handy for updating stock quotes or news that appears on a page.
- **Print** enables you to print the currently displayed page.
- **Quicken.com** takes you to the Quicken.com home page (refer to Figure 3-1).
- **Full Browser** starts and switches to your default web browser. Quicken continues to run in the background. You can switch back to Quicken at any time by clicking its icon on the Windows task bar.

Accessing Quicken.com

Quicken.com, the official Quicken site, supports Quicken users in several different ways:

- **Home** tab   This tab is the entry point to Quicken.com. It changes frequently, but Figure 3-1 is a good example. It provides links to articles, videos, and other money management information.
- **Products** tab   This tab provides links to several Quicken products and services, as seen here.
- **Support** tab   This tab displays answers to many frequently asked questions, has a direct link to Quicken support, and offers other resources for users of Intuit's personal financial products.
- **Basic Money Management** tab   As seen in Figure 3-2, this tab provides links to articles and hints for good money management, as well as videos to help you with many financial matters.
- **Set Goals & Save** tab   The information found in this tab helps you learn to manage your money and save for that future goal. See Chapters 8 and 14 through 16 for more ideas on planning for your future.
- **Invest & Track Growth** tab   This tab features advice in the form of articles, videos, and other suggestions on investment issues for you. See Chapters 9, 10, and 11 to learn how to work with your own investments.

Quicken.com is a dynamic website that changes frequently. The screen illustrations and features shown here may appear differently when you connect.

Figure 3-2 • The Money Management tab found at Quicken.com offers valuable tips for managing your finances.

In addition, brand-new features might be added after the publication of this book. The best way to learn about the features of Quicken.com is to check them out yourself.

Participating Financial Institutions

If you're interested in keeping track of your finances with the least amount of data entry, you should be considering Quicken's online features Transaction Download and Online Payment. The beginning of this chapter explained the benefits of these features. Chapters 5 and 10 tell you how to use them. But you can't use them until you've set up an account with a participating financial institution and applied for the online account services you want to use.

When you create a bank, credit card, or investment account, Quicken prompts you to enter the name of your financial institution. Quicken determines whether your financial institution is one of the participating financial institutions, as many are. If you've already set up your accounts for online account services, you can skip this section. But you may find it useful if you're shopping around for another financial institution and want one that works with Quicken.

Finding a Participating Institution

Participating financial institutions offer four types of online financial services:

- **Banking account access** enables you to download bank account transactions directly into your Quicken data file.
- **Credit/charge card access** enables you to download credit or charge card transactions directly into your Quicken data file.
- **Investment account access** enables you to download brokerage and other investment account transactions directly into your Quicken data file.
- **Payments** enables you to send payment instructions from within Quicken. This makes it possible to pay bills and send payments to anyone without writing a check.

Change Financial Institutions   If your bank or credit card company doesn't support online banking services with Quicken and you really want to use this feature, you can find a financial institution that does support them and open an account there. Here is a link to a site that lists them all: http://web.intuit.com/fisearchbasic.

Use Quicken Bill Pay and Quicken Visa credit card   If you're interested only in the Bill Pay feature, you can use Quicken Bill Pay. This enables you to process payments from your existing bank accounts from within Quicken. There's no need to change banks or wait until your bank signs on as a participating financial institution.

If you'd like to earn Quicken Rewards, consider the Quicken Visa credit card. You can learn more about Quicken Bill Pay and the Quicken Visa credit card in the Quicken Services window; choose the More From Quicken tab to display the Quicken Services window.

Applying for Online Financial Services

Before you can take advantage of the online features in Quicken, you must apply for a user name and password from your financial institution. This gets the wheels turning to put you online. It may take a few days to get the necessary access information, so apply as soon as you're sure you want to take advantage of the online financial services features.

Banking

This part of the book explains how to use Quicken Personal Finance Software to keep track of your bank and credit card accounts. It starts by explaining the basics of manually recording bank and credit card transactions, and then tells you how you can take advantage of online transaction entry and payment processing features such as Transaction Download and Online Bill Pay. It provides details about how you can tap into the power of Quicken to automate many entry tasks, thus saving you time. It also explains how to reconcile accounts and how to use Quicken's reporting features to learn more about what you have and how you're doing financially. This part has five chapters:

Part Two

Recording Bank and Credit Card Transactions

Chapter 4

In This Chapter:

- *Creating banking accounts*
- *Entering payments and other transactions*
- *Using splits and tags*
- *Writing and printing checks*
- *Entering credit card transactions*
- *Transferring money*
- *Working with existing transactions*
- *Adding notes and attachments*

At Quicken's core is its ability to manage your bank accounts. This is probably Quicken's most used feature. You enter the transactions, and Quicken Personal Finance Software keeps track of account balances and the source and destination of the money you spend. You can even have Quicken print checks for you.

Using similar transaction entry techniques, Quicken can also help you keep track of credit card accounts. You enter transactions as you make them, at the end of the month, or when you receive your statement and pay your bill. Quicken keeps track of balances and offers you an easy way to monitor what you used your credit card to buy. It also enables you to keep an eye on how much your credit cards cost you in terms of finance charges and other fees.

Getting Started

Before you can use Quicken to track bank and credit card transactions, you should prepare by creating the necessary accounts and learning how recording transactions works. This section provides an overview of the banking account types, along with examples of transactions you might make. You will also see detailed step-by-step instructions for creating banking accounts.

Overview of Accounts and Transactions

Most of the transactions you track with Quicken will involve one or more of its bank, credit card, and cash accounts. Here's a closer look at each account type, along with some transaction examples. As you read about these accounts, imagine how they might apply to your financial situation.

Bank Accounts

Quicken offers two types of accounts that you can use to track the money you have in a bank:

- **Checking** accounts include check writing privileges. These accounts usually have a lot of activity, with deposits to increase the account balance and checks that decrease the account balance.
- **Savings** accounts are for your savings. These accounts usually don't have as much activity as checking accounts. You can use a savings account to track the balance in a certificate of deposit (CD), holiday savings club, or similar savings account.

Generally speaking, bank account transactions can be broken down into three broad categories: payments, deposits, and transfers.

Payments   Payments are cash outflows. Here are some examples:

- You write a check to pay your electric bill.
- You withdraw money from your savings account to buy a gift for your mother.
- You use your ATM card to withdraw spending money from a bank account.
- You use your debit card to buy groceries.
- You pay a monthly checking account fee.

Deposits   Deposits are cash inflows. Here are some examples:

- You deposit your paycheck into your checking account.
- You sell your old computer and deposit the proceeds into your savings account.
- Your paycheck or Social Security check is deposited into your bank account as a direct deposit.
- You earn interest on your savings account.

Transfers   A transfer is a movement of funds from one account to another. Here are some examples:

- You transfer money from an interest-bearing savings account to your checking account when you're ready to pay your bills.
- You transfer money from a money market account to your home equity line of credit account to reduce its balance.

Credit Card Accounts

Credit card accounts track money you owe, not money you own. Some credit cards, such as MasterCard, Visa, American Express, and Discover, can be used in most stores that accept them. Other credit cards, such as Macy's or Shell, can be used only in certain stores. But they all have one thing in common: If there's a balance, it's usually because you owe the credit card company money.

Credit card account transactions can also be broken down into two categories: charges and payments.

Charges   Charges result when you use your credit card to buy something or the credit card company charges a fee for services. Here are some examples:

- You use your Visa card to buy a new computer.
- You use your Discover card to pay for a hotel stay.
- You use your Shell card to fill the gas tank on your boat at the marina.
- A finance charge based on your account balance is added to your Macy's bill at month's end.
- A late fee is added to your MasterCard bill because you didn't pay the previous month's bill on time.
- A fee is added to your American Express bill for annual membership dues.

The opposite of a charge is a *credit*. Think of it as a negative charge; don't confuse it with a payment. Here are two examples:

- You return the sweater you bought with your American Express card to the store you bought it from.
- In reviewing your MasterCard bill, you discover that a merchant charged you in error, and you arrange to have the incorrect charge removed.

Payments   Payments are amounts you send to a credit card company to reduce your balance. Here are three examples:

- You pay the minimum amount due on your Visa card.
- You pay $150 toward the balance on your Macy's card.
- You pay the balance on your American Express card.

Cash Accounts

Quicken also offers cash accounts for tracking cash expenditures. For example, you might create an account called My Wallet or Spending Money and use it to keep track of the cash you have on hand. Cash accounts are like bank accounts, but there's no bank. The money is in your wallet, your pocket, or the old coffee can on the windowsill.

Cash accounts have two types of transactions: receive and spend.

Receive   When you receive cash, you increase the amount of cash you have on hand. Here are some examples:

- You withdraw cash from the bank for weekly spending money.
- You sell your *National Geographic* magazine collection for cash at a garage sale.
- You get a $20 bill in a birthday card from your grandmother.

Spend   When you spend cash, you reduce your cash balance. Here are some examples:

- You buy coffee and a newspaper and pay a bridge toll on your way to work.
- You give your son his allowance.
- You put a $20 bill in the birthday card you send to your granddaughter.

Creating Banking Accounts

Chapter 2 briefly discusses how to create your primary checking account. Here are the details for creating banking accounts.

While there are several ways to add new accounts, the quickest is to use the Add An Account button found at the bottom of the Account Bar as seen here. Click the button to open the Add Account dialog seen in Figure 4-1. You can create credit card and cash accounts as well, as discussed later in this chapter. If the Account Bar is not displayed, click the plus sign to the left of the word "Accounts" on the same line as the tabs, as seen here.

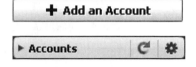

Choose the type of account, and click Next. The Add (*type of account*) Account dialog opens, as seen in Figure 4-2. This dialog includes the type of account you chose in the previous screen as part of its name so that you know you're entering the right type of account.

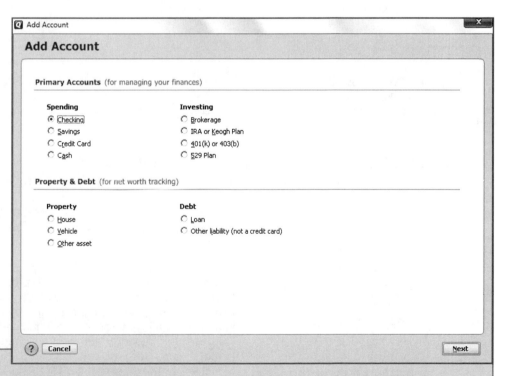

Figure 4-1 • The Add Account dialog helps you set up all types of accounts in Quicken.

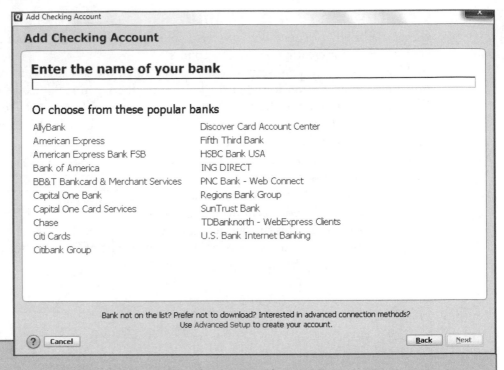

Figure 4-2 • When you add a new account, you can enter your bank's name or choose from the list provided by Quicken.

Creating Accounts with Online Features

Quicken's extensive online account access features make it possible to automate data entry and account reconciliations for accounts held in participating financial institutions. To take advantage of these features, Quicken starts the account creation process by prompting you to enter the name of your financial institution (see Figure 4-2). You can either type the name of your financial institution or simply click one of the

EXPERIENCED QUICKEN USERS

Account Setup

Earlier versions of Quicken had special setup screens and dialogs. Quicken 2011 has streamlined the way in which you can enter new accounts. With Simple Setup, you can now enter all types of accounts, including investment, property, and debt accounts, from the same dialog. You can still use dialogs similar to those used in earlier versions of Quicken by choosing Advanced Setup at the Add (*type of account*) Account dialog.

provided names. (If you do not see your bank's name, or if you prefer not to download automatically, click Advanced Setup to create your account. For further information, see "Using Advanced Setup" later in this chapter.)

Whether you have chosen to type the name or select it from the list, Quicken prompts you for the user ID and password given to you by your financial institution, as seen here.

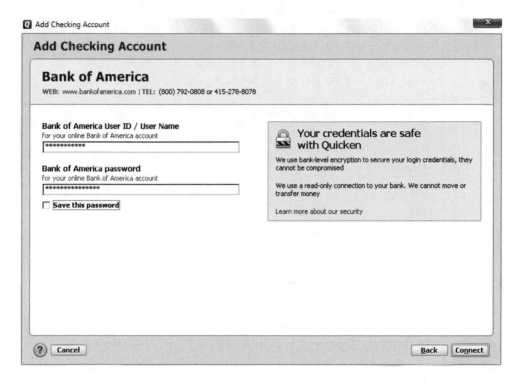

Click Save This Password to save your password into the Quicken Password Vault. Find out how to use the Password Vault in Chapter 6.

After you have entered your information, click Connect to use your Internet connection to contact your financial institution.

Each financial institution has its own method of issuing passwords and identification for their online services. Contact your bank or credit union to apply for these services, and have that information available when you set up your Quicken accounts.

Several connection information messages will appear, as shown next, and you may be prompted to enter additional information, depending on the requirements of your institution. Once you are connected, follow the instructions given by your institution to download the transactions into Quicken. After your first account is downloaded, click Add Another Account or Finish, depending on what you want to do next.

 If you have any existing accounts of the same type in your Quicken file that are not online accounts, Quicken may prompt you with a screen that lists the accounts found at the financial institution, asking if you want to add, link, or ignore each account, and asking you to select an account nickname. Once you have made your selections, click Next and the designated account downloads occur. Then the Finish screen displays.

 Once you've set up one of your accounts for online banking, Quicken will use your Internet connection to update its financial institution list each time you open the program.

Using Advanced Setup

If your bank does not appear on the list, or if you have chosen to enter your information manually, or if you simply prefer not to download at this time, click Advanced Setup to open the Advanced Setup dialog shown next. From this dialog, you have two options:

- **I Want To Select The Connection Method Used To Download My Transactions** is the selection you make if your bank has several options for downloading. Type the name of the bank in the text box, and click Next. The next dialog displays your choices for downloading, as shown on the next page. Choose the one you want to use, and click Next. Enter your user ID and password as given to you by your financial institution, and click Connect to use your Internet connection to contact your bank. Depending on your bank's requirements, you may be prompted to answer additional questions. Follow the directions of your institution and continue through the messages. If you have more than one account, transactions for all of the accounts may be downloaded. You may be offered a screen to select which of the multiple accounts you want to download and be prompted for account nicknames.

- **I Want To Enter My Transactions Manually** tells Quicken that you don't want to download your data or that your accounts are at an institution that does not offer Quicken access. Keep in mind that you won't be able to take advantage of Quicken's online banking features for this account. However, you can activate the online banking features later. See the discussion on online banking in Chapter 5. Click Next to continue. Quicken prompts you to enter a name for the account. Enter a descriptive name in the Account Name/Nickname box, and click Next. As shown next, Quicken prompts you to enter your account ending statement date and balance. Click Next to continue. Quicken displays an Account Added message. Depending on what you want to do next, click either Add Another Account or Finish.

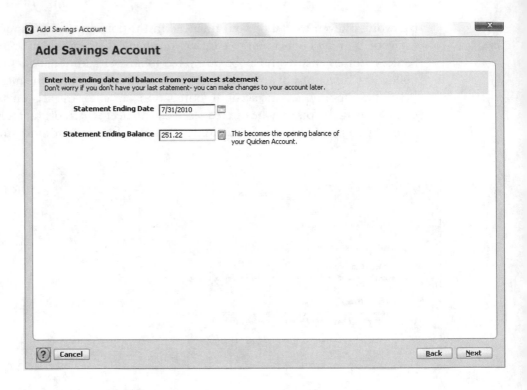

For checking, savings, and credit card accounts, you have three options:

- Enter the ending statement date and balance from your most recent account statement, as shown here. This is the quickest, most accurate way to create an account. The statement date becomes your account's start date, and you will enter only those transactions that were made after that date or that did not clear that statement.
- Enter the ending statement date and balance from an earlier account statement. This is also an accurate way to create the account, but it will require that you play "catch up" to enter more transactions into Quicken.
- Enter today's date and **0** in the dialog. This is fast, but it certainly isn't accurate. You'll eventually have to either adjust the beginning balance for the account or use the reconciliation feature to create an adjusting entry after your first reconciliation.

For a cash account, unless you plan to enter transactions you made before you created the account, you'll probably use today's date and the contents of your wallet or pocket as the starting balance information.

Tips for Creating Banking Accounts

Here are a few additional things to keep in mind when creating Quicken accounts:

- Give each account a name that clearly identifies it. For example, if you have two checking accounts, don't name them "Checking 1" and "Checking 2." Instead, include the bank name (such as "USA Bank Checking") or account purpose (such as "Joint Checking") in the account name. This prevents you from accidentally entering a transaction in the wrong account register. Remember, the name of the account register displays on the title bar of the Quicken window and at the top of each register as seen here.

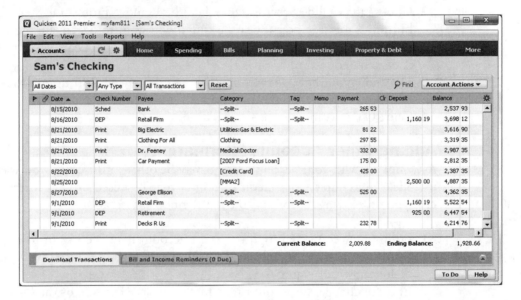

- If you create a bank or credit card account with a balance date and amount from a bank statement—the recommended way—be careful not to enter transactions that already appear on that statement or in previous statements.
- Entering your credit limit for a credit card account enables Quicken to alert you when you get close to (or exceed) your limit. If a credit card account doesn't have a credit limit—for example, an American Express card—you may want to enter your own personal spending limit. This makes it possible to take advantage of Quicken's alerts feature to prevent overspending in that account.
- Using a cash account to track every penny you spend, from the cup of coffee you buy at work in the morning to the quart of milk you pick up on your way home that evening, isn't for everyone. You may prefer to track only large cash inflows or outflows and record the rest as miscellaneous expenses.

Editing Existing Accounts

After you have added an account, you can easily make changes to it. For example, you may have entered something in error and need to correct an account with online services. You can temporarily deactivate the online services to fix your error.

Deactivating Online Services

1. From the Account Bar, right-click the account you want to edit. From the context menu that opens, click Edit Account to display the Account Details dialog.
2. Choose the Online Services tab. Click the Remove From One Step Update button. A message box appears asking if you want to deactivate the online service. Click Yes. A connection message box briefly appears while the service is deactivated.
3. Depending on the type of connection your financial institution offers, you may see a Remove Connection button. If so, click it.
4. Click OK to complete the deactivation.

Adding Other Account Information

As you work with your accounts, there may be other information you want to include. For example, your credit card limit may be raised or your interest rate changed on a savings account. To enter the new information:

1. From the Account Bar, right-click the account name you want to edit to open a context menu. Select Edit Account to open the Account Details dialog shown in Figure 4-3.
2. Enter or change the account information on the left side of the General tab. The dialog has different fields depending on the type of account.
   - Checking and savings accounts let you change the following:
     - Account name
     - Description
     - Whether the account is tax deferred
     - Interest rate
     - Maximum and minimum balances for which you can be alerted
   - For credit card accounts, you can change the following:
     - Account name
     - Description
     - Interest rate
     - Credit limit

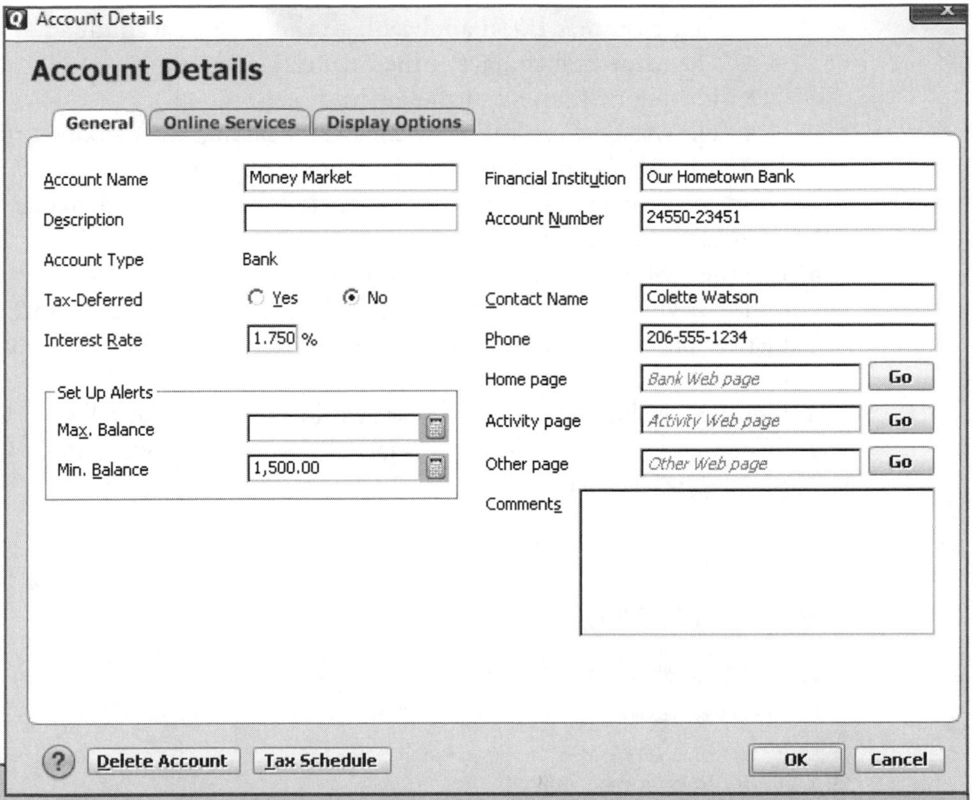

Figure 4-3 • The General tab of the Account Details dialog is used for making changes and updates to your account information.

- Investing accounts let you change the:
  - Account name
  - Description
  - Whether the account is tax deferred
  - An option to show the cash in the investment account in a checking account
- For all account types, the information on the right side of the dialog is similar, depending on the account type. You can modify all of the information if the account is not set up for online services. If the account is set up for online services, you may not change the financial, account and routing numbers, and the customer ID. You see the following:
  - The financial institution—useful if your bank merges with another
  - The account and bank routing numbers

- Your customer ID, if applicable to this type of account
- The name of a contact at the financial institution
- The phone number of the institution
- The financial institution's webpages, including the banking activity pages
- Any other comments you have about the account

From the General tab, you can also delete the account and change the tax schedule information.

3. Use the Online Services tab to add or remove online services or activate online payment services, if they are available through your financial institution. See "Deactivating Online Services" earlier in this chapter for more information.

4. Use the Display Options tab, as shown in Figure 4-4, to tell Quicken how to display this account. More information about hiding accounts in Quicken is covered in Chapter 2.

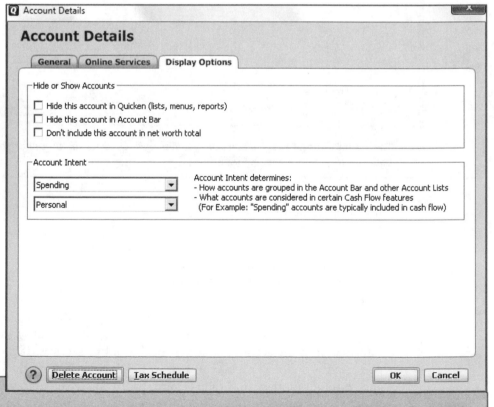

Figure 4-4 • You can tell Quicken how to display your accounts in various parts of the program.

    a. **Hide Or Show Accounts** tells Quicken how you want this account included in totals, lists, reports, and menus.

    b. **Account Intent** field #1 lets you choose in which area of the Account Bar to display the account.

    c. **Account Intent** field #2 lets you select the account as intended for personal, business, or rental property use.

5. Use the **Delete Account** button to delete the account with which you are working. See Chapter 2 for more information about deleting accounts.

6. Click the Tax Schedule button to enter any tax information about this account. This option is discussed in more detail in Chapter 2.

When you have made all of your changes, click OK to close the Account Details dialog.

Entering Transactions

To make the most of Quicken, you must enter transactions for the accounts you want to track. You can do this manually, as discussed in this chapter, or, if the account is enabled for online account services, you can track your account activity automatically via download, as discussed in Chapter 5. Either way, you'll need to know how to enter transactions for your accounts.

You can enter transactions in several ways, based on the type of transaction.

- Use registers to record virtually any type of transaction, including manual checks, bank account payments and deposits, credit card charges and payments, and cash receipts and spending.
- Use the *Write Checks* window to record checks to be printed by Quicken.
- Enter transfers to transfer money from one account to another.

Using Account Registers

Quicken's account registers offer a standard way to enter all kinds of transactions. As the name suggests, these *electronic account registers* are similar to the paper checking account register that comes with your checks.

You can open an account's register as follows:

- If the Account Bar is displayed, click the name of the account you want to open.

The account window appears with the transactions displayed. Refer to Figure 4-5.

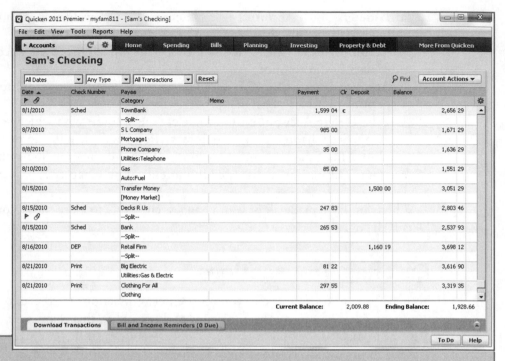

Figure 4-5 • The Account Register for a checking account can display two lines if you choose and looks very much like a paper register.

Overview of the Account Register

Before we discuss entry techniques, let's take a closer look at the account register window.

Downloaded Transactions   At the bottom of the account register are two tabs of information (see Figure 4-5). If these tabs are not visible, you can tell Quicken to show them. From the menu bar, click Edit | Preferences | Downloaded Transactions and clear the Automatically Add Downloaded Transactions To Register check box.

Download Transactions or Downloaded Transactions displays a setup form for enabling transaction download or a list of transactions that have already been downloaded but not yet accepted into the account, respectively. Learn how to set up and work with the Transaction Download and Online Payment features in Chapter 5.

Bill and Income Reminders   The Bill And Income Reminders tab displays a list of upcoming, due, and overdue scheduled transactions, as seen here. See Chapter 6 for more information about scheduled transactions.

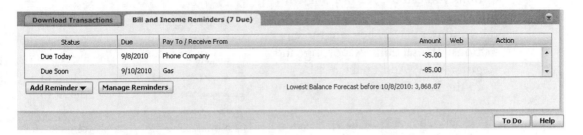

You can show or hide this information in the bottom half of the register window by clicking the small arrow button on the right end of the bar on which the tabs appear.

Button Bar Options

1. From the account register, the Dates drop-down list lets you filter the register to include all dates, specific time periods, or create a customized date range to display.
2. The next drop-down list in bank account registers gives the ability to filter for all transaction types, payments, or deposits. In credit card account registers, your choices are Charge or Payment.
3. The next drop-down list allows you to filter the register by several criteria: Uncategorized, Unreconciled, Cleared, Uncleared, and Flagged.
4. Reset sets the transactions register back to the default settings: All Dates, Any Type, and All Transactions.
5. The Find icon displays the Quicken Find dialog, which you can use to search for transactions based on a variety of criteria. Learn how to search for transactions later in this chapter, in the section titled "Searching for Transactions."

Account Actions

This window's Account Actions menu, as seen here, includes a number of options you can use for working with transactions, reporting, and changing the window's view. There are three sections: Transactions, Reporting, and Register Views And Preferences.

In the Transactions section you can:

1. Click Update Now to open the One Step Update Settings dialog for accounts that have online services. Enter the password given by your financial institution and click Update Now.
   –Or–
   Click Set Up Online to open the Add Account dialog for accounts that have not yet been activated for download.
2. Click Edit Account Details to open the Account Details dialog as described in "Editing Existing Accounts" shown earlier in this chapter.
3. Click Write Checks to open the Write Checks dialog. See "Writing Checks" later in this chapter.
4. Click Reconcile to open the Reconcile Details dialog. See Chapter 7 for complete instructions on reconciling your accounts.
5. Click Transfer Money to open the Transfer Between Quicken Accounts dialog. See "Transferring Money" later in this chapter for directions.

The Reporting section allows you to:

1. Click Account Attachments to open the Attachments dialog. See more information in the section "Adding Notes and Attachments" later in this chapter.
2. Click Account Overview to display a graphical recap of the selected account as well as the account's current status, as shown on the top of the next page.

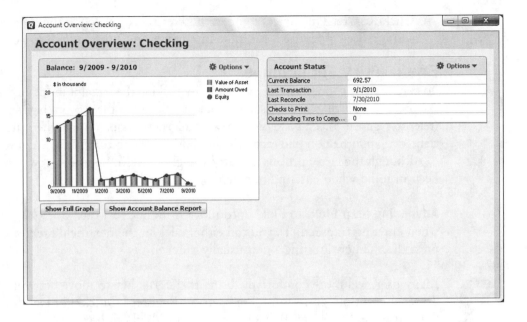

3. Click More Reports to see the information about this account in various report formats. Read more about creating reports in Chapter 8.
4. Click Print Transactions to open the Print dialog where you can print the check register for this account. See Chapter 8 for more information about printing reports and graphs.
5. Click Export To Excel Compatible File to export this file to your installed copy of Microsoft Excel. See more information in Chapter 8.

The Register Views And Preferences section lets you set how this register displays.

1. Click Two-Line Display to show your register information on two lines, as seen in Figure 4-5. If you clear that check box, you'll see the payee, the category, and the amount on just one line. One-line display is the default for Quicken 2011.
2. Click Sorting Options to tell Quicken how to organize your transactions in this register, as seen here. See "Sorting Transactions" later in this chapter for more information.
3. Click Register Columns to open the Register Columns list as seen in Figure 4-6.

4. Click Register Preferences to open the Preferences dialog at the Register section. See Appendix B for more discussion on Quicken Preferences.

Basic Entry Techniques

To enter a transaction, first, open a register by clicking the account in the Account Bar. Begin by clicking in the first empty line at the end of the account register window (refer to Figure 4-5). This activates a new, blank transaction. You can then enter transaction information into each field and press ENTER to complete the transaction.

Although the entry process is pretty straightforward, here are a few things to keep in mind when entering transactions.

Advancing from Field to Field   To move from one text box, or *field*, to another when entering transactions, you can either click in the next field's text box or press the TAB key. Pressing TAB is usually quicker.

 Many users feel more comfortable using the ENTER key to move between fields. To set this option, go to Edit | Preferences | Register | QuickFill | Data Entry. Click the Use Enter Key To Move Between Fields check box.

Using Icons   Icons appear when certain fields are active.

- When the Date field is active, a calendar icon appears, as seen here. You can click it to display a calendar, and then click calendar buttons to view and enter a date.

  8/8/2010

- When one of the two Amount fields is active, a calculator icon appears as shown. You can click it to use a calculator and enter calculated results.

- When the Payee or Category field is active, a Report button appears. Click the Report button to display a pop-up report of transactions in that category or for that payee, like the one shown here. Click the X to close the report.

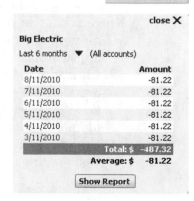

 If you do not see the calendar, calculator, or report icons, you can turn them on by going to Edit | Preferences | Register | QuickFill and ensuring that the Show Buttons On QuickFill fields check box is selected, as shown on the top of the next page.

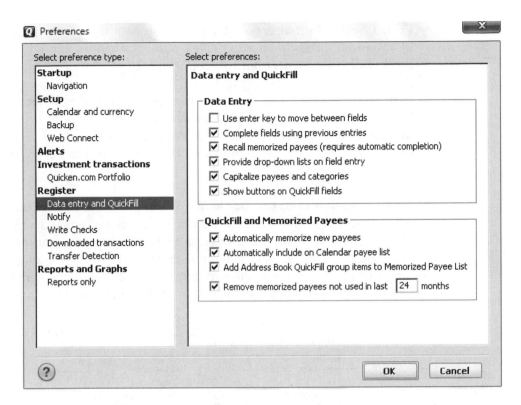

Menu buttons, which look like triangles pointing down to a horizontal line, display drop-down lists of items applicable to the active field. You can enter an item by choosing it from the list's options or by simply typing the information.

Using the Number Field   The Check Number (or Reference Number in non-banking accounts) field is where you enter a transaction number or type. You can enter any number you like or use the drop-down list (shown here) to display a list of standard entries; click an option to enter it for the transaction. You can also press the + or – key on the keyboard to increment or decrement the check number, respectively, while the field is active.

- **Next Check Num** automatically increments the most recently entered check number and enters the resulting number in the Check Number field.
- **ATM** is for ATM transactions. You may also want to use it for debit or check card transactions.
- **Deposit** is for deposits.

- **Print Check** is for transactions for which you want Quicken to print a check. Quicken automatically enters the check number when the check is printed.
- **Send Online Payments** is for accounts for which you have enabled Online Bill Pay.
- **Online Transfer** is for accounts that have been activated to transfer funds from one online account to another online account.
- **Transfer** is for a transfer of funds from one account to another.
- **EFT**, which stands for electronic funds transfer, is for direct deposits and similar transactions.

The Payee Drop-down List and QuickFill   When you begin to enter information in the Payee field, a drop-down list of existing payees or payers appears. As you type, Quicken narrows down the list to display only those names that match what you have typed. You can enter an existing name from the list by selecting it. Quicken will fill in details from the most recent transaction for that name for you. This is Quicken's QuickFill feature, which you will learn more about in Chapter 6.

Jeff's Hardware	-26.93	Home Re...
Joseph O Engineering	-250.00	Home Re...
Linens And Towels	-68.97	Recreation
Lions' Club	-25.00	Charitabl...
Loan Payment	-525.00	--Split-- N/A
Morg's Auto Repir	-304.88	Auto:Ser...

Memorized Payee List

Automatic Categorization   After entering a payee for the first time, Quicken may fill in the category for you. This is Quicken's automatic categorization feature, which enters categories based on thousands of payee names programmed into it. You'll find that in most cases, Quicken assigns an appropriate category. But you can change the category if you like and, from that point on, Quicken's QuickFill feature will use the category you assign for future transactions to that payee. Chapter 6 provides more information about QuickFill.

Using the Category Drop-down List   The Category drop-down list organizes category and transfer accounts in the Category List window (which is discussed in Chapter 2). This drop-down list may appear automatically when you begin to enter a category in the Category field of the transaction area; if it does not, you can click the menu button on the right side of the field to display it. You can narrow down the display of categories by clicking a heading on the left side of the drop-down list. Then click the category name to enter it into the field.

Entering New Categories   If you type in a category that does not exist in the Category List, Quicken displays the New Category dialog (shown here), which offers to create a new category with that name. Click Yes to use the Set Up Category dialog to create a new category, or click No to return to the register and enter a different category. If you turn off the Prompt Before Creating New Categories check box, Quicken automatically displays the Set Up Category dialog every time you enter a category that does not exist in the Category List. See more about categories in Chapter 2.

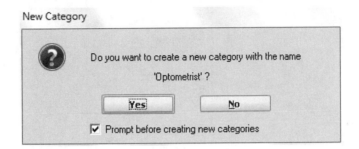

Entering Subcategories   When you choose a subcategory from the Category field's drop-down list, Quicken automatically enters the subcategory's parent category name, followed by a colon (:) and the subcategory name. To type a subcategory, use the first letter or two of the category, the colon, and then the first letter or two of the subcategory. QuickFill will match the category:subcategory. Here's what it might look like in a register entry.

Entering Multiple Categories   To enter more than one category for a transaction, click the Split button (a small, two-headed arrow pointing upwards) on the right side of the transaction entry area. See how to enter transactions with splits a little later in this chapter, in the section titled "Using Splits."

Using Register Columns   The small gear icon at the top of the balance column is used to tell Quicken which columns to display and which to hide. Click the gear icon to open the menu, as shown in Figure 4-6. Each item toggles the selected column in your register off and on. While many of the items are self-explanatory, there are several that might cause some confusion and are explained here. You can also open this dialog by clicking Register Columns in the Account Actions menu.

- **Amount**   Selecting this option adds an amount column before the balance column. It displays deposits in black and payments in red.

Figure 4-6 • Use the Register Columns menu to choose the columns to display in your register.

- **Action Buttons** When this is selected, the Save/More Actions/Split Transaction Into Multiple Categories buttons display in the selected transaction. See "Using Transaction Buttons" later in this chapter for more information.
- **Attachments, Status, and Tax-Related** If any or all of these are selected, the Sort By Attachment, Sort By Status, and/or Sort By Tax-Related buttons appear at the top of the Date column, as shown here. See "Sorting Transactions" later in this chapter for more information. The small flag and attachment icons also appear before or underneath the date when entering a new transaction.

Using Tags As discussed in Chapter 2, a tag is an optional identifier for specifying what a transaction applies to. Quicken displays a Tag field in the transaction form. To include a tag in a transaction, simply enter the tag in that field. Quicken may display a drop-down list of valid tags for you to choose from. If you type a tag name that is not on the Tag List, Quicken displays the Set Up

Tag window so you can create the tag on the fly. Review how to create tags in Chapter 2. You can use the Register Columns menu to turn off the Tag field display as seen in Figure 4-6.

Entering Memos You can enter a brief memo (up to 64 characters) about the transaction in the Memo field to the right of the Category (or Tag) field. This memo can help you recall why you made the transaction.

Using Transaction Buttons As shown here, three buttons appear on the line above or below the active transaction. You can use these buttons to work with the transaction.

- **Save** enters the transaction into the account register. If Quicken's sound option is turned on, you should hear a cash register *ch-ching* sound when you click it. (You can turn Quicken sounds on or off in the Preferences dialog, which is covered in Appendix B.)
- **More Actions**, a small black gear icon, displays a menu you can use to edit this transaction. See some of the More Action's menu commands later in this chapter, in the section titled "Changing Transactions."
- **Split Transaction Into Multiple Categories**, a small two-headed arrow pointing upward, opens the Split Transaction window. The next section explains how to enter a transaction with splits.

Using Splits

A *split* is a transaction with more than one category. For example, suppose you pay one utility bill for two categories of utilities—electricity and water. If you want to track each of these two expenses separately, you can use a split to record each category's portion of the payment you make. This enables you to keep good records without writing multiple checks to the same payee.

To record a transaction with a split, click the Split icon in the account register or the Split button in the Write Checks window when entering the transaction. The Split Transaction window, which is shown next, appears. Click in the first blank line and select a category. If desired, enter a memo for the category in the Memo field. Then enter the amount for that category in the Amount field. Repeat this process for each category you want to include in the transaction. Here's what the Split Transaction window might look like with two categories entered:

Split Transaction

Split Transaction

Enter multiple categories to itemize this transaction; use the Memo field to record more details.

	Category	Tag	Memo	Amount
1.	[Deck Loan]			171 38
2.	Interest Exp		Next Edit ▾	61 40
3.				
4.				
5.				
6.				
7.				
8.				
9.				
10.				
11.				
12.				
13.				
14.				
15.				
16.				

Add Lines   Clear All

Split Total: 232.78
Remainder: 0.00

Adjust   Transaction Total: 232.78

?   OK   Cancel

If you entered a transaction amount before clicking the Split button, you can monitor the Remainder and Transaction Total values in the Split Transaction window to make sure you've accounted for the entire transaction amount. If you entered an incorrect amount, you can click the Adjust button to adjust the transaction amount to match the split total.

When you're finished entering transaction categories, click OK or press ENTER. If you left the transaction amount empty before clicking the Split button, a dialog appears, asking if you want to record the transaction as a payment or deposit. Select the appropriate option and click OK.

As shown here, the word "Split" appears in the Category field for the transaction in the account register window.

Three buttons appear beside the Category field when you activate a transaction with a split.

- The green check mark displays the Split Transaction window so you can review and edit the transaction.

- The red X opens a message that allows you to clear all lines from the split. Use this option with care—it permanently removes all category information from the transaction.
- The Report icon prints a report about this transaction for a time period you can set.

Tracking Credit Cards with Quicken

Tracking bank account transactions and balances is just one part of using Quicken. It's also a great tool for tracking credit cards. Knowing how much you owe on your credit cards helps you maintain a clear picture of your financial situation.

How you use Quicken to track your credit cards depends on how accurate you want your financial records to be and how much effort you're willing to spend to keep Quicken up-to-date.

Credit Card Tracking Techniques

You can use either of two techniques for paying credit card bills and monitoring credit card balances with Quicken.

- Use your checking account register or the Write Checks window to record amounts paid to each credit card company for your credit card bill. Although this does track the amounts you pay, it doesn't track how much you owe or the individual charges.
- Use a credit card account register to record credit card expenditures and payments. This takes a bit more effort on your part, but it tracks how much you owe and categorizes what you bought.

Many Quicken users feel it's worth the extra effort to track your credit card expenditures and balances in individual credit card accounts. And if you utilize Quicken's Transaction Download feature for your credit card accounts, as discussed in Chapter 5, it won't take much time or effort to get the job done.

Recording Strategies

You can also use two strategies for recording transactions in credit card accounts. Choosing the strategy that's right for you makes the job easier to handle.

Enter as You Spend   One strategy is to enter transactions as you spend. To do this, you must collect your credit card receipts—which might be something you already do. Don't forget to jot down the totals for any telephone and online shopping you do. Then, every day or every few days, sit down with Quicken and enter the transactions.

While this strategy requires you to stay on top of things, it offers two main benefits.

- Your Quicken credit card registers always indicate what you owe to credit card companies. This prevents unpleasant surprises at month-end or at the checkout counter when you're told you've reached your limit. It also enables you to use the alerts feature to track credit card balances. Learn more about those features in Chapter 8.
- At month-end, you don't have to spend a lot of time entering big batches of transactions. All (or at least most) of them should already be entered.

Many just don't like holding on to all those pieces of paper. (Of course, once you have signed up for Transaction Download, all of the information is entered automatically. You can learn more about Transaction Download in Chapter 5.)

Enter When You Pay   The other strategy, which you may find better for you, is to enter transactions when you get your monthly statement. With this strategy, when you open your credit card statement, you'll spend some time sitting in front of your computer with Quicken to enter each transaction. If there aren't many, this isn't a big deal. But it could take some time if there are many transactions to enter.

Of course, the main benefit of this strategy is that you don't have to collect credit card receipts and spend time throughout the month entering your transactions. But you still have to enter them!

Entering Credit Card Transactions

Entering credit card transactions isn't very different from entering checking account or savings account transactions. Here are a few examples, which are illustrated in Figure 4-7.

Entering Individual Charges   Open the account register for the credit card account. Then enter the charge transaction, using the name of the merchant that accepted the charge as the payee name. If you don't want to include a transaction number or receipt number, you can leave the Reference Number field empty.

Entering Credits   Enter the transaction just as if it were a charge, but put the amount of the credit in the Payment box. This subtracts it from your account balance.

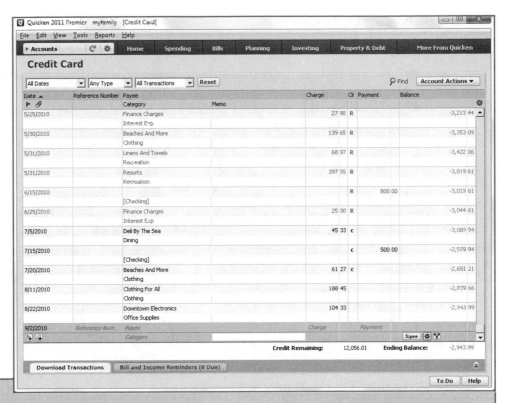

Figure 4-7 • Your credit card register looks very much like your bank account register.

Entering Finance Charges   In the credit card account register, enter the name of the credit card company as the payee and the amount of the finance charge as a charge. You can use the Interest Exp category for the transaction.

Entering Payments   In the account register for your checking account or in the Write Checks window, enter a payment transaction with the credit card company name in the Payee box. Enter the credit card account name in the Category text box; you should find it as a transfer account in the Category drop-down list that appears when you activate the field. The checking account register transaction should look like the one shown here.

| Bank Of The Island | 800 | 00 |
| [Credit Card] | | |

Recording Credit Card Rebates   Some credit card companies offer rebates for purchases. How you record a rebate depends on how the rebate is received.

- To record a rebate received as a check, deposit the check as usual and enter the amount of the rebate as a deposit in that account.
- To record a rebate received as a reduction in the credit card account balance, enter the amount of the rebate in the credit card account as a payment. (Just remember that a rebate is not a payment that counts toward your monthly obligation to the credit card company.)

What you use as a category for this transaction is completely up to you. You may want to use the Interest Exp account, thus recording the rebate as a reduction in your interest expense. Or, perhaps, if the rebate applies to a certain purchase only, use the category you originally used for that purchase. For example, if you have a credit card that gives you a 5 percent rebate on fuel purchases, you might record the rebate using the Fuel category you created to track fuel expenses. If you have a lot of credit cards that offer rebates, you may want to create a Rebate income account and use that as the category for all rebate transactions. These are just suggestions. There is no right or wrong way to do it.

Entering Cash Transactions

Although Quicken enables you to keep track of cash transactions through the use of a cash account, not everyone does this. The reason: Most people make many small cash transactions every day. Is it worth tracking every penny you spend? That's something you need to decide.

Many people track only expenditures that are large or tax-deductible. You may want to do the same. If so, you still need to set up a cash account, but you don't need to record every transaction. Figure 4-8 shows an example.

Cash Receipts   Cash receipts may come from using your ATM card, cashing a check, or getting cash from some other source. If the cash comes from one of your other accounts through an ATM or check transaction, when you record that transaction, use your cash account as the transfer in the Category field. That increases your cash balance.

Important Cash Expenditures   In your cash account, record large, tax-deductible, or other important cash expenditures like any other transaction. Be sure to assign the correct category.

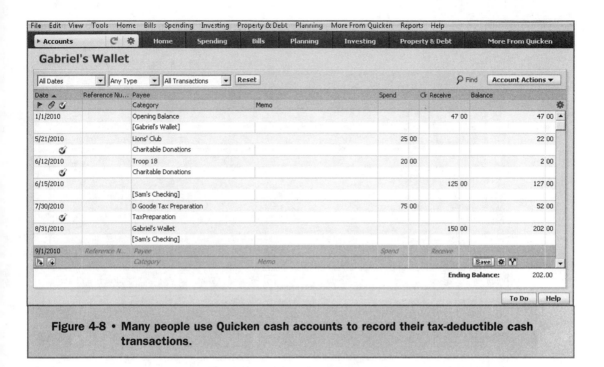

File Edit View Tools Home Bills Spending Investing Property & Debt Planning More From Quicken Reports Help								

▶ Accounts	C ✿	Home	Spending	Bills	Planning	Investing	Property & Debt	More From Quicken

Gabriel's Wallet

All Dates ▾	Any Type ▾	All Transactions ▾	Reset				𝒫 Find	Account Actions ▾

Date ▲	Reference Nu...	Payee		Spend	Clr	Receive	Balance	
▶ 𝒪 ✓		Category	Memo					✿
1/1/2010		Opening Balance				47 00	47 00	▲
		[Gabriel's Wallet]						
5/21/2010		Lions' Club		25 00			22 00	
✓		Charitable Donations						
6/12/2010		Troop 18		20 00			2 00	
✓		Charitable Donations						
6/15/2010						125 00	127 00	
		[Sam's Checking]						
7/30/2010		D Goode Tax Preparation		75 00			52 00	
✓		TaxPreparation						
8/31/2010		Gabriel's Wallet				150 00	202 00	
		[Sam's Checking]						
9/1/2010	Reference N...	Payee		Spend		Receive		
▶ ◄		Category	Memo				Save ✿ Y	▼

Ending Balance: 202.00

To Do   Help

Figure 4-8 • Many people use Quicken cash accounts to record their tax-deductible cash transactions.

Other Cash Expenditures   Throughout the week, you may spend 50¢ for a newspaper, $3 for a cup of coffee, and about $12 for lunch at your favorite hamburger joint. Recording transactions like these can be tedious, so don't bother if you don't want to. Instead, at the end of the week, compare your cash on hand to the balance in your cash account register. Then, enter a transaction to record the difference as an expenditure. You can use the Misc category and enter anything you like in the Payee field.

Writing Checks

Quicken's Write Checks window uses a basic checklike interface to record checks. You enter the same information that you would write on an actual check. You then tell Quicken to print the check based on the information you entered. (See how to print checks later in this chapter, in the section titled "Printing Checks.")

To open the Write Checks window, from your account register, click Account Actions | Write Check or press CTRL-W. The Write Checks window, which is shown in Figure 4-9, appears. The name of the account from which you are writing this check appears in the drop-down list near the top of the window.

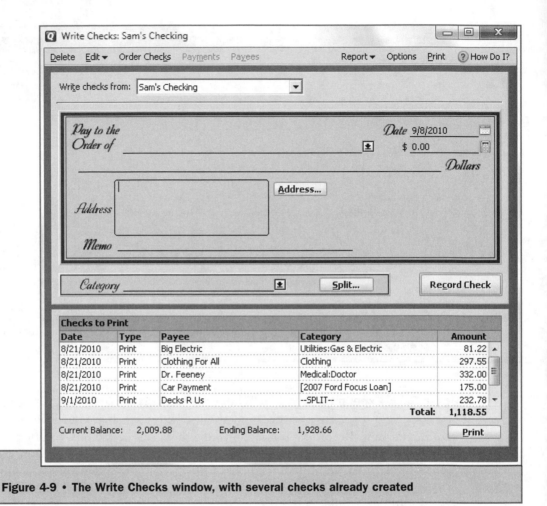

Figure 4-9 • The Write Checks window, with several checks already created

If you need to choose another account, click the down arrow. Enter the necessary information for a check and record the transaction.

Overview of the Write Checks Window

The Write Checks window is a busy place, with a lot of information and options. Before you learn how to use it to enter transactions, let's take a look at its options.

The Button Bar   The Write Checks window's button bar includes a number of buttons and menus for working with transactions and changing the window's view.

- **Delete** deletes the selected transaction. When you click this button, a dialog appears to confirm that you really do want to delete the transaction.
- **Edit** is a menu full of commands for creating, editing, and working with transactions. I discuss many of these commands later in this chapter, in the section titled "Working with Existing Transactions."
- **Order Checks** displays the Checks & Supplies page of the Intuit Market window, with information on how you can order check stock that is compatible with Quicken.
- **Payments** displays the Bills & Deposits list, which is discussed in Chapter 6. This option is only available if you are using the Write Checks window to send an online payment instruction.
- **Payees** displays the Online Payee List window, which is covered in Chapter 5. This option is only available if you are using the Write Checks window to send an online payment instruction.
- **Report** displays a menu of reports that are available for the selected transaction. Use commands to generate reports from within the Write Checks window. Learn more about Quicken's reporting features in Chapter 8.
- **Options** displays the Write Checks Preferences dialog, which you can use to customize the way the Write Checks window looks and works; learn more about customizing Quicken Preferences in Appendix B.
- **Print** enables you to print checks. Learn more about that later in this chapter, in the section titled "Printing Checks."
- **How Do I?** displays the Quicken Personal Finances Help window, with a list of topics related to the Write Checks window.

Account List   The Write Checks From drop-down list near the top of the window displays a list of accounts from which you can write checks. Be sure to choose the correct account from the list before entering check information.

Check Form   The middle of the window displays a form that looks and works a lot like a paper check. This is where you enter transaction information.

Checks To Print   The Checks To Print area of the window lists all of the checks that have been entered in the Write Checks window that have not yet been printed. When you enter a transaction in the Write Checks window, it is added to this list.

Entering Transactions in the Write Checks Window

The Write Checks window (refer to Figure 4-9) is like a cross between a paper check and Quicken's account register window. You fill in the check form like you would fill in the blanks on a paper check. Quicken's QuickFill feature makes data entry quicker and easier by recalling entry information from similar transactions to the same payee, and its automatic categorization feature can automatically "guess" the category for many new transactions. You must enter a valid Quicken category in the Category field, just as you would when entering a transaction in the account register. Clicking the Record Check button completes the transaction and adds it to the Checks To Print list (see Figure 4-9), as well as the account register.

Consult the section "Using Account Registers," earlier, for details about the information that should be entered into most fields. Here are a few additional things to consider when entering transactions in the Write Checks window.

Addresses on Checks   If you enter an address on the check, you can mail the check using a window envelope. The address is automatically added to the Quicken Address Book. You can click the Address button in the Write Checks window to display the Edit Address Book Record dialog, which you can use to modify an address in the Address Book.

Check Memos   If you enter a note on the memo line of a check, it may be visible if you mail the check in a window envelope.

Transferring Money

You can also record the transfer of funds from one account to another. You might find this feature especially useful for recording telephone or ATM transfers.

Using the Transfer Dialog

One way to record a transfer is with the Transfer dialog. Open the account register window for one of the accounts involved in the transfer transaction and click Account Actions | Transfer Money. The Record A Transfer Between Quicken Accounts dialog, which is illustrated on the next page, appears. Choose the source and destination accounts from the drop-down lists, enter a transaction date and amount, and click OK.

Recording a Transfer in the Account Register Window

The Transfer dialog isn't the only way to record a transfer. You can also record a transfer in the account register window of either the source or destination account. When you choose Transfer (TXFR) from the Check Number drop-down list, the Category drop-down list displays only transfer accounts. Choose the other transfer account from the list and complete the transaction.

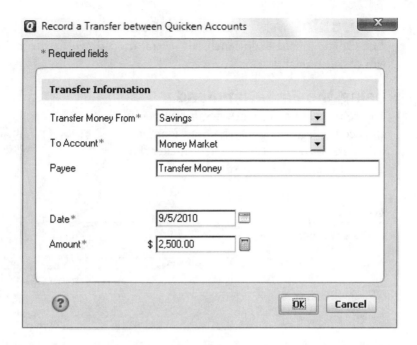

The following illustrations show a transfer from a savings account to a money market account. Here's what the source (Savings) account transaction looks like:

| TXFR | Transfer Money | 2,500 | 00 |
| | [Money Market] | | |

And here's what the corresponding destination (Money Market) account transaction looks like:

| 9/5/2010 | | Transfer Money | | | 2,500 | 00 |
| | | [Savings | | | | |

Working with Existing Transactions

So far, this chapter has concentrated on entering transactions. What do you do when you need to modify a transaction you already recorded? That's what this section is all about.

Searching for Transactions

The Quicken Find dialog includes several drop-down lists to help you locate and work with transactions.

Using the Find Command

To use the Find command, begin by opening an account register. Click the Find icon, as seen here, or press CTRL-F. The Quicken Find dialog appears, shown next.

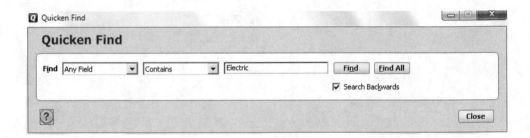

Start by choosing an option from the Find drop-down list, which includes all register fields for a transaction. Then choose the matching option from the next field to indicate how the search criteria should be matched (this field is not labeled, but the first choice on the list is "Contains"). Enter the search criteria in the next field. To search backward (relative to the currently selected transaction), turn on the Search Backwards check box.

After setting up the search, if you click the Find button, Quicken selects the first match found in the window. If you click the Find All button, Quicken displays the Search Results window, which lists all the matches it found. You can double-click a match to view it in the account register window. See illustration at the top of the next page.

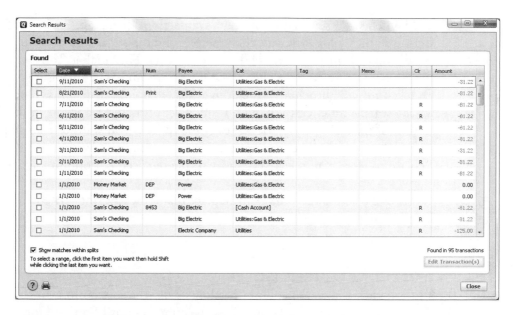

Using the Edit Transaction Command

To edit transactions, first find them and then in the Search Results window, select the transaction(s) by clicking the check box(es) in the Select column. Then click the Edit Transaction(s) button in the Search Results window. The Find And Replace dialog appears with the items you selected, as shown here.

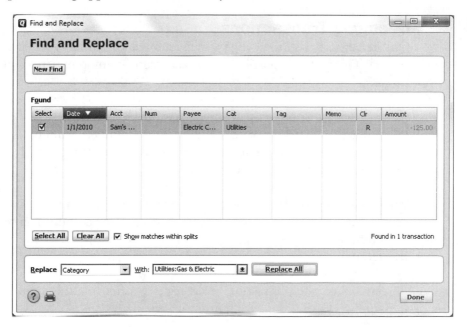

The items you selected in the Edit Transactions dialog appear in the Found section of the dialog. You can click the New Find button to make the top part of the dialog look and work much like the Quicken Find dialog. You can turn on the Show Matches In Split check box at the bottom of the dialog if you want Quicken to find all matches, including those that appear in splits. Once you set up the search and click the Find button, a list of matches appears in the Found section of the dialog. Click beside each found item you want to change to place a check mark there. Then set options in the Replace and With boxes. Click Replace to replace all selected items with the replacement option you specified.

 You can also access the Find And Replace dialog by pressing CTRL-H or clicking Edit | Find/Replace.

Sorting Transactions

You can click a register's column heading or use the sort options to change how your transactions are displayed. Click Account Actions | Sorting Options in an account's register to open the menu from which you can change the sort order of transactions, as seen here. For example, sorting by check number groups the transactions by the Check Number field, making it easy to find a specific check. You can quickly move to a specific date or transaction number by dragging the scroll box on the scroll bar.

Changing Transactions

Quicken enables you to change a transaction at any time—even after it has been cleared. This makes it possible to correct errors in any transaction you have entered.

Making Simple Changes   If all you want to do is change one of the fields in the transaction—such as the category, date, or number—simply find the transaction in the appropriate account register, make changes as desired, and click the Save button to record them.

Using the More Actions Menu   The More Actions menu appears, as shown next, when you click the More Actions button in the account register window for the currently selected transaction. It offers other options for working with a selected transaction.

- **Save** enters the transaction in the register. Choosing this command is the same as clicking the Save button or pressing ENTER.

- **Restore Transaction** enables you to change a transaction back to the way it was before you started changing it. This option is available only if you have made changes to the selected transaction.
- **Split** opens the Split window for the transaction. Choosing this command is the same as clicking the Split button. You learned how to use the Split feature earlier in this chapter, in the section titled "Using Splits."
- **Notes And Flags** displays the Transaction Notes And Flags dialog (which is shown later in this chapter, in the section titled "Adding Notes, Flags, and Alerts") so you can add transaction notes, flag the transaction in a specific color, or create an alert for follow-up.
- **Attachments** displays the Transaction Attachment dialog (shown later in this chapter, in the section titled "Attaching Checks, Receipts, or Other Images") so you can attach checks, receipts, and other images to the transaction.

Save	
Restore transaction	
Split...	Ctrl+S
Notes and flags...	
Attachments...	
Tax Line Item Assignments	
Copy transaction(s)	
Cut transaction(s)	
Paste transaction(s)	
Edit transaction(s)	
New	Ctrl+N
Delete	Ctrl+D
Undo delete	
Insert transaction	Ctrl+I
Move transaction(s)	
Undo Accept All Transactions	
Memorize payee...	Ctrl+M
Schedule bill or deposit	
Void transaction(s)	
Reconcile	▶
Find...	Ctrl+F
Find Next	Ctrl+Shift+F
Go To matching transfer	
Go to specific date...	Ctrl+G
View as a check	

- **Tax Line Item Assignments** displays the dialog with which you can assign a line item to the transaction's category as discussed in Chapter 17.
- **Cut Transaction(s)** copies the selected transaction and removes it from the account register.
- **Copy Transaction(s)** copies the selected transaction without removing it from the account register.
- **Paste Transaction(s)** pastes the last-copied transaction into the current account register. This option is available only after a transaction has been cut

or copied. You might want to cut a transaction to paste it into another register if you realize that you entered it in the wrong register.

- **Edit Transaction(s)** displays the Find And Replace dialog (shown earlier in this chapter, in the section titled "Searching for Transactions") so you can use the Replace feature to modify the selected transaction(s).

- **New** enables you to create a new transaction for the account. This does not affect the currently selected transaction.

- **Delete** deletes the selected transaction. This is the same as clicking the Delete button in the button bar. Remember that deleting a transaction removes the transaction from the Quicken data file, thus changing the account balance and category activity.

- **Undo Delete** restores the transaction you just deleted. You must use this command immediately after deleting a transaction to restore it.

- **Insert Transaction** enables you to insert a transaction before the selected transaction in the account register. This does not affect the currently selected transaction.

- **Move Transaction(s)** displays the Move Transactions(s) dialog, which you can use to move a transaction from the current account register to a different account register. Simply choose an account name from the drop-down list and click OK to complete the move.

- **Undo Accept All Transactions** restores accepted transactions to unaccepted status. This command is available only if the last thing you did was accept transactions. Learn more about accepting transactions in Chapter 5.

- **Memorize Payee** tells Quicken to add the selected transaction to its list of memorized payees.

- **Schedule Bill Or Deposit** enables you to schedule the transaction for a future date or to set up the transaction as a recurring transaction. Learn more about scheduling transactions in Chapter 6.

- **Void Transaction(s)** marks the selected transaction as void. This reverses the effect of the transaction on the account balance and category activity without actually deleting the transaction.

- **Reconcile** enables you to indicate whether the transaction should be marked as Not Reconciled, Cleared, or Reconciled. Learn how to reconcile accounts in Chapter 7.

- **Revert To Downloaded Payee Name** (not shown) enables you to revert to the transaction payee downloaded from your financial institution's server. This option only appears if the transaction has been downloaded and its payee name has changed.

- **Find** displays the Find dialog, which is discussed earlier in this chapter, in the section titled "Searching for Transactions."

- **Find Next** searches for transactions matching the previously entered Find criteria.
- **Go To Matching Transfer** displays the selected transaction in the account register for the other part of a transfer. For example, if the selected transaction involves the checking and savings accounts and you are viewing it in the checking account register, choosing the Go To Transfer command displays the same transaction in the savings account register. This command is available only if the selected transaction includes a transfer.
- **Go To Specific Date** enables you to move to a different date within the register. This does not affect the currently selected transaction.
- **Cancel Payment** (not shown) sends a cancel payment instruction to your bank to stop an online payment. This option is available only for online payments that have not yet been made.
- **Amount Spent On** *category* will display a Category Report for this category if your cursor is in the category field in the selected transaction. If your cursor is in the payee field, the report will be Payments Made To *payee name*.
- **Utilities:Gas & Electric Budget** displays budget information about the selected category, if your cursor is in the category field.
- **Launch Mini-Report For** displays a small report window of the current payee's or category's transactions. The option that appears depends on the field that is selected when you display the menu.
- **Use Calculator** (not shown) opens the Quicken calculator. This option is available if your cursor is in a field other than the category or payee fields.

Selecting More Than One Transaction   You may need to work with more than one transaction at a time. To do this, you need to select multiple transactions. Here's how:

- To select several individual transactions in an account register, hold down CTRL and click each transaction you want to include. The transactions change color to indicate they are selected.
- To select a range of transactions, click to select the first transaction in the range. Then hold down SHIFT and click the last transaction in the range. All transactions between the first and the last transaction change color to indicate they have been selected.

Adding Notes and Attachments

Quicken's attachment feature enables you to add notes, flags, reminders, and image files to a transaction or account. This makes it possible to store all kinds of digital information in your Quicken data file, including cancelled checks, receipts, or photographs.

Adding Notes, Flags, and Alerts

You can add a note, color-coded flag, or follow-up alert—or all three—to any Quicken transaction. First, select the transaction you want to add the item to. Then click the More Actions button, and from the menu, click Notes And Flags to open the Transaction Notes And Flags dialog seen here. You can also use the small flag or paper clip icons beneath or to the left of the date on a register line.

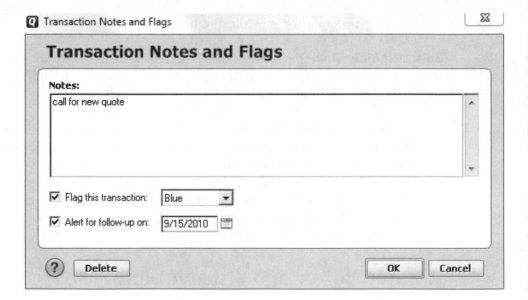

- To add a note, type the text of the note into the Notes box. This adds a flag icon to the transaction beneath the date. Pointing to the icon displays the note in a screen tip box.
- To flag the transaction, click the Flag This Transaction check box. Then choose a color from the drop-down list. This colors the flag icon placed above.
- To create a follow-up alert, turn on the Alert For Follow Up On check box and enter a date in the box beside it. (You can add a follow-up alert only if the transaction is already flagged.) This adds an alert to the Alerts Center window, which is discussed in Chapter 8.

Click OK to save your settings.

Attaching Checks, Receipts, or Other Images

Quicken also enables you to attach image files from a file on disk, a scanner, or the clipboard to transactions or accounts. You can use this feature to file digital copies of important documents with the transactions or accounts they relate to.

Attaching Images to Transactions

You attach an image to a transaction in the account register window. Begin by selecting the transaction you want to attach the item to. Then click the More Actions button and select Attachments.

In the Transaction Attachments dialog that appears (see Figure 4-10), use the Attach New or Attach Another drop-down list to choose the type of attachment you want to add: Check, Receipt/Bill, Invoice, Warranty, or Other. Then click one of the Image From buttons.

- **File** displays the Select Attachment File dialog, which you can use to locate, select, and open a file on disk. The file must be in a format readable by Internet Explorer, such as JPG, GIF, TXT, HTML, PDF, or PNG. When you click Open, the file's content appears in the Transaction Attachment dialog.
- **Scanner** may display the Select Source dialog, which you can use to select your scanner. It then displays your scanner's standard scanning interface, which you can use to scan an image. When the scan is complete, the image appears in the Transaction Attachment dialog.
- **Clipboard** pastes the contents of the clipboard into the Transaction Attachments dialog. (To use this option, you should select and copy an image *before* opening the Transaction Attachment dialog.)

Figure 4-10 • Use the Transaction Attachment dialog to attach important documents to a transaction.

Quicken allows you to add as many attachments as you like to a transaction. To add other attachments, just repeat the process. When you're finished, click Done to close the Transaction Attachments dialog. An Attachment icon appears beneath the transaction date to indicate that items are attached.

Working with Attachments

Once a file has been attached to a transaction, you can view, remove, replace, or print it at any time.

To work with a transaction attachment, click the More Actions icon for the transaction and select Attachments. The Transaction Attachments dialog (refer to Figure 4-10) opens. Click the thumbnail image or icon for the attached item to work with it.

You can use buttons in the Transaction Attachments dialog to work with attachments.

- **Help** (which appears as a question mark) displays the Quicken Personal Finances Help window, with links to topics about attaching digital images to transactions and accounts. Click a link to view the help information.
- **Print** (which appears as a small printer icon) prints the attachment.
- **Encryption** allows you to encrypt the attachment.
- **Export** saves the attachment as a file on your disk.
- **Delete** removes the attachment.
- **Done** closes the dialog.

Printing Checks

Quicken's ability to print checks enables you to create accurate, legible, professional-looking checks without picking up a pen (or a typewriter). In this section, you'll learn how to print the checks you enter in the Write Checks window, discussed earlier in this chapter.

Getting the Right Checks

Before you can print checks from Quicken, you must obtain compatible check stock. Quicken supports checks in a number of different styles.

- **Standard checks** print just checks. There's no voucher or stub.
- **Voucher checks** pair each check with a similarly sized voucher form. When you print on a voucher check, the transaction category information, including splits and tags, can be printed on the voucher part.
- **Wallet checks** pair each check with a stub. When you print on a wallet check, the transaction information is printed on the stub.

In addition to these styles, you can get the checks in two different formats for your printer.

- **Page-oriented** checks are for laser and inkjet printers.
- **Continuous** checks are for pin-feed printers.

A catalog and order form for checks may have been included with your copy of Quicken. You can use it to order checks. If you have an Internet connection, you can order checks online from within Quicken by clicking the Order Checks button in the button bar of the Write Checks window (see Figure 4-9).

Setting Up

Quicken must also be set up to print the kind of checks you purchased. You do this once, and Quicken remembers the settings.

Choose File | Printer Setup | For Printing Checks to display the Check Printer Setup dialog, shown next. Use the drop-down lists and option buttons to specify settings for your printer and check stock. The following are a few things to keep in mind when making settings in this dialog.

Partial Page Printing Options

If you select the Page-Oriented option and either Standard or Wallet checks in the Check Printer Setup dialog, you can also set options for Partial Page Printing Style. This enables you to set up the printer for situations when you're not printing an entire page of checks.

- **Edge** is for inserting the page against one side of the feeder. The left or right edge of the checks enters the feeder first.
- **Centered** is for centering the page in the feeder. The left or right edge of the checks enters the feeder first.
- **Portrait** is also for centering the page in the feeder, but in this case, the top edge of each check enters the feeder first.

If your printer supports multiple feed trays, you can also set the source tray for partial and full pages by choosing options from the Partial Page Source and Full Page Source drop-down lists.

Continuous Printing Options

If you select the Continuous option and either Standard or Wallet checks in the Check Printer Setup dialog, the dialog changes to offer two Continuous options.

- **Bypass The Driver** should be turned on for a continuous printer that skips checks or prints nothing.
- **Use Low Starting Position** should be turned on for a continuous printer that cuts the date or logo off your checks.

Checking the Settings for Page-Oriented Checks

If you're using page-oriented checks, you can check your settings by printing a sample page on plain paper. Here's how:

1. Click the Alignment button in the Check Printer Setup dialog.
2. In the Align Checks dialog that appears, click the Full Page Of Checks button.
3. In the Fine Alignment dialog, click the Print Sample button.
4. When the sample emerges from your printer, hold it up to the light with a sheet of check stock behind it. The sample should line up with the check.
5. If the sample does not line up properly with the check stock, set Vertical and/or Horizontal adjustment values in the Fine Alignment dialog. Then repeat steps 3 through 5 until the alignment is correct.
6. Click OK in each dialog to accept your settings and close it.

Printing

Once setup is complete, you're ready to print checks.

Open the account register for the account you want to print checks for. Then insert the check stock in your printer and choose File | Print Checks, or click the Print button in the Write Checks window. The Select Checks To Print dialog, which is shown next, appears. Enter the number of the first check that will be printed in the First Check Number box. Then set other options as desired. If you select the Selected Checks option, you can click the Choose button to display a list of checks and mark off the ones you want to print. Click Done in that window to return to the Select Checks To Print dialog.

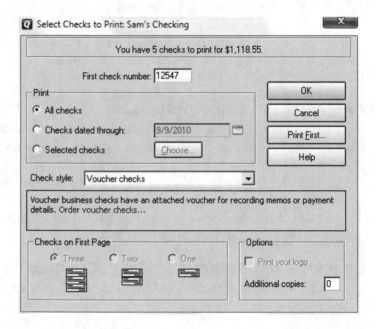

When you click Print First or OK, Quicken sends the print job to your printer. It then displays a dialog asking if the checks printed correctly. You have the following two options:

- If all checks printed fine, just click OK.
- If a problem occurred while printing the checks, enter the number of the first check that was misprinted, and then click OK. You can then go back to the Select Checks To Print dialog and try again.

Using Online Banking Features

Chapter 5

In This Chapter:

- *Benefits and costs of online banking*
- *Setting up Online Account Services*
- *Downloading and comparing transactions*
- *Setting up payees*
- *Processing online payments and transfers*

Life can be pretty hectic sometimes—too hectic to keep track of your bank accounts, pay bills before they're overdue, and buy stamps to mail your bills. Quicken Personal Finance Software's Online Account Services enable you to do most (if not all) of your banking from the comfort of your own home so banking can be a lot less of a chore. Several features can be used separately or together.

- **Transaction Download** enables you to download bank and credit card account activity, and transfer money online between accounts.
- **Online Payment** enables you to pay bills online without manually writing or mailing a check. (Quicken Bill Pay offers the features of Online Payment, even if your bank does not support it.)

This chapter explains how these features work and how you can use them to save time while keeping track of your finances.

The instructions in this chapter assume that you have already configured Quicken for an Internet connection. If you have not done so, do it now. This chapter also assumes that you understand the topics and procedures discussed in Chapters 2 and 4. This chapter builds on many of the basic concepts discussed in those chapters.

Online Account Services

Here's a closer look at Quicken's Online Account Services, including what the services are, how they work, and how you can expect to benefit from them.

Transaction Download

Quicken's Transaction Download feature can perform several tasks, depending on your financial institution. Here's the scoop.

How It Works

Generally speaking, financial institutions can support Transaction Download three ways.

Direct Connect   Many financial institutions support direct communication between Quicken and the financial institution's server. This so-called *Direct Connect* method is the most powerful way to use the Transaction Download feature. To download transactions, you simply click a button in Quicken's Online Center window, provide brief instructions and a PIN, and wait while Quicken gets the information you want. At the same time, Quicken can send information such as payment or transfer instructions to your bank for processing. In this two-way communication, Quicken does all the work.

Express Web Connect   If a financial institution does not support Direct Connect but does support the download of transactions from its website, it may support a download method called *Express Web Connect*. This one-way communication downloads transactions directly into Quicken without requiring you to manually visit the financial institution's website.

If you're already using Quicken with Web Connect and your financial institution supports Express Web Connect, Quicken will prompt you to convert the download method to Express Web Connect. While Express Web Connect may simplify the download of transactions from your financial institution to your Quicken data file, some users have reported a delay in transaction dates, depending on when the transactions are downloaded by your financial institution.

Web Connect   Many financial institutions that don't support Direct Connect or Express Web Connect enable you to manually download specially formatted *Web Connect* files. To do this, you must log in to your financial institution's website using the information your financial institution supplies, navigate to a download page, and indicate what data you want to download. Once the Web Connect file has been downloaded, Quicken reads it and knows exactly which Quicken account it applies to.

Downloaded Transactions

Bank account transaction downloads include all deposits, checks, interest payments, bank fees, transfers, ATM transactions, and debit card transactions. Credit card transaction downloads include all charges, credits (for returns or adjustments), payments, fees, and finance charges. Quicken displays all of the transactions, including those you have not yet entered in your account register, as well as the current balance of the account. A few clicks and keystrokes is all it takes to enter the transactions you missed. This feature makes it virtually impossible to omit entries, while telling you exactly how much money is available in a bank account or how much money you owe on your credit card account—no more surprises in that monthly statement.

Additional Features of Direct Connect

If your financial institution supports Direct Connect, you may also be able to take advantage of the following two features.

Transfer Money Between Accounts   If you have more than one bank account at the same financial institution, you can use Online Account Access to transfer money between accounts. Although many banks offer this feature by phone or on their websites, initiating the transaction from within Quicken is quicker and easier and has the added benefit of entering it into your Quicken data file. Just enter a transfer transaction and let Quicken do the rest.

Send E-mail Messages to Your Financial Institution   Ever call the customer service center at your bank or credit card company to ask a question? If you're lucky, real people are waiting to answer the phone. But if you're like most people, your financial institution uses a call routing system that requires you to listen to voice prompts and press telephone keypad keys to communicate with a machine. Either way, when a real person gets on the line, you have to provide all kinds of information about yourself just to prove that you are who you say you are. *Then* you can ask your question. Some financial institutions offer an e-mail feature that's part of Direct Connect which enables you to exchange e-mail messages with your bank or credit card company's customer service department. You normally get a response within one business day.

Online Payment and Quicken Bill Pay

Online Payment enables you to send a check to anyone without physically writing, printing, or mailing a check. You enter and store information about the payee within Quicken. You then create a transaction for the payee that includes the payment date and amount. You can enter the transaction weeks or months in advance if desired—the payee receives payment on the date you specify.

Online Payment is one of the least understood Quicken features. Many folks think it can be used to pay only big companies like the phone company or credit card companies. That just isn't true. You can use Online Payment to pay any bill, contribute to your retirement account, donate money to a charity, or send your brother a birthday gift.

How It Works

Suppose you use Quicken to send online payment instructions to pay your monthly bill at Jim's Hardware Store. You've already set up Jim's as a payee by entering the name, address, and phone number of his store, as well as your account number there. Quicken sends your payment instructions to your bank, which stores it in its computer with a bunch of other online payment instructions. When the payment date nears, the bank's computer looks through its big database of payees that it can pay by wire transfer. It sees phone companies and credit card companies and other banks. But because Jim's store is small, it's probably not one of the wire transfer payees. So the bank's computer prepares a check using all the information you provided. It mails the check along with thousands of others due to be paid that day.

Jim's wife, who does the accounting for the store (with Quicken Home & Business, in case you're wondering), gets the check a few days later. She deposits it with the other checks she gets that day. The amount of the check is deducted from your bank account and your account balance at Jim's. If you use Transaction Download, the check appears as a transaction. It also appears on your bank statement. If your bank returns canceled checks to you, you may get the check along with all your others.

When the Money Leaves Your Account   The date the money is actually withdrawn from your account to cover the payment varies depending on your bank. There are four possibilities:

- One to four days before the payment is processed for delivery
- The day the payment is processed for delivery

- The day the payment is delivered
- The day the paper check or electronic funds transfer clears your bank

To find out when funds are withdrawn from your account for online payments, ask your bank.

The Benefits of Online Payment

Online Payment can benefit you in several ways. You can pay your bills as they arrive, without paying them early—the payee doesn't receive payment before the payment date you specify. You don't have to buy stamps, and the bank never forgets to mail the checks.

Quicken Bill Pay

If your bank does not support Online Payment, you can still take advantage of this feature by signing up for Quicken Bill Pay. This service works with your checking account like Online Payment does.

Costs

The cost of Quicken's Online Account Services varies from bank to bank. Check with your bank to determine the exact fees. Here's what you can expect:

- Transaction Download is often free to all customers or to customers who maintain a certain minimum account balance. Otherwise, you could pay a fee for this service.
- Online Payment is sometimes free, but more often it costs from $5 to $10 per month for 20 to 25 payments per month. Each additional payment usually costs 40¢ to 60¢. Again, some banks waive this fee if you maintain a certain minimum balance.
- Quicken Bill Pay is $9.95 for up to 20 payments and $2.49 for each set of five payments after that. (These prices are subject to change.)

NEW TO QUICKEN?

Online Payment Costs

If you think Online Payment sounds expensive, do the math. Here's an example. Let's say you get 20 payments per month for $5. If you had to mail 20 checks, it would cost $8.80 in postage. So you'd actually save $3.40 per month if you made 20 online payments. Even if you don't make 20 payments a month, you also don't have to stuff envelopes, apply return address labels, or stick on stamps. Your bills get paid on time, you earn more interest income, and never bounce a check.
Does this feature sound useful?

Security

If you're worried about security, you must have skipped over the security information in Chapter 3. Go back and read that now. It explains how Quicken and financial institution security works to make Online Account Services safe.

Setting Up Online Account Services

To use the Online Account Services supported by Quicken, you must configure the appropriate Quicken accounts. This requires that you enter information about your financial institution and the account with which you want to use these features.

Applying for Online Account Services

Before you can use one of the Online Account Services, you must apply for it—learn how at the end of Chapter 3. Normally, all it takes is a phone call, although some banks and credit card companies allow you to apply online.

To learn more about and apply for Quicken Bill Pay, choose the More From Quicken tab and click Get Started in the Quicken Bill Pay section. After reading the information about Quicken Bill Pay that appears in your browser window, click the 1 Month Free, Start Now! button to begin the process.

The application process for these services usually takes a week, but may take less. You'll know that you're ready to go online when you get a letter with setup information. The setup information usually consists of the following.

PIN (Personal Identification Number)   You'll have to enter this code into Quicken when you access your account online. This is a security feature, so don't write down your PIN on a sticky note and attach it to your computer monitor. Many financial institutions send this information separately for additional security.

Customer ID Number   This is often your Social Security number or taxpayer identification number.

Bank Routing Number   Although your bank might send routing number information, Quicken won't need it. It knows what financial institution you're using based on the information you provide when you create the account. That's why it's so important to choose the correct financial institution when you create an account.

Account Number for Each Online Access–Enabled Account   This tells your financial institution which account you want to work with. In many instances, Quicken may not need this information either.

Setting Up Online Account Services

With customer ID and PIN in hand, you're ready to set up your account (or accounts) for Online Account Services. You can set up the account in a number of ways; rather than cover them all, this section covers the most straightforward method.

Keep in mind that if you set up an account using the online method, as discussed in Chapter 3, and you already have online account access enabled at your bank, your account may already be set up for online access. You can tell if it is by following the instructions in the "Checking Online Account Service Status" section, later in this chapter.

Setting Up for Direct Connect, Express Web Connect, and Quicken Bill Pay

If you entered the account manually, in the Account Bar, click the account you want to set up to open its register. Click Account Actions | Set Up Online, as shown here. If the account is already set up for online access, the Account Action menu will show Update Now instead of Set Up Online.

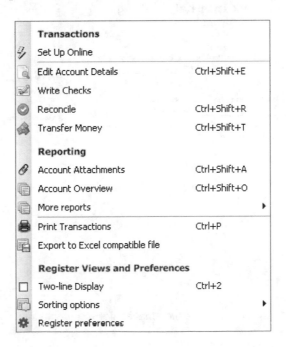

The Add [*type of account*] Account dialog appears as seen in Figure 5-1. Type the name of your financial institution, or choose from the list. Quicken uses your Internet connection to connect to your bank. Depending on your bank, you may be prompted to choose the branch or account type for this account. If so, choose from the list or drop-down list (what you see depends on your bank) and click Next.

Enter the user ID and password furnished to you by your bank and click Connect. Quicken connects to the Internet again to fetch more information. You may be asked for additional information by your financial institution. If so, enter that information and click OK.

A list of the accounts held at this financial institution displays as shown on the next page. Choose the account and add a nickname for this account if you choose. Otherwise, Quicken will use the name shown by the bank. If you want to link one of these accounts to an account you originally added manually, click Add to open a menu from which you can link to any of the accounts you've already added into Quicken. Click Next.

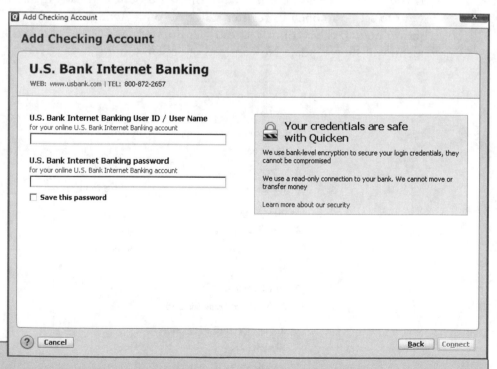

Figure 5-1 • The Add Account dialog makes setting up online services easy.

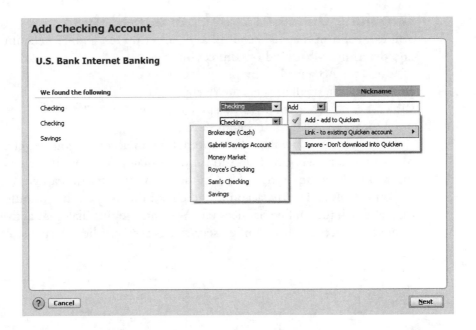

After the download has completed, the Account Added dialog appears with the name of your account and the number of transactions that were downloaded as shown here. Click Finish to return to the register.

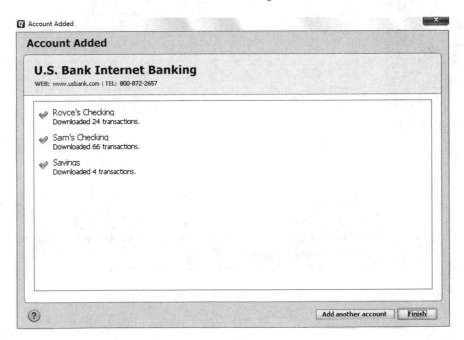

Checking Online Account Service Status

You can confirm that an account has been set up for Online Account Services and determine what kind of connection it uses.

Open the Account List by pressing CTRL-A or by clicking the small gear on the Account Bar as shown here. Each account will display the type of connection, as shown in Figure 5-2.

If the Activate Download link appears for an account, you can click the link to set up online services. The Add Account dialog will appear. Follow the directions shown in "Setting Up Online Account Services" earlier.

You can also select the account and click Edit to open the Account Details dialog. Click the Online Services tab. You can use this dialog to activate or remove this account from online services, as seen on the next page.

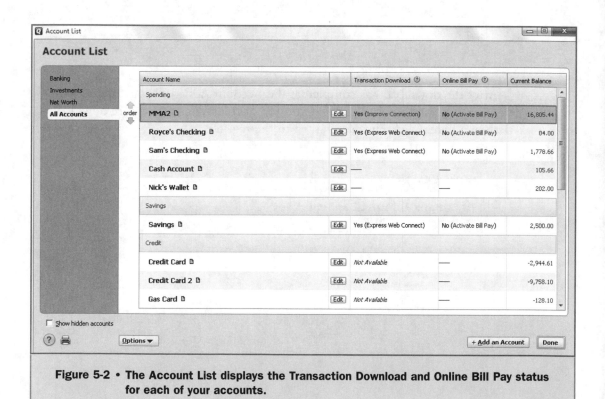

Figure 5-2 • The Account List displays the Transaction Download and Online Bill Pay status for each of your accounts.

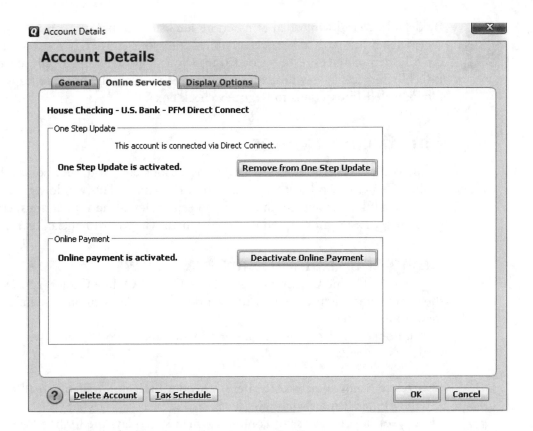

More About Transaction Download

Quicken makes a distinction between two types of downloaded transactions:

- **Online transaction instructions** are those transactions that have been sent to your financial institution but have not yet cleared your account. For example, suppose you used your bank's website to pay one of your bills. This transaction is in your bank's computer server, but it hasn't been completed or cleared. After the bill has been paid, when you download transactions for that account, Quicken downloads the payment.

- **Cleared transactions** are those transactions that have cleared your account and are included in your current account balance. For example, suppose you made a deposit at the bank. As soon as the bank accepts the deposit, the deposit is said to have "cleared" and is included in your current bank account balance. Cleared transactions can include deposits, checks, online payments, ATM transactions, debit card transactions, bank or interest fees, and interest earnings.

By default, your downloaded transactions are listed so that you can review and accept them before they have been entered into your register. If you want all downloaded transactions to be loaded into your register automatically, click Edit | Preferences | Downloaded Transactions and select the Automatically Add Downloaded Transactions to Registers check box.

The Online Center

While you can access online services in the various tabs, you can also use the Online Center to work with Quicken's online features. This window gives you access to all the lists and commands you need to download transactions, create payments, transfer money, and exchange e-mail with your financial institution.

Using the Online Center Window

To open the Online Center window, choose Tools | Online Center. Figure 5-3 shows what the Payments tab of this window looks like with one financial institution selected.

A number of button bar buttons and menus enable you to work with the window's contents.

- **Delete** removes the selected item. This button is not available in all tabs of the Online Center window.
- **Payees** (if you have set up online payments) displays the Online Payee List window, which is discussed later in this chapter in the section titled "Entering Online Payee Information."
- **Repeating** (if you have set up online payments) displays the Repeating Online tab of the Bill and Income Reminders list window. Learn more about using this feature later in this chapter, in the section titled "Scheduling Repeating Online Payments."
- **Contact Info** displays the Contact Information dialog for the currently selected financial institution, if it is offered. You can use the information in the dialog to contact the bank or credit card company by phone, website, or e-mail. Not all financial institutions have these options.
- **Password Vault** gives you access to Quicken's Password Vault feature, which is discussed in Chapter 6. (This option may appear only if you have online banking features enabled for accounts at more than one financial institution.)
- **Renaming Rules** displays the Renaming Rules dialog. Learn how to use the renaming feature later, in the section titled "Renaming Downloaded Payees."

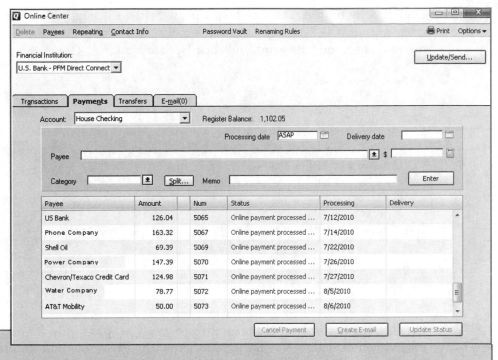

Figure 5-3 • The Online Center gives you access to online features for your accounts.

- **Print** prints the transactions that appear in the window. It may also print previously accepted transactions for some financial institutions.
- **Options** displays a menu of commands for working with the current account or window.

Downloading Transactions

One of the main features of Online Account Services is the ability to download transactions from your financial institution into Quicken. You do this with the Update/Send button of the Online Center window (refer to Figure 5-3). Here's how you can take advantage of this feature.

Connecting to the Financial Institution with Direct Connect or Express Web Connect

If your financial institution supports Direct Connect or Express Web Connect, you can download all transactions from within Quicken.

In the Online Center window, choose the name of your bank or credit card company from the Financial Institution drop-down list. If necessary, click the

Update/Send button. The One Step Update Settings dialog, which is shown next, appears. Click to toggle the check marks beside the instructions you want to send, enter your password, and click Update Now.

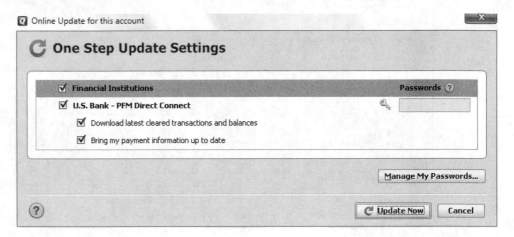

 Quicken might display a dialog offering to save your passwords. If you click Yes, follow the instructions in Chapter 6 to set up the Password Vault feature. You may then need to reinitiate the download procedure.

Wait while Quicken connects to your bank. A status dialog appears while it works. When Quicken has finished exchanging information, the status dialog disappears and the One Step Update Summary window takes its place. Continue following the instructions later in the chapter, in the section titled "Comparing Downloaded Transactions."

Downloading a Web Connect File

If your financial institution supports Web Connect but not Express Web Connect, you'll have to log in to your financial institution's website and manually download the statement information, just as you did when you first set up the account for Online Account Services.

In the Online Center window, choose the name of your bank or credit card company from the Financial Institution drop-down list. If necessary, click the Update/Send button. Quicken connects to the Internet and displays your financial institution's login page. Log in, navigate to the page where you can download statements, and download the statement or transactions you want. If necessary, switch back to Quicken. It should automatically import the transactions you downloaded into the correct account. If you have chosen to automatically accept your downloaded transactions, you will see a small blue ball icon. Transactions that have been matched to scheduled transactions have a calendar icon.

If Express Web Connect is available for an account, you may also see a dialog offering to upgrade your connection.

Click the Close button in the One Step Update Summary window to dismiss it. Then, use the Account Bar or some other method to open the account with downloaded transactions.

Unless you have chosen to turn on the Automatically Add Downloaded Transactions To Register preference, your downloaded transactions will appear in the Downloaded Transactions tab at the bottom of the register window. From there, you can use the directions in "Comparing Downloaded Transactions to Register Transactions."

Keep in mind that the first time you connect via Direct Connect, the bank normally sends all transactions from the past 60 or more days. (Some banks send a full year of transactions!) After that, only new transactions will be downloaded. For Web Connect downloads, you can often specify the transaction period when you set up the download.

Comparing Downloaded Transactions to Register Transactions

Your job is to compare the downloaded transactions to the transactions already entered in your account register. This enables you to identify transactions that you neglected to enter or that you entered incorrectly. In addition, because Quicken will automatically enter a date, transaction number, and amount—and in the case of some transactions, the payee and category (based on previously memorized transactions)—using this method to enter a transaction can be much faster than entering it manually in the account register window.

The Status column in the bottom half of the account register window (refer to Figure 5-4) identifies three types of transactions:

- **Match** identifies transactions that match those in the register. This will happen if the transaction has already been entered in the Quicken register.
- **New** identifies transactions that are not in the register.
- **Accepted** identifies matched transactions that you have accepted. When a downloaded transaction has been accepted, a small c appears in the Clr column of the account register to indicate that the item has cleared the bank but has not yet been reconciled.

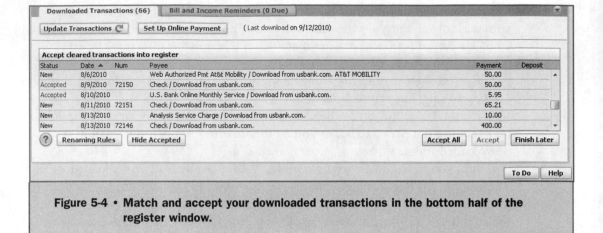

Figure 5-4 • Match and accept your downloaded transactions in the bottom half of the register window.

When you select a transaction in the bottom half of the window, the transactions below it shift down to make room for a blank line with an Accept button and an Edit menu. You can use these to work with the selected transaction.

Accepting a Matched Transaction   If a transaction matches one in the register, you can accept it by selecting it in the list at the bottom of the window and clicking the Accept button.

Entering and Accepting a New Transaction   To enter and accept a new transaction, select the transaction in the bottom half of the window. Fill in any missing details, including the payee, category, and memo. Then click Enter in the top half of the window or Accept in the bottom half. Quicken enters and accepts the transaction.

Unmatching a Matched Transaction   If a matched transaction really shouldn't be matched, select it in the bottom half of the window and choose Unmatch from the Edit pop-up menu.

- **Unmatch** tells Quicken that it got the match wrong, but this command lets Quicken attempt to match it to another transaction. As a result, it may come up with another match. It's your job to determine whether the new match is correct. If it can't find a match, the status changes to New.
- **Make New** tells Quicken that the transaction shouldn't match any existing transaction. The status changes to New and Quicken can then treat it as a new transaction.

- **Make All New** tells Quicken to make all of the downloaded but not yet accepted transactions new so you can manually match them.

Manually Matching a Transaction   If a downloaded transaction identified as New should match one in the register, or if a single transaction corresponds to multiple transactions in your account register, you can manually match them up. In the bottom half of the window, select the transaction that you want to match manually, and click the Edit button, which is shown here. Click Match Manually to open the Manually Match Transactions dialog. Turn on the check box(es) for the transaction(s) you want to include in the match. When you click Accept, Quicken creates an entry for the transaction. If the transaction included multiple register transactions, the entry Quicken creates includes each of the register transactions on a separate split line. You can click the Split button for the transaction to edit it as desired. Learn how to work with splits in Chapter 4.

You can also use the match process on a transaction that Quicken fails to match correctly, or just use the manual match process before the unmatch process. See Figure 5-5 for an example of matching transactions manually. If there is a small error between you and the bank, you are prompted to accept one or the other, or correct your register, as seen here.

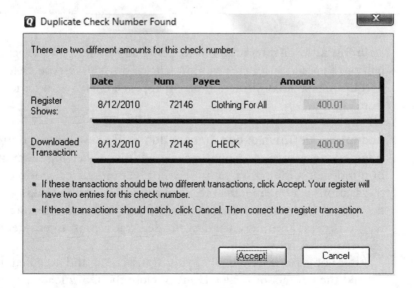

Figure 5-5 • Use the Manually Matching Transactions dialog to match transactions that have been downloaded.

Deleting a New Transaction   To delete any transaction, select it in the bottom half of the account register window, click Edit, and choose Delete from the Edit pop-up menu. A confirmation dialog appears; click Yes to remove the transaction from the list.

Accepting All Downloaded Transactions   The Accept All button accepts all transactions into your account register without reviewing them one by one. Keep in mind that some transactions may not be properly categorized, and some transactions may be matched to the wrong transaction, making it appear as if the downloaded transaction disappeared. Most Quicken users don't use Accept All without first examining each downloaded transaction to ensure it matched to the proper register transaction.

After you have reviewed all of your transactions and accepted, matched, and deleted the transactions, click Done to close the Downloaded Transactions dialog.

Renaming Downloaded Payees
One of the potentially annoying things about entering transactions by accepting downloaded activity information is the way your bank identifies payees. For

example, one bank identifies the payee for a cable television company as "NationalCableofAmerica{026-144710}" instead of plain old "CableAmerica."

Fortunately, Quicken's renaming rules feature can automatically rename bank-assigned payee names with names you prefer.

You can also create and apply your own renaming rules. You do this with the Renaming Rules dialog, which is shown here.

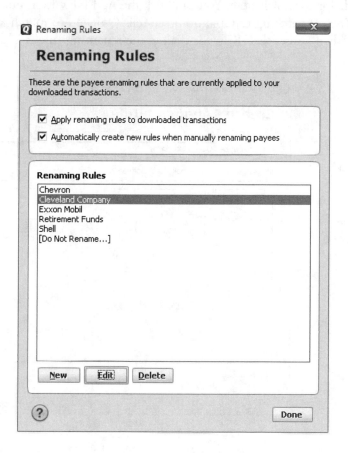

To open this dialog, click the Renaming Rules button at the bottom of the Downloaded Transactions tab of the register window, or choose Tools | Renaming Rules. The dialog lists all the renaming rules that have already been created. At the top of the dialog are options enabling the Renaming feature and letting Quicken automatically create renaming rules for you. These are turned on by default, and most Quicken users opt to leave them turned on.

You can use buttons at the bottom of the list to add, modify, or remove renaming rules.

New   Clicking the New button displays the Create Renaming Rule dialog. Enter the name you want to see as the payee name in the Change Payee box. Then choose an option from the first drop-down list to determine which field Quicken should match, choose a match option from the middle drop-down list, and enter match text in the text box. For example, if we wanted to change every downloaded item containing the text *QuickFuel* to *Quick Stop Fuel*, we'd set the dialog as shown here. You can click the Add New Item button to add another line of matching criteria; doing so tells Quicken to match *any* criteria you enter. When you click OK in the dialog, the renaming rule is added to the list.

Edit   Clicking the Edit button displays the Edit Renaming Rule dialog, which looks and works just like the Create Renaming Rule dialog just shown. This dialog enables you to modify settings for the selected renaming rule.

Delete   Clicking the Delete button removes the selected renaming rule from the list. You'll have to click OK in the confirmation dialog that appears to remove the rule.

Making Online Payments

The Add Transaction Reminder feature enables you to enter online payment instructions for accounts for which you have enabled the Online Payment feature. Figure 5-6 shows what it looks like.

The rest of this section explains how to set up online payees, enter payment information for one-time and repeating payments, and work with payment instructions.

Entering Online Payee Information

To send payments from your account, your bank must know who and where each payee is. To ensure that your account with the payee is properly credited, you must also provide account information. You do this by setting up online payees.

- From the Tools menu, click Online Center to open the Online Center dialog. Click Payees to open the Online Payee List. You can also choose Online Payee List from the Tools menu to open the list.
- **Financial Institution** offers a drop-down list of all the institutions for which you have enabled Online Bill Pay. Choose the institution that has the account from which you will be paying this payee. The payees you have

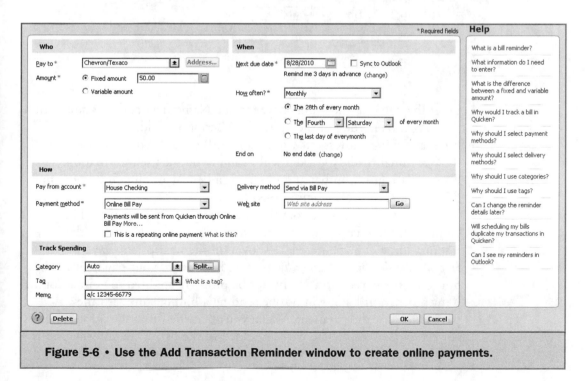

Figure 5-6 • Use the Add Transaction Reminder window to create online payments.

added for the displayed institution are listed, showing the payee name, the lead time for this payee, and the account number. Some financial institutions do not provide the lead time for online bill payments.

- **New** opens the Set Up Online Payee dialog, shown next.

- Enter the name of the online payee in the Name field and any description that might be needed in the optional Description field.
- Enter a mailing address, city, state, and ZIP code. If you skip over one of these required fields, Quicken will prompt you for the information.
- Enter an account number and phone number. Again, if you do not enter this information, you are prompted for it.
- Click OK when you have completed entering the information. The Confirm Online Payee Information message appears displaying the information you just entered, as shown on the next page. *Check the information in this box carefully.* If there is an error, your payment might not reach the payee, or it might not be properly credited to your account. Remember, your bank will not be sending a billing stub with the payment—just the payment. When you're satisfied that the information is correct, click Accept. The payee is added to the list. If the information is not correct, click Cancel to return to the Set Up Online Payee dialog.

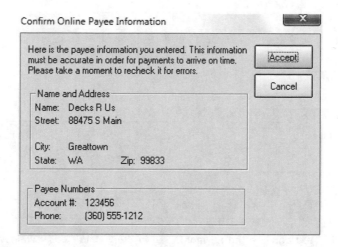

- **Edit** enables you to modify the information for the selected online payee. However, note that you cannot change the account number without deleting the payee and setting up a new payee.
- **Use** switches you back to the Payments tab of the Online Center window and inserts the selected payee into the payment form.
- **Report** displays a report of all payments made to the selected online payee.
- **Delete** removes the selected online payee. Deleting a payee simply deletes the payee's information from the Online Payee List window. It does not change any transactions for a payee. You cannot delete a payee for which unsent payment instructions exist.
- **Print** prints a list of online payees.

Entering Payment Instructions

To enter additional online payment instructions, click Tools | Online Center | Payments, as seen in Figure 5-7. Ensure you are using the correct financial institution if you have more than one set up for online payments. Fill in the fields in the middle of the window with the following payment information:

- **Processing Date** is the date the bank should begin processing the payment. For some banks, this date is fixed based on the Delivery Date field and can't be changed.
- **Delivery Date** is the date you want the payee to receive payment. This should be before the date the bank will either create and mail the check or make the electronic funds transfer. The check may be received before the delivery date, depending on the mail (if the check is mailed). The date you enter, however, must be at least the same number of business days in advance

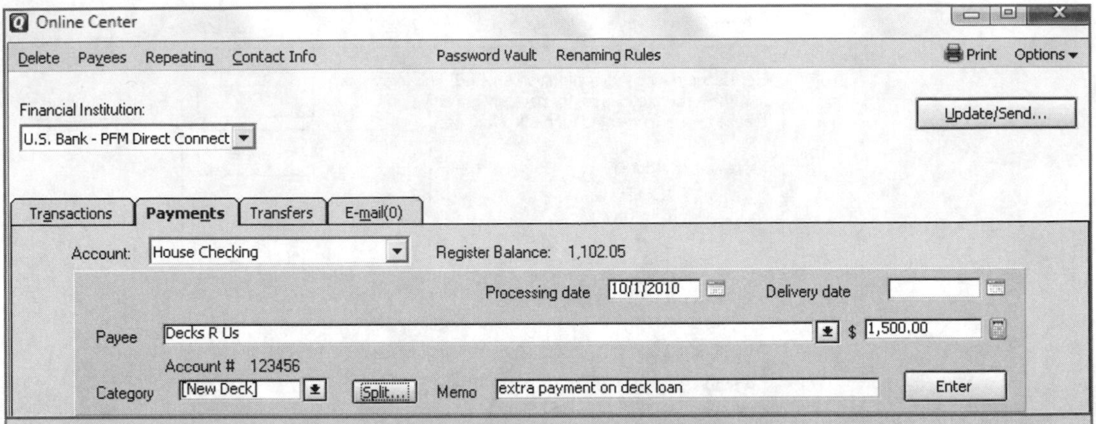

Figure 5-7 • **You can use the Payments tab in the Online Center window to enter information about online payments.**

as the lead time for the payee—usually four days. That means if you want to pay a bill on Wednesday, June 29, you must enter and send instructions to your bank on or before Friday, June 24. To process the payment as soon as possible, just enter today's date and Quicken will adjust the date for you. For some banks, the delivery date cannot be changed; instead, specify a processing date that allows enough time for the payment to be made on a timely basis.

- **Payee** is the online payee to receive payment. Quicken's QuickFill feature fills in the payee's name as you type it. If desired, you can choose it from the drop-down list of online payees. If you enter a payee that is not in the Online Payee List window, Quicken displays the Set Up Online Payee dialog so you can add the new payee's information. This enables you to create online payees as you enter payment instructions.
- **$** is the amount of the payment.
- **Category** is the category for the transaction. You can enter a category, choose one from the drop-down list, or click the Split button to enter multiple categories.
- **Memo**, which is optional, is for entering a note about the transaction.

When you've finished entering information for the transaction, click Enter. A message box appears reminding you that you need to allow enough time for the payment to be processed by your financial institution, as seen here. Click OK to continue or Cancel to return to the payment. Click the Don't Show This Message Again check box to keep the message from appearing.

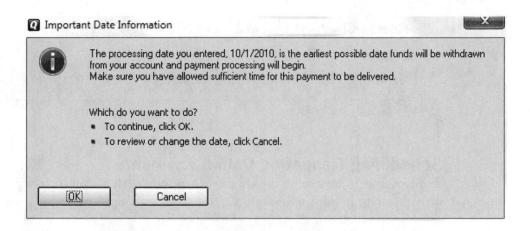

The transaction appears in the list in the bottom half of the window with the words "Payment request ready to send" in the Status column beside it. You can repeat this process for as many payments as you want to make.

Entering Online Payments in the Account Register

Another way to enter an online payment instruction is to simply enter the transaction in the appropriate account register. Click the Bills tab, click Manage Reminders, and double-click the transaction on the list or click Enter. The Enter Transaction dialog appears with SEND in the Method/Check Number field, as seen on the following page. Make any changes or additions in the dialog, and Click Enter Transaction to enter it into the register. You may find this method quicker, especially if you've worked with Quicken for a while and are familiar with the account register window.

NEW TO QUICKEN?

Payment and Delivery Dates

Don't let the Processing Date and Delivery Date options confuse you. The Delivery Date is the important date. It determines whether your payment will make it to the payee on time. Whenever possible, give the bank an extra two days. So, for example, if a bill is due on June 29, instruct the bank to pay on June 25. This isn't because of a lack of confidence in Quicken or the bank. It's because the Postal Service must still deliver the check.

If the Delivery Date field on your form can't be changed, don't panic. Just enter a processing date at least four days (or more) before the date you want the payment to arrive. That should give your bank enough time to get the payment to the payee without getting you in trouble.

House Checking

| All Dates ▼ | Any Type ▼ | All Transactions ▼ | Reset |

Date ▲	Check Number	Payee		Payment
▶ 🖉 ✓		Category	Memo	
10/1/2010	Send	Decks R Us		1,500 00
🖉		[New Deck]		

Scheduling Repeating Online Payments

Some payments are exactly the same every month, such as your rent, a car loan, or your monthly cable television bill. You can set these payments up as repeating online payments.

Here's how it works. You schedule the online payment once, indicating the payee, amount, and frequency. Quicken sends the instructions to your bank. Thirty days before the payment is due, your bank creates a new postdated payment based on your instructions and notifies you that it has created the payment. Quicken automatically enters the payment information in your account register with the appropriate payment date. The payment is delivered on the payment date. This happens regularly, at the interval you specify, until you tell it to stop. Because you don't have to do a thing to continue paying regularly, the more payments you make with this feature, the more time you save.

(Using this feature to pay an amortized loan such as a mortgage works a little differently. Learn about it later in this chapter, in the section titled "Linking a Repeating Online Payment to an Amortized Loan.")

In the Add Transaction Reminder window, click the Repeating Online Payment check box under the Payment Method field. The delivery method will immediately change to Automatic. You can also click Tools | Online Center | Repeating to open the Add Transaction Reminder window.

There are two very important things to remember when using the Add A Transaction Reminder dialog to create a repeating online payment:

- Choose Online Bill Pay from the Payment Method drop-down list. This tells Quicken that the payment will be made online.
- Turn on the This Is A Repeating Online Payment check box. This tells Quicken to send one instruction for multiple repeating payments.

When you click OK to save the payment instruction, it appears in the Repeating Online tab of the Bill And Income Reminder list window, as shown in Figure 5-8.

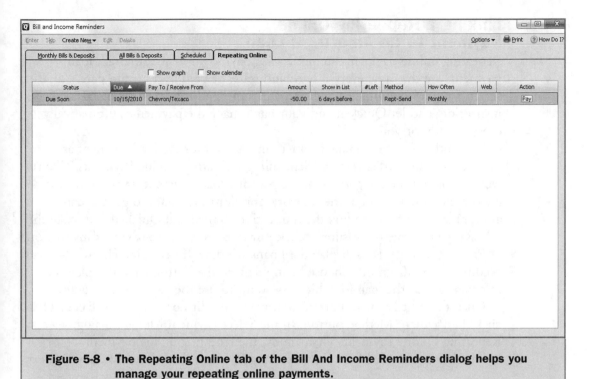

Figure 5-8 • The Repeating Online tab of the Bill And Income Reminders dialog helps you manage your repeating online payments.

You can use button bar options to work with items listed in the Bill And Income Reminders list window.

- **Enter** records the selected repeating online payment in the register.
- **Skip** skips payment of the selected repeating online payment.
- **Create New** enables you to create a new scheduled transaction or paycheck. Learn more about this menu in Chapter 6.
- **Edit** displays the Edit Repeating Online dialog so you can modify the details of the repeating online payment.
- **Delete** removes the repeating online payment from the list, thus canceling future payments. You must click Delete in the confirmation dialog that appears to remove the transaction.
- **Options** offers commands for changing the sort order of payments in the list.
- **Print** prints a list of repeating online payments.
- **How Do I?** displays the Quicken Personal Finances Help window with instructions for completing tasks with the Bill and Income Reminder list.

Linking a Repeating Online Payment to an Amortized Loan

Repeating online payments are perfect for paying off loans. After all, loan payments are the same every month and must be paid by a certain date. You can set up a repeating online payment instruction, send it to your financial institution, and let Quicken and your bank make the payments automatically every month for you.

Set up the repeating online payment instruction for the loan payment as instructed in the earlier section "Scheduling Repeating Online Payments." Don't worry about all the categories that are part of a loan payment transaction. Just choose the loan account as the category. You don't even have to get the date or amount right. When you link the transaction to the loan, Quicken will make the necessary adjustments. Be sure to click Authorize to save the payment instruction.

Press CTRL-SHIFT-H to display the Loans window. If necessary, choose the loan account's name from the Choose Loan menu in the button bar to display the information for the loan for which you want to use the payment instruction.

Click the Edit Payment button to display the Edit Loan Payment dialog. Then click the Payment Method button. In the Select Payment Method dialog, select Repeating Online Payment. Then choose the repeating online payment instruction you created from the Repeating Payment drop-down list, as seen next.

Click OK in each dialog to dismiss it. Click Done at the View Loans dialog. Quicken links the loan payment to the repeating online payment instruction. It makes changes to the payment instruction, if necessary, to match the payment categories and split information. The next time you connect to your financial institution, the instruction will be sent and payments will begin.

Sending Payment Instructions

Once your payment instructions have been completed, you must connect

---

NEW TO QUICKEN?

Repeating Online Loan Payments

Setting up a loan payment as a repeating online payment has got to be one of the best timesaving features available in Quicken. It does all kinds of neat things for you.

First, it ensures that your loan payment is made regularly, on a timely basis, with no monthly effort on your part. Second, it automatically adjusts the balance of your loan principal account (a debt account) by accurately calculating interest and principal paid for every entry. (You know these amounts change every month, right? Can you imagine doing the entries manually? Egads!) And since the loan account balance is updated with every payment, your net worth is always up to date.

Just set it and forget it. That should be this feature's slogan. And if you're confused about how to set up a loan in Quicken, you'll see how in Chapter 12.

---

to your bank to send the instructions. In the Online Center window, click the Update/Send button. Quicken displays the One Step Update Settings dialog, which lists all of the payment instructions, including any repeating payment instructions, as seen next. Enter your password and click the Update Now button.

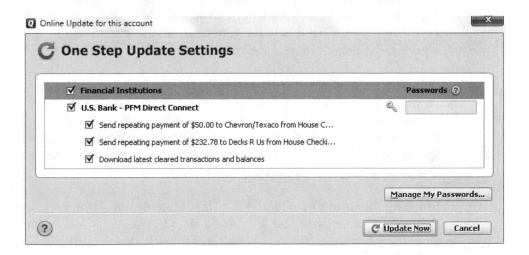

Wait while Quicken connects to your bank's server and sends your payment (or payment cancellation) instructions. When it has finished, it displays the Online Update Summary window. Click Done.

In the Payments tab of the Online Center window, the words "Scheduled for delivery on" followed by the payment date appear in the Status column beside the payment instructions that have been sent to your bank.

Canceling a Payment

Occasionally, you may change your mind about making a payment. Perhaps you found out that your spouse already sent a check or that you set up the payment for the wrong amount. For whatever reason, you can cancel an online payment that you have sent to your bank—as long as there's enough time to cancel it.

Here's how it works. When you send a payment instruction to your bank, it waits in the bank's computer. When the processing date (determined by the number of days in the payee's lead time and the payment date) arrives, the bank makes the payment. Before the processing date, however, the payment instructions can be canceled. If you send a cancel payment instruction to the bank before the processing date, the bank removes the instruction from its computer without sending payment to the payee. Quicken won't let you cancel a payment if the processing date has already passed. If you wait too long, the only way to cancel the payment is to call the bank directly and stop the check.

Keep in mind that canceling a payment instruction isn't the same as stopping a check. If you send the cancel payment instruction in time, the bank should not charge a fee for stopping the payment.

Canceling a Regular Online Payment   In the Online Center window, click the Payments tab, select the payment that you want to cancel, and click the Cancel Payment button. Click Yes in the confirmation dialog that appears. Use the Update/Send button to send the cancel payment instruction.

Stopping a Single Repeating Online Payment   In the Online Center window's Payments tab, select the payment you want to stop, and click the Cancel Payment button. Click Yes in the confirmation dialog that appears. Use the Update/Send button to send the cancel payment instruction. Note that the payment may not appear in the Online Center window unless you have reviewed and approved all downloaded payment transactions, as instructed earlier in this chapter.

Stopping All Future Payments for a Repeating Online Payment   In the Repeating Online tab of the Bill And Income Reminders window, select the payment you want to stop and click Delete. Click Delete in the confirmation dialog that appears. The transaction is removed from the list. Then use the Update/Send button in the Online Center window to send the cancel payment instruction.

Transferring Money Between Accounts

If you have more than one account enabled for Online Bill Pay via Direct Connect at the same financial institution, you can transfer money from one account to the other directly from Quicken.

- From the Account Bar, select the account you from which you want to transfer the funds.
- Click Account Actions | Transfer Money or press CTRL-SHIFT-T.
- The Record A Transaction Between Quicken Accounts dialog appears, as seen here.

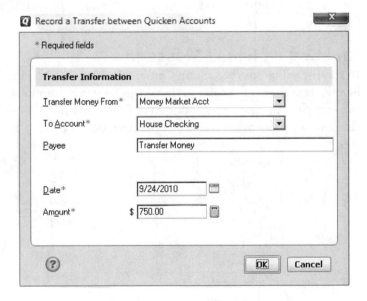

Enter the transfer information—source account, destination account, and amount—in the fields in the middle of the window. When you click Enter, the information is added to the list of transfers at the bottom of the window. The transaction will appear in both check registers with TXFR in the Check or Reference Number field.

Like payment instructions, you must send transfer instructions to your bank in order for the transaction to take place. Click the One Step Update button on the Account Bar to send the information.

Exchanging E-mail with Your Financial Institution

You can use the E-mail tab of the Online Center window to exchange e-mail messages with financial institutions for which you have enabled Online Account Services via Direct Connect. Keep in mind that not all financial institutions support this feature. Also, remember that this communication is between you and your financial institution, not Intuit (the makers of Quicken). It is intended primarily for exchanging information about your account, not technical support for using Quicken.

Creating an E-mail Message

In the E-mail tab of the Online Center window, click Create. If a Create dialog like the one shown here appears, use it to set general options for your e-mail message. If your message is about an online payment, choose the account from the Account drop-down list and select the payment from the Payments scrolling list.

When you click OK, a Message window appears. Use it to compose your e-mail message. When you click OK, the message is saved. It appears in the bottom half of the E-mail tab of the Online Center window, ready to be sent to your financial institution.

Exchanging E-mail Messages   Using e-mail is a lot like having a box at the post office. When you write a letter, you have to get it to the post office to send it to the recipient. When you receive a letter, you have to go to the post office and check your box to retrieve it. E-mail works the same way. Connecting is a lot like going to the post office to send and retrieve messages.

In the Online Center window, click the Update/Send button. Quicken displays the Online Update window, which includes any e-mail messages you may have created that need to be sent. Enter your password and click the Update Now button. Then wait while Quicken establishes an Internet connection with your bank and exchanges e-mail.

Reading an E-mail Message

When your bank sends you an e-mail message, it appears in the E-mail tab of the Online Center window. To read the message, select it and click Read. The message appears in a message window. If desired, you can click the Print button to print the message for future reference.

Automating Transactions and Tasks

In This Chapter:

- *Scheduled transactions*
- *QuickFill and memorized payees*
- *Calendar*
- *Billminder*
- *Paycheck Setup*
- *Address Book*
- *One Step Update and the Password Vault*
- *Scheduling updates*

Quicken Personal Finance Software includes a number of features to automate the entry of transactions. This chapter tells you about QuickFill, Billminder, and the other features you can use to automate transaction entries or remind yourself when a transaction is due. It also explains how you can use Quicken's One Step Update feature to handle all of your online tasks at once. These features can make data entry and other Quicken tasks quicker and easier.

Before you read this chapter, make sure you have a good understanding of the data entry techniques covered in Chapter 4. This chapter builds upon many of the basic concepts discussed there.

Bills and Income Reminders

A favorite Quicken feature is the ability to tell Quicken about the bills, deposits, and other transactions that need to be made in the future—especially the ones that happen on a regular basis. This feature, when fully utilized, doesn't just prevent you from forgetting to pay bills; it can completely automate the transaction entry process. Starting from the time you first create your Quicken file, scheduling transactions helps you stay on top of your monthly bills, as seen in Figure 6-1.

This part of the chapter tells you more about bill and income reminders, including how to set up and use them.

Overview of Scheduled Transactions

Generally speaking, you can use two types of scheduled transactions:

- **One-time transactions** are future transactions that you expect to record only once. For example, suppose you are arranging to purchase some furniture. You have already paid a deposit for the furniture and you know that the balance will be due at month-end, when the furniture is delivered. You can schedule that month-end payment in advance.

Some Quicken users prefer to enter this future transaction in their check register with the month-end date.

- **Recurring transactions** are transactions that occur periodically on a regular basis. Many of your monthly bills are good examples: rent or mortgage payments, car payments, utility bills—unfortunately, there are too many to list!

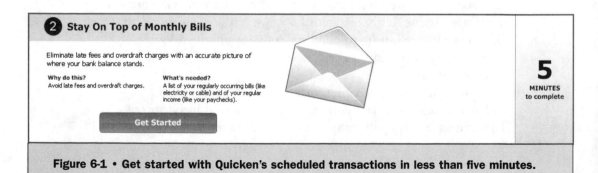

Figure 6-1 • Get started with Quicken's scheduled transactions in less than five minutes.

Reminders aren't only for payments. You could create a reminder for incoming funds, too, such as an expected bonus or a monthly child-support check you receive. You can even schedule your paycheck—but it's better to use Quicken's Paycheck Setup feature, which is discussed later in this chapter, to do that.

Making the Most of Bill and Income Reminders

Quicken's Reminders feature is one of the best timesaving features Quicken offers. By taking full advantage of this feature, you can minimize the time you spend entering transactions into Quicken. That's a good thing, right? After all, you have better things to do with your time than punch numbers into a computer.

Here are a few suggestions from seasoned Quicken users about how you can make the most of the feature. See how many you can use—and how much time they can save you.

Set up all recurring transactions as scheduled transactions *Recurring payments* are things like monthly and quarterly bills for rent, mortgage, insurance, utilities, and other regular bills. *Recurring deposits* are things like your paycheck, commissions, and other regular income. Set them all up, even if the amounts vary from one payment or deposit to the next. Not only does having these transactions set up in advance make them quick and easy to enter, but it also enables you to take advantage of Quicken's budgeting and forecasting features, which are covered in Chapter 16.

Use Paycheck Setup to track gross pay and deductions Paycheck Setup may take a bit of time to set up, but it can save you a lot of time and effort while keeping close track of your gross pay and all deductions. This enables you to utilize Quicken's tax planning and reporting features, which are discussed in Chapter 18, without spending a lot of time entering data. Be sure to set up all paychecks for the people included in your Quicken data file—normally, you and, if you're married, your spouse.

Let Quicken automatically enter transactions whenever possible If Quicken automatically enters transactions for you, entering recurring transactions is a real no-brainer. Quicken does all the entry work; all you do is make the payment or deposit. The only unfortunate thing about this option is that it works best with transactions that have the same amount each time they are made.

Use the Online Payment or check printing feature Scheduled transactions seem to work best when coupled with either Quicken's Online Payment feature, which is covered in Chapter 5, or its check printing feature, which is covered in

Chapter 4. (Of the two, many Quicken users prefer online payments.) Once the transaction is entered, Quicken can either automatically send payment instructions when you connect to your financial institution or automatically print checks for payments when you print all checks. So not only is Quicken entering the transaction details for you, but ensuring the payments are made!

Record transactions several days in advance   You don't have to wait until you make a payment or deposit to record the associated transaction. You can enter transactions in advance so your account register reflects both the current and future balances. Just be sure to enter the transaction due dates rather than entry dates when entering them into Quicken. This is especially useful for payments, because Quicken can clearly show that even if there is a nice fat balance today, transactions due over the next few days may leave considerably less to work with. This can be used as a short-term forecasting tool.

Set up reminders based on how often you use Quicken   When you schedule a transaction and indicate that Quicken should prompt you to enter it, you can specify the number of days in advance that you should be reminded. Set this value based on how often you use Quicken. For example, if you use Quicken only once a week, set this value to 10. If you use Quicken every other day, set it to 4. This way, you're sure to be reminded in time to enter a scheduled transaction and make the payment or deposit associated with it.

Remember that creating a reminder is not the same as recording a transaction   You must record a transaction to have it appear in the appropriate register, print a check for it, or send an online payment instruction for it. Creating the reminder is only part of the job. You still have to make sure each transaction is entered in a timely manner.

Creating a Reminder

You can create a scheduled transaction in Quicken in several ways. One is to press CTRL-J to display the Bill And Income Reminders window, seen in Figure 6-2. Click Create New and from the drop-down menu, shown next, select Bill, Income, Paycheck, or Transfer reminder to open the Add Transaction Reminder dialog. As shown in Figure 6-3, from the top of this dialog, select the type of transaction you want to enter. You can enter a Bill or Payment, Income or Deposit, or Transfer reminder.

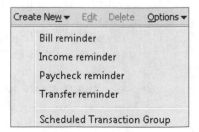

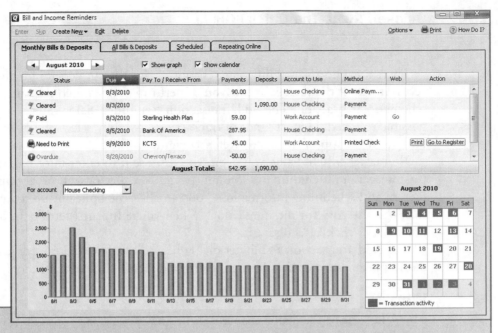

Figure 6-2 • The Bill And Income Reminders window lists recurring and one-time bills, deposits, scheduled transactions, and repeating online payments.

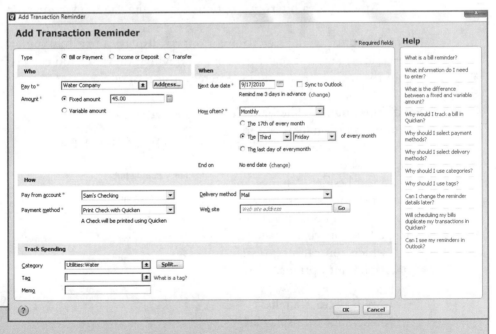

Figure 6-3 • Use one of the three options along the top of the Add Transaction Reminder dialog to add transactions for bills, deposits, and other items.

There are a number of different versions of this dialog, depending on how you access it. All of the dialogs enable you to perform pretty much the same task: schedule a transaction. The Add Transaction Reminder dialog, however, makes it possible to schedule most kinds of transactions—simply select one of the Type options at the top of the dialog (refer to Figure 6-3).

No matter which dialog you open, you can use it to enter information about the transaction, including the account, payee, category or transfer account, memo, and scheduling information. You can click the Split button to enter more than one category for the transaction. When you're finished setting up the transaction, click OK to save it.

The Add Transaction Reminder dialog has quite a few options, some of which don't appear elsewhere in Quicken. Here's a closer look at each of them.

Who

The Who part of the dialog enables you to specify who you are paying (for bill or payment) or who has paid you (for income, deposit, or transfer). You can enter text in the field or choose a QuickFill transaction from the drop-down list. (See "QuickFill and Memorized Payees" later in this chapter.) Clicking the Address button enables you to enter an address for the person or entity in the field.

The Amount area offers two options for setting the transaction amount.

Fixed Amount   The Fixed Amount option displays a text box you can use to enter a dollar amount that the transaction will always use. You can change the amount when the transaction is entered, if necessary.

Variable Amount   The Variable Amount option enables you to estimate the amount. When you select this option, an estimate may appear beside a Change link. To set or change the estimate, click the link. This displays the Change Estimate dialog (shown here), which you can use to set variable amount options.

- **Do Not Estimate** tells Quicken not to display an estimated amount.

- **Estimated Amount** enables you to enter an estimated amount. This is useful for expenses that are always approximately the same, such as a cable television bill, which may vary slightly from month to month.
- **Estimate From Last *N* Payments** enables you to specify how many previous transactions Quicken should average to calculate an amount. This is a rolling average; Quicken's calculation will change every time the payment is made. If you select this option, be sure to enter the number of transactions Quicken should include for average calculation purposes. This is useful for bills that may vary from month to month on a trend, such as electricity or natural gas. Note that until you have entered the payment N times, the estimate may not be what you expect.
- **Estimate From One Year Ago** tells Quicken to estimate based on your payment to the same payee last year around the same time. This is useful for seasonal expenditures.
- **Use Full Credit Card Balance** tells Quicken to use the credit card account's balance when calculating a payment. This is especially useful for credit card accounts that must be paid in full when due, such as American Express. This option is available only if the transaction is to make a credit card payment.

When

The When area enables you to set transaction scheduling options. How you set these options determines when you will be reminded about the transaction. They can also make it possible for the transaction to be entered automatically.

Next Due Date   The next due date is the transaction date or the first date for a repeating transaction.

Sync to Outlook   If you use Microsoft Outlook, check this box to synchronize your due date reminder with the Outlook calendar.

Reminder   The Reminder area enables you to set how far in advance you should be reminded about the transaction or whether Quicken should just enter it automatically. Click the Change link beside the reminder description to display a dialog like the one shown on the next page. Set options as desired and click OK.

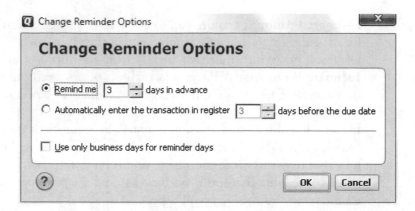

- **Remind Me *N* Days In Advance** enables you to set the number of days Quicken should remind you in advance. The default setting is 3.
- **Automatically Enter The Transaction In Register *N* Days Before The Due Date** lets you enter the number of days in advance that Quicken should automatically enter the transaction in the appropriate register.
- **Use Only Business Days For Reminder Days** excludes weekends and holidays from the calculation of the number of days in advance to remind you about or enter the transaction.

How Often?   Use the How Often? options to set up a recurring transaction. First, choose an option from the drop-down list. Your options are Only Once, Weekly, Every Two Weeks, Twice A Month, Every Four Weeks, Monthly, Every Two Months, Quarterly, Twice A Year, Yearly, Estimated Tax (which follows the IRS estimated tax payment schedule), Variable Weeks, and Variable Months. Then set options in the area beneath the list; the options change based on the frequency you select.

End On   For a recurring transaction, you can click the Change link beside the end date to display the End Reminders dialog (shown here) to specify when the recurring transaction should end.

- **No End Date**, which is the default option, keeps the transaction scheduled until you delete it or set another option in this dialog.

- **End On** enables you to set a specific date for the last transaction.
- **End After** *N* **Reminders** enables you to specify the number of transactions before they automatically end.

How

The How area of the dialog enables you to set options that control how the payment, deposit, or transfer will be made. The options that appear vary depending on the type of transaction you are setting up a reminder for.

Pay From Account/Add To Account/From Account   This is the account you will pay from (for a bill or payment), add funds to (for income or a deposit), or transfer money from (for a transfer). All accounts except hidden accounts will appear in the drop-down list.

Payment Method   For bills or payments, you can choose a payment method. The method you choose determines how the transaction will appear in your account register when it is entered, and it may trigger other Quicken features. You can choose from the following three options on the Payment Method drop-down list:

- **Manual Payment** records the transaction as a payment, which decreases the balance in a banking account. The Check Number field in the account register for the transaction remains blank; you can always fill it in later if desired. Use this option for handwritten checks or cash payments.
- **Online Bill Pay** records the transaction as an online payment, which decreases the balance in a banking account. The Check Number field in the account register is set to SEND, which signals Quicken to send the transaction with other payment instructions. If you choose this option, you can turn on the This Is A Repeating Online Payment check box to set up the payment as a repeating online payment. Learn more about repeating online payments in Chapter 5.
- **Print Check With Quicken** records the transaction as a payment using a check to be printed. This decreases the balance in a banking account. The Check Number field in the account register is set to PRINT, which signals Quicken to include the transaction with other checks to be printed. Use this option for scheduling transactions using Quicken's check printing feature, which Chapter 4 discussed in greater detail.

Delivery Method   Quicken enables you to specify a delivery method for bills, payments, income, deposits, or transfers. Use the Delivery Method drop-down list to choose from options such as Automatic, Bank Web Site, In Person, Mail, Other, or Payee website. Although this does not affect how Quicken records the transaction, it helps you keep track of how a transaction was completed.

Web Site   This option enables you to enter the URL for the payee or payor's website. You can click the Go button beside the web address to open the site in your default web browser. The website Go button is also available in the Bill And Income Reminders dialog.

Track Spending

The Track Spending area of the dialog enables you to set the category or account, tag, and memo for the transaction.

Category/Account   For a bill, payment, income, or deposit, you can use the Category field to set the category or transfer account for the transaction. For a transfer transaction, this field becomes the Account field, which you can use to set the account that funds are being transferred into.

Split   If you want to assign more than one category to this transaction, click Split to open the Split Transaction dialog. See Chapter 4 for detailed information about split transactions.

Tag   If you have selected to display the Tag field, you can use the Tag drop-down list to assign a tag to the transaction. Using the tag feature of Quicken is completely optional.

Memo   To provide just a little bit more detail about the transaction, you can enter a short note in the Memo field. This is also optional.

Viewing Reminders

Quicken displays reminders in several places.

- In the Home tab, the Stay On Top Of Monthly bills section displays your reminders.
- From the Bills tab, click the Manage Reminders button.
- From the Quicken menu bar, click Tools | Manage Bill & Income Reminders.

The Home Tab

The Main View of the Home tab displays your reminders for the next 7, 14, or 30 days as you designate. As seen in Figure 6-4, the view shows each scheduled

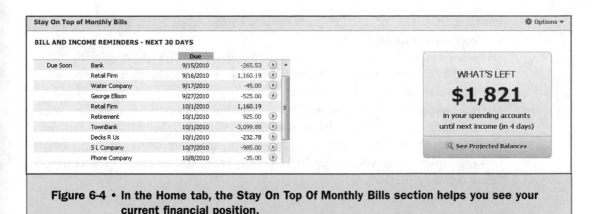

Figure 6-4 • In the Home tab, the Stay On Top Of Monthly Bills section helps you see your current financial position.

transaction for the time period and lets you know how much money you have available in your spending accounts until the next income is due. There are several ways you can work with this information.

Options   Click Options to open a menu from which you can:

- Choose to display the reminders for the next 7, 14, 30, or 90 days, or 12 months
- Open the Add Reminder dialog
- Go directly to the Bills tab

Enter or Edit Reminders   Each reminder displayed on the list is a link. Click the amount to open the Edit Reminder dialog. Click the arrow to the right of the amount to see a menu, shown here, from which you can:

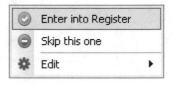

- Enter the reminder into the appropriate register.
- Skip this one entry.
- Click Edit to open a submenu from which you can:
    - Edit this one reminder—and open the Edit Reminder dialog.
    - Edit this and all future reminders, which opens the Edit Bill Reminder dialog.
    - Delete this and all future reminders, which opens a message that you are about to delete a scheduled bill or deposit. You must click OK to delete the reminder or Cancel to close the message without deleting the reminder.

What's Left   The What's Left section shows how much is available until your next income comes in.

If any of your accounts are overdrawn you will see "Risk of Overdraft" displayed at the bottom of the What's Left section. Click the link to see which of your accounts are currently overdrawn.

If your accounts are all positive (not overdrawn), you will see a See Projected Balances link instead of the Risk of Overdraft link. Click See Projected Balances to display the balances in each of your spending accounts, as shown here. This is the same information you see in the Bills tab's Projected Balances view as seen in Figure 6-6 on page 169.

The Bills Tab

You can use the Bills tab, shown in Figures 6-5 and 6-6, to view upcoming bills and other scheduled transactions in a number of different ways. Each view is a different look at your bills, with two options that appear in the button bar.

- Add Reminder enables you to add a bill, income, paycheck, or transfer reminder as discussed earlier in this chapter.
- Manage Reminders displays the Bill And Income Reminders window (refer to Figure 6-2).

The Bills tab has two subtabs.

Upcoming The Upcoming subtab (shown in Stack view in Figure 6-5) shows each upcoming scheduled transaction with a note-like interface. Click one of the transactions and its details appear in the middle of the window. Use the horizontal scroll bar at the bottom of the window to display upcoming transactions. You can use a transaction's buttons to enter, skip, or edit the transaction. Clicking a Show History button displays a payment history for that payee.

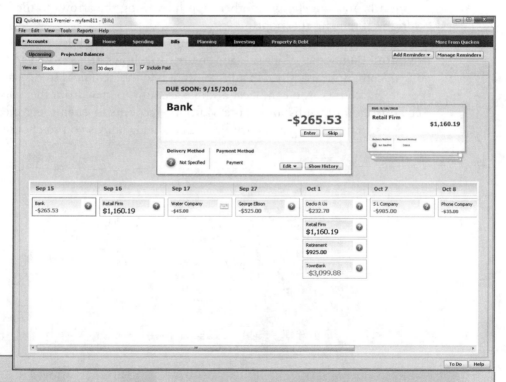

Figure 6-5 • The Upcoming subtab in the Bills tab displays what bills are coming due.

You may change the way the information is displayed by clicking the View As drop-down list, as seen here.

- **Stack** displays each item in a "stack" as if they were papers on top of each other. You can use the Due drop-down list to choose the time period. Your options are 7, 14, and 30 days. You can choose to not include items that have been paid by clearing the Include Paid check box.
- **List** displays information about the status, due date, pay to or receive from information, and amount of each transaction. From this view you can enter, edit, or skip the transaction. The Due and Include Paid options are the same as in the Stack view.
- **Calendar** view shows all transactions in a calendar view that includes transactions and their amounts, as well as the ending total banking account balance. You can use the arrows by the current month area to scroll through months. Learn more about how the Calendar works later in this chapter.
- **Monthly List** shows all scheduled transaction reminders for the current month. You can choose another month by using the arrows to the left and right of the current month.

Projected Balances   This subtab (Figure 6-6) shows projected balances and your upcoming transactions in a list view. While the default is to display all spending accounts, you can select a single account to view from the Select Accounts drop-down list or choose Multiple Accounts to open the Projected Balance selection dialog as shown here. This dialog allows you to choose two or

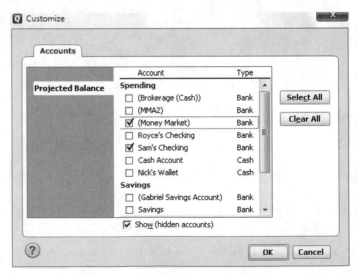

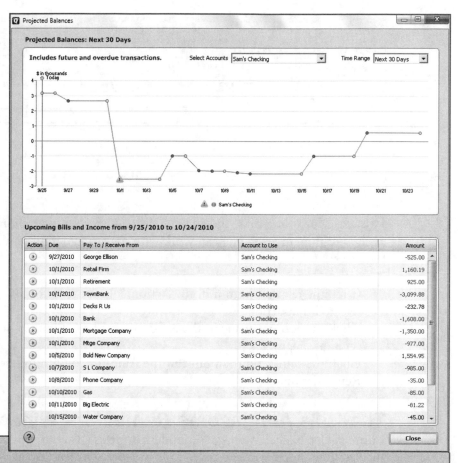

Figure 6-6 • The Projected Balances subtab shows both your projected balances and upcoming bills and income for the time period you have selected.

more spending or credit card accounts to display. You can choose Show Hidden Accounts so that they may be included in the cash flow view.

Click Select All to choose all displayed accounts or Clear All to start over with your selection. Click OK to close the dialog.

You may choose a time period to display by clicking the Time Range drop-down list. You may choose the next 7, 14, 30, or 90 days; the next 12 months; or you may create a customized time period.

The Projected Balances section of the subtab includes all of the accounts you have selected for the time period selected. A legend showing the account or accounts represented in the line graph appears at the bottom of the section as shown on the next page.

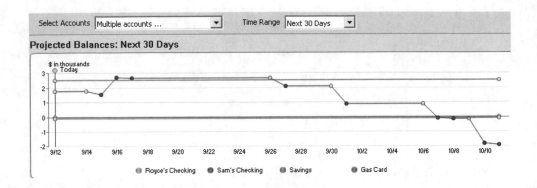

In the Upcoming Bills And Income From *nn/nn/nnnn* to *nn/nn/nnnn* section, as shown in Figure 6-6, you can work with your transaction reminders as follows:

- Click the relevant button in the Action column to enter, skip, or edit the selected transaction.
- Click the account name in the Account To Use column to be taken to that account's register.
- Click the transaction's amount in the Amount column to open the Edit Reminder dialog.

The Bills And Income Reminders Window

In the Bills tab, click Manage Reminders or press CTRL-J to open the Bill And Income Reminders window (refer to Figure 6-2), which displays current and future transactions. If you have previously scheduled transactions or repeating online transactions, the Bill And Income Reminders window has four tabs. Until you have created either one or both, there are only two tabs visible. See the section "Window Tabs" for more information.

Bills and Income Reminder Button Bar Options　You can use button bar options in both the Monthly Bills & Deposits and the All Bills & Deposits tabs to enter, skip, create, edit, or delete scheduled transactions. You must select a transaction to activate all but the Create New option.

- **Enter** opens the Enter Transaction dialog shown next. Enter the appropriate information and click Enter Transaction. If the reminder is for an investment income, you may see a dialog titled Edit Income – Income (Div, Int, etc.).

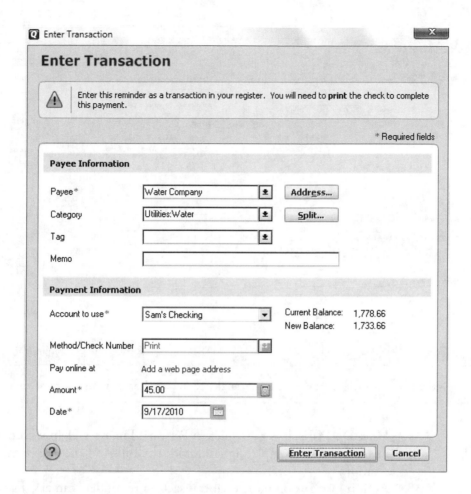

- **Skip** enables you to skip the payment (or next payment) of that transaction.
- **Create New** enables you to create a new scheduled transaction or paycheck. Learn how to add a scheduled transaction earlier in this chapter and how to add a paycheck later in this chapter.
- **Edit** opens the Edit Bill (or Income) Reminder dialog in which you can modify each area of the reminder as shown in Figure 6-7.
- **Delete** removes the scheduled transaction. It does not remove any transactions that have already been entered in a register.
- **Options** offers commands for changing the way the Bill And Income Reminders window is sorted. You can also change the sort order by clicking the Due, Pay To/Receive From, Payments, or Deposits column header.
- **Print** prints a list of scheduled transactions.

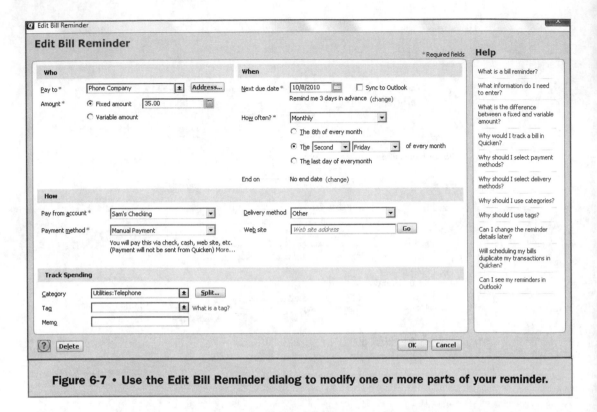

Figure 6-7 • Use the Edit Bill Reminder dialog to modify one or more parts of your reminder.

- **How Do I?** displays the Quicken Personal Finances Help window with instructions for completing tasks with the Bill And Income Reminders window.
- **Action buttons** on individual transaction reminders can also be used. To access the action buttons, select a reminder and choose from the following:

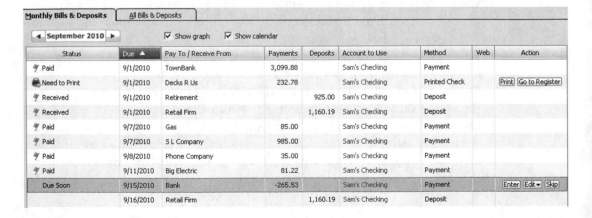

- **Enter** opens the Enter Transaction dialog discussed earlier in this chapter.
- **Edit** opens a menu that gives you the option to change the reminder only this time or for this and all future reminders as seen here.

> Only this instance
> This and all future reminders

- **Skip** tells Quicken to skip the reminder for this time only.
- **Print** opens the Print dialog so that you can print this transaction. See Chapter 4 for more information on printing checks from Quicken.
- **Go To Register** opens the check register for this reminder at this transaction.

Window Tabs

- **All Bills & Deposits** (refer to Figure 6-2) displays all types of scheduled reminders.
- **Monthly Bills & Deposits** displays all reminders for the month. You can click the arrows beside the name of the month to view reminders for other months.

If you have scheduled transactions or online payments, you will see two additional tabs.

- **Scheduled** displays the deposits and payments that have been scheduled for this month.
- **Repeating Online** lists repeating payments you have scheduled to be paid online.

Display Check Boxes   Two check boxes enable you to display additional information in the window, as shown in Figure 6-2.

- **Show Graph** displays a column chart showing cash flow for selected accounts for the month.
- **Show Calendar** displays one or two calendars that indicate dates on which transactions will be made.

Schedule These?   The Schedule These? list in a Bill And Income Reminders list, when present, displays transactions that Quicken "thinks" you might want to schedule for the future. It builds this list based on categories used in the transactions or transactions you have entered more than once. Here are a few things you can do to work with this list:

- To schedule a transaction in the list, click the Yes button beside it. Quicken displays the Edit Bill Reminder dialog so you can turn the transaction into a scheduled transaction.
- To remove a transaction from the list, click the No button beside it.

QuickFill and Memorized Payees

As you enter transactions, Quicken is quietly working in the background, memorizing transaction information for each payee. It creates a database of memorized payees. It then uses the memorized payees for its QuickFill feature.

How It Works

QuickFill works in two ways:

- When you enter the first few characters of a payee name in the Write Checks or account register window, Quicken immediately fills in the rest of the name. When you advance to the next text box or field of the entry form, Quicken fills in the rest of the transaction information based on the last transaction for that payee.
- You can select a memorized payee from the drop-down list in the Payee field of the Write Checks or account register window. Quicken then fills in the rest of the transaction information based on the last transaction for that payee.

QuickFill entries include amounts, categories, and memos. They can also include splits and tags. For example, you might pay the cable or satellite company for television service every month. The bill is usually the same amount each month. The second time you create an entry with the company's name, Quicken fills in the rest of the transaction automatically. You can make adjustments to the amount or other information as desired and save the transaction. It may have taken a minute or so to enter the transaction the first time, but it'll take only seconds to enter it every time after that.

By default, the QuickFill feature is set up to work as discussed here. If it does not, check the QuickFill options to make sure they are set properly. You can learn how in Appendix B.

Working with the Memorized Payee List

If desired, you can view a list of memorized payees, as shown in Figure 6-8. Just choose Tools | Memorized Payee List or press CTRL-T. The list displays the last transaction you entered for each payee.

Select a memorized payee to display the Edit and Delete action buttons as seen here.

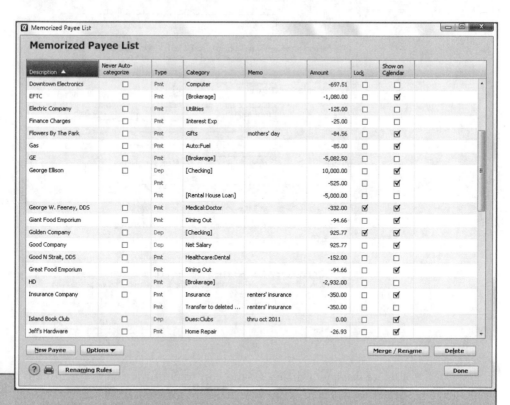

Figure 6-8 • Each line in the Memorized Payee List represents the last transaction recorded for a payee.

- **Edit** displays the Edit Memorized Payee dialog, shown next, for the currently selected transaction. The Payee Name field displays the payee name as it is currently entered. You may change the name or any of the other fields as required. You may also leave the Category, Memo, or Amount fields blank so that data can be changed each time you use this payee. If the amount paid to this payee changes each time, leave the amount blank. Click Lock And Leave This Payee Unchanged When It Is Edited In A Register to ensure the transaction stays blank in the Memorized Payee list. The remaining two check boxes, which are also cleared by default, tell Quicken not to auto-categorize this payee and not to display this payee in the Memorized Payee list in the Calendar.

- **Delete** displays a dialog asking you to confirm that you really do want to delete the selected item. If you delete the transaction, it is removed from the Memorized Payee list only—not from any register in the Quicken data file.

Button Bar Buttons

You can use buttons at the bottom of the window to add, change what displays in the list, merge, rename, or delete memorized payees on the Memorized Payee list.

- **New Payee** displays the Create Memorized Payee dialog, shown next, which you can use to create brand-new transactions without actually entering them into any register of your Quicken data file. Just fill in the fields to enter transaction information, and click OK. The new transaction appears in the Memorized Payee List window.

- **Options** opens a menu, seen here, that allows you to choose to display the transaction on the Financial Calendar. The Calendar is covered in more detail later in this chapter. You can also choose to lock the transaction. This means that on the Memorized Payee list, the transaction is

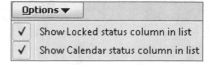

the same each time. However, a locked transaction can be changed in the register when the payment is actually made.

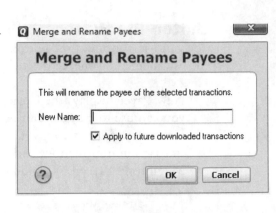

- **Merge/Rename** displays the Merge And Rename Payees dialog, shown here, which you can use to enter a new name for the selected payee.
- Use the **Delete** button to delete one or more payees from the list.
- **How Do I?** displays the Quicken Personal Finances Help window with additional information for completing tasks with the Memorized Payee List window.
- **Print** prints a list of memorized payees.
- **Renaming Rules** opens the Renaming Rules dialog shown next. Learn about Renaming Rules in Chapter 5.

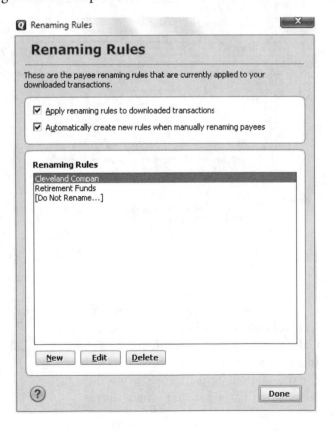

Calendar

Quicken's Calendar, shown in Figure 6-9, keeps track of all your transactions—past and future—by date. You may open the Calendar by choosing Tools | Calendar or by pressing CTRL-K.

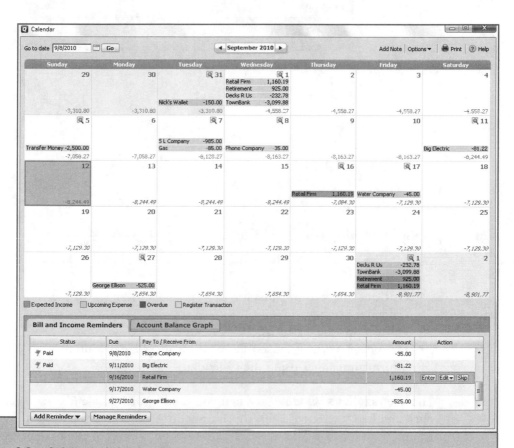

Figure 6-9 • Quicken's Calendar shows each day's transactions.

Calendar Button Bar Options You can use button bar options to work with the window's contents.

- **Go To Date** enables you to go to a specific calendar date. Click the Calendar icon and use the tiny calendar that appears to locate and select the date you want. Or enter the date in the edit box and click the Go button.
- **Arrow** buttons on either side of the month name enable you to move from one month to another.
- **Add Note** enables you to enter a note for the selected date. The note you enter appears on the Calendar. To view a note, click it as seen here.

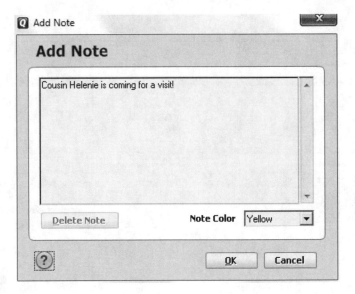

- **Options** offers commands for viewing and working with the contents of the Calendar window.
- **Print** prints the Calendar.
- **Help** displays the Quicken Personal Finances Help window with information about using the Calendar.

The Transactions Window When you double-click a calendar date (or single-click an already selected date), the Transactions window, which lists all the transactions for that date, appears, as shown on the top of the next page.

You can use buttons in the window to work with transactions.

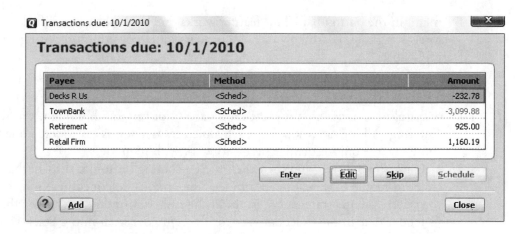

- **Add** enables you to enter a new transaction or create a new scheduled transaction. The dialog that appears when you click this button offers all the options of the Add Scheduled Transaction dialog shown earlier.
- **Enter** takes you to the currently selected transaction in the appropriate account register, if the transaction has already been entered, and enters the transaction in the register if it has not already been entered into the register. If the transaction has already been entered into the account register, this button changes to Go To Register.
- **Edit** enables you to modify the currently selected transaction. If this transaction has not been entered into the register, the Edit <type> Reminder dialog displays. If it has been entered into the register, the Edit Register Transaction dialog appears.
- **Delete** removes the selected transaction. This option is only available for transactions that have already been entered into the register.
- **Skip** lets you skip the transaction for this date. This option is only available for transactions that have not been entered.
- **Schedule** enables you to create a new scheduled transaction based on the selected transaction. This option is only available if the currently selected transaction is not a scheduled transaction.
- **Close** closes the window.

Account Balances   The dollar amounts that appear in the bottom of each calendar date box show the total account balances for the accounts displayed in the window, taking all payments into consideration. (You can specify which accounts to include by choosing Select Calendar Accounts from the Options menu in the button bar.) This feature works, in effect, like a simplified forecasting tool. Learn how to use Quicken's more powerful forecasting feature in Chapter 16.

Working with Reminders

Scheduling a transaction was the hard part. (Not very hard, though, was it?) Entering, editing, and skipping a scheduled transaction is easy. Here's one way, some say, the quickest and easiest—to work with reminders.

Click the Bills tab, and then click the Upcoming button to display that view (refer to Figure 6-5). Select a reminder. The options described here may be on the selected item's transaction list, as in the List or Monthly List views, the Calendar date in the Calendar view, or the reminder itself in the Stack view.

Enter   In all views except the Calendar view, if the transaction has not already been entered, the Enter button displays the Enter Transaction dialog. Use this dialog to finalize settings for a transaction. When you click Enter Transaction, the transaction is entered into the account register.

Skip   In all views except the Calendar view, the Skip button skips the transaction if it has not already been entered into the account register. The transaction moves down in the list and its due date changes to the next due date.

Edit   In all views except the Calendar view, the Edit button displays the Edit Transaction Reminder dialog when the transaction has not yet been entered into the account register. This dialog looks and works very much like the Add Transaction Reminder dialog, shown earlier in Figure 6-3. Use this dialog to modify settings for the transaction's future entries. If the transaction is an instance of a recurring transaction, the Edit button appears as a menu with the following two options:

- **Only This Instance** displays the Edit Reminder dialog that enables you to change the date and amount of the transaction.
- **This And All Future Reminders** displays the Edit Transaction Reminder dialog, as discussed earlier.

Billminder

Quicken's Billminder feature makes it possible for you to monitor upcoming bills and scheduled transactions without starting Quicken. Let's take a quick look at it.

Quicken Billminder

The Quicken Billminder application, seen in Figure 6-10, displays a window that summarizes upcoming transactions, as shown next. It also includes a convenient button to run Quicken, should you decide to take action on a listed item.

To open Billminder, you can choose Start | All Programs | Quicken 2011 | Billminder. But to make the most of Billminder, you may want to configure it so it automatically starts each time you start your computer. To do this, click the Options button in the Billminder button bar to display Billminder options as shown on the next page. Turn on the Enable Billminder On Windows Startup check box. You can set other configuration options as desired to determine when Billminder should appear. Then click OK.

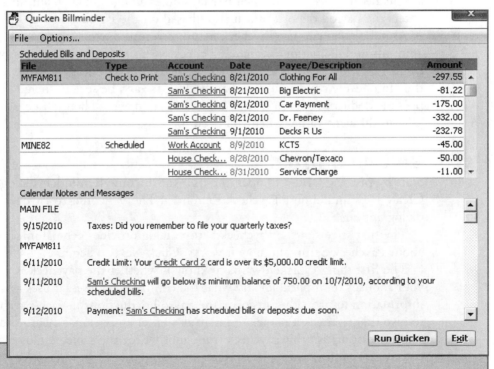

Figure 6-10 • The Billminder can help you remember scheduled bills and deposits.

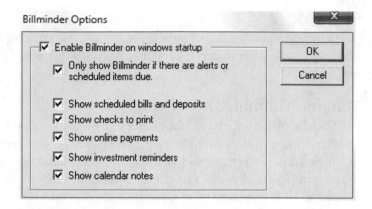

Using Paycheck Setup

Quicken's Paycheck Setup feature offers yet another way to automate transactions. You use it to enter information about your regular payroll check and its deductions. Then, when payday comes along, Quicken automatically enters the payroll deposit information based on the Paycheck Setup transaction.

Although you can use Paycheck Setup to record payroll checks with varying amounts and deductions—such as a check with varying hourly wages or overtime pay—it can be a real timesaver if your paycheck is the same (or almost the same) every payday. If your paycheck does vary, be sure to include all possible deductions, even if their values are often zero. Then it'll be easy to just plug in different values when you need to.

Getting Started

Start by pressing CTRL-J to open the Bill And Income Reminders dialog. Click Create New and choose Paycheck Reminder. The Welcome To Paycheck Setup dialog appears.

The first screen of the Paycheck Setup dialog provides general information about Paycheck Setup and how it works. Click Next to begin.

The first thing Quicken wants to know is whether the paycheck is yours or your spouse's (if applicable) and what the company name is. It uses this information to properly categorize the payroll deductions in each paycheck and to give the paycheck a name. You may also enter an optional memo should you want to distinguish this paycheck from another for the same employer. After entering this information, click Next.

Next, Quicken asks what you want to track. You have two options:

- **I Want To Track All Earnings, Taxes, And Deductions** tells Quicken you want to keep track of all payroll deductions when recording a paycheck. This option makes it possible to take advantage of Quicken's tax planning features, which are discussed in Part Six of this book. If you select this option, continue following the instructions in the next section, "Tracking All Earnings and Deductions," after clicking Next.
- **I Want To Track Net Deposits Only** tells Quicken that you just want to track the net take-home pay, not the gross pay and deductions. This option makes setting up a paycheck a bit quicker, but it doesn't tap into Quicken's full power for automatically recording detailed information. If you select this option, continue following the instructions in the section titled "Tracking Net Deposits Only" after clicking Next.

Tracking All Earnings and Deductions

When you indicate that you want to track all earnings and deductions, Quicken displays the Paycheck Setup dialog (see Figure 6-11). Use this dialog to enter

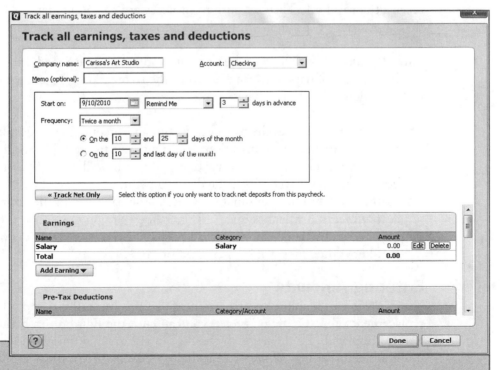

Figure 6-11 • You can use the Set Up Paycheck dialog to enter all details for your paycheck.

detailed information about the paycheck. It's a good idea to have a recent pay stub on hand when entering information because you'll want it to be as accurate as possible.

Setting Options

Start with the following information.

Account Use the Account drop-down list to choose the account to which the net pay will be deposited. If the check will be deposited to more than one account—for example, if part of the paycheck is deposited to a company credit union savings account—make sure you add the other account and indicate how much is deposited to each account in the Deposit Accounts area near the bottom of the dialog.

Start On Enter the date of the next paycheck (or the current paycheck, if you plan to enter this one after setting it up) in the Start On field.

Frequency Use the Frequency drop-down list to indicate how often you receive the paycheck. Then set options, if necessary, to specify dates. The options that appear vary depending on the frequency you select.

Entry Options Select one of the two entry options in the Scheduling area and set the number of days in advance to enter the transaction. The entry options on the drop-down list are as follows:

- **Remind Me** includes the paycheck in Bill and Income Reminders lists as a reminder to enter the transaction. You may want to use this option if the paycheck's amounts vary each payday or if you have the nasty habit of not depositing your paycheck on the day you get it.
- **Automatically Enter** automatically enters the paycheck in the appropriate account register when it's due. This is the best option to select if the paycheck is the same each payday, especially if you have direct deposit and you know the funds will be deposited on time.

Entering Amounts

You can enter an amount by clicking the default amount (0.00) and typing in a replacement value. Or, if you prefer, you can click the Edit button beside an item to display an Edit dialog, which you can use to enter information.

To add another type of item to the dialog, use the Add pop-up menu in the appropriate section. (You can see an example of the pop-up menus in the next illustration.) For example, to add a pretax deduction, display the Add Pre-Tax Deduction pop-up menu and choose an option. Then enter the details for that item in the dialog that appears. This may seem like a lot of work, but once the paycheck is set up properly, Quicken will take over and do all the hard work for you.

Scroll through the entire pay stub and enter all deductions into the dialog. When you're finished, the net pay amount at the bottom of the dialog should match your take-home pay amount.

Entering Year-to-Date Amounts

When you click Done, Quicken displays a dialog asking if you want to enter year-to-date information as shown next. If year-to-date totals appear on the pay stub you used to set up the paycheck, I highly recommend entering this information so all the earnings and deduction information for the current year is included in your Quicken data file.

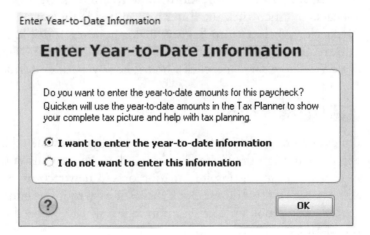

Select I Want To Enter The Year-To-Date Information, and click OK. The Paycheck Year-To-Date Amounts dialog appears. Edit the values in the Year To Date column by clicking each one to select it and entering a replacement value. When you're finished, click Enter.

Tracking Net Deposits Only

When you indicate that you want to track just the net payroll deposits, Quicken displays a Set Up Paycheck dialog. Use this dialog to enter information about the amount you expect to deposit. If you're not sure what the amount will be—commission checks, for example, may vary from one quarter to the next—you can leave the Amount field set to 0.00; if you do so, don't tell Quicken to enter the paycheck without prompting you, or it will enter 0 each payday!

When you're finished, click Done.

Editing Paychecks

Once you have at least one paycheck set up, you can use the Edit Future Paychecks dialog to modify it or delete it. Open Bill And Income Reminders by pressing CTRL-J. Select a paycheck, and click Edit on the menu bar to open the Track All Earnings, Taxes And Deductions dialog. You can also use the Edit button in the Action column and select This And All Future Reminders.

Make whatever changes are necessary, and click Done.

Entering Paycheck Transactions

Entering a paycheck transaction is just as easy as entering a scheduled transaction. Display a Bill And Income Reminders list in which the paycheck appears, and then click the Enter button beside the paycheck. The Edit Current Paycheck And Enter Into Register dialog appears. It displays all of the information you entered when you set up the paycheck. Modify values and options as necessary, and click Enter. The paycheck's information is recorded.

Address Book

Quicken's Address Book feature automatically stores the address information you enter when using the Write Checks window. You can also use this feature to modify or delete existing information or add new records. Keeping track of addresses with the Address Book makes it easy to insert addresses when writing checks and to look up contact information when you need to follow up on transactions.

Displaying the Address Book Window

Choose Tools | Address Book to display the Address Book window (see Figure 6-12). It lists all the records in the Address Book.

You can use button bar buttons and menus to work with Address Book window contents.

- **New** enables you to create a new Address Book record.
- **Edit** enables you to edit the selected record as shown next.

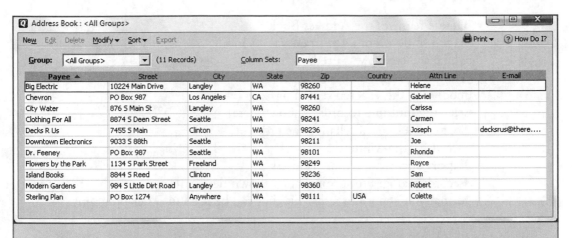

Payee ▲	Street	City	State	Zip	Country	Attn Line	E-mail
Big Electric	10224 Main Drive	Langley	WA	98260		Helene	
Chevron	PO Box 987	Los Angeles	CA	87441		Gabriel	
City Water	876 S Main St	Langley	WA	98260		Carissa	
Clothing For All	8874 S Deen Street	Seattle	WA	98241		Carmen	
Decks R Us	7455 S Main	Clinton	WA	98236		Joseph	decksrus@there....
Downtown Electronics	9033 S 88th	Seattle	WA	98211		Joe	
Dr. Feeney	PO Box 987	Seattle	WA	98101		Rhonda	
Flowers by the Park	1134 S Park Street	Freeland	WA	98249		Royce	
Island Books	8844 S Reed	Clinton	WA	98236		Sam	
Modern Gardens	984 S Little Dirt Road	Langley	WA	98360		Robert	
Sterling Plan	PO Box 1274	Anywhere	WA	98111	USA	Colette	

Figure 6-12 • Use the Address Book to keep track of the organizations and individuals with whom you do business.

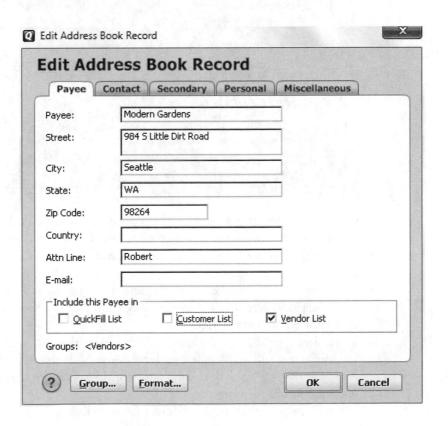

- **Delete** removes the Address Book record. It does not affect transactions in which the record was used.
- **Modify** offers several commands for modifying the selected record or selecting multiple records as shown here.
- **Sort** enables you to change the order of records in the window.
- **Export** opens the Export Address Records dialog. From this dialog, shown here, you can send the records in a format you choose to a text file that can be used in other programs.

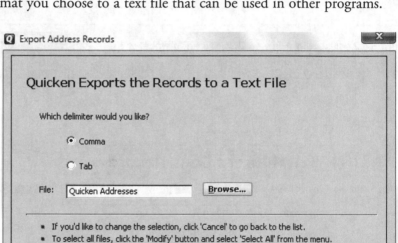

- Choose the format you want, either comma- or tab-delimited. Your choice depends on the program in which you want to use the data.
- Type in the name of the file, or click Browse to locate it.
- Click Next to continue.
- Select the fields from the list on the left you want to include in your text file. Click Add after each field you select and it will appear in the Field To Be Exported list on the right.
- To remove a field from the exported list, select the field and click Remove. You can use standard Windows selection methods to select the fields for Add/Remove: CTRL-click to select noncontiguous items and SHIFT-click to select a contiguous range.
- Click Done to return to the Address Book dialog.

- **Print** offers commands for printing Address Book record information.
- **How Do I?** displays the Quicken Personal Finances Help window with instructions for working with the Address Book.

Adding or Modifying Address Book Records

To add a new Address Book record, click New on the button bar of the Address Book window. The Edit Address Book Record dialog, shown earlier, appears.

You also use the Edit Address Book Record dialog to edit an existing record. Simply select the record in the Address Book window and click the Edit button in the button bar.

The Edit Address Book Record dialog has five tabs for record information. Click a tab to display its options, and then enter the information you want to store. Here's what you can enter in each of the five tabs:

- **Payee** is for the information that would normally appear in a Write Check window, as well as some additional contact information.
- **Contact** is for the name, title, phone numbers, and website of a specific person.
- **Secondary** is for a secondary mailing address and e-mail address.
- **Personal** is for personal information, such as spouse and children's names, birthday and anniversary, and still more phone numbers.
- **Miscellaneous** is for additional information, such as user-defined fields and notes.

Printing Entry Information

You can print the information in the list in three formats: list, labels, and envelopes.

Start by selecting a record and the Group drop-down list at the top of the Address Book window to display the records that you want to print.

If you want to change the format of a specific record, choose that record and click Modify | Format Address to open the Format Print Check Address dialog seen on the top of the next page. Set the options and click OK.

Click Print to open a drop-down list of printing options.

List Choosing List displays a Print dialog just like the one that appears when printing Quicken reports. Use it to enter printing options, and then click OK to print the list. Consult Chapter 8 for more information about printing lists and reports.

Labels Choosing Labels displays the Print Labels dialog. It includes a list of commonly used Avery label products; be sure to select the right one before you click the Print button. To print a sheet of return address labels, choose an address from the drop-down list in the Return Address area and select the Return Address (Whole Sheet) option in the Print Selection area.

Envelopes Choosing Envelopes displays the Print Envelope dialog. Use it to print #10 envelopes for Address Book records. Just set options in the dialog, put envelope stock into your printer, and click the Print button.

One Step Update and the Password Vault

As discussed in Chapters 5 and 9, the Bank Account Update, Portfolio Export, and WebEntry features use One Step Update to update information on the Web and download transactions entered on the Web. But that's not all One Step

Update can do. This feature makes it possible to handle many of your connection chores at once. When used in conjunction with the Password Vault feature, you can click a few buttons, enter a single password, and take a break while Quicken updates portfolio and account information for you. You can even schedule updates to occur automatically when Quicken isn't running.

Using One Step Update

The idea behind One Step Update is to use one command to handle multiple online activities. This eliminates the need to use update commands in a variety of locations throughout Quicken. One command does it all.

Setting Up the Update

Choose Tools | One Step Update or click the Update button in the Account Bar. If a dialog appears, asking if you want to set up the Password Vault, click No for now. You'll see how to use this feature later in this chapter, in the section titled "The Password Vault." The One Step Update dialog, which is shown in Figure 6-13, appears. It lists all of the items that can be updated. Check marks appear for each item that will be updated when you connect. You can click the check boxes to toggle the check marks there.

The dialog is split into three areas.

Download Quotes, Asset Classes, Headlines and Alerts   This area offers one option to download security quotes, asset classes, financial headlines, and security-related alerts. You can select which quotes should be downloaded by clicking the Select Quotes link. Learn more about downloading quotes in Chapter 12.

Financial Institutions   The Financial Institutions area lists all of the financial institutions for which Online Account Services have been enabled. Your list will differ from the one shown here—unless we have the same financial institutions! You can enter your password in a box to the right of each institution name when you're ready to update your data. Note that this part of the dialog scrolls; be sure to scroll down if necessary to set options for financial institutions at the bottom of the list.

Quicken.com   The Quicken.com area lists preferences for uploading or exporting your Quicken data with Quicken.com. You can access these Quicken Preferences by clicking the Select Quicken.com Data To Update link. Your options are:

- Selecting accounts you want to view online. All of the investing accounts you have entered into Quicken are displayed. You can choose which, if any, you want to view.

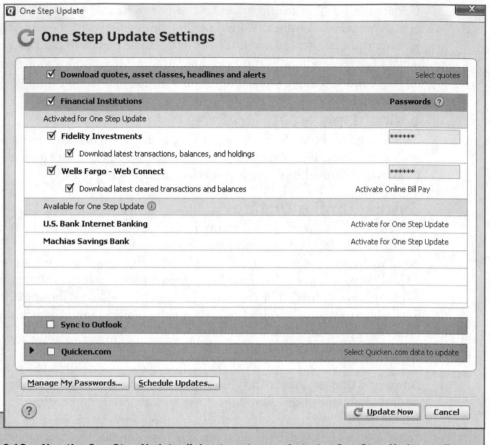

Figure 6-13 • Use the One Step Update dialog to set up and start a One Step Update online session.

- Click Send My Shares to track the value of your current holdings.
- Click Send Only My Symbols if you want general information about your stock holdings.
- By default, your Watch List (see Part Three for more information) is tracked in Quicken.com. Clear this check box if you don't want it tracked.
- Click OK to close Preferences and return to the One Step Update dialog.

Updating Information

Make sure check marks appear beside the items you want to update in the One Step Update dialog. If necessary, enter passwords in the text boxes beside financial institutions for which you want to update data. Then click Update Now. If Quicken offers to save your passwords, click No for now. Learn how to use the Password Vault feature later in this chapter. Quicken establishes a connection to the Internet and begins transferring data.

When the update is complete, the One Step Update Summary dialog appears. As shown in Figure 6-14, it summarizes the activity for the update. Click the disclosure triangles to the left of financial institution names to reveal a list of accounts and activity. You can click the name of an account in the window to go to that account's register, or click the Close button at the bottom of the window to dismiss it.

The One Step Update Summary dialog does not appear if you have previously told Quicken to display the summary only when there is an error.

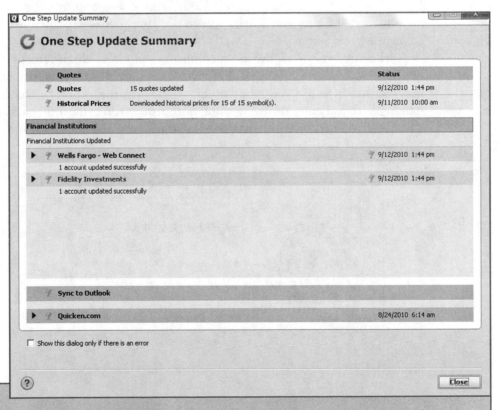

Figure 6-14 • The One Step Update Summary displays the results of your One Step Update.

The Password Vault

You might find it a nuisance to have to type in each password when you use the One Step Update feature—especially if you connect to more than one or two financial institutions. This is when the Password Vault can help.

Quicken's Password Vault feature enables you to store all your financial institution passwords in one central location. The passwords are then protected with a single password. When you use One Step Update, you enter just one password to access all financial institutions. You must have Online Account Access or Online Payment set up with at least one institution to use the Password Vault feature.

Setting Up the Password Vault

Choose Tools | Online Center | Password Vault or Tools | Password Vault | Setup New Password Vault. The Password Vault Setup dialog appears. It provides some introductory information. Click Next to display the first window of the Password Vault Setup.

As shown next, follow the instructions in each tab to choose financial institutions and enter corresponding passwords. You'll enter each password twice because the characters you type do not appear on screen; this is a secure way of making sure you enter the same thing both times. You can do this for any combination of financial institutions for which you have set up online access.

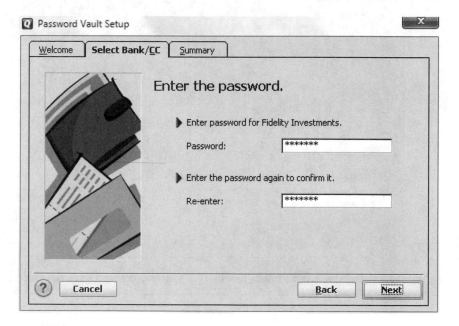

When you've finished, select the No option if you have no other passwords to enter. Select Yes if you have other accounts you wish to include in the Password Vault. Enter as many as you choose, and when all have been entered, click Next when asked whether you want to enter additional passwords.

You are prompted to enter a password to protect the Password Vault. Enter it in each box and click Next.

When you click Next, the Summary tab of the Password Vault Setup window appears. It displays a list of your financial institutions and indicates whether a password has been stored for each one.

You can use buttons in this dialog to change or delete a selected password, print all passwords, or change the Vault password. When you've finished working with the window's contents, click Done. Quicken creates the Password Vault.

Using the Password Vault

Using the Password Vault is easy. Simply choose Tools | One Step Update or click the Update button in the Account Bar. You will no longer be prompted for any passwords. Simply continue using One Step Update in the usual way with one difference: You don't have to enter passwords for any of the financial institutions for which a password has been entered in the Password Vault.

You can also use the Password Vault in conjunction with the Update/Send button in the Online Center window, which is discussed in Chapters 5 and 10. Clicking that button automatically displays the Password Vault dialog. Enter your password and click OK; Quicken performs the update.

Editing the Password Vault

Once you've created a Password Vault, you can modify it to change passwords or add passwords for other financial institutions. Choose Tools| Password Vault | Add Or Edit Passwords. In the Edit Password Vault dialog that appears, click the Change Vault Password button to change the password to your Password Vault. Click Change Password to change the passwords for any account. Click Delete Password to delete an account's password. When you've finished, click Done.

Deleting the Password Vault

You can delete the Password Vault if you decide you no longer want to use it. Choose Tools | Password Vault | Delete Vault And All Saved Passwords. Then click Yes in response to the confirmation dialog that appears. Quicken deletes the Password Vault. From then on, you'll have to enter passwords for each financial institution when you use One Step Update.

Scheduling Updates

You can schedule updates to occur when you're not using Quicken. Then, when you start Quicken, your data file is already updated with information from your financial institutions, and, if you've disabled automatic transaction download, ready to review and accept into your account registers. Your Quicken.com information can also be automatically updated based on information in your Quicken data file.

Setting Up the Schedule

To set up a schedule, begin by choosing Tools | Schedule Updates. The Schedule Updates dialog, which is shown next, appears. Set options in each area of the dialog and click OK.

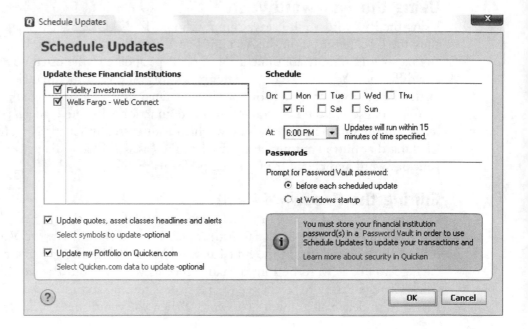

The following sections look at each of the options.

Items To Schedule   The update area lists all of the items in the One Step Update dialog discussed earlier in this chapter. Click to toggle check marks beside each item you want to include in the schedule.

Schedule   The Schedule area determines when the updates will occur. Turn on check boxes for each day of the week you want the updates to occur, and then choose a time from the At drop-down list. Since your computer must be running for the updates to take place, set options for when you know your computer will be turned on. Updates will not occur, however, if Quicken is running; this ensures that the automated feature does not interrupt your work with Quicken.

Security   Security options enable you to indicate when your computer should prompt you for the Password Vault password. (The Password Vault feature must be set up and used in conjunction with scheduled updates.) You have two options:

- **Before Each Scheduled Update** displays the Password Vault Password dialog just before each update. You may want to select this option if the update is scheduled for a time when you expect to be at work on your computer. This is a more secure option, since it requires you to be present just before the update takes place. If you're not around, however, the update will not take place as scheduled.
- **At Windows Startup** displays the Password Vault Password dialog when you start Windows. This option can make scheduled updates more convenient, since you don't have to be around when they occur.

Using the Schedule

Using the schedule is easy. First you must exit Quicken, since a scheduled update will not occur when Quicken is running. Eventually, the Password Vault dialog will appear. When it appears depends on the schedule and security options you set. Enter your password in the dialog and click Update. Quicken does the rest.

Changing the Schedule

To change the schedule, choose Tools | Schedule Updates to display the Schedule Updates dialog. Make changes in the dialog as desired to modify settings. To cancel scheduled updates, turn off the check boxes beside each day of the week. When you're finished making changes, click OK.

Reconciling Your Accounts

Chapter 7

In This Chapter:

- *Starting a reconciliation*
- *Comparing transactions*
- *Making adjustments*
- *Reconciling credit card accounts*
- *Printing a reconciliation report*
- *Identifying reconciled items*

Often, the task of manually balancing, or *reconciling*, your bank account each month is not your favorite chore. However, you probably open your bank statement each month and using the paper form and a hand calculator, total all the checks and deposits. There's a lot of adding when it comes to totaling the outstanding checks and deposits, and the longer you wait to do the job, the more adding you'll need to do. And for some reason, it hardly ever comes out right the first time you try. Maybe you've even failed so many times that you've given up.

In this chapter, you will learn why it is important to reconcile your bank statements and how you can do it—quickly and easily—with Quicken Personal Finance Software.

Reconciling Bank Accounts

Reconciling an account refers to the process of comparing transactions in your account register to transactions on the account statement sent to you by your bank. Transactions that match are simply checked off. Transactions that appear only in one place— your account register or the bank's account statement—need to be accounted for.

In this section, you'll review the basics of reconciling a bank account with Quicken: comparing transactions, making adjustments, and finishing up.

Getting Started

To reconcile a bank account with your paper statement, you must have the statement. Paper bank statements usually come monthly, so you won't have to wait long to begin.

With statement in hand, open the account register for the account you want to reconcile. Click the Account Actions button and choose Reconcile. What happens next depends on whether the account is enabled for online access.

Accounts Without Online Account Access

If the account is not enabled for online access, the Statement Summary dialog, which is shown next, appears. It gathers basic statement information prior to reconciling the account. Enter information from your bank statement in the appropriate boxes. (Enter service charge and interest earned information only if you have not already entered it in the account register.) Then click OK to continue.

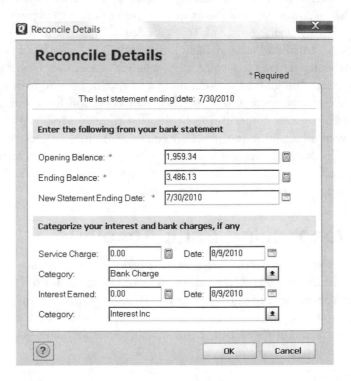

EXPERIENCED QUICKEN USERS AND NEW TO QUICKEN?

Reconciling Accounts

If you have been reconciling your bank statements for a long time, you may be tempted to skip this chapter. But, please reconsider. This information can save you time, money, and frustration, so please rethink your decision and take the few minutes to read through the chapter.

Reconciling your checking account is important. It helps you locate differences between what you think you have in the account and what the bank says you have. It can help you track down bank errors (which do happen once in a while) or personal errors (which, unfortunately, seem to happen more frequently). Completely balancing your checking account and making adjustments as necessary can prevent you from accidentally bouncing checks when you think you have more money than you really do. That can save you the cost of bank fees and a lot of embarrassment.

If you keep track of all bank account activity with Quicken, reconciling your bank accounts is easy. You don't need to use the form on the back of the bank statement. You don't even need a calculator. Just use Quicken's reconciliation feature to enter beginning and ending balances, check off cleared transactions, and enter the transactions you missed. You'll find you're successful a lot more often with Quicken helping you out.

You can use Quicken's reconciliation feature to balance any Quicken banking account— including credit card accounts. Although this chapter concentrates on checking accounts, you'll find information for reconciling other accounts, including credit cards, as well. You can also reconcile checking accounts linked to investment accounts. This is useful if you write checks or pay bills with the linked account.

Accounts with Online Account Access

If the account is enabled for online account access, Quicken may begin by displaying a suggestion that you download transactions to update your check register, as seen here. If your account is not up to date, take a moment to go online and update your account. It's the only way you can be sure that all transactions recorded by the bank are included in your account register. Choose Download Transactions For This Account to go online and download the latest

transactions for this account. Click Reconcile Without Downloading to continue with the reconciliation. After you have made your selection, click OK to continue. Click Cancel if you want to stop the reconciliation process entirely.

If you have not yet registered your copy of Quicken, you may be prompted to go online and do so before you can download transactions. This requires Internet access.

If you are up to date, Quicken displays the Reconcile Online Account dialog:

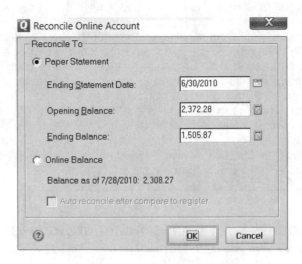

As you can see, this dialog offers two options for reconciling the account:

- **Paper Statement** enables you to reconcile the information in your Quicken account register to your bank statement. It is a traditional account reconciliation, and it works just like the account reconciliation you perform for an account without online account access. If you select this option, you must enter the bank statement ending date and ending balance in the appropriate boxes.
- **Online Balance** enables you to reconcile the account to the balance that was last downloaded for the account. If you select this option, you don't have to enter anything in the boxes. Turning on the Auto Reconcile After Compare To Register check box tells Quicken to reconcile the account to your financial institution's online balance automatically each time you download

and accept transactions. With this Auto Reconcile feature enabled, you never have to reconcile the account again. However, you are trusting the bank to make no mistakes.

After setting options in this dialog, click OK to continue.

Comparing Transactions

The next step in reconciling the account is to compare transactions that have cleared on the statement with transactions in your account register. For this, Quicken displays the Reconcile window (shown in Figure 7-1), which displays all payments, checks, and deposits for the account you are reconciling.

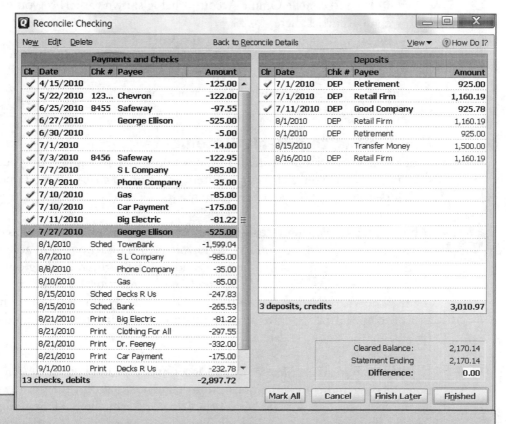

Figure 7-1 • **The Reconcile window helps you easily compare the transactions on your register to the items on your paper bank statement.**

You can use button bar buttons within this window to work with its contents:

- **New** switches you to the account register window for the account you are reconciling so you can enter a new transaction. To return to your reconciliation, click the Reconcile:name of account button at the bottom left of the check register, as seen here.

  `Reconcile: Checking`   `X`

- **Edit** switches you to the account register window for a selected transaction so you can modify it.
- **Delete** removes the selected transaction from the account register.
- **Back To Reconcile Detail** displays the Statement Summary dialog shown earlier or the Reconcile Paper Statement dialog (which is similar to the top half of the Reconcile Online Account dialog shown earlier) so you can check or change entries there.
- **View** offers options to change the sort order of the window's contents, as seen here.
- **How Do I?** displays the Quicken Personal Finances Help window with instructions for reconciling accounts.

> View ▾   ⑦ How Do I?
>   Sort by Check Number
> ✓   Sort by Date
>   Sort by Payee
>   Sort by Amount

Reconciling to a Bank Statement

Your job is to check off the items in the window that also appear on your bank statement. While you're checking off items, be sure to check off the same items with a pen or pencil on your bank statement.

A hidden field—Posting Date—controls which transactions are presented in the Reconcile window for accounts with downloaded transactions. You access this hidden field by right-clicking the transaction in the register, holding down the CTRL key on the keyboard, and clicking Copy Transaction from the context menu. The View Posting dialog appears. This is handy info if transactions you expect to appear in the current reconcile do not appear—their posting date may be outside the reconcile date range.

If the account is enabled for online account access and you have been downloading and comparing transactions regularly to accept them into your account register, many of the transactions in the Reconcile Bank Statement window may already be checked off. This speeds up the reconciliation process.

While you're checking off transactions in Quicken and on your bank statement, look for differences between them. Here are some of the differences you might encounter:

- An item that appears on the bank statement but not in your account register is an item that you did not enter. You may have omitted the transaction for a number of reasons. Perhaps it was a bank adjustment that you were not informed about. Or maybe you simply forgot to enter a check. To enter an omitted transaction, click New on the button bar to switch to the register window. Enter the transaction in the register, click Enter, and click the Reconcile:accountname button at the bottom of the register to continue the reconciliation. Then click to place a check mark in the Clr column beside the item to mark it cleared.

- An item that appears on both your account register and bank statement but has a different amount or date could be due to an error—yours or the bank's. If the error is yours, you can edit the transaction by double-clicking it in the Reconcile window. This displays the account register window with the transaction selected. Edit the transaction and click the Enter button. Then click the Reconcile:accountname button at the bottom of the register to continue the reconciliation.

- Items that appear in your account register but not on the bank statement are items that have not yet cleared the bank. These are usually transactions prepared just before the bank's closing date, but they can be older. Do not check them off. Chances are you'll check them off the next time you complete a reconciliation. If, during a bank reconciliation, you discover any uncleared items that are older than two or three months, you should investigate why they have not cleared the bank. You may discover that a check (or worse yet, a deposit) was lost in transit.

Reconciling to an Online Balance

If you've recently downloaded and accepted transactions for the account, reconciling to an online balance shouldn't take much time. Items you've already reviewed and accepted will be checked off. Some more recent transactions may not be checked off because they haven't cleared your bank yet. Your job is to look for older transactions that appear in your Quicken account register that aren't checked off. These could represent stale payments that may have been lost in transit to the payee or errors (or duplications) you made when manually entering information into your Quicken account register. Follow up on all transactions more than 60 days old to see why they haven't been included with your downloaded transactions.

Finishing Up

When you reconcile a bank account with Quicken, your goal is to make the difference between the Cleared Balance and the Statement Ending Balance zero. You can monitor this progress at the bottom of the Reconcile window, as shown here.

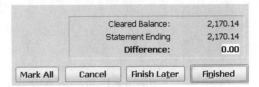

When the Difference Is Zero

If you correctly checked off all bank statement items and the difference is zero, you've successfully reconciled the account and you can click the Finished button.

If You Can't Get the Difference to Zero

Sometimes, try as you might, you just can't get the difference to zero. Here are a few last things to check before you give up:

- Make sure all the amounts you checked off in your account register are the same as the amounts on the bank statement. Keep in mind that if you made a transposition error—for example, 24.19 instead of 24.91—the difference between the two amounts will be evenly divisible by 9.
- Make sure you included any bank charges or earned interest.
- Make sure the beginning and ending balances you entered are the same as those on the bank statement.

If you checked and rechecked all these things and still can't get the difference to zero, click Finished. Quicken displays a dialog like the one shown here that indicates the amount of the difference and offers to make an adjustment to your account register for the amount. Click Adjust to accept the adjustment. The amount of the adjustment will be recorded without a category.

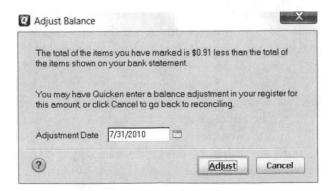

First-Time Reconciliations

A while back, a client was having difficulties understanding how to reconcile an account for the first time. He seemed to think he needed to come up with some kind of "plug figure" to get the reconciliation to work. He hadn't even *tried* performing the reconciliation, too worried about what *might* happen. He may have been over-thinking the situation, but his concern was valid and is discussed here.

Suppose you have a checking account that you've been using for several years. Recently, you purchased and installed Quicken. You set up your checking account as a Quicken account, using the ending balance on your most recent bank statement—say it was dated 5/11/10—as the beginning balance in the account. After setting up the account, you entered all transactions dated after 5/11/10 into the account register.

June arrives and you receive your 6/11/10 bank statement. Following the instructions in this chapter, you reconcile the account for the first time. But you discover that the 6/11/10 bank statement includes checks you wrote *before* 5/11/10 that were outstanding (had not cleared the bank) as of the 5/11/10 bank statement. If you don't consider these transactions in your reconciliation, there is a difference between the cleared balance and the statement ending balance. What do you do about these transactions?

It was this fact that confused my client. He thought he needed to make some kind of adjusting entry in Quicken *before* starting the reconciliation. Instead, consider the following two options:

- If you want to record the transactions in your Quicken data file—perhaps to make charges to categories more complete—record them. You can do this during the reconciliation by clicking the New button on the Reconcile window's button bar (refer to Figure 7-1) as explained earlier in this chapter. Once the transactions have been entered, be sure to check them off in the Reconcile window. The difference should go away.
- If you don't want to record the transactions—perhaps you don't care about the categories that would be affected—let Quicken make an adjusting entry for you at the end of the reconciliation. That's the "plug figure" my client was looking for. He didn't realize that Quicken would take care of it for him.

Once that first reconciliation is complete, you should have no further problems—unless, of course, the 7/12/10 bank statement includes one or more very old checks from before 5/11/10. Then the same situation results, with the same options and resolution.

The moral of this story: Trust Quicken. Even if you can't figure out the accounting procedures behind your finances, Quicken can.

Other Reconciliation Tasks and Features

Quicken offers a number of other reconciliation features that you might find useful. Here's a quick look at them.

Reconciling Credit Card Accounts

You can reconcile a credit card account the same way you reconcile a bank account. If you try to enter all credit card transactions as you make them throughout the month, it's a good idea to use the reconciliation feature to compare your entries to the credit card statement, just to make sure you didn't miss any. If you simply enter all credit card transactions when you get your statement, reconciling to the statement really isn't necessary.

When you begin the reconciliation process, Quicken displays either the Statement Summary dialog or the Reconcile Online Account dialog, depending on whether the credit card account has online account access features enabled. The dialogs are similar to the ones that appear when you reconcile a bank account.

If you have a card for which you do not download transactions, you are prompted to enter the total charges you have made during the billing period as well as any payments or credits that have been made on the account, as shown here. You can find this information on your paper credit card statement. Enter

Reconcile: Credit Card

Reconcile: Credit Card

* Required

The last statement ending date: 7/23/2010

Enter the following from your statement.

Charges, Cash Advances: * (other than finance charges)	425.00
Payments, Credits: *	2,500.00
Ending Balance: *	969.61
New Statement Ending Date: *	8/25/2010

Enter and categorize your interest charges, if any.

Finance Charges: 24.55   Date: 7/25/2010

Category: Interest Exp

OK   Cancel

the payment date and any finance charges and click OK to move to the Reconcile window, which looks and works almost exactly like the Reconcile window that was shown in Figure 7-1.

 If you download transactions for a card, simply enter the date from the paper statement, the ending balance, and zeros in the Charges and Payments fields. Quicken will compute the rest for you! (However, make sure to enter the zeros, as leaving the fields blank will cause an error message to display.)

If you can't successfully get the credit card reconciliation to work, Quicken offers to make adjustments. The following illustration shows the Adjusting Register To Agree With Statement dialog for a hopelessly messed-up account that needs adjustments to opening balance, payments, and charges. Choose a category for each adjustment and click Adjust to make the adjusting entries.

Adjusting Register to Agree with Statement	X

In order to bring your records into balance with the statement, Quicken is about to make the following entries in your register.

Opening balance difference

-421.21   Category (optional): Home Repair

Register missing one or more payments

-50.00   Category (optional): [Credit Card]

Register missing one or more charges

-5.78   Category (optional): Home Repair

Adjust   Cancel

At the conclusion of a credit card reconciliation, Quicken may display the Make Credit Card Payment dialog (shown on the top of the next page), offering to prepare a credit card payment for you. This is particularly handy if you like to pay your credit card bill after reconciling your statement to your entries. Select an account and payment method and click Yes. Quicken prepares the transaction for you.

If you do not wish to make a payment now, click No to close the dialog box.

If your credit card balance is zero, a message box appears that says there is an outstanding balance of zero. Click OK to close the message box.

Be careful about clicking the Don't Show Me This Screen Again check box. You only get one chance to do this, and at some point, you may want to see the dialog. To do so, you will need to reset the Quicken Warnings preference. Click Edit | Preferences | Alerts | Reset Quicken Warnings.

Printing a Reconciliation Report

At the end of a reconciliation Quicken displays a dialog that offers to create a reconciliation report. If you click Yes, the Reconciliation Report Setup dialog, shown here, appears. Set report options in the dialog and click OK to open the Print dialog and print the report.

Even if you don't normally print reconciliation reports, if your reconciliation required an adjusting entry, it might be a good idea to document it by printing one. You can then file the report with your bank statement and canceled checks.

If you don't want a printed copy, print the reconciliation report as a .pdf file and store it with the electronic copy of your statement and pictures of your processed checks.

Identifying Reconciled Items

As shown in Figure 7-2, Quicken uses the Clr column in an account register to identify items that either have cleared the bank or have been reconciled:

- **c** indicates that the item has cleared the bank. You'll see a c in the Clr column beside items that you have checked off during a reconciliation if you have not completed the reconciliation. You'll also see a c beside items downloaded and accepted using Quicken's online account access feature, as discussed in Chapter 6.
- **R** indicates that the item has been reconciled.

If you want to change a transaction's cleared status, click in the Clr column to see several choices, as shown here. Choose from:

- **Uncleared** to indicate that the transaction has not yet been cleared by the bank.
- **Cleared** to indicate that the bank has cleared the item, but the item has not yet been reconciled.
- **Reconciled** to show that the item has been reconciled. The item will then appear in gray print as seen in Figure 7-2. To make it even more obvious that a transaction either has cleared your financial institution or has been reconciled, reconciled transactions appear in gray print rather than black.
- **Reconcile This Account** to open the Reconcile Online Account dialog, discussed earlier in this chapter.

You can toggle the gray color of reconciled transactions to black via Quicken preference Register | Register Appearance | Gray Reconciled Transactions. The "Standard" view for new users is Gray Reconciled Transactions by default.

To prevent errors in your account registers, do not edit transactions that have been reconciled.

Figure 7-2 • Outstanding transactions in your check register are in black, while items that have cleared your bank are in gray.

Examining Your Banking Activity

Chapter 8

In This Chapter:

- *Spending tab overview*
- *Types of reports and graphs*
- *Creating reports and graphs*
- *Customizing and saving reports and graphs*
- *Printing reports and graphs*
- *Planning your spending*
- *Viewing your spending*
- *Using alerts*

At this point, you'll probably agree that entering financial information into Quicken Personal Finance Software is a great way to organize it. But sometimes organizing information isn't enough. Sometimes you need to see concise summaries of the information you entered in the form of balances, activity reports, and graphs.

Quicken provides the kind of information you're looking for in the form of snapshots, reports, and graphs. This chapter concludes the discussion of Quicken's Spending tab by telling you about the snapshots of information it offers and how you can take advantage of its alerts. It also explains how you can create, modify, and save standard and custom reports and graphs for all Quicken tabs.

A Closer Look at the Spending Tab

The previous chapters in this part of the book have explored many aspects of Quicken's banking area, including accounts, transaction entry, Online Account Services, automation features, and reconciliations. But the Spending tab also offers a place for examining the results of your work with banking accounts and features.

In this part of the chapter you will go on a guided tour of the Spending tab's reporting and graphing features so you can learn about the information you can find there.

The Spending Graph

The Spending graph (see Figure 8-1) shows the total of what you have spent for the last 30 days by default. The top of the window shows the total in all categories. Next is a colorful pie chart with a legend to the right explaining the category associated with each of the "pie slices." The lower part of the window is a register displaying all of the transactions.

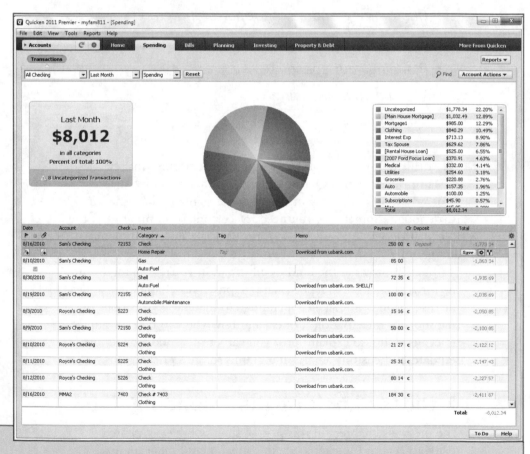

Figure 8-1 • The Spending tab displays a graph of your spending.

Accounts   The Accounts drop-down list, seen next, lets you decide which accounts to display in the Spending graph. You can choose from:

- **All Accounts**, which includes all of the accounts that appear in the Banking section of the Account Bar. Note: This list includes accounts that you have marked as "Hidden" in the Account Detail dialog.
- **All Checking/Savings/Cash/Credit Cards** includes the accounts you have so named in Quicken.
- **Custom** opens the Customize *nnnnnn* dialog, which allows you to choose which accounts to display in your graph. In the example shown here, we've chosen to display only the two credit cards.

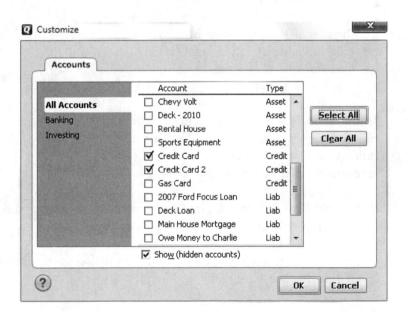

The other menu options display all of checking, savings, cash, or credit card accounts so you can choose to use just one in your Spending graph.

Time Period   While the default for your Spending graph is the last 30 days, you can use this drop-down list to choose any time period you wish. Your options are:

- **All Dates**, which includes every date for which you have entered a transaction into Quicken.
- **This Month**, which displays just the spending you've done since the first of the current month.
- **Last Month** includes your expenditures in the last calendar month.
- **Last 30/60/90 Days** options are self-explanatory.
- **Last 12 Months** includes all of your expenditures for the last 365 days (or 366 days in leap years).
- **This Quarter** includes the information from the first day of this calendar quarter through today.
- **Last Quarter** presents your spending for the most recent calendar quarter before this quarter.
- **This Year** presents all of your spending since the first of January through today.
- **Last Year** displays all of last year's spending.
- **Custom** lets you set the date range for your graph as seen here.

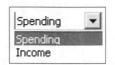

Transaction Types   The Income/Spending drop-down list, shown here, lets you choose to display either your expenditures or your income. You can choose both the accounts and the date range to include.

Reset and Find Buttons   The Reset button, located next to the Spending/Income drop-down list, resets your graph to the default of All Accounts, Last 30 Days, and Spending.

The Find button opens the Quicken Find dialog as seen here. Learn more about the Quicken Find dialog in Chapter 4.

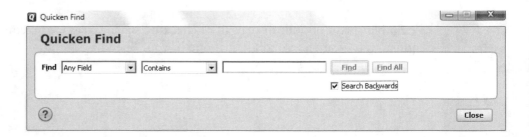

The Spending Register

The register shown at the bottom of the Spending tab view is similar to the All Transactions register, in that it displays all of the transactions from the accounts you have chosen in the Accounts drop-down list at the top of the Spending graph. It includes, as does the All Transactions register, an Account column, in which Quicken displays the account into which the transaction was entered.

By default, this register is sorted by date, with the earliest date first. You can tell Quicken which columns to display and which columns to hide by using the Register Columns gear at the upper-right corner of the register, as seen in Figure 8-2. The choices displayed on the Register Columns list vary, depending on the type of account. For example, if you do not have any accounts activated for download, the Downloaded Amount option may not appear.

Figure 8-2 • Use the gear tool in your register to tell Quicken what columns you wish to display.

When you have made your selections, click Done. To return the columns to the Quicken default settings, click Default.

You can adjust the width of each of these columns by placing your cursor on the line between two columns and dragging to the left or right as shown here.

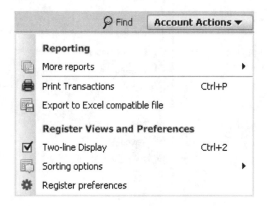

Date ▲	⟵Account	Check Number
7/27/2010	MMA2	9008
7/27/2010	Checking	

If you have upgraded from a previous version of Quicken, your columns may not be in the same order.

If you have chosen the Two-Line Display in the Account Actions menu, as shown next, instead of the default single-line display, you see a shorter menu. See "Reports and Account Actions Button" later in this chapter for more information. The two-line display shows the Category, Tag, and Memo columns on the second line instead of the first. If you choose to show two lines, the columns in the second line are not adjustable.

Reports and Account Actions Button

The Reports button provides links to many useful Quicken reports. See "Quicken Reporting Overview" later in this chapter for complete information about the reports Quicken can create.

When you select the Account Actions button in the Spending tab, the menu provides links to many of the reporting features of Quicken, covered next in this chapter. The Register Views And Preferences section lets you choose the following:

- **Two-Line Display** This choice shows each transaction on two lines as described earlier. Its keyboard shortcut is CTRL-2.

- **Sorting Options**   By default, registers are sorted by date. This option allows you to choose another column by which to sort your register as seen here.
- **Register Preferences**   When you select this option, the Preferences dialog opens to Register Preferences from which you can tell Quicken how you want your register to appear. As seen below, there are several choices that affect the register's display. See Appendix B for more detailed information.

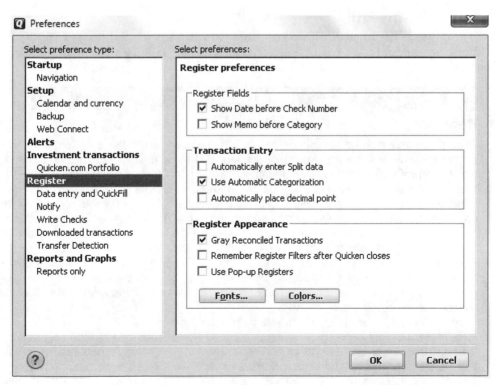

Quicken Reporting Overview

Quicken offers a variety of reports and graphs, each of which can be customized to meet your needs. When you spend time entering data into Quicken, Quicken crunches the numbers for you and provides reports and graphs to analyze your spending habits, help you find ways to save money, and format your data to submit information to financial institutions when you apply for loans or credit cards.

In this section, you'll learn about the types of reports and graphs Quicken offers. Then you'll see how you can use a variety of techniques to quickly create reports and graphs based on the information in your Quicken data file. The techniques in this part of the chapter apply to the reports and graphs you create for any Quicken data, regardless of where it appears.

Types of Reports and Graphs

Within Quicken are two kinds of reports and graphs: standard and saved. Here's an overview of each one.

Standard

When you click Reports on the menu bar, Quicken displays a number of standard reports and graphs, organized by topic: Banking, Comparison,

---

NEW TO QUICKEN?

Reporting

Okay, perhaps you're not a corporation with stockholders and SEC reporting requirements. And maybe you're not even involved in any kind of business where reports could help you maximize profits. But that doesn't mean you won't find Quicken's reporting features useful.

One Quicken user found out how useful the reports can be when she and her husband applied for a mortgage for a rental property they wanted to buy. They had been faithfully entering transactions into Quicken for years and had a complete record of everything they owned and owed. Rather than manually filling out the lengthy forms required by the lender, they created Quicken reports that provided the same information. In addition, they quickly created reports summarizing their current net worth, detailing their investment portfolio, and totaling their year-to-date income and expenses. They sent all these reports to the bank with copies of their recent tax returns and got a positive answer within a few days. And not once did they have to find the calculator.

In the old days, before Quicken, you might spend hours with your tax preparer each year, answering questions and shuffling through piles of paper and handwritten notes. With Quicken you can create reports of income and expenses, including detailed reports for things like charity contributions and medical expenditures. Take all of these reports to your tax person, and you may find that your tax preparation bill is much less than what it used to be.

As you can see, reports aren't just for businesses.

Investing, Net Worth & Balances, Spending, Tax, EasyAnswer, and Graphs. If you do not see the Net Worth & Balances reports section, turn on the Property & Debt tab. To turn on this tab, click View | Tabs To Show | Property & Debt.

If you are using the Home and Business or Rental Property Management versions of Quicken, you have additional reports available.

For example, the Banking topic includes Banking Summary, Cash Flow, Cash Flow By Tag, Missing Checks, Reconciliation, and Transaction reports. These reports and graphs clearly show banking-related information. EasyAnswer reports and graphs answer specific, predefined questions, such as, "Where did I spend my money during the period…?" and "How much did I spend on…?" You select a question and then provide optional information, such as a date range, payee, or account. Quicken gathers the information and generates the report or graph.

Saved

You can create custom reports and graphs by customizing the standard reports and graphs. This multiplies your reporting capabilities, enabling you to create reports or graphs that show exactly what you need to show. When you save your custom reports and graphs, they can be re-created quickly, with just a few mouse clicks, to display current information.

Creating Reports and Graphs

With Quicken, creating a report or graph is as simple as clicking a few buttons. You can use several techniques: choosing a report or graph from the Reports menu, setting options in the Reports & Graphs Center window, using the Report button or menu on button bars, and choosing commands from contextual menus. In this section, you'll learn to use all of these techniques.

Reports & Graphs Center

The Reports & Graphs Center window (see Figure 8-3) offers one way to create reports and graphs. Open the Spending, Planning, or the Investing tab and from the Reports button, choose All Reports | Reports & Graphs Center to display it. You can also access the Reports & Graphs Center from the Quicken menu bar by clicking Reports | Reports & Graphs Center.

Click one of the topics on the left side of the window to display a list of the available reports and graphs. The icon that appears to the left of the report name indicates whether you can create a report, a graph, or both.

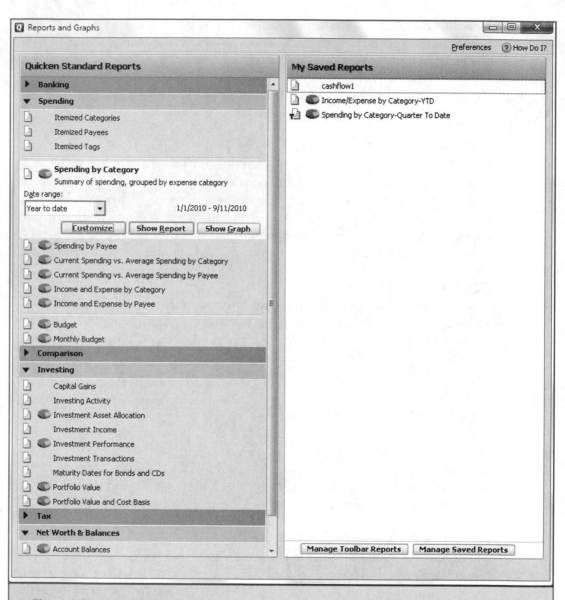

Figure 8-3 • Use the Reports & Graphs Center window to create reports or graphs.

To create a report or graph, click its name on the left side of the window and then set the Date Range option in the settings area that appears beneath it. You can click the Customize button to further customize the report or graph, as explained later, in the section titled "Customizing Reports and Graphs." Then click Show Report or Show Graph to display the report or graph. Figure 8-4 shows an example of a report.

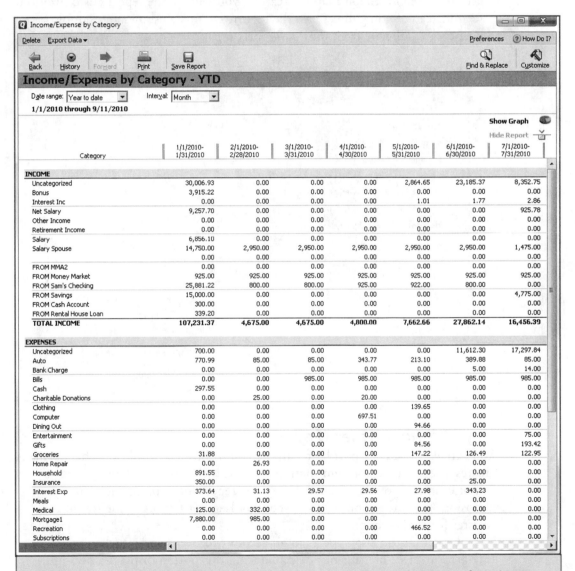

Category	1/1/2010-1/31/2010	2/1/2010-2/28/2010	3/1/2010-3/31/2010	4/1/2010-4/30/2010	5/1/2010-5/31/2010	6/1/2010-6/30/2010	7/1/2010-7/31/2010
INCOME							
Uncategorized	30,006.93	0.00	0.00	0.00	2,864.65	23,185.37	8,352.75
Bonus	3,915.22	0.00	0.00	0.00	0.00	0.00	0.00
Interest Inc	0.00	0.00	0.00	0.00	1.01	1.77	2.86
Net Salary	9,257.70	0.00	0.00	0.00	0.00	0.00	925.78
Other Income	0.00	0.00	0.00	0.00	0.00	0.00	0.00
Retirement Income	0.00	0.00	0.00	0.00	0.00	0.00	0.00
Salary	6,856.10	0.00	0.00	0.00	0.00	0.00	0.00
Salary Spouse	14,750.00	2,950.00	2,950.00	2,950.00	2,950.00	2,950.00	1,475.00
	0.00	0.00	0.00	0.00	0.00	0.00	0.00
FROM MMA2	0.00	0.00	0.00	0.00	0.00	0.00	0.00
FROM Money Market	925.00	925.00	925.00	925.00	925.00	925.00	925.00
FROM Sam's Checking	25,881.22	800.00	800.00	925.00	922.00	800.00	0.00
FROM Savings	15,000.00	0.00	0.00	0.00	0.00	0.00	4,775.00
FROM Cash Account	300.00	0.00	0.00	0.00	0.00	0.00	0.00
FROM Rental House Loan	339.20	0.00	0.00	0.00	0.00	0.00	0.00
TOTAL INCOME	**107,231.37**	**4,675.00**	**4,675.00**	**4,800.00**	**7,662.66**	**27,862.14**	**16,456.39**
EXPENSES							
Uncategorized	700.00	0.00	0.00	0.00	0.00	11,612.30	17,297.84
Auto	770.99	85.00	85.00	343.77	213.10	389.88	85.00
Bank Charge	0.00	0.00	0.00	0.00	0.00	5.00	14.00
Bills	0.00	0.00	985.00	985.00	985.00	985.00	985.00
Cash	297.55	0.00	0.00	0.00	0.00	0.00	0.00
Charitable Donations	0.00	25.00	0.00	20.00	0.00	0.00	0.00
Clothing	0.00	0.00	0.00	0.00	139.65	0.00	0.00
Computer	0.00	0.00	0.00	697.51	0.00	0.00	0.00
Dining Out	0.00	0.00	0.00	0.00	94.66	0.00	0.00
Entertainment	0.00	0.00	0.00	0.00	0.00	0.00	75.00
Gifts	0.00	0.00	0.00	0.00	84.56	0.00	193.42
Groceries	31.88	0.00	0.00	0.00	147.22	126.49	122.95
Home Repair	0.00	26.93	0.00	0.00	0.00	0.00	0.00
Household	891.55	0.00	0.00	0.00	0.00	0.00	0.00
Insurance	350.00	0.00	0.00	0.00	0.00	25.00	0.00
Interest Exp	373.64	31.13	29.57	29.56	27.98	343.23	0.00
Meals	0.00	0.00	0.00	0.00	0.00	0.00	0.00
Medical	125.00	332.00	0.00	0.00	0.00	0.00	0.00
Mortgage1	7,880.00	985.00	0.00	0.00	0.00	0.00	0.00
Recreation	0.00	0.00	0.00	0.00	466.52	0.00	0.00
Subscriptions	0.00	0.00	0.00	0.00	0.00	0.00	0.00

Figure 8-4 • You can create reports that show both your income and expenses by category.

The All Reports Menu

The All Reports menu, shown next, can be opened from the Reports subtab of the Spending, Planning, and Investing tabs. It includes a number of submenus, each of which corresponds to a report topic. To create a report or graph from the All Reports menu, click a topic submenu, and then click a report name. Quicken creates the report with default date settings. If you have your preferences set to Customize Report/Graph Before Creating, you will see the report customization screen instead of going directly to the report. Figure 8-5 shows an example of a report created directly from the All Reports menu.

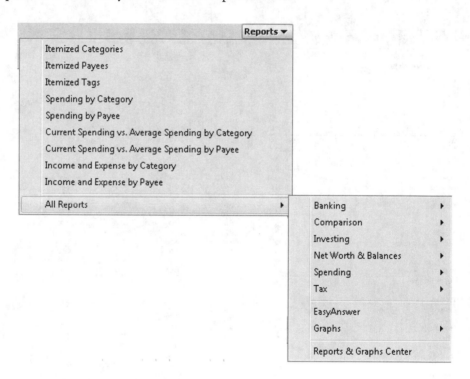

Reports from Other Menus

You can also create a report by using the menus in some windows. This normally creates a report based on information selected within the window.

For example, you could create a Register report for a specific account by choosing Account Actions | More Reports | Register Report at the top of the register for that account.

A Report button also appears in an account register window when you activate the Payee or Category field. Clicking this button displays a pop-up *mini report* of recent activity for the payee or category, as discussed briefly in

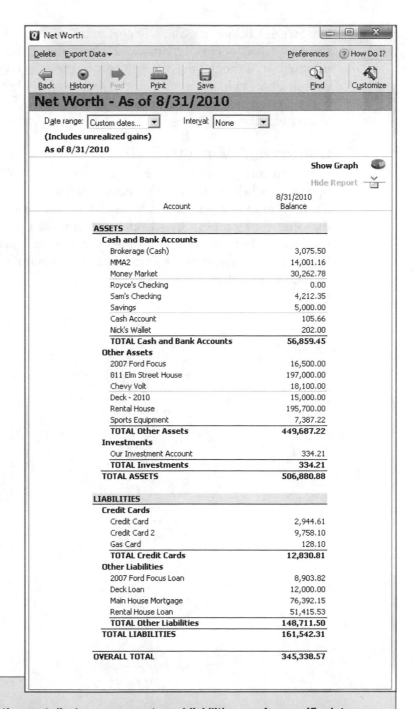

Figure 8-5 • A Net Worth report displays your assets and liabilities as of a specific date.

Chapter 4. Clicking the Show Report button in the mini report opens a report window with the information, although the Show Report button does not display in the mini report if you clicked a Category field with a split. See the illustration here.

Contextual Menus

The contextual menu that appears when you right-click (click the right mouse button) while pointing to an item sometimes includes a command that will create a report for the item. For example, right-clicking the name of a payee in the account register window displays a menu that includes the Payments Made To and Launch Mini-Report For Payee *nnnnn*. These commands are shown at the bottom of the menu, as shown here.

Working with Reports and Graphs

Although Quicken's standard reports and graphs can often provide just the information you need on-screen, you may want to do more with them. In this section, you will see how you can customize reports and graphs, save the reports and graphs you create so they're easy to re-create, and print reports and graphs so you have hard copies when you need them.

Working with a Report Window

When you create a report or graph, it appears in a report window as seen in Figures 8-4 and 8-5. This window has a number of features and options you can use to work with reports.

Button Bar Buttons

The report window includes a number of button bar buttons that work with report contents.

- **Delete** deletes the report from the Report History List. This button is gray if the report has not been added to the report list. See more about the report list in the section titled "Saving Reports and Graphs," later in this chapter.
- **Export Data** is a menu that includes commands for exporting the report's contents in three ways: Export Report To Excel Compatible Format, Copy Report To Clipboard, and Export To PDF Format. See more information about exporting in "Exporting Your Reports" later in this chapter.
- **Preferences** displays the Quicken Preferences dialog for reports and graphs so you can set preferences for all reports and graphs you create. Reports And Graphs preferences are described in Appendix B.
- **How Do I?** displays the Quicken Personal Finances Help window with information about creating reports and graphs.

Toolbar Buttons

The report window also includes a number of toolbar buttons.

- **Back**, which is available only if you are viewing a subreport (see Figure 8-6), returns to the parent report. See how to create subreports later in this chapter.
- **History** displays a list of the parent report and all subreports you have created. Choose the name of a report to display it. If you choose the Show Report List command, a Report History navigation bar appears, listing all

reports related to the window (see Figure 8-6). You can click the Hide Report List button to hide the list.

- **Forward**, which is available only if you have clicked the Back button, displays the previously viewed report in the window.
- **Print** sends the report or graph to the printer.
- **Save Report** saves the report. Learn more about saving reports in the section titled "Saving Reports and Graphs," later in this chapter.
- **Find & Replace** displays the Find And Replace dialog, which you can use to modify transactions that make up the report. The Find And Replace feature of Quicken is discussed in Chapter 4.
- **Customize** displays the Customize dialog, which you can use to customize the currently displayed report. The Customize dialog is covered later in this chapter, in the section titled "Customizing Reports and Graphs."

Hide/Display Graph/Report

If a report includes a graph, the graph or a Show Graph button will appear at the top of the report window. Clicking the Show Graph button will display the graph. The button will then turn into a Hide Graph button; clicking it hides the graph. Similarly, the report window may include a Hide Report or Show Report button, depending on whether the report is displayed or hidden.

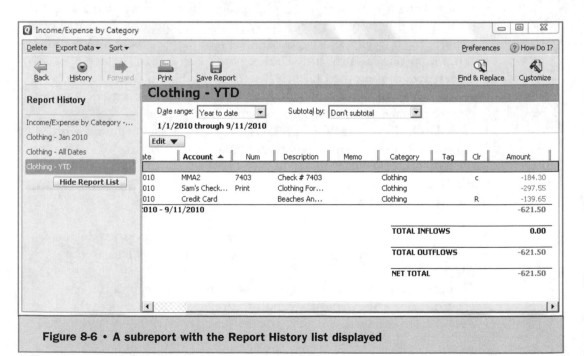

Figure 8-6 • A subreport with the Report History list displayed

You can display a large graph instead of a report, as shown in Figure 8-7, by clicking the Show Graph button and then clicking the Hide Report button.

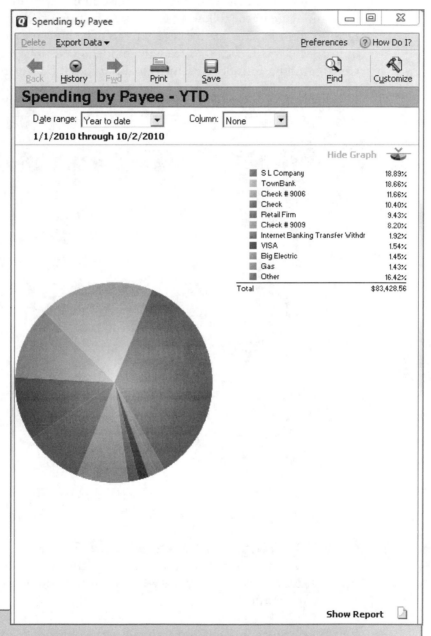

Figure 8-7 • The Spending By Payee graph with the corresponding report hidden

Hiding or Displaying Report Detail

You can show or hide the details for some reports by clicking a plus (+) or minus (–) button beside a report line. For example, clicking the – button beside Auto In Figure in the following illustration collapses the subcategories beneath Auto to show just the main category totals. The button then turns into a + button, which you click to display the hidden detail. The Expand All and Collapse All buttons do the same thing, but for all categories and subcategories.

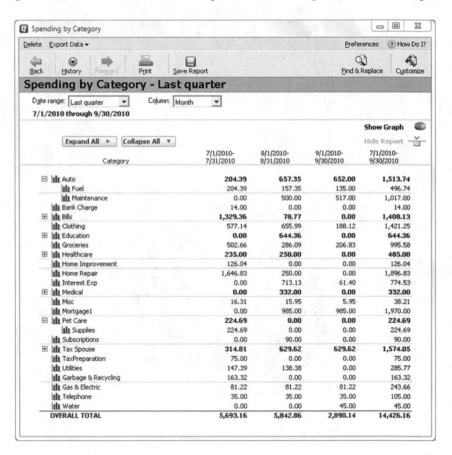

Customizing Reports and Graphs

You can customize just about any report or graph you create so it shows only the information you want to display. When you can customize it, however, depends on how you create it.

- When you create a report or graph using the Reports & Graphs Center window (refer to Figure 8-3), you can customize it before or after you create it.

- When you create a report using other commands, you may be able to customize it only after you create it.

Customization options vary from one type of report or graph to another. It's impossible to cover all variables in this chapter. Here are the most common options so you know what to expect. You will probably agree that Quicken's reporting feature is very flexible when you go beyond the basics.

Using the Customize Dialog

To customize a report or graph, click the Customize button in the options area for the report or graph in the Reports & Graphs Center window (refer to Figure 8-3) or the Customize button at the top of the report window (refer to Figures 8-4 through 8-7). The Customize dialog, which is shown next, appears. The dialog's full name includes the name of the report or graph.

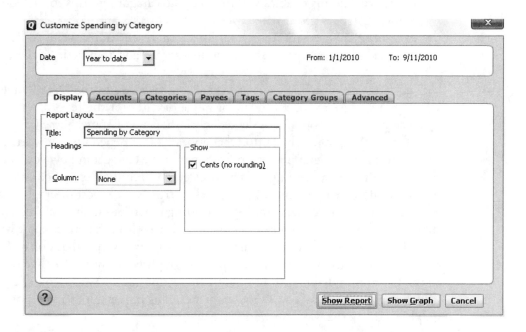

The Customize dialog includes up to seven tabs of options that you can set to customize the report.

- **Display** enables you to set display options for the report, such as the title, row and column headings, organization, number formatting, and columns.

- **Accounts** enables you to select the accounts that should be included in the report. Quicken will include transactions or balances in only the accounts you specify in the report.
- **Categories** enables you to select the categories to include in the report. If desired, you can use this tab to include only transactions for which the payee, category, or memo contains certain text.
- **Payees** makes it possible to select the payees to include in the report. If desired, you can use this tab to include only transactions for which the category, payee, or memo contains certain text.
- **Tags** enables you to select the tags to include in the report. If desired, you can use this tab to include only transactions for which the payee, tag, or memo contains certain text. This tab, which appears only if you have at least one tag defined, makes it possible to generate reports by tag. You learn about tags in Chapter 2.
- **Category Groups** enables you to select the category groups to include in the report. Category groups are covered in Chapters 2 and 16.
- **Advanced** enables you to set additional criteria for transactions to be included in the report, such as amount, status, and transaction type.

No matter which tab is selected, you also have access to the Date Range area, which you can use to specify a date or range of dates for the report.

Once you have set options as desired, click the Show Report, Show Graph, or OK (for both) button. (The button that appears varies depending on whether you can create a report, a graph, or both from within the dialog and how you opened the dialog.) If you are creating the report or graph from the Reports & Graphs Center window (refer to Figure 8-3), Quicken creates the report or graph to your specifications. If you are customizing an existing report or graph, Quicken creates a subreport of the original report or graph and displays it in the same report window.

If the custom report or graph isn't exactly what you want, that's okay. Just click the Customize button in the report or graph window and change settings in the Customize dialog to fine-tune the report or graph. When you click OK, Quicken creates a new report. You can repeat this process until the report or graph is exactly the way you want it.

Using the Customize Bar

The Customize bar near the top of a report window, as seen in Figures 8-4 through 8-7, offers another way to customize a report or graph. Use it to change date ranges, modify subtotal settings, or set columns for the report. Quicken immediately creates a subreport based on your revised settings and displays it in the same report window. For example, Figure 8-8 shows Income/Expense By

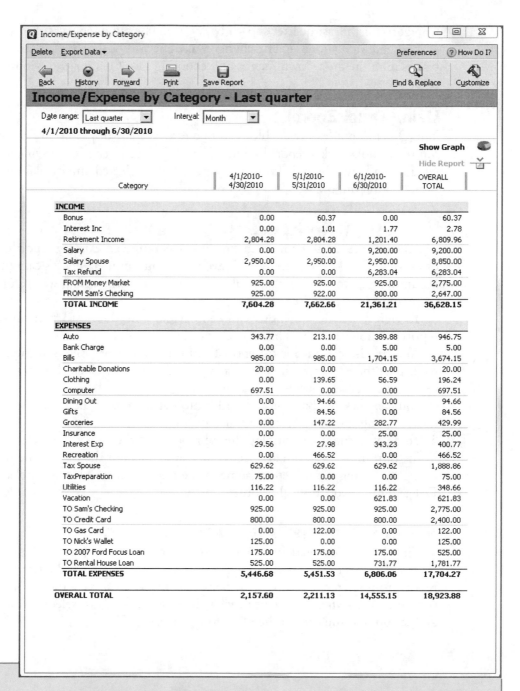

Income/Expense by Category	□ ▣ ✕

Delete   Export Data ▾   Preferences   ⑦ How Do I?

⇦ Back   ◉ History   ⇨ Forward   🖨 Print   💾 Save Report   🔍 Find & Replace   🔧 Customize

Income/Expense by Category - Last quarter

Date range: | Last quarter ▾ | Interval: | Month ▾ |
4/1/2010 through 6/30/2010

Show Graph ⬭
Hide Report

Category	4/1/2010- 4/30/2010	5/1/2010- 5/31/2010	6/1/2010- 6/30/2010	OVERALL TOTAL
INCOME				
Bonus	0.00	60.37	0.00	60.37
Interest Inc	0.00	1.01	1.77	2.78
Retirement Income	2,804.28	2,804.28	1,201.40	6,809.96
Salary	0.00	0.00	9,200.00	9,200.00
Salary Spouse	2,950.00	2,950.00	2,950.00	8,850.00
Tax Refund	0.00	0.00	6,283.04	6,283.04
FROM Money Market	925.00	925.00	925.00	2,775.00
FROM Sam's Checking	925.00	922.00	800.00	2,647.00
TOTAL INCOME	**7,604.28**	**7,662.66**	**21,361.21**	**36,628.15**
EXPENSES				
Auto	343.77	213.10	389.88	946.75
Bank Charge	0.00	0.00	5.00	5.00
Bills	985.00	985.00	1,704.15	3,674.15
Charitable Donations	20.00	0.00	0.00	20.00
Clothing	0.00	139.65	56.59	196.24
Computer	697.51	0.00	0.00	697.51
Dining Out	0.00	94.66	0.00	94.66
Gifts	0.00	84.56	0.00	84.56
Groceries	0.00	147.22	282.77	429.99
Insurance	0.00	0.00	25.00	25.00
Interest Exp	29.56	27.98	343.23	400.77
Recreation	0.00	466.52	0.00	466.52
Tax Spouse	629.62	629.62	629.62	1,888.86
TaxPreparation	75.00	0.00	0.00	75.00
Utilities	116.22	116.22	116.22	348.66
Vacation	0.00	0.00	621.83	621.83
TO Sam's Checking	925.00	925.00	925.00	2,775.00
TO Credit Card	800.00	800.00	800.00	2,400.00
TO Gas Card	0.00	122.00	0.00	122.00
TO Nick's Wallet	125.00	0.00	0.00	125.00
TO 2007 Ford Focus Loan	175.00	175.00	175.00	525.00
TO Rental House Loan	525.00	525.00	731.77	1,781.77
TOTAL EXPENSES	**5,446.68**	**5,451.53**	**6,806.06**	**17,704.27**
OVERALL TOTAL	**2,157.60**	**2,211.13**	**14,555.15**	**18,923.88**

Figure 8-8 • Many reports can be broken out by month or some other time period with the Column menu.

Category for the last quarter shown by month. The same report is shown for the year to date in Figure 8-4. The change was done with a couple of mouse clicks by opening the drop-down menus and choosing Last Quarter and Month, respectively.

Using QuickZoom

The QuickZoom feature enables you to create a report or graph on the fly. Simply double-click a report line item, graph bar, or legend item. Quicken generates a new subreport for the item you double-clicked and displays it in the same report window.

Working with Subreports

Quicken creates a subreport each time you customize an existing report or graph, or create a QuickZoom report and save it. As you can imagine, it's easy to accumulate quite a few of these subreports when experimenting with Quicken's reporting features.

To view a specific subreport, choose its name from the History menu in the report window's toolbar. The view changes to the report.

You can also choose Show Report List from the History menu in the toolbar to display the Report History List, shown in Figure 8-6. Click the name of the report you want to view to display it.

You can click the Back or Forward button at the top of the navigation bar to move among subreports you have already viewed.

To delete a subreport, display the subreport and then click the Delete button in the button bar. You can also delete any subreport but the first in the report list by right-clicking the subreport name in the Report History List and selecting Delete This Report from the context menu.

Saving Reports and Graphs

You'll often create a predefined report and customize it to create a report you want to be able to see again and again. Rather than creating and customizing the report from scratch each time you want to see it, you can save the report's settings. Then, when you want to view the report again, just select it from a list and it appears. You can do the same for graphs.

Saving a Report or Graph

To save a report or graph, start by creating, customizing, and displaying it. When it looks just the way you want, click the Save Report button in the report window's toolbar. The Save Report dialog, which is shown next, appears.

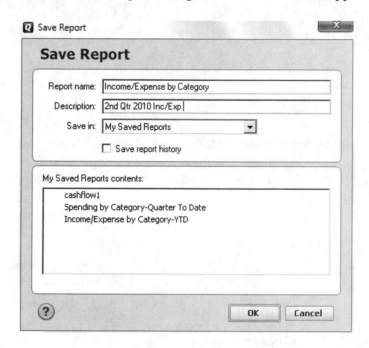

Enter a name and description for the report or graph in the appropriate boxes. To save the report or graph in a specific folder, choose the folder name from the Save In drop-down list. You can create a new folder by clicking the Create Folder button, entering a name for the folder in the dialog that appears, and clicking OK. To save all versions of the report that you create, turn on the Save Report History check box. When you're finished setting options, click OK to save the report.

Viewing a Saved Report or Graph

When you save a report or graph, it appears in a number of places throughout Quicken, organized by folder if you have saved them into specific folders.

The Reports & Graphs Center Window   Saved reports and graphs appear in the My Saved Reports area of the Reports & Graphs Center window as seen on the next page. Click the name of the report or graph, and click Show Report or Show Graph to display it.

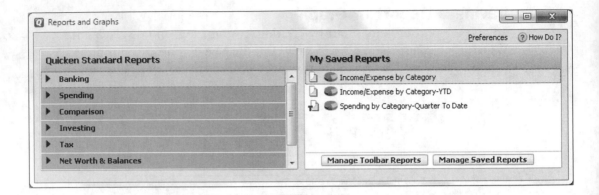

The My Saved Reports & Graphs Submenu Saved reports and graphs also appear on the Reports menu as My Saved Reports & Graphs. (This submenu appears only if at least one report has been saved.) Choose a report name to display it.

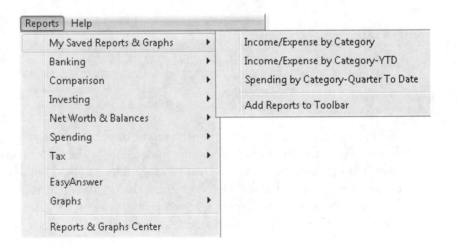

The Quicken Tool Bar If you use the Manage Toolbar Reports dialog to add saved reports to the toolbar, as discussed in the section titled "Managing Toolbar Reports" later in this chapter, they appear as toolbar buttons. Click the button to display the report. If you display a saved report folder on the toolbar (also selected in the Manage Toolbar Reports dialog), it appears as a pop-up menu button that lists the reports within it. You can learn more about customizing the Quicken Tool Bar in Appendix B.

Managing Saved Reports

Quicken offers two tools for managing saved reports: the Manage Saved Reports and Manage Toolbar Reports dialogs. You can open both of these dialogs by clicking the appropriate button within the Reports And Graphs Center window as seen in Figure 8-3.

Managing Saved Reports   The Manage Saved Reports dialog, shown next, enables you to organize saved reports by folder, edit report settings, or delete reports. Select the item you want to work with in the report list and click a button.

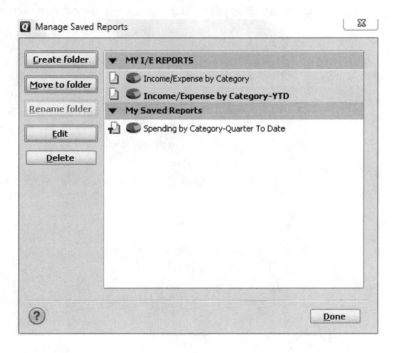

- **Create Folder** displays the Create New Report Folder. Enter a name for the folder in the Name box and click OK. The folder appears in the list.
- **Move To Folder** displays the Move To Report Folder dialog. Choose a different folder from the Name drop-down list and click OK. The item moves to that folder.
- **Rename Folder** displays the Rename Report Folder dialog. Enter a new name for the folder in the Name box and click OK. The folder's name changes.
- **Edit** displays the Edit Saved Report dialog, which enables you to enter a new name and description for the report. Click OK to save your changes.

- **Delete** removes the selected item. When you click this button, a confirmation dialog appears. You must click OK to permanently delete the item.
- **Done** closes the Manage Saved Reports dialog and returns you to the Reports And Graphs screen.

Managing Toolbar Reports   The Manage Toolbar Reports dialog, shown next, enables you to specify which saved reports and folders should appear on the toolbar. This option appears only when you have chosen to show the Quicken Tool Bar. Click View | Show Tool Bar. Turn on the check box beside each folder or report you want to appear. Then click OK to save your settings.

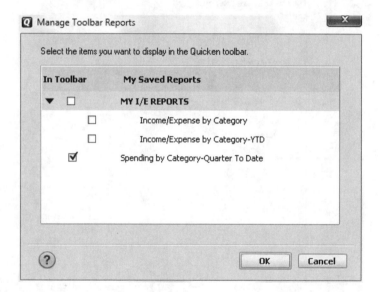

Exporting Your Reports

Another method of working with your reports is to export them into other formats or programs. From your report window, choose Export Data as shown here.

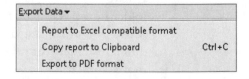

You have three choices, each of which is explained in the sections that follow.

Report To Excel Compatible Format

This option saves your report into a .txt file that can be used with the Microsoft Office Excel program. The file is saved as a tab-delimited file with the file extension .txt. To save your file in this format:

1. From the Export Data menu, choose Report To Excel Compatible Format to open the Create Excel Compatible File dialog, as seen next.

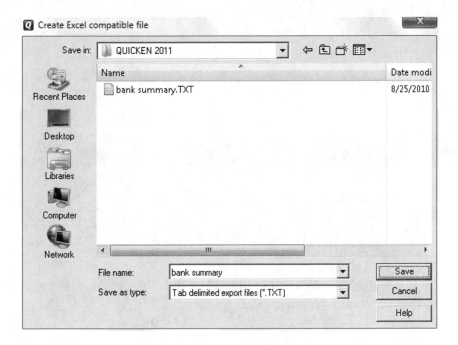

2. Browse to find the folder into which you want to save this file, and click that folder.
3. Enter a name for your file and click Save. The file will have a .txt extension. The new file is saved into the folder you designated and you are returned to your report window. See "Work with Your Saved Excel File" next to see how to open the file in Excel.

Work with Your Saved File

Once you have saved the file, you can work with it in Microsoft Excel. To do so:

1. Open Microsoft Excel. (The illustrations in this section refer to Microsoft Excel 2010, but the application works in similar ways with earlier versions of Excel.)

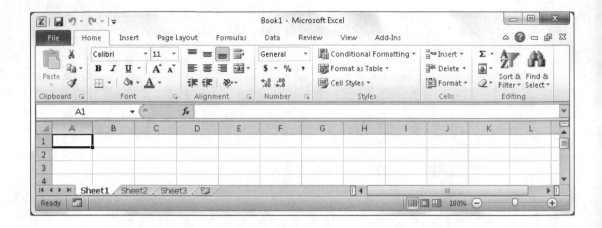

2. Click File | Open. Choose All
Files instead of All Excel Files as
the type of file for which you want
Excel to look. (See the next
illustration.) Locate the folder into

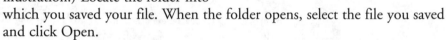

which you saved your file. When the folder opens, select the file you saved
and click Open.
3. The Text Import Wizard appears as shown next.

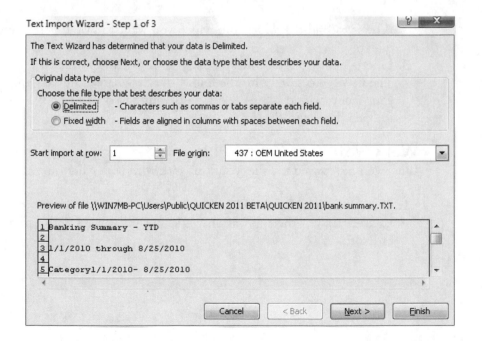

4. Ensure that Delimited is selected, which it may be by default. Click Next.
5. Make sure that Tab is selected from the Delimiters column. Click Next to continue.
6. At the last step (shown next), choose General and then click Finish to complete the import.

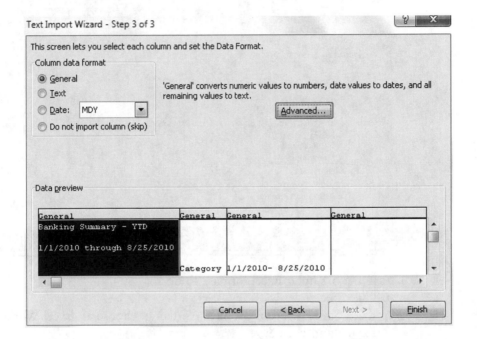

7. Your Excel worksheet appears, as shown on the next page. You may have to make the columns wider to see the report. If so, place your cursor on the line between the column letters and drag to the right.

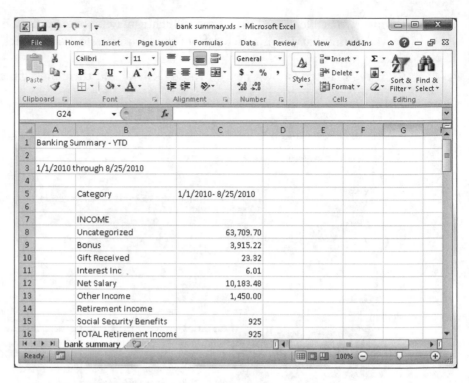

8. Save the file in an Excel format. To do so:
   a. Click File.
   b. Click Save As. From the Save As dialog, choose an Excel Workbook format and click Save.

Copy the Report to the Clipboard

Use this option to copy the report into another Windows program. You can also use the keyboard shortcut CTRL-C. To "paste" this report into another program, use the keyboard shortcut CTRL-V. You can use this method to copy the report into Microsoft Excel—a much easier process than the one described earlier.

Export to PDF Format

PDF stands for Portable Document Format. This format, invented by Adobe Systems, allows the reader to print a document from nearly any computer or word processor. This option is particularly useful if you are saving the report to e-mail it or sharing the file with someone who does not have either Quicken or Microsoft Office. To save as a .pdf file:

1. From the Export Data menu, click Export To PDF Format.

2. The Print dialog appears as shown next. In the Printer field you will see "Quicken PDF Printer on *nnnn*" rather than your regular printer.

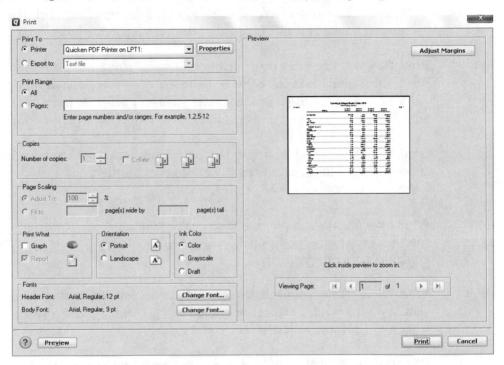

3. Click Print. The Save To PDF File dialog appears. Type a name for your file, and click Save. Your file is now saved with a .pdf extension.

Printing Reports and Graphs

You can print reports and graphs. This enables you to create hard copies for your paper files or for use when applying for loans or completing your tax returns.

To print a report, subreport, or graph, begin by displaying it in the report window. Then click the Print button in the window's toolbar. The Print dialog appears. Set options as desired and click Print.

Here's a look at the available options.

Print To   Print To options determine the destination of the printed report or graph. You have two choices:

- **Printer** prints to the printer you choose from the drop-down list, which includes all printers, faxes, and related devices set up in Windows. This is the option you'll probably select most often. Clicking the Properties button displays the Properties dialog for the currently selected printer.

- **Export To** makes it possible to export the report information in one of three formats you choose from the drop-down list: Text File, Tab-Delimited (Excel-Compatible) Disk File, or PRN (123-Compatible) Disk File. This option is only available if you are printing a report without a graph.

Print Range   The print range determines which pages will print. You can use this if the printout is expected to be more than one page. The default setting is All, which prints all pages of the report. To print a range of pages, select Pages, and then enter the page numbers for the page range you want to print.

Copies   The Copies box determines how many copies of the report will print. If you enter a value greater than 1, you can turn on the Collate check box to collate the copies as they are printed.

Page Scaling   Page Scaling options enable you to resize a report or graph to a specific percentage or to fit on a certain number of pages. These options are only available for certain printers.

Print What   You can toggle two check boxes to determine whether Quicken should print a graph or report or both. The options that are available depend on what's in the report window.

Orientation   Orientation determines how the printed report will be viewed. The options are Portrait or Landscape. These are standard options offered by all programs. The icon beside each orientation option illustrates it.

Ink Color   Select one of three options to determine the ink color and quality of the printout: Color (available only if a color printer is selected from the Printer drop-down list), Grayscale, or Draft.

Fonts   Use the two Change Font buttons to change the header and body typefaces of the report or graph. Clicking the button displays the Font dialog, which you can use to set standard font options, such as font, size, and style.

Preview   The Preview area shows a thumbnail preview of the document. You can click the buttons in the Viewing Page area to scroll through all pages of the report. To change the margins for the document, click the Adjust Margins button. The Preview area changes, as shown next, to offer boxes for entering margin values. To view a full-size preview, click the thumbnail in this area or click the Preview button at the bottom of the dialog.

Planning Your Spending

Another tool provided by Quicken to help you take control of your spending is found in the Planning tab. Quicken's Spending Planner, which you can see in Figure 8-9, is like a live budget where you can easily see income and spending based on payee and category. You can use this feature to help you take control of your spending and to save money.

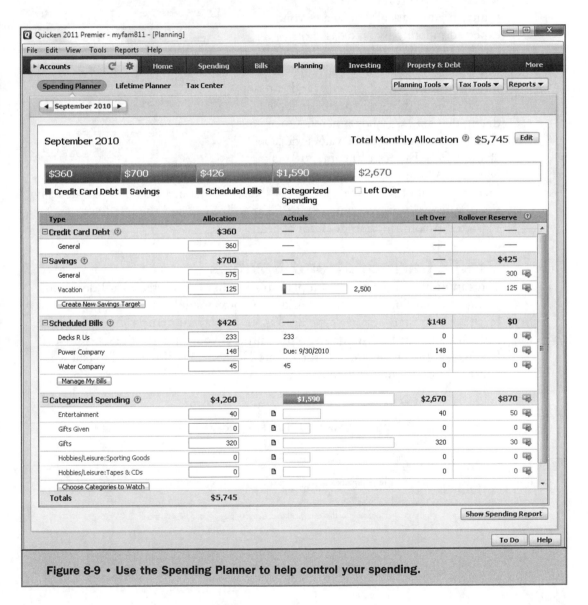

Figure 8-9 • Use the Spending Planner to help control your spending.

You may have already started your plan if you used the Track Spending Goals To Save Money section of the Home tab's Main View. If so, the information you entered in that section is reflected in the Categorized Spending section of your Spending Planner. If necessary, click the Spending Planner button in the Planning tab to display the Spending Planner.

Expected Income

Quicken automatically calculates your expected monthly income based on scheduled paychecks and other income. You can change this amount by clicking the Edit button near the top of the view and entering a new value in the Set Expected Income dialog that appears (shown here). When you set a new monthly income value, the label changes from Expected Income to Total Monthly Allocation. Setting a new monthly income also affects the fields in the Set Expected Income dialog. If you are using the default amount, you only see the Change To field and the Use Default Expected Amount option does not appear.

Credit Card Debt and Savings

You can indicate how much you plan to allocate to your credit card debt and savings by entering values in the Allocation box beside each item. (You may have to click the + sign beside a type heading to display an item as shown in Figure 8-9.) If you want to save for a specific purpose, you can click the Create New Savings Target button and use the Create New Savings Target dialog (shown next) to enter a name and amount to save.

Scheduled Bills

Quicken lists your scheduled bills and other transactions in the Scheduled Bills area so you know what expenses to expect for the month. You can adjust the allocation for a payee by entering a different value in the Allocation column box beside it. You can display the Bill And Income Reminders window, which is discussed in detail in Chapter 6, by clicking the Manage My Bills button at the bottom of the Scheduled Bills List.

Categorized Spending

Quicken also displays expenses by category, showing allocated and actual amounts graphically. This makes it easy to see if you've already spent more for a category than you've allocated for it. You can change a category's allocation by entering a new value in the Allocation box beside it. To change the list of categories that appears in the view, click the Choose Categories To Watch button and use the Choose Categories dialog that appears (shown next) to check off the categories you want to monitor.

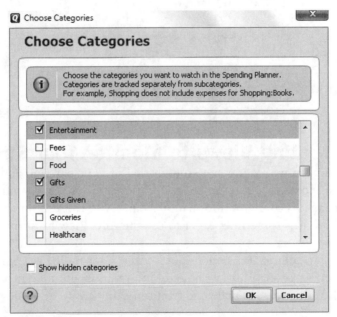

Rollover Reserve

The far-right column of the Spending Planner worksheet shows the rollover reserve. This is the difference between an allocated amount and the actual amount. Rollover reserves can accumulate from one month to the next.

For example, suppose you allocated $150 per month for entertainment. This month, however, you only spent $100. The remaining $50 goes into a rollover reserve so you can spend it in the future without exceeding your allocation for that category. Of course, if you spent more than $150 this month for entertainment, the rollover is a negative value, meaning you must spend less next month.

You can move a rollover reserve from one payee or category to another. Click the button in the Rollover Reserve column at the far-right end of the worksheet for a payee or category. Then use the Edit Rollover Reserve dialog (shown next) to indicate how you want the rollover moved. When you click OK, Quicken adjusts the rollover reserve as you specified.

Creating Views to Monitor Your Spending

Quicken makes it easy to monitor all of your banking and spending activities. In the Home tab, you can create additional views that include a number of snapshots of useful information. While you can customize the default Main View, it is sometimes easier to use the Add View button to create one or two new views.

For example, in versions of Quicken prior to 2011, a Summary view displayed a number of snapshots with useful information about your banking accounts. If you liked this view, as many did, you can easily create it, as shown on the next page.

1. Open the Home tab, and click Add View. The Customize View dialog appears. In View Name field, type **Summary View**. By default, the Main View information (or the information from the last view you created) appears in the Chosen Items list. Click the first item, hold down your SHIFT

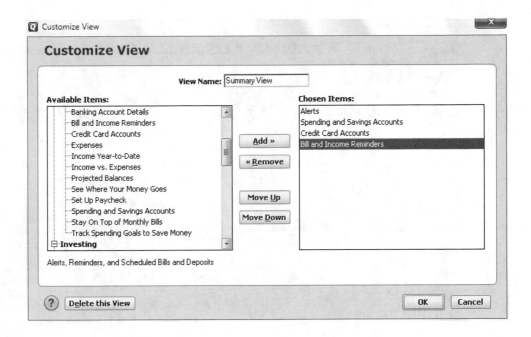

key, and click the bottom item to select the entire list. Then, click Remove to remove these items. You are only removing them from the Chosen Items list in the current view. They are still available in the Available Items list on the left.

2. Start by selecting alerts in the Available Items list and click Add. You will note that all of the items are in alphabetic order within the six sections: Overview, Banking, Investing, Property & Debt, Planning, and Tax.

3. Add the following from the Banking section of the Available Items list: Spending And Savings Accounts, Credit Card Accounts, and Bill And Income Reminders, in that order. When you click OK, you'll see a Summary View, similar to the one that was in previous Quicken versions, as shown in Figure 8-10.

   In your new Summary View, all snapshots include an Options menu and possibly buttons that you can use to work with that snapshot. For example, the Alerts snapshot at the top of the view has buttons and Options menu commands for showing, setting up, and deleting alerts. Many of these options are discussed throughout this part of the book; you can explore the others on your own.

   Here's a brief summary of each snapshot in your new Summary View.

Figure 8-10 • The Summary View includes useful information about your current balances and planned spending.

Alerts

The Alerts snapshot lists alerts you have set up. You can click blue links to go to the account or other items the alert applies to. See how to set up and use banking-related alerts later in this chapter, in the section titled "Banking Alerts Overview."

Spending And Savings Accounts

The Spending And Savings Accounts snapshot lists all of your checking, savings, and cash accounts, along with their current and ending balances. You can click links to view the account register, set up balance alerts, and set interest rates.

Credit Card Accounts

The Credit Card Accounts snapshot lists all of your credit card accounts along with their current and ending balances. You can click links to view the account register, set the credit limit, and specify the interest rate.

Bill And Income Reminders

The Bill And Income Reminders snapshot lists all of your bills, deposits, and other scheduled transactions. It may also display a list of transactions that Quicken thinks you may want to schedule. Buttons beside each item enable you to enter, edit, or skip a scheduled transaction, or to schedule or ignore a suggested transaction. See more about working with scheduled transactions in Chapter 6.

Creating an Analysis & Reports View

Another popular view can be created easily in Quicken 2011. This Analysis & Reports View includes both graphs and reports that explain your current financial position.

1. From the Home tab, click Add View to open the Customize View dialog. Type **Analysis & Reports View** in the View Name field. Remove all items in the Chosen Items list.
2. Add the following from the Available Items list: Expenses, Income vs. Expenses, and Budget, in that order. When you click OK, you'll see an Analysis & Reports View, as shown in Figure 8-11.

The Analysis & Reports View includes snapshots that summarize and help you analyze entries into your banking accounts. Most of these snapshots give you a glimpse of Quicken's extensive and highly customizable reporting features, as discussed earlier in this chapter, in the section titled "Working with Reports and Graphs."

Here's a quick look at the snapshots in the Analysis & Reports View.

Expenses

The Expenses snapshot displays a pie chart of your expenses for the current or previous month.

Income vs. Expenses

The Income vs. Expenses snapshot displays a column chart of your year-to-date income and expenses.

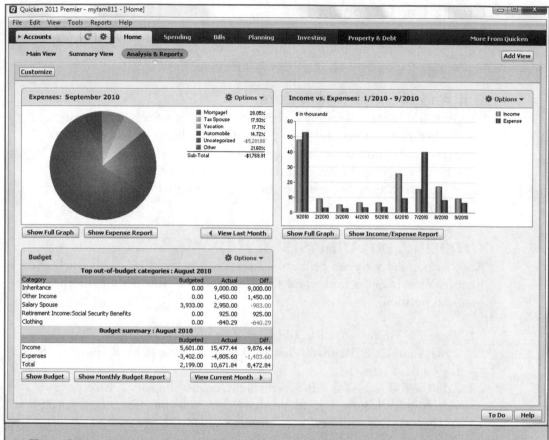

Figure 8-11 • Create an Analysis & Reports View to better understand your spending.

Budget

The Budget snapshot displays information from your budget, including the top five out-of-budget categories and a summary of your budgeted and actual income and expenses. To use this snapshot, you must set up a budget using Quicken's budgeting feature, as discussed in Chapter 16. Otherwise, this area will display instructions on how to do that.

Alerts

The Alerts snapshot in the Summary View (refer to Figure 8-10) lists alerts that have been established. Having them at the top of the window helps make sure that you don't miss them.

This section discusses the kinds of alerts Quicken offers for banking and explains how to set them up.

Banking Alerts Overview

Quicken offers seven different alerts that you can set up for cash flow accounts. To enable them, open the Tools menu, choose Alerts Center, click the Setup tab, and then open the Banking category. Here's an explanation of each of them:

- **Account Min. Balances** enables you to set minimum balances for your checking and savings accounts. You can set a minimum amount and a reminder amount for each account, as shown in Figure 8-12. Quicken will alert you when the account balance falls below the reminder amount you specify.

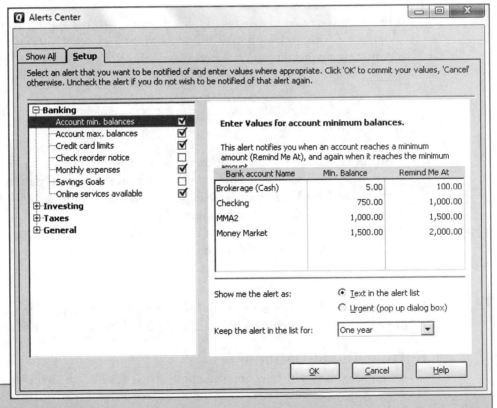

Figure 8-12 • Quicken alerts can notify you of many financial deadlines.

- **Account Max. Balances** enables you to set maximum balances for your checking and savings accounts. Quicken alerts you when the account balance climbs above the amount you specify.
- **Credit Card Limits** enables you to set limits for your credit card accounts. You can set a limit amount and a reminder amount. Quicken alerts you if the balance exceeds the reminder amount.
- **Check Reorder Notice** tells Quicken to alert you when you reach a certain check number. You can set this option for checking and savings accounts. This feature can be used whether you use checks provided by your bank or another printer, or checks you purchase exclusively for use with Quicken.
- **Monthly Expenses** enables you to specify maximum monthly spending amounts for any Quicken expense category. If you exceed the limit you specified, Quicken alerts you to this fact.
- **Savings Goals** tells Quicken to alert you when you fall behind on a savings goal. This option works directly with Quicken's Savings Goals feature, which you learn about in Chapter 16.
- **Online Services Available** tells Quicken to alert you when one of your financial institutions supports Online Account Services. Quicken can learn about new financial partners when you connect to the Internet to utilize other features. Online Account Services are discussed at length in Chapter 5.

In addition, Quicken offers three other general-category reminder alerts that fall in the spending area.

- **Online Transactions** tells Quicken to remind you to download transactions from your financial institution if you haven't done so for 30 days or more.
- **Scheduled Bills Or Deposits Due Soon** tells Quicken to remind you in advance of any scheduled transactions that are due.
- **Send To Quicken.com** tells Quicken to remind you to export your portfolio to Quicken.com when holdings change.

Setting Up Alerts

You set up alerts from the Setup tab of the Alerts Center window, as seen in Figure 8-12. You can then click the name of one of the alerts to view and set it.

Setting Basic Options

To set an alert, begin by selecting the name of the alert on the left side of the window. If necessary, click the check box to place a check mark within it. Then click the value you want to change on the right side of the window and enter a

NEW TO QUICKEN?

Cash Flow Alerts

If you're juggling multiple bank and credit card accounts, Quicken's banking alerts can really help you keep your sanity. After all, who can keep track of all those balances and keep them where they should be? Quicken can! Financial superhero!

For example, suppose you have a checking account and a money market account. The checking account may be free, but only if the balance is at least $1,000. The money market account earns interest, but you're allowed to make only a limited number of monthly expenditures, so it can't replace the checking account. This kind of situation is perfect for Quicken's Alerts feature. Set it up so Quicken tells you when your checking account balance is getting too low—so you can transfer money from your money market account and avoid paying fees—or too high—so you can transfer money to your money market account and earn interest on it.

The Alerts feature can also prevent embarrassment at a checkout counter by warning you when a credit card balance is getting dangerously close to its limit. Likewise, it can remind you to pay your credit card bill so even if your balance is relatively low, you won't forget to make that monthly payment on time.

If you're trying to keep spending under control, Quicken can be a good friend. You can use its Alerts feature to set up maximum spending amounts for specific categories. Find yourself dining out too often? Set the maximum Dining category expenditure for the month. Just can't resist another pair of shoes in the mall? Set the maximum Clothing category expenditure. Then, when you enter the expenditure that puts you over the maximum for the month, Quicken firmly informs you that it's time to stop.

It's like having an impartial financial manager looking over your shoulder.

new value. Not all alerts have values you can change; for example, the Online Services Available alert is a simple on or off setting made with the check mark.

Setting Other Options

You can set two additional options in the bottom half of the window.

Show Me the Alert As   Choose from two options for showing the alert:

- **Text In The Alert List** displays the alert as an item in an Alerts snapshot only, which you can see in the Alerts Center Show All tab and when you add alerts to another view.
- **Urgent (Pop Up Dialog Box)** displays the alert in a dialog when you start Quicken. You must dismiss this in-your-face alert by clicking the OK button in the dialog before continuing to work with Quicken.

Keep the Alert in the List For   You can set the amount of time the alert should remain in the Cash Flow Alerts snapshot. The default setting is One

Month, but you can use the drop-down list to choose One Day, One Week, One Month, One Quarter, or One Year.

Finishing Up

When you're completely finished setting alerts, click OK to close the Alerts Center window. The alerts will work quietly in the background, watching your finances. When it's time to go to work, they appear as you specified.

Working with Alerts

Once you've set up alerts, you can view, modify, or delete them as desired. Here's how.

Viewing Alerts

As shown in Figure 8-12, you can add alerts so they will appear in a snapshot in any custom view.

You can also view alerts in the Show All tab of the Alerts Center window (see Figure 8-13). Click the Show All Alerts button in any alerts snapshot or open the Tools menu and choose Alerts Center | Show All to display them.

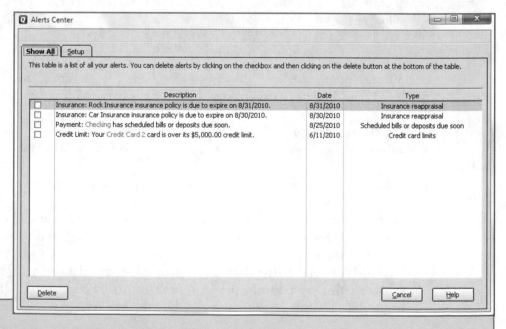

Figure 8-13 • The Show All tab of the Alerts Center window enables you to view and delete specific alerts.

Modifying Alerts

You can change the way an alert works at any time. Open the Tools menu and choose Alerts Center | Setup (refer to Figure 8-12). Then follow the instructions in the earlier section titled "Setting Up Alerts" to change alert settings.

Deleting Alerts

To delete an alert, display the Show All tab of the Alerts Center (refer to Figure 8-13). Turn on the check box beside each alert you want to delete, and click the Delete button. A confirmation dialog appears, as shown next. Click OK to delete the alert.

To prevent a deleted alert from getting reestablished and appearing again in the future, use the Setup tab of the Alerts Center window to turn off the check box for the alert in the list on the left side of the window.

Investing

This part of the book explains how you can use Quicken Personal Finance Software to track your investments. It begins by explaining the basics of tracking investments in Quicken and then goes on to explain how you can use Quicken's online investment tracking features to download investment information from your brokerage firm and exchange information with Quicken.com. Along the way, it provides a wealth of information you can use to invest wisely and maximize your investment returns. Finally, it explains how you can use Quicken's Investing tab and reporting features to keep an eye on your portfolio and investment returns. This part has three chapters:

Chapter 9:   Entering Your Investment Transactions

Chapter 10:   Downloading Transactions and Researching Tools

Chapter 11:   Evaluating Your Position

Part Three

Entering Your Investment Transactions

Chapter 9

In This Chapter:

- *Setting up investment accounts*
- *Recording investment transactions*
- *Adding and editing securities*
- *Using the Security Detail View window*

Investments offer individuals a way to make their money grow. Although more risky than deposits made to an FDIC-insured bank, stocks, bonds, mutual funds, and other types of investments have the potential to earn more. That's why many people build investment portfolios as a way to save for future goals or retirement.

In this chapter, you will be introduced to investments and portfolio management and then you will learn how to use Quicken Personal Finance Software to keep track of the money you invest.

Quicken Investment Basics

An *investment* is a security or asset that you expect to increase in value and/or generate income. There are many types of investments—Table 9-1 lists some of them. This chapter concentrates on the investments you can track with the features in Quicken's Investing tab.

Type of Investment	Type of Account
CD	Savings account or standard brokerage account
Money market fund	Savings account or standard brokerage account
Stocks in your possession	Standard brokerage account
Brokerage account with one or more securities, with or without an associated cash, checking, or interest-earning account	Standard brokerage account
Employee stock options	Standard brokerage account
Employee Stock Purchase Plan (ESPP)	Standard brokerage account
Dividend Reinvestment Program (DRIP)	Standard brokerage account
Bonds, including U.S. Savings Bonds	Standard brokerage account
Treasury bills	Standard brokerage account
Single mutual fund with no cash balance	Single mutual fund account
Variable or fixed annuities	Standard brokerage account
401(k) or 403(b) plan	401(k) or 403(b) account
529 Educational Savings Plan	529 plan account or Educational IRA (529) account
Traditional IRA, Roth IRA, Education IRA	IRA account
Keogh Plan, SEP-IRA, or SIMPLE-IRA	Keogh plan or SEP-IRA account
Real estate	Asset account
Real estate investment trusts (REITs) or partnerships	Standard brokerage account

Table 9-1 • Quicken Accounts for Various Investment Types

Before you learn how to use Quicken to track your investments, here's a review of Quicken's investment accounts and a more detailed explanation of why investment tracking is so important.

Your Quicken Portfolio

The term *portfolio* refers to the total of all of your investments. For example, if you have shares of one company's stock, shares in two mutual funds, and a 401(k) plan account, these are the items that make up your portfolio.

Types of Investment Accounts

Your Quicken portfolio can include four types of investment accounts. You can have as many investment accounts as you need to properly represent the investments that make up your portfolio.

Standard Brokerage   A standard brokerage account is for tracking a wide variety of investments handled through a brokerage firm, including stocks, bonds, mutual funds, and annuities. Like the account at your brokerage firm, it can track income, capital gains, performance, market values, shares, and cash balances for multiple securities.

IRA or Keogh Plan   An IRA or a Keogh account is for tracking a variety of retirement accounts, including standard IRA, Roth IRA, Coverdell Education Savings Account (formerly known as Education IRA), SEP-IRA, SIMPLE-IRA, and Keogh plans.

401(k) or 403(b)   A 401(k) or 403(b) account is for tracking 401(k), 403(b), or 457 plans, in which you make regularly scheduled, pretax contributions toward investments for your retirement. This type of account can track performance, market value, and distribution among investment choices. If you (and your spouse) have more than one plan, you should set up a separate account for each.

529 Plan   A 529 plan account is for tracking 529 Educational Savings Plans. These plans enable multiple family members to make pretax contributions to invest money for a family member's college education. This type of account enables you to track cash, money market, and securities activity and balances.

Choosing the Right Type of Account

Sometimes, it's not clear which kind of account is best for a specific type of investment. Table 9-1 offers some guidance.

   Keep in mind that you can also track many types of investments in asset accounts. But Quicken's investment accounts enable you to better track and report on the income, capital gains, and performance of your investments.

   This chapter concentrates on investment accounts tracked in standard brokerage, IRA or Keogh, 401(k) or 403(b), and 529 plan accounts. Consider what type of account your financial institution requires for downloading transactions as you decide between a single mutual fund account and a standard brokerage account.

   If you want to track the maturity dates of your CDs, you may need to use the standard brokerage account.

The Importance of Portfolio Management

At this point, you may be wondering why you should bother including investment information in your Quicken data file. After all, you may already get quarterly (or even monthly) statements from your broker or investment firm. What you may not realize, however, is how you can benefit from keeping a close eye on your investments. Take a look at what portfolio management with Quicken can do for you.

Centralizing Your Investment Records

Unless you have only one brokerage account for all your investments, you probably get multiple statements for the stocks, bonds, mutual funds, and other investments in your portfolio. No single statement can provide a complete picture of your portfolio's worth—however, Quicken can. By entering the transactions and values on each statement within Quicken, you can see the details of your entire portfolio in one place.

Knowing the Value of Your Portfolio on Any Day

Brokerage statements can tell you the value of your investments on the statement's ending date, but not what they're worth today—or what they were worth on July 1, 2008. Quicken, however, can tell you what your portfolio is worth on any day for which you have entered—or, better yet, downloaded—security prices, and it can estimate values for dates without exact pricing information. If you like to keep your portfolio's value up-to-date with the latest security prices, you can retrieve prices online. Chapter 10 shows you how to take advantage of this feature.

Keeping Track of Performance History

Manually compiling a complete pricing and performance history for an investment is no small task, especially for periods spanning multiple statements. If you consistently enter investment information in your Quicken data file, however, preparing performance charts and reports is as easy as choosing a menu command or clicking a button.

NEW TO QUICKEN?

Automatic Download of Quotes

New to Quicken 2011, those using Quicken Premier or higher can opt to update stock quotes every 15 minutes. Other new features are the ability to create reports that show both CD and bond maturity information and a subtotal of shares in your Investment Transactions reports.

Calculating Capital Gains Quickly and Easily

Calculating the gain on the sale of an investment isn't always easy. Considerations include not only the purchase and selling prices, but also commissions, fees, stock splits, and purchase lots. Quicken can take all the work out of calculating capital gains, even if you're just considering the sale and want to know what its impact will be. This is extremely helpful at tax time, as Chapter 17 explains.

Creating Investing Accounts

Before you can begin tracking your investments with Quicken, you must set up the investment accounts you'll need. Basic information about setting up accounts is contained in Chapter 2. This chapter provides the specifics for creating investing accounts. As you'll see on the following pages, when you create an investment account, Quicken not only prompts you for basic account information, but also gathers information about your security holdings. When you're finished creating an account, it's all ready to use for entering transactions and creating reports.

Choosing the Type of Investing Account

Begin by clicking Add An Account from the Account Bar. If you have not yet run One Step Update for the day, Quicken uses your Internet connection to retrieve financial institution information. The Add Account dialog opens as seen in Figure 9-1. The first thing you need to do is indicate the type of account you want to create. Select the appropriate option; you can refer to Table 9-1 if you need help deciding. The option you select will determine certain settings for the account. For example, if you choose an IRA or Keogh plan, Quicken will set tax-deferred options that would not be set if you selected a standard brokerage account. Then click Next.

Using Simple Start to Create an Account

Quicken's extensive online account access features make it possible to automate data entry for accounts held in participating financial institutions, including many brokerage firms. To take advantage of these features, Quicken starts the account creation process for standard brokerage, IRA or Keogh Plan, or 401(k) or 403(b) accounts by prompting you to enter the name of your brokerage firm or choosing one from the list provided.

If you have chosen the default Simple Start method of creating your account, after you have chosen the name of your broker, click Next. With your Internet connection, Quicken verifies the connection to your broker and opens a window in which you are prompted to enter the user ID and password given to you by your broker. Quicken may display dialogs that prompt you for additional

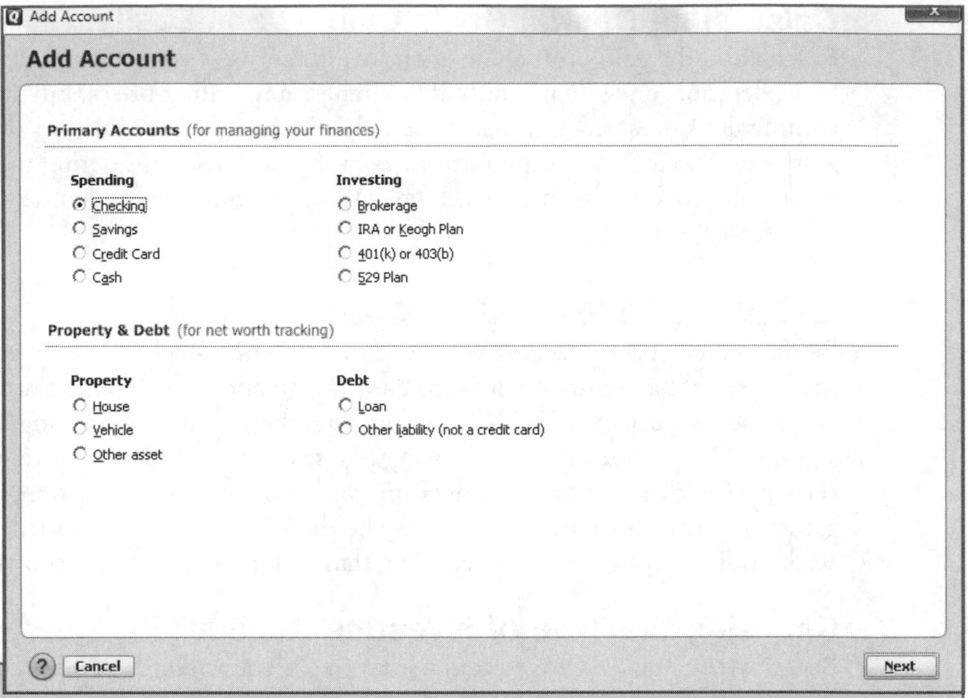

Figure 9-1 • There are four types of investing accounts available in the Add Account dialog.

information about the account. The dialogs that appear and the order in which they appear vary, depending on the financial institution you indicated. Once you have entered your login info (see Figure 9-2), click Connect to proceed with the account setup. After you have proceeded through any dialogs prompting for additional info, Quicken retrieves the account info and transactions, creates the account, and displays an Account Added screen.

Using Advanced Setup   If your institution's name is not on the Simple Setup list, has other connection methods, or you just prefer not to download, you can set up your account manually. After you have chosen the type of investing account you want to set up, at the dialog where you are prompted for your institution's name, click Advanced Setup, as seen in Figure 9-2.

The dialog shown in Figure 9-3 appears. You have two options:

- **I Want To Select The Connection Method Used To Download My Transactions**   Select this option if your institution offers more than one

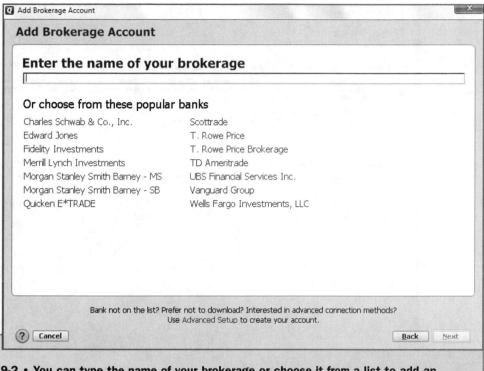

Figure 9-2 • **You can type the name of your brokerage or choose it from a list to add an investing account.**

online service or if you have been given specific instructions how to connect to their website.

- **I Want To Enter My Transactions Manually**   Select this option if your account is held by an entity that does not offer online services, or you just prefer to enter your transactions by hand. Use this option as well if the account you are creating is not held at a financial institution—for example, an account to track the value of securities in your safe deposit box.

Account Name and Other Basic Information   Depending on your account, you'll be asked for other information. Quicken displays dialogs that prompt you to enter certain types of accounts and other basic information, including the account name, statement ending date, and cash and money market balances. Depending on the type of account, you may also be prompted for additional information as discussed next.

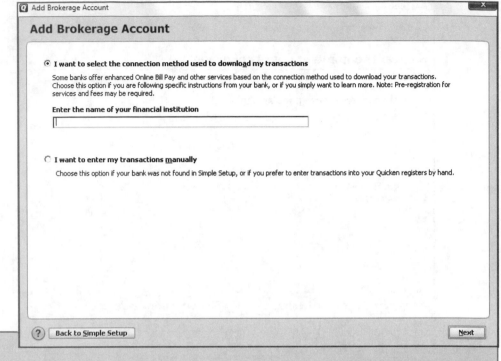

Figure 9-3 • You can choose to enter manually transactions for your investing account.

For IRAs

- Who owns the IRA
- What type of an IRA it is
- Whether this is a single mutual fund account

For 401(k) or 403(b) Accounts You will need to enter variations of this basic information for several types of accounts, most notably 401(k)s:

- Statement ending date
- Employer name
- Who owns the account
- Whether you have loans (and how many) against the account
- What securities you have in the account
- Whether you want to set up your paycheck information
- If the account tracks the number of shares, whether the statement lists the number of shares of each security

For 401(k) or 403(b) accounts, Quicken displays a dialog that asks whether you want to track loans against the account. If you have any loans against the account, be sure to indicate how many you have. Quicken will then display one or more dialogs prompting you for information about your loan(s).

Securities Held   A dialog like the one shown next prompts you to enter security ticker symbols and names. Enter one security per line, using the tab key to move from one box to the next. If you don't know the ticker symbol for a security, you can click the Ticker Symbol Lookup button to look it up online. If you need to enter more than five securities in the dialog, click the Add More button to add more lines. Don't enter bonds in this dialog; you can add them later.

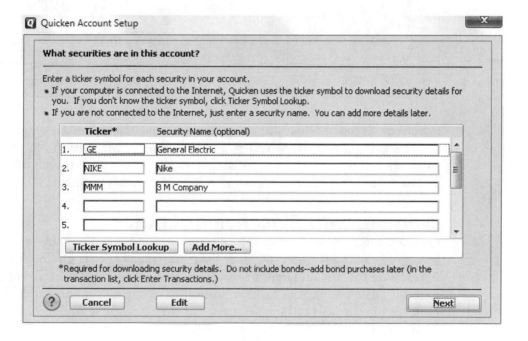

Current Holdings   After you have entered the ticker symbols for your securities, click Next. With your Internet connection Quicken updates and verifies the symbols and displays a dialog like the one shown on the next page. Enter the total number of shares for each security. If the type of security—Stock, Mutual Fund, or Other—is incorrect, select the correct option. When you click Next, Quicken displays a summary dialog confirming your entries. Click Done. Quicken displays an Account Added window. Click Finish to close the window.

Paycheck Setup When you create a 401(k) or 403(b) account, Quicken displays a dialog that asks whether you want to set up your paycheck. Quicken's Paycheck Setup feature is great for automatically entering 401(k) contributions and loan payments. Chapter 6 contains more about this feature.

Working with Placeholder Entries

Quicken automatically creates special transactions, called *placeholder entries*, in investment accounts when you enter—either manually or via Online Account Access—current holding information for securities as part of the account setup process. These transactions make it possible to get up and running quickly with Quicken's investment tracking features, but they lack the information Quicken needs to create accurate investment reports.

Here's how it works. When you create an investment account, you tell Quicken what securities are in the account and how many shares of each security you currently own. But Quicken doesn't know when you bought those shares or what you paid for them. Without this historical cost information, Quicken can't calculate your return on investment or your capital gains (or losses) when you sell the security.

Although you can work with a Quicken investment account as soon as it's created, to get the most out of Quicken's investment tracking features, you should replace the placeholder entries it creates with investment cost

information. This section
explains how.

Viewing Placeholder Entries for an Account

You can find an account's
placeholder entries with the
rest of the transactions for
that account. Click the
Investing tab, and then
choose the name of the
account you want to work
with from either the Account
Bar or the Account List in
the Portfolio view. You will
see the placeholder
transactions on the

> ### EXPERIENCED QUICKEN USERS AND NEW TO QUICKEN?
>
> The placeholder "locks" the number of shares
> and cash balance for the given date to the
> number specified in the placeholder. If you
> enter transactions before the placeholder
> date, the cash balance will not be affected.
> This can be a good thing, as you don't have to
> account for where the cash came from for
> securities purchased long before you started
> tracking in Quicken, but it can also be a bad
> thing if you don't understand how the
> placeholder works. Many Quicken users
> wonder why cash is not subtracted from the
> account when they enter a buy transaction.
> Thus, many users don't use placeholders to
> avoid these sorts of complications.

transaction list. Figure 9-4 shows an example of an investment account that
includes several placeholder entries.

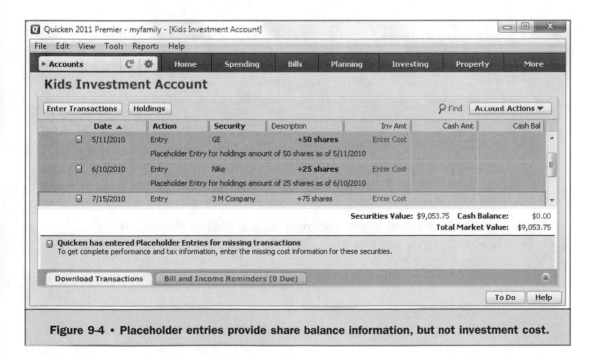

Figure 9-4 • Placeholder entries provide share balance information, but not investment cost.

If placeholder entries are not visible, you may need to set the preference for viewing hidden investment transactions. Select Edit | Preferences. Click Investment Transactions, and then select the Show Hidden Transaction check box. Click OK to save the preference.

Entering Cost Information for Placeholder Entries

To enter security cost information, begin by selecting the placeholder entry you want to work with. Click the Enter Cost link to display the Enter Missing Transactions dialog shown here.

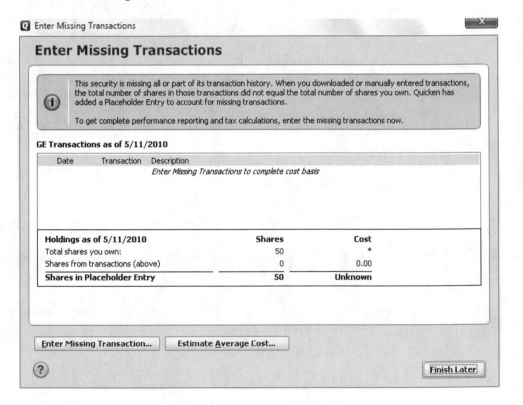

Transactions entered in the investment account before the date of the placeholder entry will not affect the cash balance of the investment account. It is often better to just enter all the historical transactions dated before the placeholder entry and delete the placeholder.

Two buttons at the bottom of the dialog offer methods for entering historical cost information for a security: Enter Missing Transaction and Estimate Average Cost.

Enter Missing Transactions   This option enables you to enter the individual transactions that make up the total number of shares you hold. In many cases, these transactions include purchases, stock dividends, and stock splits. This option gives you the most accurate records, but if you have many transactions, entering them all could be time-consuming. When you click this button, Quicken displays the Shares Bought dialog, shown next, which enables you to enter transaction details for a security acquisition. If the account is a 401(k) account, you may see an extra button labeled Cash Source. You will find how to enter transactions, such as purchases and stock dividends, later in this chapter, in the section titled "Recording Investment Transactions."

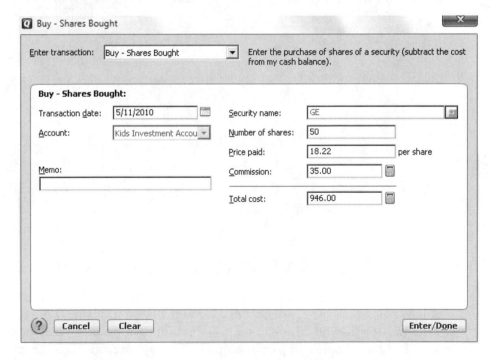

Estimate Average Cost   This option enables you to enter an average estimated cost for all of the shares you hold. Although this method is less accurate than entering individual transactions, it's a lot quicker and may be sufficient if you don't need detailed records of stock costs. You can always go back later and use the Enter Missing Transaction button to record more accurate acquisition details.

When you click this button, a dialog like the one shown next appears. Enter either the total cost of the shares in the Cost box or the average price per share in the Price/Share box. Quicken makes any necessary calculations. Click OK to save the entry.

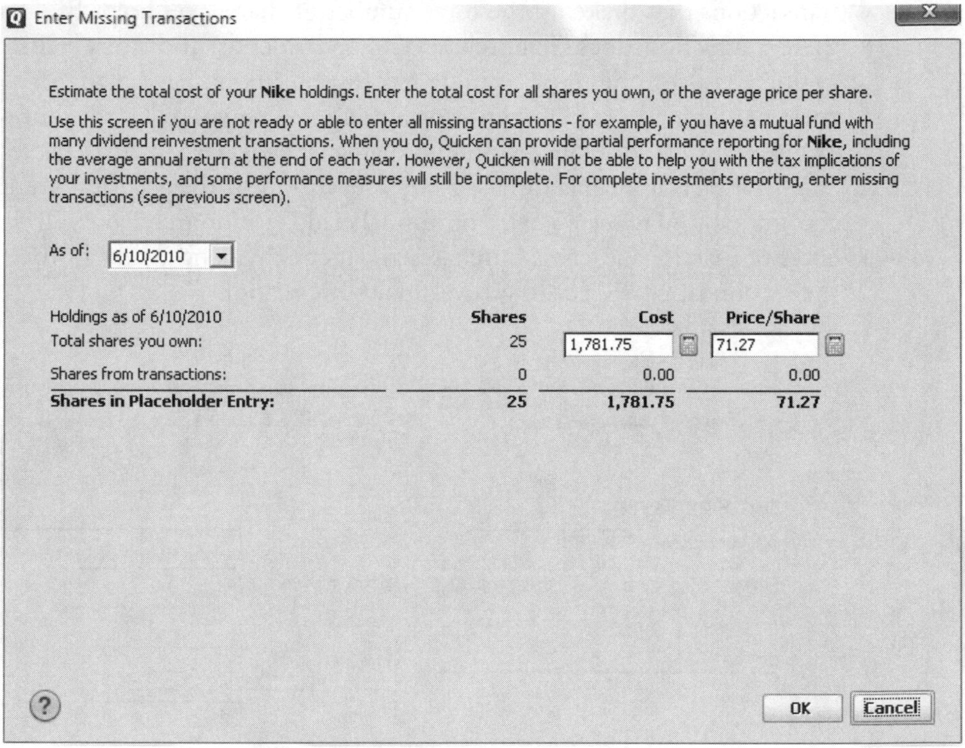

Working with Investment Accounts

To view an account's information, select the account name from the Account Bar. This opens the register for this account as seen in Figure 9-5. From this transaction list you can enter transactions and perform other activities.

The most important part of properly tracking investments is recording all investment transactions. This includes purchases, sales, dividends, and other activity affecting your portfolio's value. This will make life much easier when you are ready to sell the security.

Before you enter a transaction, you must have all of its details. In most cases, you can find the information you need on a monthly statement, confirmation form, or receipt you receive from your broker or investment firm. The

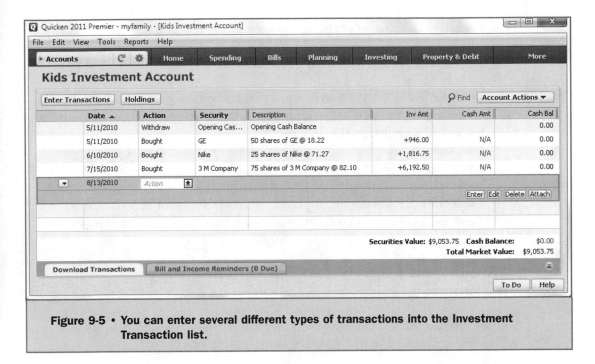

Figure 9-5 • You can enter several different types of transactions into the Investment Transaction list.

information varies, depending on the transaction, but it generally should include the security name, transaction date, number of shares, price per share, and any commissions or fees.

This section provides some information and advice for understanding the Investment Transaction list and entering the most common transactions into investment accounts.

Understanding the Investment Transaction List

The Investment Transaction list looks very much like the check registers. However, instead of the familiar Date, Check Number, and Payee fields, the Investment Transaction list has fields that pertain to your investing activities. See Figure 9-5 for an example.

The Investment Transaction list includes the following:

- **Date**   The date of the transaction is on this line of the register. Click the small arrow to sort transactions by date.
- **Action**   What this transaction represents. See "Investment Actions" later in this chapter for more information. This column can also be sorted by clicking the small arrow. It sorts in alphabetical order by action.

- **Security** The name of the security for this line of the register. Since a single investment account can contain a wide variety of securities, each one is identified. This column can be sorted using the small arrow. It is sorted alphabetically.
- **Description** What action is represented. For example, if the Action column says "Bought," the number of shares of the named security and the price paid is shown in this column.
- **Inv Amt** Shows the amount of the investment in dollars. For example, if you purchased 50 shares of stock at $18.22 per share with a $35.00 commission/fee, this amount would be 946.00.
- **Cash Amt** This column displays cash transactions for this account.
- **Cash Bal** This column displays any cash balance in the account after the transaction on this line of the register.

Working with the Button Bar Options

In addition to the register lines, the button bar has two options.

Enter Transactions Clicking the Enter Transactions button opens the Investment Transaction dialog as described later in this chapter.

Holdings Clicking the Holdings button opens an Account Overview window for this account. Similar to the Portfolio view in the Investing tab, you can see the current value, recent and historical performances, and the tax implications of the transactions in this account, as seen in Figure 9-6.

Using the Account Actions Menu

The Account Actions menu (seen here) gives you access to several investment-related activities. The menu is divided into three sections: Transactions, Reporting, and Register Views and Preferences. Each is described next.

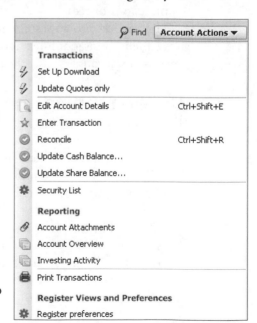

- **Set Up Download** will appear if you have not yet activated this investing account for online services. Click Set Up Download to do so.

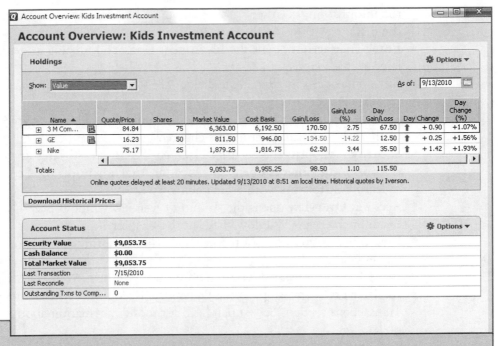

Figure 9-6 • You can see an overview of each of your investing accounts using the Holdings button.

- **Update Transactions** opens the One Step Update Settings dialog. Enter your password and click Update Now to update your accounts.
- **Update Quotes Only** prompts Quicken to use your Internet connection to download the latest quotes on your holdings and Watch List. Learn more about the Watch List in Chapter 10.
- **Edit Account Details** displays the General Information tab of the Account Details dialog, which you can use to enter or edit basic information about the account, including its name, tax-deferred status, account number, and contact information. From this dialog you can also enter information about fees and commission charges for this account. Click Transaction Fees to open the Transaction Fees dialog shown here. After you have entered

the information, as either a dollar amount or a percentage, click OK to close the dialog.

- **Enter Transaction** opens the Investment Transaction dialog as described later in this chapter.
- **Reconcile** opens the Reconcile dialog. See Chapter 7 for information on reconciling accounts.
- **Update Cash/Share Balance** works as described in "Updating an Account's Cash/Share Balance" later in this chapter.
- **Security List** opens the Security List. See "Security List" later in this chapter.
- **Account Attachments** opens the Account Attachment dialog. See Chapter 4 to learn how to work with attachments.
- **Account Overview** opens the Account Overview window. See "Using the Account Overview Window" later in this chapter.
- **Investing Activity** opens a report about your investing activity for time ranges you can set.
- **Print Transactions** gives you the opportunity to print your transaction list.
- **Register Preferences** opens the Preferences dialog to the Investment Transactions section. See Appendix B for more information about preferences.

Using the Investment Transaction Dialog

You enter transactions into an investment account with the investment transaction dialog. This dialog, which is named for the type of transaction you are entering, is a fill-in form with all of the fields you need to enter transaction details.

To open the investment transaction dialog, click the Enter Transactions button in the register for the account in which you want to enter the transaction (refer to Figure 9-5). It looks like the dialog shown on the top of the next page when you first open it. If the account is a 401(k) account, you may see a Cash Source button in the dialog.

Investment Actions

To use the investment transaction dialog, you must begin by choosing a transaction type (or *action*) from the Enter Transaction drop-down list. There are dozens of action types organized into two categories: investment transactions and cash transactions.

Investment Transactions Investment transactions directly affect your security or investment account balances, unless you have placeholders. See "About Placeholders" elsewhere in this chapter.

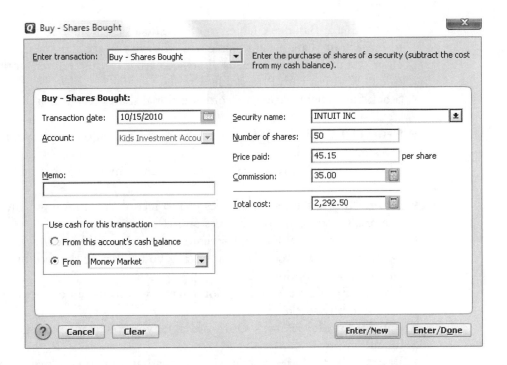

- **Buy – Shares Bought** (shown above) enables you to add shares to an investment account. The cost of the shares (plus any commissions) is deducted from the account's cash balance (or another account's cash balance).
- **Sell – Shares Sold** enables you to remove shares from an investment account. The proceeds from the sale (net of any commissions) are added to the account's cash balance (or another account's cash balance).
- **Div – Stock Dividend (Non-Cash)** enables you to add shares of a security paid as a dividend.
- **Reinvest – Income Reinvested** enables you to account for investment income (such as dividends) that is reinvested in the security. This is common with dividend reinvestment plans and mutual funds.
- **Inc – Income (Div, Int, Etc.)** enables you to record income from interest, dividends, and capital gain distributions.
- **Add – Shares Added** enables you to add shares to an investment account without an exchange of cash. You might use this option to add shares received as a gift.
- **Remove – Shares Removed** enables you to remove shares from an investment account without an exchange of cash. You might use this option to remove shares you have given to someone else as a gift.

- **Adjust Share Balance** enables you to create a placeholder entry transaction to make your share balance agree with your brokerage statement. You can enter cost information later, as discussed earlier in this chapter, in the section titled "Working with Placeholder Entries."
- **Stock Split** enables you to record additional shares received as a result of a stock split.
- **Return Of Capital** enables you to record the return of part of your investment capital.
- **Miscellaneous Expense** enables you to record investment expenses other than commissions.
- **Margin Interest Expense** enables you to record the amount of interest paid as a result of purchasing securities on margin.
- **Bonds Bought** enables you to record the purchase of bonds.
- **Grant Employee Stock Option** enables you to record the receipt of an employee stock option.
- **Exercise Employee Stock Option** enables you to use an employee stock option to buy stock.
- **Reprice Employee Stock Option** enables you to change pricing information for stock options.
- **Bought ESPP Shares** enables you to buy shares in an employee stock purchase program.
- **Sold ESPP Shares** enables you to sell shares purchased through an employee stock purchase program.
- **Short Sale** enables you to record a short sale of a security.
- **Cover Short Sale** enables you to record the purchase of stock to cover a short sale.
- **Corporate Name Change** enables you to record the change of the name of a company for which you own stock. This preserves the old name information; simply editing the security name in the Edit Security dialog does not.
- **Corporate Securities Spin-Off** enables you to record securities obtained through a spin-off of a smaller company from one of the companies in which you own securities.
- **Corporate Acquisition (Stock For Stock)** enables you to record securities obtained in exchange for other securities you own, normally as a result of a corporate acquisition.
- **Cash Transferred Into Account** enables you to record the transfer of cash into the investment account.
- **Cash Transferred Out Of Account** enables you to record the transfer of cash out of the investment account.

- **Shares Transferred Between Accounts** enables you to move shares from one Quicken investment account to another.
- **Reminder Transaction** enables you to enter an investment reminder. You may find this option useful if you want to conduct a transaction at a future date and are worried that you may forget to do it. If the Reminder Transaction has a future date, the reminder will not appear in the alert list until that future date.

Cash Transactions   Cash transactions affect the cash balance in an investment account. These actions make it possible to track an investment account's cash balance without using a linked cash account.

- **Write Check** enables you to record a check written from an investment account.
- **Deposit** enables you to record a cash deposit to an investment account.
- **Withdraw** enables you to record the withdrawal of cash from an investment account.
- **Online Payment** enables you to record an online payment from the investment account's cash balance. To use this feature, the account must be enabled for Online Payment or Online Bill Pay. Chapter 6 discusses Online Payment.
- **Other Cash Transaction** enables you to record any type of transaction that affects the investment account's cash balance.

Completing the Transaction

Investment transaction dialogs and forms are generally self-explanatory and easy to use. Simply fill out the fields in the form, and click one of the Enter buttons.

- **Enter/New** enters the current transaction and redisplays the investment transaction dialog so you can enter another transaction.
- **Enter/Done** enters the current transaction and dismisses the investment transaction dialog.

Entering Common Transactions

Although page count limitations make it impossible to review every kind of investment transaction in this book, here's a look at a few common transactions. They should give you a solid understanding of how the investment transaction dialogs work so you can enter your transactions.

Buying Shares

A security purchase normally involves the exchange of cash for security shares. In some cases, you may already own shares of the security or have it listed on your Watch List. In other cases, the security may not already exist in your Quicken data file, so you'll need to set up the security when you make the purchase.

Start by choosing Buy – Shares Bought in the investment transaction dialog to display the Buy – Shares Bought dialog shown earlier. Enter information about the shares you have purchased.

- **Transaction Date** is the date of the transaction.
- **Account** is the name of the account in which the transaction should be recorded. You cannot change the option chosen from this drop-down list if you are entering a transaction from within the account's Transaction View window; if it's wrong, click Cancel, open the correct transaction list, and start over.
- **Security Name** is the name of the security. If you enter the name of a security that doesn't already exist in Quicken, the Add Security To Quicken dialog, which is discussed later in the section titled "Adding a New Security," appears so you can add the security to Quicken.
- **Number Of Shares** is the number of shares purchased.
- **Price Paid** is the per-share price.
- **Commission** is the amount of commissions you paid to your brokerage or investment firm.
- **Total Cost** is calculated by Quicken. Enter the total cost and number of shares, and let Quicken calculate the price paid. The total cost and number of shares is what gets reported on IRS Schedule D when you sell the shares. However, if you're recording the purchase of a fractional number of shares and this amount is off by a penny or two, use the Commission field to adjust the total cost. The net effect of tiny adjustments like this is negligible.
- **Use Cash For This Transaction** enables you to specify an account from which the total cost should be deducted. By default, this option is set to use cash from the same investment account.
- **Memo** lets you enter any comments about this transaction.

When you're finished entering information about the transaction, click one of the Enter buttons. The transaction appears in the Transactions tab for the account.

If you want to add security shares to an account without an exchange of cash, use the Add – Shares Added action. Its form asks for most of the same information but does not affect any cash balances.

Selling

A security sale also involves the exchange of cash for security shares. Normally, you dispose of shares you already own, but in some instances, you may sell shares you don't own. This is called *selling short*, and it is a risky investment technique sometimes used by experienced investors. (To record short sale transactions, use the Short Sale or Cover Short Sale action.)

To sell shares, choose Sell – Shares Sold in the investment transaction dialog to display the Sell – Shares Sold dialog, which is shown next. Enter information about the shares you have sold.

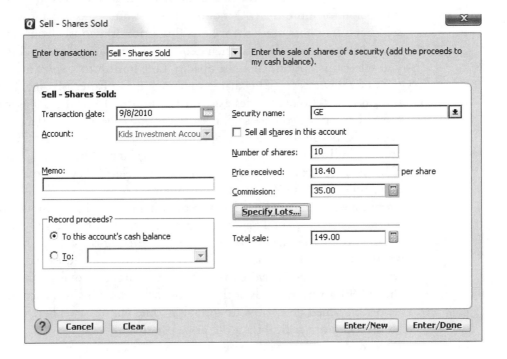

- **Transaction Date** is the date of the transaction.
- **Account** is the name of the account in which the transaction should be recorded. You cannot change the option chosen from this drop-down list if you are entering a transaction from within the account's Transaction View window; if it's wrong, click Cancel, open the correct account register, and start over.
- **Security Name** is the name of the security. You can choose an option from the drop-down list.

- **Sell All Shares In This Account** tells Quicken to automatically enter the total number of shares you own in the Number Of Shares box.
- **Number Of Shares** is the number of shares sold.
- **Price Received** is the per-share price.
- **Commission** is the amount of commissions you paid to your brokerage or investment firm.
- **Specify Lots** enables you to specify which shares you are selling when you have multiple purchase lots. You can use this option for additional control over capital gains. For example, if you want to take advantage of long-term capital gains tax breaks, you could sell shares that have been in your possession for more than 12 months. If you want to record a loss, you could sell shares that cost more than the selling price. Obviously, your options will vary, depending on the lots, their acquisition prices, and your selling price. If you select this option, click the Specify Lots button to display a dialog like the one shown next. (This dialog may include an Enter Missing Transactions button if placeholder entries exist for the security.) Use the dialog to enter shares in each lot you are selling, or select one of the Auto Select options and click OK. If you don't use the Specify Lots button to select lots, Quicken automatically sells the oldest shares (First In, First Out, or FIFO, method). Consult your tax professional if you want to select lots other than FIFO to determine what the IRS limitations might be.
- **Total Sale** is calculated by Quicken dividing the total sale amount by the number of shares. Total Sale can also be determined by multiplying the per-share price by the number of shares and deducting the commission. These are the proceeds from the sale. The technique Quicken uses is determined by the data you enter. However, your broker reports the total sale amount on the 1099B Form he sends at the end of each year. This is the number you report on Schedule D of your annual income tax report. Therefore, total sale amount is more critical than the price per share.
- **Record Proceeds?** enables you to specify an account to which the net proceeds should be added.
- **Memo** lets you enter any comments about this transaction.

When you click one of the Enter buttons, Quicken records the transaction.

Dividend Payments and Other Income

Many investments pay dividends, interest, or other income in cash. (That's why they're so attractive to an investor!) Recording this activity in the appropriate transaction list enables Quicken to calculate performance accurately while keeping account balances up-to-date, as well as helping you at tax time.

Keep in mind that many mutual funds are set up to reinvest income rather than pay it in cash. Do not use the steps in this section to record a reinvestment of income. Instead, use the Reinvest Income action to enter transaction information.

To record dividend or interest income, choose Inc – Income (Div, Int, Etc.) from the drop-down list in the investment transaction dialog to display the Inc – Income dialog, shown next. Enter information about a cash payment on an investment.

- **Transaction Date** is the date of the transaction.
- **Account** is the name of the account in which the transaction should be recorded. You cannot change the option chosen from this drop-down list if you are entering a transaction from within the account's Transaction View window; if it's wrong, click Cancel, open the correct transaction list, and start over.
- **Transfer Account** enables you to specify an account into which the income is deposited. Leave this blank if the cash is deposited directly into the investment account.
- **Memo** enables you to enter a brief note about the transaction.

- **Security Name** is the name of the security. You can choose an option from the drop-down list. If the transaction isn't related to a specific security—for example, interest paid on a cash balance in a brokerage account—you can leave this field blank.
- **Dividend**, **Interest**, **Short-Term Cap Gain Dist**, **Mid-Term Cap Gain Dist**, **Long-Term Cap Gain Dist**, and **Miscellaneous** are fields for entering various types of income. In most cases, you'll use only one or two of these boxes.
- **Total Proceeds** is the total of all income amounts calculated by Quicken.
- **Category For Miscellaneous** is the category you want to use to record miscellaneous income. This field is available only if you enter a value in the Miscellaneous field.

When you click one of the Enter buttons to record the transaction, it appears in the transaction list.

Other Transactions

Other transactions are just as easy to enter as purchases, sales, and income. Simply choose the appropriate option from the drop-down list in the investment transaction dialog and enter the transaction information in the form that appears. If you have the transaction confirmation or brokerage statement in front of you when you enter the transaction, you have all the information you need to record it.

If you need additional guidance while entering a transaction, click the Help button (question mark icon) in the Enter Transaction dialog to learn more about the options that must be entered.

Entering Transactions in the Transaction List

Quicken also enables you to enter investment transactions directly into the Transaction List window. This feature makes entering transactions quicker for experienced Quicken users.

To begin, scroll down to the blank line at the bottom of the register. Click the line to activate it, and enter the transaction date in the Date column. Then choose an action from the pop-up menu in the Action column and press TAB. The two lines for the transactions fill in with italicized reminders of the information you should enter into each field. Fill in the fields with transaction details and click Enter.

Editing Transactions

You can quickly edit transactions from your account's register. In the register for the account (refer to Figure 9-5), select the transaction you want to edit. Click in the field you want to modify, and make the desired change. When you're finished, click Enter.

You can also select the transaction and select the Edit action button, as shown next. The Edit dialog appears. Change any of the fields and click Enter/Done.

Nike	25	71...	35...	1,816.75	N/A	0.00
Memo					Enter Edit Delete Attach	

You can also right-click the transaction to open the context menu. Choose Edit to open the Edit dialog.

A few transaction types cannot be edited: Exercise Employee Stock Option and Sold ESPP Shares. These transactions must be deleted and re-entered if a change is needed.

Adjusting Balances

Occasionally, you may need to adjust the cash balance or number of shares in an investment account or update the balance in a 401(k) account. Here's how.

Updating an Account's Cash Balance

You can adjust the balance in an investment account with a cash balance. In the Account Bar, click the name of the account you want to adjust. From the register that opens, choose Account Actions | Update Cash Balance. The Update Cash Balance dialog appears. (Note that this dialog will not display downloaded cash balance information if the account is not enabled for online access.) Enter the date and the correct balance in the text boxes, and click Done. Quicken creates an adjusting entry.

Updating an Account's Share Balance

You can adjust the number of shares in an investment account. In the Account Bar, click the name of the account you want to adjust. From the transaction list, choose Account Actions | Update Share Balance to display the Adjust Share Balance dialog, shown on the next page. (This is the same as choosing the Adjust Share Balance action in the investment transaction dialog.) Enter the adjustment date, security, and correct number of shares in the dialog. When you click

Enter/Done, Quicken creates a placeholder entry that adjusts the share balance. Learn more about placeholder entries in the section titled "Working with Placeholder Entries," earlier in this chapter.

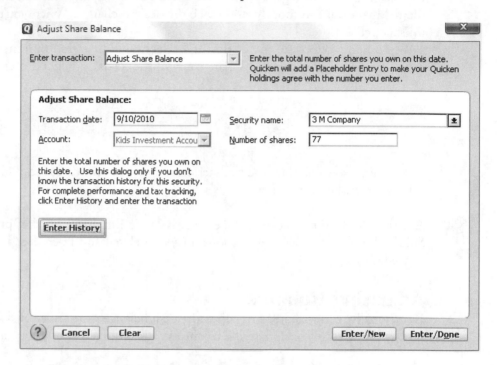

Updating 401(k) or 403(b) Balances

401(k) or 403(b) account balances change every time you make a contribution through your paycheck. To adjust the balance, click the name of the 401(k) or 403(b) account in the Account Bar to open its register. Click the Account Actions menu and choose Update 401(k) Holdings. Then follow the prompts in the Update 401(k)/403(b) Account dialog that appears to update the information. Click Next to display the next page. When you're finished, click Done to record the adjustment.

You will only see the Update 401(k) Holdings item in the Account Actions menu if the 401(k) account is manual. You will not see the item if the 401(k) account is enabled for transaction download.

Remember, if you set up your paycheck as discussed in Chapter 6, Quicken will automatically record contributions to your 401(k) or 403(b) account every payday.

Working with Securities

This chapter talks a lot about securities. But exactly what are they?

In Quicken, a security is a single investment that has a share price. Examples of securities include stock shares for a specific company, bonds for a specific company, and mutual funds offered by investment firms. Normally, when you own a security, you own a certain number of shares. To calculate the total value of the security, you'd multiply the number of shares you own by the most recent per-share price.

This part of the chapter explains how you can use the Security List to add a new security, choose market indexes, download quotes, edit security details, and more.

Security List

The Security List window (see Figure 9-7) simply lists the securities in Quicken's data file. You can use this window to add, edit, delete, or hide securities, including *Watch List securities*—securities you don't own but want to monitor.

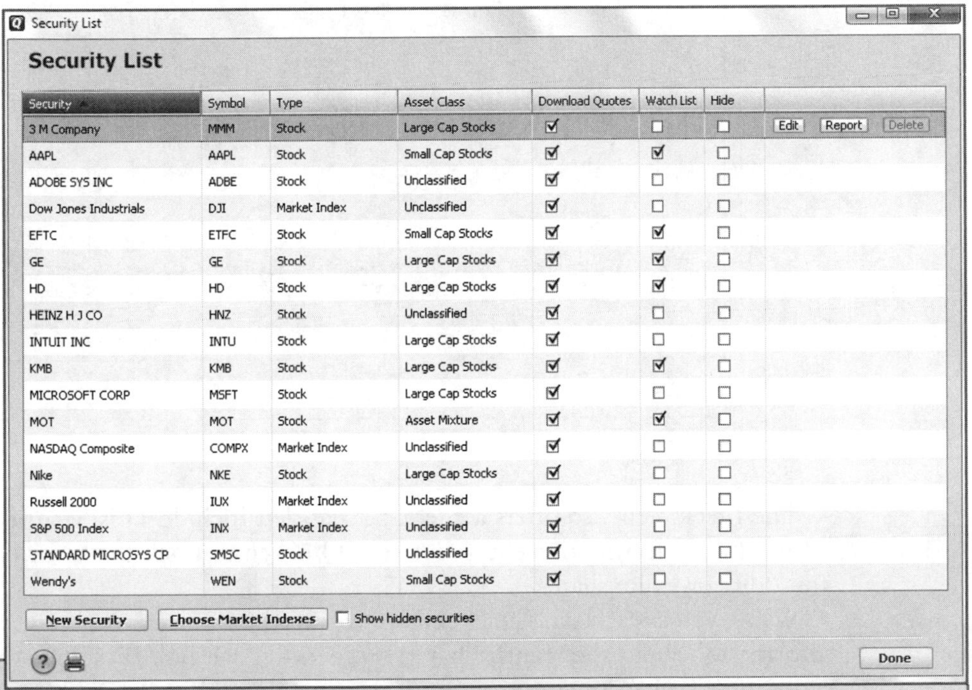

Figure 9-7 • **Use the Security List window to view, add, edit, or remove securities that you own or watch.**

To open this window, press CTRL-Y. You can also access the list from the Account Actions menu in an Investment Transaction list or from the Investing tab's Tools menu.

Adding a New Security

To add a new security to your Quicken data file—either as a holding or a Watch List item—click the New Security button at the bottom of the Security List window (refer to Figure 9-7). The Add Security To Quicken dialog appears, displaying screens that prompt you for information about a security.

As shown next, Quicken starts by prompting you for the security's ticker symbol and name. Entering the correct ticker symbol when you have an Internet connection can automate much of the security setup process. If you don't know the ticker symbol and have an Internet connection, you can click the Look Up button to connect to the Internet and look up the symbol.

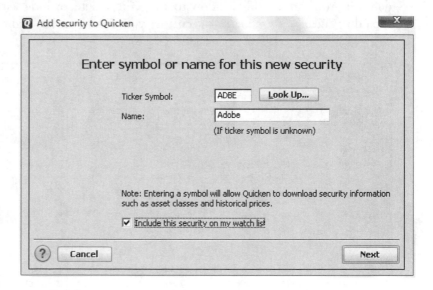

The first screen also offers a check box labeled Include This Security On My Watch List. Selecting this check box tells Quicken to track the security, even if you don't own any shares.

When you click Next, Quicken connects to the Internet to obtain information about the security based on its ticker symbol. If it finds the ticker symbol, it displays the information it has downloaded in the Add Security To Quicken dialog. Click Done to add the security to the Security List.

If Quicken can't find information about the security on the Internet, it displays a dialog like the one shown here, enabling you to correct the ticker symbol or add the security manually. If you made an error when entering the ticker symbol, you can enter the correct symbol in the Ticker Symbol text box and click Next to try looking it up on the Internet again.

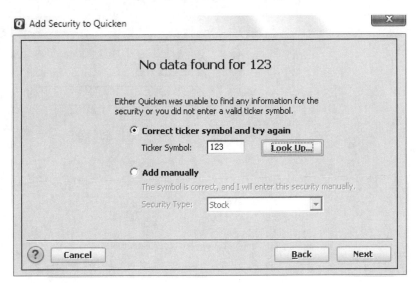

If you select the Add Manually option, select a security type—Bond, CD, Emp. Stock Option, ESPP, Market Index, Mutual Fund, Other, Stock, or U.S. Savings Bond—and click Next. Another dialog appears, prompting you for additional information about the security, such as its asset class (for a stock), asset class mixture (for a mutual fund), and bond type and maturity and call dates (for a bond). Enter whatever information you have for the security, and click Done to add the security to the Security List.

Choosing a Market Index

Choose Market Indexes enables you to add common market indexes, such as the Dow Jones Industrial Average and the S&P 500 Index, to the Security List. This lets you download quotes for these indexes when you download security prices, as discussed in Chapter 10.

Working with Individual Securities

When you select a security on the list, three action buttons appear. It is with these buttons that you can edit or delete a security as well as run a report. You can also access these actions by right-clicking the security name.

Editing a Security   You can edit a security to correct or clarify information you previously entered for it. Select the security's name in the Security List window (refer to Figure 9-7), and click the Edit button. The Edit Security Details dialog appears; the illustration shown next shows what it looks like for a stock. Enter or edit information in the dialog, and click OK to save your changes.

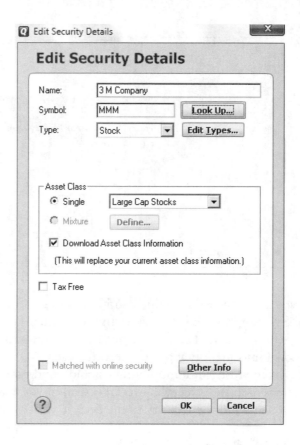

Deleting a Security   Delete removes the currently selected security from your Quicken data file. You cannot delete a security that has been used in a transaction.

Creating a Report   Report displays a Security Report, which summarizes all activity for the security. From the Report window, you can customize, save, or print this report. See more about working with reports in Chapter 8.

In addition to the actions and buttons already discussed, there are two more buttons on the Security List.

- The **Help icon** displays the Help window open to the Manage Securities section.
- **Print** opens the Print dialog from which you can print your Security List.

Security Type List   Each security in the Security List must be assigned a security type. To see the Security Type List, open your Security List and select any security. Choose the Edit action button to open the Edit Security Details dialog. Click the Edit Types button to open the Security Type List, which is shown here, to display a list of security types.

You can use buttons to modify the list.

- **New** enables you to create a new security type. Clicking this button displays the Set Up Security Type dialog, which you can use to enter a name for the security type.
- **Edit** enables you to change the name of the currently selected security type.
- **Delete** enables you to remove the currently selected security type from the list.

Be cautious about editing or deleting security types. You can cause yourself some serious headaches by doing so.

- The **Help icon** displays the Quicken Personal Finances Help window with instructions for working with the Security Type List.
- **Print** prints the Security Type List.

Investing Goal List   As illustrated next, the Investing Goal List window displays a list of all investment goals. You may find investment goals useful for organizing your investments based on what you expect them to do for you. You can assign a goal to a security by clicking the Other Info button in the Edit Security Details dialog for the security.

To see the Investing Goal List, open your Security List and select any security. Choose the Edit action button to open the Edit Security Details dialog. Click the Other Info button to open the Additional Security Information dialog. From this dialog, click Edit Goals to display the Investing Goal List dialog. Use the following buttons to work with the list:

- **New** enables you to create a new investment goal. Click this button to open the Set Up Investing Goal dialog in which you can enter a name for the goal.
- **Edit** enables you to change the name of the currently selected investment goal.
- **Delete** enables you to remove the currently selected investment goal from the list.

- **Print** prints the Investing Goal List.
- The **Help icon** displays the Quicken Personal Finances Help window with instructions for working with the Investing Goal List.

Using the Account Overview Window

The Account Overview window displays the holdings and status of a brokerage account. To access this window, select an account from the Account Bar, and from the Account Actions menu, choose Account Overview or the Holding button. As seen in Figure 9-6, this window is organized into snapshots of information about the currently selected security. The Holdings and Options areas are explained more fully in Chapter 11.

Holdings   The Holdings area lists each of the securities held in the account, along with information about each one. You can use various buttons and menus in the Holdings area to work with this information.

- **Options** offers commands to change the view preferences, include sold security lots in the display, include exercised and expired employee stock option grants, get quotes online, or display a complete portfolio.
- **Show** enables you to display a variety of information about the securities, including Value (the default selection), Recent Performance, Historic Performance, or Tax Implications. Tax Implications is not a choice for tax-deferred accounts.
- **As Of** enables you to see the account's status on a certain date. Change the date in this box, and Quicken recalculates the information as of that date.
- **Download Historical Prices** displays the Get Historical Prices dialog, which you can use to get price history for securities you own or watch. Learn more about downloading stock prices in Chapter 10.

Account Status   The Account Status area provides information about the status of the account, including the account's value and transactions and download dates. The Options menu in this area offers commands to reconcile the account or view all accounts in the Account List window.

Using Transaction Download and Research Tools

Chapter 10

In This Chapter:

- *Downloading transactions*
- *Comparing downloaded transactions to register transactions*
- *Reviewing account balance details*
- *Comparing downloaded holdings to recorded holdings*
- *Downloading stock quotes*
- *Exporting your portfolio to Quicken.com*
- *Using online research tools*

Quicken offers three separate features for tracking investments online.

- **Downloading Transactions** enables you to download transactions and balances for your investment accounts. This helps automate the entry of investment transactions and keeps your Quicken records in sync with your brokerage firm's records.
- **Quotes, News, And Alerts Download** enables you to obtain current and historical quotes; asset allocation information; and news headlines about individual stocks, mutual funds, and other investments. This automates the tracking of market values and provides valuable information you can use to make better investment decisions. This feature can also alert you to important information about securities you own or watch.

299

- **Quicken.com Update** enables you to put a copy of your investment portfolio on the Quicken.com website, where you can track its value from any computer connected to the Internet—without Quicken.

This chapter tells you about each of these features and explains how they can help you save time and stay informed about your investments. It also tells you about some of the features on Quicken.com that can help you research investments.

The instructions in this chapter assume that you have already configured your computer for an Internet connection. If you have not done so, do it now. This chapter also assumes that you understand the topics and procedures discussed in Chapters 2 and 6, and it builds on many of the basic concepts discussed in those chapters.

Transaction Download

You can download transactions, balance details, and holdings information directly from the financial institutions with which you maintain investment accounts. Each transaction can then be entered into your Quicken investment account with the click of a mouse button. You can also review downloaded account balance details and compare downloaded holdings information to the information recorded in your portfolio.

Reviewing Your Investing Accounts

When you click the Investing tab for the first time, you are taken to the Portfolio view of your investing accounts, as seen in Figure 10-1. This allows you to view information about an account. Learn more about the individual views of the Investing tab in Chapter 11.

Click an account name, either in the Portfolio view or from the Account Bar, to be taken to the account's transactions list. See "Reviewing and Accepting Transactions" later in this chapter for more information about investing account transactions.

To see the securities held in an investing account, click the small folder to the left of each account as seen here. The folder opens to show each of the securities within that account.

Click a security's name to open the Security Detail View. Clicking the small plus sign to the left of a security shows you all the lots of that security you have entered in Quicken listed from oldest purchase to newest purchase.

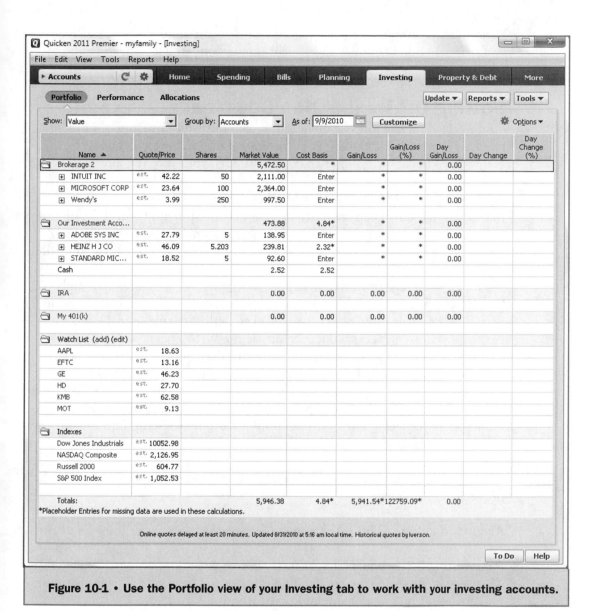

Figure 10-1 • Use the Portfolio view of your Investing tab to work with your investing accounts.

Many brokerage and investment firms support the downloading of transactions. If you set up your investing account as a manual account using Advanced Setup as described in Chapter 9, consider changing to online services if your brokerage offers them. Downloading transactions saves time and effort, and ensures that your Quicken records match those of your broker. However, your broker's records, or at least the records your broker will download, may not be accurate or complete, especially in the case of corporate mergers, ESPP buys and sells, and other complex investment transactions. You'll want to ensure that what gets downloaded makes sense.

Setting Up Transaction Downloads

To download transactions for an account, you must first configure the account for this. This requires that you enter additional information for the account(s) you want to track, including the account number, your user ID, and a password.

Applying for Transaction Downloads

Before you can download transactions, you may need to apply for it. Learn how at the end of Chapter 3. Normally, all it takes is a phone call, although many brokerage and investment firms allow you to apply online through the company website.

Not all brokerage firms have an application process. Some brokers simply provide Quicken access information on their websites. To access your account with Quicken, you simply configure Quicken with the same user ID and password you use to access your account via the Web. There's no need to wait for an application to be processed and additional information to be sent. Check your brokerage firm's website to see if these instructions apply to you.

If you do need to apply for Quicken access to your account, it may take up to a week for the application to be processed. You'll know that you're ready to go online when you get a letter with setup information. The setup information may consist of the following.

Customer ID   This may be your Social Security number or some other ID the brokerage firm provides.

Account Number   This is the number for your account at the brokerage firm.

Password or PIN   You'll have to enter your password or PIN into Quicken when you download transactions. If your brokerage firm sends this information, they may send it separately for additional security.

Setting Up the Account and Downloading Transactions

Setting up to download your transactions is a simple process, once you have your identification numbers. When the information is correctly set up, the process happens quickly.

From the Account Bar, right-click the account name you want to set up, and from the context menu, click Edit Account. The Account Details dialog appears. In the General tab, enter the name of your financial institution. Then click the Online Services tab. The services available from your broker are shown in the One Step Update section. Depending on your brokerage, you may see one of the following:

- One Step Update is not available. Transaction download is available via Web Connect.
- One Step Update is available.

Activate Web Connect   If your institution does not offer One Step Update services yet, you may be able to use Web Connect services. You may recall from Chapter 5 that Web Connect services enable you to download information from your institution's website. To do this, you must log in to your financial institution's website using the information your financial institution supplies, navigate to a download page, and indicate what data you want to download. Once the Web Connect file has been downloaded, Quicken reads it and knows exactly which Quicken account it applies to.

From the Online Services tab of the Account Details dialog, click Activate, as shown next. With your Internet connection, you are connected to your broker's website. While each institution is slightly different, at some point you will be prompted to enter your user ID and/or password, as shown here. Depending on your institution, you may be asked for additional information, such as your security question, before you have access to your account.

One Step Update

One Step Update is not available.

Transaction download is available via Web Connect.   [**Activate**]

LOG IN FOR SECURE ONLINE ACCESS

User ID: [   ]   Forgot User ID?

[NEXT]

Activate for One Step Update   If your institution is like many, you will be able to use Quicken's One Step Update to download your transactions with one or two mouse clicks. To use this service, from the Online Services tab of the Account Details dialog, click Activate One Step Update as shown.

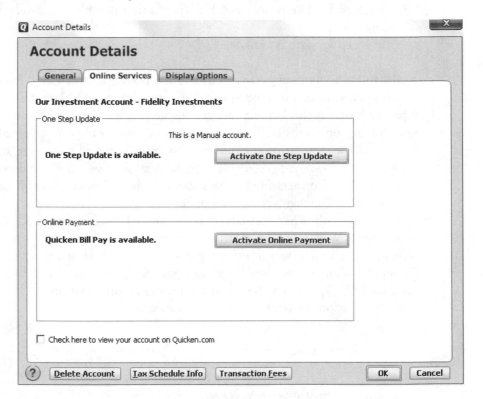

Quicken verifies your Internet connection to your institution and opens the Add Account dialog. You are prompted to enter your user ID and password as shown on the top of the next page. Enter them and click Connect.

Any accounts that Quicken finds at the institution are listed. You may be prompted to enter a nickname for each account. If so, type in the name you want to use and click Next. Quicken connects to the Internet to download transactions and balances for your account. When it's finished, you see the Account Added dialog with the name of your account as well as the number of transactions that were downloaded. Click Finish to close the dialog.

In addition to the account nicknames, you may need to decide if you wish to add, link, or ignore accounts found at the financial institution. And if you decide to link them, you see a list of all unlinked investment accounts, including hidden accounts, as seen on the bottom of the next page.

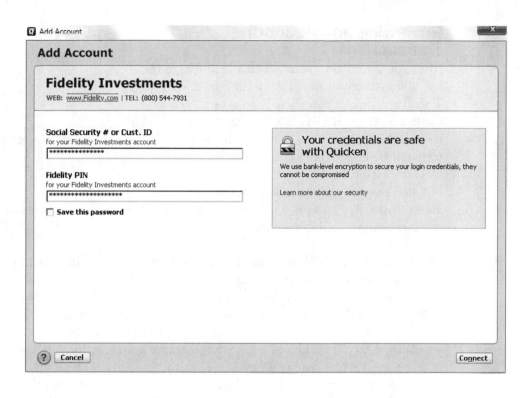

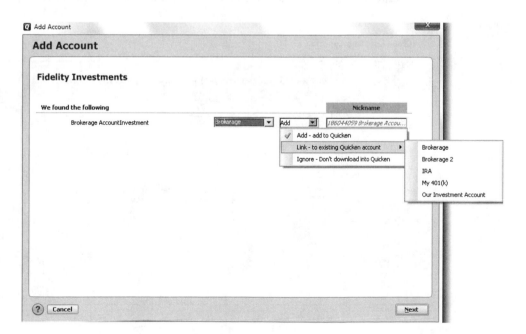

Reviewing and Accepting Transactions

After you download, there is a small red flag to the left of your account in the Account Bar, as seen here. This flag indicates that there is an action necessary for this account. If you click the flag, there are one or more links you can click to review the downloaded transactions or go to the transaction reminder list. This is new for 2011.

Click the account name and the New Data Download dialog appears, as shown below. You may handle your downloaded transactions in two different ways:

- **Review First** This method is best used if your account information is currently up to date. It allows you to look at each of the downloaded transactions before deciding to accept them into your "official" Transaction List. Consult Chapter 5 for details. In most cases, you'll simply select a new or matched transaction and click the Accept button to accept it.
- **Accept All** This choice is best the first time you download transactions because it is the fastest. When you click this, all of the transactions are transferred to the Transaction List and the Cash Amt and Cash Bal fields are updated. The Downloaded Transactions pane will disappear. When you click

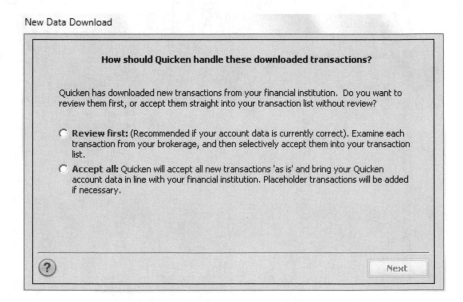

Accept All, if there are sold or removed transactions in the download, you may need to follow prompts in a dialog so you can enter additional required information. However, after the first time you download, be sure to back up before you accept all the transactions. If you have been entering transactions manually, the download may be slightly different, causing duplication and incorrect balances.

Remember that downloaded transactions that have not been accepted may not be entered in your Investment Transaction list. Thus, your register and portfolio balances may be misstated until you accept all downloaded transactions.

 If your account balance as downloaded does not match your Quicken balance, an extra adjusting transaction will be added.

Renaming Transactions

Renaming rules are not very helpful in investment accounts. The rules only affect payee names, and only cash transactions have payees. However, you may want to rename some transactions in order to make them consistent with your naming conventions, or to avoid cluttering your Transaction List with a variety of names that don't give you the information needed. In this case, you can create rules telling Quicken how to change the names of downloaded transactions. You can "rename" securities in downloaded transactions by matching the downloaded security to a security in your Security List. Once the Matched With Online Security link is established, the security will be renamed to the name from the Security List. For example, TD Ameritrade downloads GE as GENERAL ELECTRIC CO COM, but you may prefer your Security List to use "General Electric," so transactions for GE are renamed to General Electric.

To rename transactions, click the Renaming Rules button in the Downloaded Transactions tab or choose Tools | Renaming Rules. The Renaming Rules dialog is displayed. It shows the list of existing rules—by default, "Do Not Rename" is initially the only rule.

To create a new rule, click New. The Create Renaming Rule dialog is displayed, as shown on the top of the next page.

1. In the Change Payee text box, type the name you want to use.
2. In the next text box, click the down arrow to choose between Payee and Memo.
3. Next click the down arrow to choose between Is Equal To, Starts With, and Contains.
4. In the last text box, type the text you want to change.

Upon creating the rule, click OK and then click Done to make the renaming action happen.

Using the Online Center Window

You can also use the Online Center to download account information and compare it to data in your Quicken file. From the menu bar, choose Tools | Online Center. If necessary, choose the name of your brokerage firm from the Financial Institution drop-down list near the top of the window.

The button bar offers a number of options you can use for working with the Online Center window.

- **Delete** deletes a selected item.
- **Contact Info** displays the Contact Information dialog for the currently selected financial institution. You can use the information in the dialog to contact the bank or credit card company by phone, website, or e-mail if this service is offered by your financial institution.
- **Password Vault** gives you access to Quicken's Password Vault feature, as discussed in Chapter 6. (This option only appears if you have enabled Online Account Services for accounts at more than one financial institution and have not yet set up the Password Vault feature.)
- **Renaming Rules** displays the Renaming Rules dialog, which is discussed in this chapter.
- **Trade**, if offered by your financial institution, connects to the Internet and displays your brokerage firm's home page in an Internet window. You can then log in to make online trades.
- **Print** prints the transactions listed in the window as well as transactions that have been previously downloaded with a Direct Connect connection.
- **Options** displays a menu of commands for working with the current window.

Downloading Transactions

To download transactions, make sure the brokerage firm is selected in the Online Center window and then click the Update/Send button. The One Step Update Settings dialog appears as shown next.

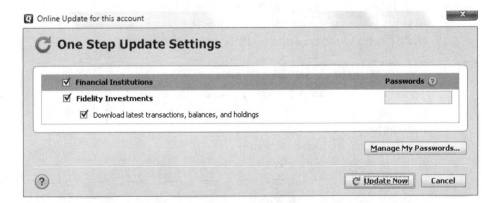

Enter your password and click Update Now. Wait while Quicken connects to your financial institution. You may be prompted to save your password as shown on the next page. If you click Yes, you are taken to the Password Vault dialog. See Chapter 6 for more information about the Password Vault.

Click Don't Ask Me This Again to hide this message in future updates.

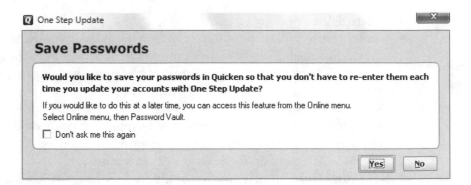

If you click No, a Quicken One Step Update Status window appears during the connection.

When Quicken is finished exchanging information, a One Step Update Summary window appears to summarize the activity that took place while you waited. Click Close. If you display the Online Center window again, you'll see the transactions you downloaded in the bottom half of the window's Transactions subtab.

Adjusting the Cash Balance

If the cash balance in your Quicken account doesn't match the cash balance at your brokerage firm, you can adjust the cash balance with the Update Cash Balance dialog. From the Investing tab, click the account you want to adjust. The Transaction List appears. From the account transaction list, click Account Actions | Update Cash Balance. Enter the correct cash balance and the date, and click Done. Quicken adjusts the account accordingly.

Reconciling Your Account

To keep your electronic investing accounts reconciled to your statement, you can perform a periodic reconciliation. If your account does not match your statement, you can adjust it with the Reconcile dialog. Select the account in the Account Bar to open the register. From the Account Actions menu, select Reconcile. The Reconcile dialog will appear as shown here. Enter the starting and ending cash balance amounts and the statement ending date, and click OK.

A list of the transactions is displayed. On the left are those transactions that decrease the cash balance, and on the right are those that increase it. As you click each transaction, the difference in the lower-right area of the dialog reflects the increase or decrease. Your account is successfully reconciled when the difference is equal to zero as shown here. If you want to start by marking all of the transactions, click Mark All. This is particularly helpful when you have a lot of transactions. When you have marked all and are finished, click Finished. If you want to return to this at a later time, click Finish Later.

When you have reconciled your account, a message will be displayed offering you the opportunity to create a reconciliation report. Click Yes or No.

- If you choose Yes, you are prompted to enter a title name and choose whether to have all transactions included in the report or only the uncleared transactions and a summary of the cleared items, as seen here. Make your choices and click OK to create the report.

- If you choose No, you are returned to your account's Transaction List.

Adjusting Holdings

If the holdings amounts in Quicken don't match what you've downloaded, the Enter Transactions dialog, which is shown on the next page, can be used to adjust your holdings. Select the account you want to adjust from the Account Bar to open the register. Click Enter Transactions. On the Enter Transaction

Buy - Shares Bought

Enter transaction: Buy - Shares Bought ▾   Enter the purchase of shares of a security (subtract the cost from my cash balance).

Buy - Shares Bought:

Transaction date: 8/18/2010

Account: Our Investment Accou ▾

Memo:

Security name: GE ▼

Number of shares: 100

Price paid: 15.61 per share

Commission: 25.00

Total cost: 1,586.00

Use cash for this transaction

⦿ From this account's cash balance

○ From

(?) Cancel   Clear   Enter/New   Enter/Done

drop-down menu, select the type of transaction you want. Buy – Shares Bought and Sell – Shares Sold are the most typical. Fill in the information needed, and when you are finished, click Enter/Done.

If you enter a transaction more than one year in the past to correct an account, you will see a warning message. If you are sure the information you are entering is correct, click Yes.

Reviewing the Account Overview

When you download transactions from your financial institution, you also receive detailed account balance information. To review this information, select the account in the Account Bar to open the

NEW TO QUICKEN?

Reset Quicken Warnings

In earlier versions of Quicken, once you turned off a warning message, such as the "Don't Show Me This Screen Again" message in the reconciliation report dialog, that message would no longer be available. In some cases, one would have to create a new account to see the warning again. However, in Quicken 2011, you can easily reset the Quicken warnings. Click Edit | Preferences | Alerts | Warnings, and click the Reset Quicken Warnings button.

register. From the Account Actions menu, select Account Overview. The Account Overview dialog for this account appears as seen in Figure 10-2.

Reviewing Holdings

Your financial institution also sends you information about your individual holdings. You can review this information in the Account Overview window and compare it to the information in your portfolio. You can choose several ways of viewing your holdings as seen here. Click the Show menu to see the options.

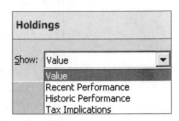

- **Value** displays the following:
  - **Quote/Price** as of the last time you downloaded.
  - **Shares** shows the number of shares you currently hold.
  - **Market Value** displays today's value of these shares.

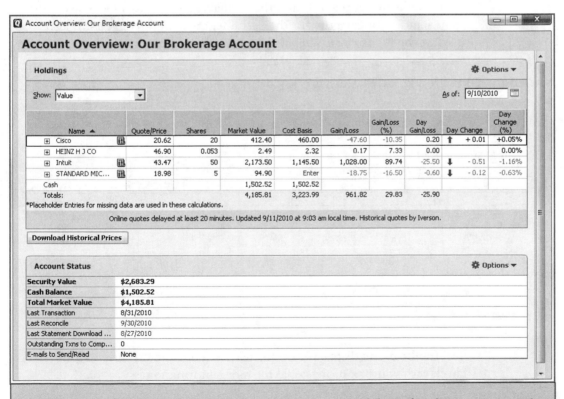

Figure 10-2 • The Account Overview dialog displays detailed information about your account.

- **Cost Basis** shows what you paid for these shares when you bought them.
- **Gain/Loss** displays your unrealized gain or loss as of the last time you downloaded.
- **Day Gain/Loss** indicates today's gain or loss based on the latest download prices.
- **Day Change** shows the trend for today for each security and the dollar amount of the change.
- **Day Change %** displays the percent of gain or loss for the day.
- **Recent Performance** shows the following:
  - **Market Value** shows today's (or as of the last download) information.
  - **Gain/Loss** shows the total gain or loss in dollars for today.
  - **Gain/Loss 1-Month** shows the gain or loss in dollars for the past month.
  - **Gain/Loss 1-Month %** shows the percent of the gain or loss for the past month.
  - **Gain/Loss for % 3-Month** and **12-Month** show the gain or loss for these time periods.
- **Historic Performance** indicates the annual return for this security compared to its industry or category for the past one, three, and five years. It also displays the industry and/or category of each holding as seen here.

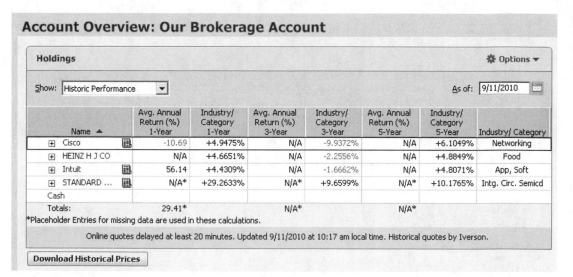

- **Tax Implications** displays tax information about each security. However, check with your tax professional for more information.

If you want to adjust your holdings, refer to the section "Adjusting Holdings" earlier in this chapter.

Seeing the Options

The Account Overview Options menu allows you to do the following:

- **Preferences** opens the Portfolio View Options dialog. See Chapter 11 for further information about this dialog.
- **Show Closed Lots** and **Show Exercised And Expired Grants** are also discussed in Chapter 11.
- **Get Online Quotes** uses your Internet connection to update your holdings.
- **Go To Full Portfolio** takes you to the Investing tab's Portfolio view.

If you are using Quicken Premier edition and have chosen to update your quotes every 15 minutes, your holdings are automatically updated. To turn on this useful feature, select Edit | Preferences | Investment Transactions, and select the Automatically Update Quotes Every 15 Minutes check box.

Checking Your Account's Status

As seen in Figure 10-2, the current status of your account is displayed on the bottom of the Account Overview window. It includes all of the following as of the date you choose in the As Of field at the top of the window:

- The **Security Value** of this entire account
- The **Cash Balance** held in this account
- The **Total Market Value**

This section also includes the Last Transaction, Last Reconcile, and Last Statement Download dates. You can also see any transactions that need to be compared, as well as any e-mails to the account's financial institution that you need to send or read from the Online Center.

Downloading Quotes, Headlines, and Alerts

Quicken enables you to download up-to-date stock quotes, news headlines, and alerts for the securities in your portfolio and on your Watch List. You set up this feature once and then update the information as often as desired. You can even download historical price information so you can review price trends for a security that only recently caught your eye.

Because the quote and headline download feature is built into Quicken, it doesn't rely on your brokerage firm for information. That means you can download quotes, headlines, and alerts even if your brokerage firm doesn't offer the downloading of transactions. All you need is an Internet connection.

Setting Up the Download

Before you can get quotes online, you must tell Quicken to download the information. Click the One Step Update symbol on either the Account Bar or the Tool Bar to open the One Step Update dialog. Click the Download Quotes, Asset Classes, Headlines And Alerts check box and click Update Now.

When the download is complete, the One Step Update Progress dialog will appear showing that the update was successful, as seen here.

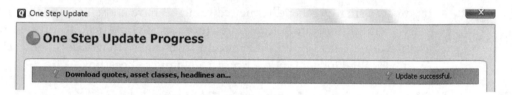

Setting Up a Watch List

To set up a group of securities you don't own but want to track, create a Watch List. Click Investing | Portfolio. Look in the Name column for the Watch List area as seen here.

Click the closed folder to the left of Watch List if necessary to open your current list. All of your current securities are shown on the list as well as any you have previously chosen to display.

To add a new security to the list, click Add to see the Add Security To Quicken dialog as shown next.

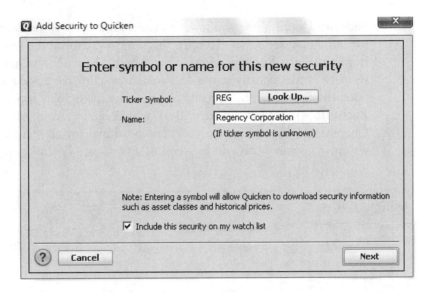

Enter the stock symbol or click Look Up to have Quicken find it for you. Once you have entered the name of the security you want to watch, click Next. The Quicken Update Status message will appear as Quicken uses your Internet connection to obtain information about this security. After the message closes, you will see the Add Security To Quicken message as shown here. Click Done to add the new security to your list.

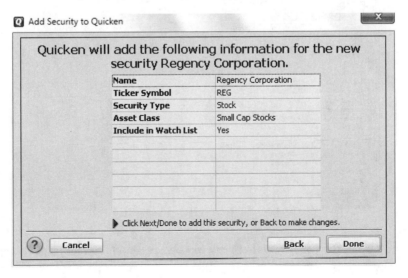

Viewing Downloaded Quotes and Headlines

You can view quotes and news headlines for a security in two places:

- **Security Detail View** window, shown in Figure 10-3, displays information for individual securities. To open this window, choose the Investing tab and from either the Portfolio view or the Watch List, click the name of the security. If the security name does not show, click the closed folder icon to open the account. The Security Detail View dialog will appear.
- **Portfolio** window (see Figure 10-4), which is covered in greater detail in Chapter 11, displays quotes and news headlines for all securities you own or watch. To display this window, choose Investing | Portfolio, or press CTRL-U.

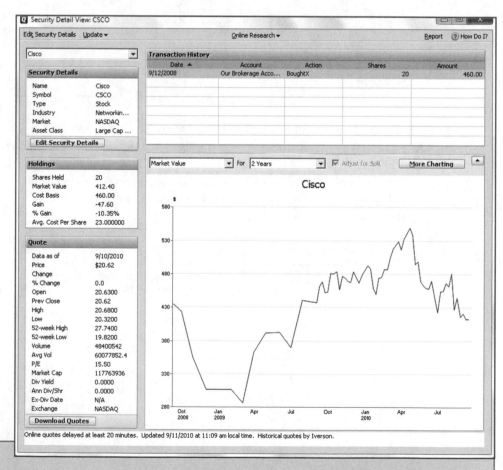

Figure 10-3 • The Security Detail View window shows information about a security.

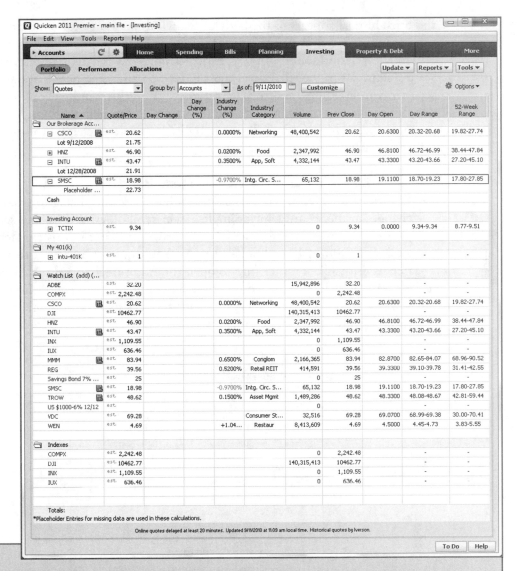

Figure 10-4 • You can view quotes with the Quotes view in the Portfolio window.

Using the Security Detail View

The Security Detail View window (see Figure 10-3) offers the most detailed quote information. You can find detailed information in the left side of the window. If you have been faithfully downloading quotes for your securities (or you have downloaded historical quotes, as discussed in the section titled "Downloading Historical Quote Information" later in this chapter), a chart of the price history appears in the body of the window. You can use the drop-down list in the top-left corner of the window to switch from one security to another.

The information found in the Security Detail View is extensive. As you can see in Figure 10-3, the left side of the window discusses the details about the security, your holdings, and the latest quotes. From this window you can edit the details of your security, download quotes, create additional charts, and do online research. (See "Using Online Research Tools" later in this chapter for more information about online research.)

Working with the Security View Detail Menu Bar

- **Edit Security Details** appears as shown here. Use this dialog to make any changes in the security, including its ticker symbol, asset class, and security type. See "Downloading Asset Class Information" later in this chapter for additional information about that topic. You can tell Quicken if this is a tax-free security. Click Other Info to open the Additional Security Information dialog in which you can indicate how much income you expect from this security, your goal for this security, your broker's name and phone number, its rating, and any other comments as seen next.

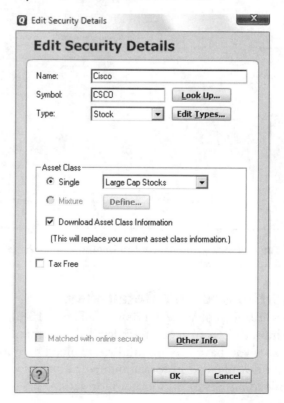

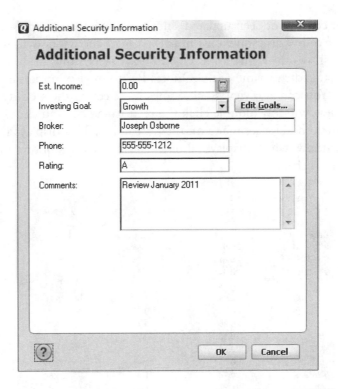

- **Update** opens a menu, shown here, from which you can download quotes, send information to Quicken.com, download both asset classes and historical prices, and if necessary, edit the price history of this security.

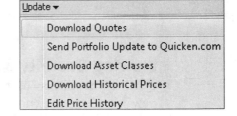

- **Online Research** offers several tools as discussed in "Using Online Research Tools" later in this chapter.
- **Report** creates a security report that you can customize to fit your needs.
- **How Do I** opens the Quicken Help window that discusses securities and security prices.

Viewing Stock Quotes

In the Investing tab's Portfolio view, downloaded quotes appear beside the security name or ticker symbol. Stock quotes are delayed 20 minutes or more during the trading day. Quotes for mutual funds are updated once a day by around 6:00 P.M. Eastern Standard Time. Prior to that, you'll see the previous day's prices with "est" beside the price (short for *estimate*), indicating that the price has not been updated since the previous trading day. Choose Quotes from the Show drop-down list near the top of the window to see more quote details, as shown in Figure 10-4. (If you don't see Quotes in the list, you probably changed the name of the Quotes Portfolio view sometime in the past.)

You can also view stock quotes by selecting the security in the Security Detail View window (double-click the security name) and choosing Edit Price History from the Update menu on the button bar. This displays the Price History window, which displays all of the recorded stock quotes for the security, as shown here.

Date	Price	High	Low	Volume
9/10/2010	**20.62**	20.68	20.32	48,400,542
9/9/2010	**20.61**	21.05	20.58	43,594,282
9/8/2010	**20.64**	20.89	20.55	40,609,070
9/7/2010	**20.58**	20.99	20.53	60,552,661
9/3/2010	**21.04**	21.13	20.76	54,469,373
9/2/2010	**20.52**	20.70	20.31	59,425,647
9/1/2010	**20.26**	20.70	20.25	80,126,649
8/31/2010	**19.985**	20.37	19.82	94,443,034
8/30/2010	**20.32**	20.89	20.29	58,934,741
8/27/2010	**20.81**	20.94	20.36	62,118,397
8/26/2010	**20.70**	21.31	20.69	53,476,384
8/25/2010	**21.21**	21.35	20.82	54,300,586
8/24/2010	**21.13**	21.45	21.10	74,398,112
8/23/2010	**21.68**	22.48	21.65	49,305,457

Price History for: Cisco — New Edit Delete Print How Do I?

Viewing Security News

Quicken may display up to three icons in the Name column of the Portfolio view window; one example is shown in the illustration. Each icon displays pertinent information when you hover the cursor over it. If an information box includes a link, clicking the link opens a webpage with more information with your Internet connection.

CSCO
DJI
HNZ
INTU

Intuit Inc (INTU)
Intuit Small Business Employment Index Shows Job Growth but at Slower Rate Than Earlier in Year
  Business Wire
Intuit GoPayment and mophie marketplace Offer Complete Credit Card Solution for iPhone
  Business Wire
more...

- The exclamation point icon displays alert information about the security, such as major price fluctuations and information about earnings announcements.

- The newspaper icon displays news headlines related to the security. Click the title to download the whole article.
- The H (shown) or L icon indicates that the security has reached a 52-week price high or low.

Downloading Historical Quote Information

Quicken enables you to download up to five years of historical quotes for any security you own or watch. Choose Investing | Update | Historical Prices. Quicken displays the Get Historical Prices dialog, shown here.

Choose a time period from the drop-down list at the top of the dialog. Your choices are Month, Year, Two Years, and Five Years. Make sure check marks appear beside all securities for which you want to get historical quotes. (Click Mark All to get prices for all on the list.)

Some Quicken users have reported trouble when selecting five years of prices for many securities at the same time. Several have suggested that you request data for five years for a single security or one month for several securities.

Then click the Update Now button. With your Internet connection, Quicken retrieves the information you requested. When it's done, it displays the One Step

Update Summary window. Click Close to dismiss the window. You can review the quotes that were downloaded in the Security Detail View window (refer to Figure 10-3).

Downloading Asset Class Information

For each security you own or watch, you can include asset class information. This enables you to create accurate asset allocation reports and graphs. Chapter 9 explains how to enter asset class information manually; Chapter 11 explains how you can use this information to diversify your portfolio to meet your investment goals.

The trouble is that most mutual funds consist of many investments in a variety of asset classes. Manually looking up and entering this information is time-consuming and tedious. Fortunately, Quicken automatically downloads this information for you, including your mutual funds.

However, you can change the information at any time. To do so, choose the Investing tab and click Tools | Security List. Click the security you want, and then click the Edit action button. This opens the Edit Security Details dialog seen earlier in this chapter. Make sure the Download Asset Class Information check box is selected, and close the dialog. The next time you update, asset classes are automatically updated.

Use Quicken.com for Updates

Using Quicken.com enables you to track your portfolio's value on the Web. Although you can do this without Quicken by manually customizing and updating the default portfolio webpage at Quicken.com, it's a lot easier to have Quicken automatically send updated portfolio information to Quicken.com for you.

To use the Quicken.com update feature, you must register Quicken. (Quicken will remind you if you haven't completed this step.) During the registration process, you will enter a member ID and password that you need to remember. The registration process sets up a private Quicken.com account for you to store your portfolio data.

Exporting Your Portfolio

In Quicken, choose Investing | Update | Update Portfolio On Quicken.com. The Preferences dialog, open to Quicken.com Portfolio, appears as shown next.

Click to place green check marks beside each account that you want to track on the Web. If you also want to track Watch List items on the Web, turn on the

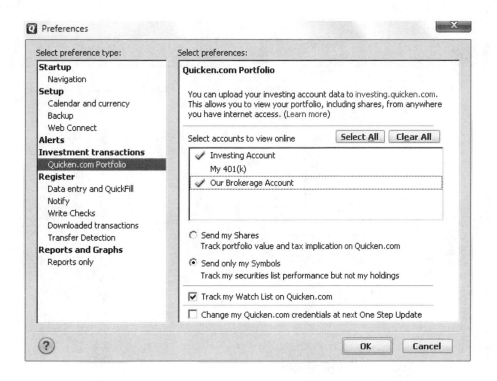

Track My Watch List On Quicken.com check box. Finally, select one of the
following upload options:

- **Send My Shares** exports the ticker symbols and the number of shares of
  each security you own for your portfolio. This enables you to track both
  prices and portfolio values.
- **Send Only My Symbols** exports just the ticker symbols for your portfolio.
  This enables you to track prices but not portfolio values.

When you're finished, click OK. The next time you run One Step Update,
your account will be updated.

To access your Quicken.com account, go to the Internet from any location. In
the address bar of your browser, type in **http://investing.quicken.com**. You are
prompted for your Quicken.com registration member ID and password. Type
the information and click Sign In. Your Investing Home page will appear as seen
in Figure 10-5.

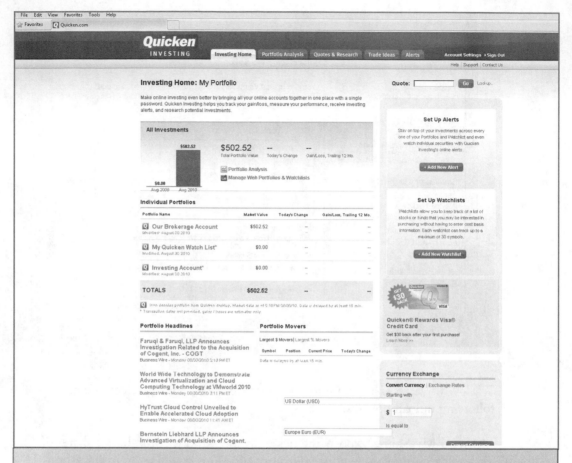

Figure 10-5 • After you have exported your portfolio, you can access it from anywhere with an Internet connection, using your member ID and password.

Updating the Password Vault

You may want to use Quicken's Password Vault to store the different passwords that you have for your various financial institutions. Your passwords are protected with encryption. Click Tools | Password Vault | Set Up New Password Vault. The Password Vault Setup dialog will appear. Click Next. The Select Bank/CC tab will display, as shown on the next page. The financial institutions for which you currently have established Internet connections are listed. Click the financial institution you want, and click Next.

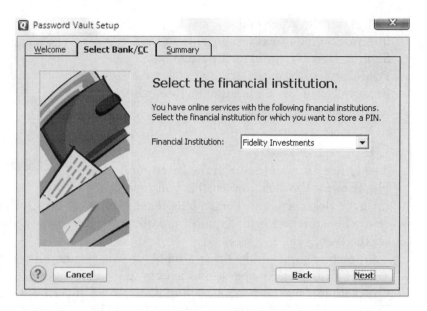

You'll next see the Enter The Password dialog. Enter the password you use to access your financial institution account, and then reenter it to confirm it is accurate. Click Next. After you have created the password for the first financial institution, Quicken asks if you want to enter additional passwords. If so, follow the same steps.

After you have entered all the passwords, you are asked to enter and reenter a password for the Password Vault itself. Click Next. The Summary tab is now displayed, showing your account and its user ID. At this point you can change or delete your passwords. Click Done to finish.

Using Online Research Tools

Quicken offers access to a number of research tools at Quicken.com. You can use these tools to find and learn about securities before you invest.

This part of the chapter tells you a little about Quicken's online research tools so you can explore them. Most Quicken users find them valuable resources for making wise investment decisions.

You can find these tools from the Classic menu. Click View | Classic Menus to display the extended menu list. Choose Investing | Online Research to open the Quicken.com login page. Enter your member ID and password, and click Sign In. Your Quicken.com page appears. Note the tabs on the top of the page as seen in Figure 10-5. Each tab has research tools and information to help you with your investing decisions.

You can also access online research
information for a specific security from the
Security Detail View. In the Investing tab
Portfolio view, select the security to open the
Security Detail View. Click Online Research to
see the menu shown here.

Online Research ▾
Get full quote
News
Quotes and research
One-Click Scorecard
Set up Alerts
Stock Evaluator
Multiple security Charting

Quote Lookup

The Quote Lookup feature in the Investing
Home tab at Quicken.com enables you to look
up stock ticker symbols. These symbols are required to use Quicken's online
research features for getting quotes and obtaining information about securities
on the Web.

In each tab, type in the ticker symbol for your security. If you don't know the
symbol, or it does not appear on the pop-up list that appears, click Lookup.
Quicken displays the Symbol Lookup dialog in a Quicken browser window.
Type all or part of the security name in the text box, and click Search. Quicken
organizes the results by security type: Stocks, Mutual Funds, ETFs, and Indices.
Click the tab of the security type you want, and examine the securities it found
that matched the criteria you entered.

One-Click Scorecard

One-Click Scorecard instantly prepares reports that help you evaluate a security
before you invest, using a variety of well-known analysis techniques and strategies.

From your Quicken Investing site, click the Quotes & Research tab of the
Quicken Investing pages on Quicken.com. In the Quote text box, type the ticker
symbol for the security you want to evaluate, and click Go. After a moment,
Quicken displays a snapshot of the requested security. About halfway down the
page, you'll see the One-Click Scorecard. Click The Complete Scorecard For
(*ticker symbol of your security*) to open a more complete analysis. The report that
appears automatically displays the results based on the recommended investing
strategy for that type of investment. For example, the recommended strategy for
a stock with strong growth and value characteristics is Robert Hagstrom's *The
Warren Buffett Way*. Read through the report to learn more about the analysis.

Tracking Security Values

As the individual views within the Investing tab illustrate, Quicken can automatically do the math to tell you what your investments are worth—*if* you take the time to enter the per-share prices of each of your securities.

When you record transactions, Quicken automatically records the security price. It uses the most recently entered price as an estimate to calculate the current value of the investment. You may see this in the portfolio—gray "est." characters indicate that the price is an estimate. These characters appear if the current date is on a weekend or holiday, or if you haven't entered or downloaded the current day's prices. Of course, the Portfolio view and all of Quicken's investing reports and charts are a lot more valuable with up-to-date security price information and a history of prices.

You can enter price information in two ways: manually (the hard way) and automatically (the easy way). This section discusses how to enter security prices manually. See "Setting Up Transaction Downloads" earlier in this chapter to learn how to enter prices automatically via Internet download.

Manually Entering Security Prices

Manually entering security prices isn't difficult—it's just time-consuming. And the more securities you track, the more time-consuming it is. But without an Internet connection, this may be the only way you can enter prices into Quicken.

If you track more than one or two securities and want to update price information more often than once a week, skip the rest of this section. You don't want to enter security prices manually. It's an extremely tedious task. Quicken's ability to download stock prices directly from the Internet—even five-year price histories—can save you tons of time and prevent data entry errors. And best of all, it's free. All you need is an Internet connection.

To enter a security's price manually, start from the Investing tab. Click the name of the security for which you want to enter the information. From the Security Detail View window, choose Edit Price History from the Update button on the button bar. The Price History window for the security appears, as shown on the top of the next page, showing all the price information stored within the Quicken data file for the security.

Date	Price	High	Low	Volume
8/17/2010	**46.48**	46.56	45.61	2,324,652
8/16/2010	**45.63**	45.785	45.09	2,122,233
8/13/2010	**45.64**	45.84	45.17	1,799,399
8/12/2010	**45.30**	45.41	44.62	2,164,149
8/11/2010	**45.30**	45.37	44.82	3,238,665
8/10/2010	**45.70**	45.96	45.30	1,844,141
8/9/2010	**45.65**	45.81	45.34	1,345,829
8/6/2010	**45.34**	45.495	45.02	2,738,057
8/5/2010	**45.43**	45.73	45.18	2,503,809
8/4/2010	**45.88**	45.99	45.30	2,632,611
8/3/2010	**45.30**	45.47	44.65	3,068,323
8/2/2010	**44.95**	44.97	44.62	3,511,550
7/30/2010	**44.48**	44.69	44.35	4,559,554
7/29/2010	**44.68**	45.58	44.63	3,886,803

Price History for: HEINZ H J CO — New Edit Delete Print How Do I?

If you want to enter prices for several securities for a single day, it's easier to use the Portfolio Quotes view. You can enter the prices and volumes directly.

You can also import prices in comma-separated variable (CSV) format. In some cases, importing prices may be the best way to reconstruct your price history.

You can also press CTRL-Z to recalculate investment transactions, which will enter prices in your price history.

Evaluating Your Position

Chapter 11

In This Chapter:

- *Using the Investing tab*
- *Understanding the Portfolio view*
- *Using the Portfolio Rebalancer*
- *Using the Portfolio Analyzer*
- *Setting investment alerts*
- *Using investment analyses and reports*
- *Using the Asset Allocation Guide*
- *Previewing your buy/sell decisions*
- *Estimating capital gains*

As you enter transactions into Quicken—whether manually or automatically via the Transaction Download—Quicken builds a portrait of your investment portfolio and performance. If you're serious about investing, you can use this information to evaluate your investing position and fine-tune your portfolio to diversify and maximize returns.

Quicken's Investing tab offers a wide range of tools—including reports, graphs, alerts, analysis tools, and reference materials—that you can use to evaluate and strengthen your investment positions. This chapter takes a closer look at the features that can make you a better investor.

Using the Investing Tab

The Investing tab should be your first stop for evaluating your investment position. Each of its views includes snapshots with calculated information and links to more information on Quicken and Quicken.com features. Because the Investing tab always displays the most recent information it has, its windows are most useful immediately after downloading quotes, news, and research information, as discussed in Chapter 10. If you are using Quicken Premier or a higher version, you can tell Quicken to download quotes for you every 15 minutes.

To open the Investing tab window, click the Investing tab near the top of Quicken's main window. The Portfolio view appears. Additional information is available in the views found by clicking the Performance or Allocations button as discussed later in this chapter.

This part of the chapter takes you on a guided tour of Quicken's Investing tab so you know exactly how you can use it to monitor your investments.

Understanding Your Portfolio View

The Portfolio view of the Investing tab (see Figure 11-1) displays all of your investments in one place. Information can be viewed in a wide variety of ways to show you exactly what you need to see to understand the performance, value, or components of your portfolio.

Open the Portfolio window by clicking the Portfolio button in the Investing tab or by pressing CTRL-U.

Using Portfolio View Options

You can quickly customize the Portfolio window's view by using the Show, Group By, and As Of options right beneath the button bar. There are many view combinations—far too many to illustrate in this book. Here's a brief overview so you can explore these options on your own.

Using Show Options   The Show drop-down list enables you to specify the view that should be used to display the information. Each of the nine predefined views can be customized with the Customize Current View dialog, discussed later in this section. You can also create nine "custom" views to see data in ways most useful to you.

Using Group By Options   The Group By options enable you to select the order in which securities appear. The drop-down list offers seven options: Accounts, Industry, Security, Security Type, Investing Goal, Asset Class, and Sector. These options correspond to information entered as part of a security's definition, either manually when you add the security to Quicken or automatically when you download asset class information. Learn how to add securities to Quicken in Chapter 9 and how to download security information in Chapter 10.

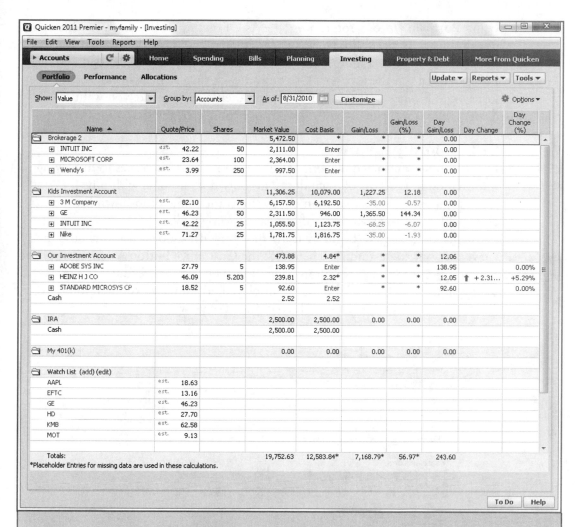

Figure 11-1 • Use the Investing tab's Portfolio view to see all of your investments in one place.

Using Portfolio Date   You can use the As Of box to set the date for which you want to view the portfolio. For example, suppose you want to see what your portfolio looked like a month ago, before a particularly volatile market period. Enter that date in the text box. Or you can click the calendar button beside the text box to display a calendar of dates, and then click the date you want to display. The view changes to show your portfolio as of the date you specified.

Customizing a View

Quicken offers an incredible amount of flexibility when it comes to displaying information in the Portfolio window. Not only does it come with nine preconfigured views that you can choose from the Show drop-down list, but it also enables you to create nine additional custom views.

To customize a view, begin by using the Show drop-down list to choose the view you want to customize. Then click the Customize button to the right of the Show, Group By, and As Of drop-down lists. The Customize Current View dialog appears with the Columns tab displayed, as shown next. Set options as desired in the dialog and click OK to change the view.

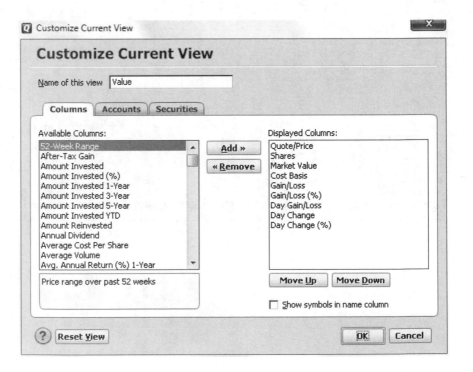

Changing the View Name   To change the name of the view, enter a new name in the Name Of This View box.

Selecting Columns to Show   To display a column of information, select it in the Available Columns list and click the Add button beside it. To hide a column of information, select it in the Displayed Columns list and click the Remove button. You can change the order in which columns appear by selecting a column name in the Displayed Columns list and using the Move Up or Move Down button to change its order in the list.

Displaying Symbols Rather Than Names   To display a security's ticker symbol rather than its name, turn on the Show Symbols In Name Column check box.

Return to Default   Click the Reset View button to return this view to the default settings.

Selecting Accounts to Include   To specify which accounts should appear, click the Accounts tab, as shown next. Toggle the check marks to the left of the account names in the Accounts To Include In This View list. Only those accounts that are selected will appear. You can change the order in which accounts appear by selecting an account name in the Accounts To Include list and clicking the Move Up or Move Down button.

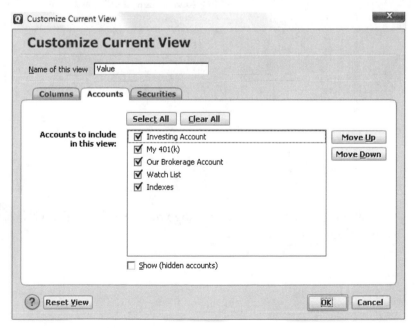

Click Select All to include all of your accounts, or click Clear All to clear all of the check marks and start over. To include hidden accounts in the Accounts To Include list, turn on the Show (Hidden Accounts) check box. To reset the view to the default settings, click the Reset View button.

Selecting Securities to Include   Click the Securities tab, shown next, to specify which securities should appear. Toggle the check marks to the left of the security names in the Securities To Include In This View list. Only those securities that are selected will appear. To include hidden securities in the Securities To Include list, turn on the Show (Hidden Securities) check box.

Click Select All to include all of your accounts, or click Clear All to clear all of the check marks and start over. To reset the view to the default settings, click the Reset View button.

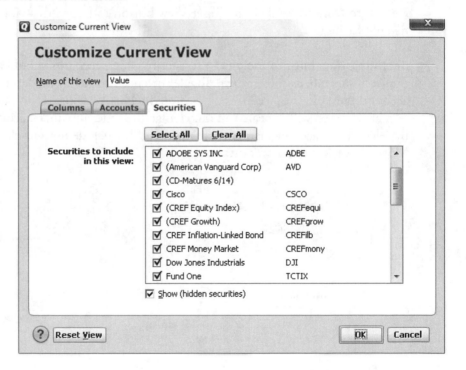

When you have finished creating your new view, click OK to return to the Investing tab's Portfolio view.

Setting Portfolio View Options

Use the Options button at the far right of the Portfolio view, shown here, to customize your views as explained earlier, as well as to do the following.

Portfolio Preferences   This option enables you to specify the period for return calculations and the tax rate used in the Portfolio window, as shown next. Setting these options enables you to fine-tune the way Quicken makes Portfolio window calculations.

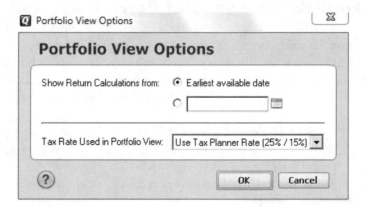

From the Investing tab Portfolio view, click Options | Portfolio Preferences to open the Portfolio View Options dialog.

The Show Return Calculations From area offers options for determining the period and tax rate for which Quicken calculates the return on investment:

- **Earliest Available Date**, the default, includes all periods for which you have entered transactions into Quicken.
- A blank field allows you to enter a starting date for calculations. All transactions between that starting date and the current date are included in the calculations. Alternatively, you can use the calendar icon to set the date.
- **Tax Rate Used In Portfolio View** allows you to choose tax rates that should be used in tax calculations for capital gains. If you are utilizing Quicken's Tax Planner, which is covered in Chapter 18, keep the default, Use Tax Planner Rate, selected. Otherwise, choose the rates that are appropriate for your financial situation. Check with your tax professional for further information about your specific situation.

Show Closed Lots   This option tells Quicken that you want to display lots that have been closed.

Studying Your Performance

The Performance button's view in the Investing tab (see Figure 11-2) displays graphs and tables of information about your investment performance. You can customize many of the snapshots that appear in the Performance view using commands on each snapshot's Options menu. You can further customize the Performance view window by using the drop-down list options at the top of the Performance view window.

Portfolio Value vs. Cost Basis

The Portfolio Value vs. Cost Basis graph uses a line graph and a bar graph to illustrate your portfolio's cost basis—what you've invested—and its market value. Ideally, you want the tops of the bars to appear above the line, indicating that your account is worth more than you spent to buy the securities.

The Options menu offers additional choices for this graph.

- **Go To Full Screen View Of This Graph** displays a graph, as seen on page 340, with only your Portfolio Value vs. Cost Basis information as of a date you choose.
- **Show Value/Cost Basis Report** tells Quicken to show the information in a report format.
- **Go To Full Portfolio** returns you to the Investing tab's Portfolio view.

Growth Of $10,000

The Growth Of $10,000 chart illustrates how an investment of $10,000 in your portfolio has grown over the period you choose. You can turn on check boxes beside popular investment indexes to compare your investment performance to one or more indexes, as shown in Figure 11-2.

Average Annual Return

The Average Annual Return chart displays the one-year, three-year, and five-year return on each of your investment accounts. If the account has one or more securities in the one-, three-, or five-year period, there will be an average annual return reported for the account. If the account did not exist or no lots of the account's securities existed during the one-, three-, or five-year period, the average annual return will show as N/A.

Figure 11-2 • The Performance view of the Investing tab shows you, at a glance, how your investments are doing.

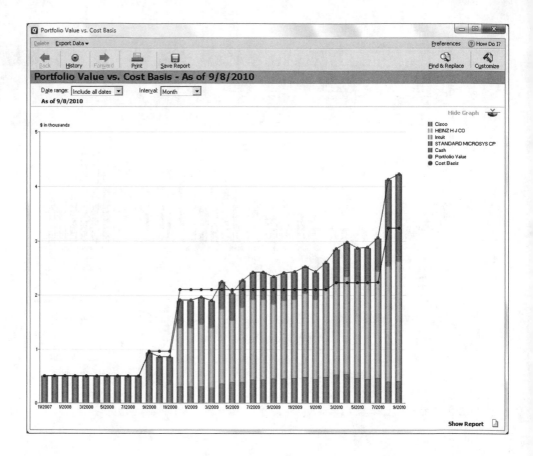

The options for this section, shown next, let you change the information's display.

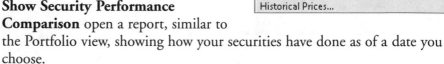

- **Show Security Performances** and **Show Security Performance Comparison** open a report, similar to the Portfolio view, showing how your securities have done as of a date you choose.
- **Historical Prices** opens the Get Historical Prices dialog, shown here, where you can tell Quicken to download historical prices for one or more of your securities for the last month, year, two years, or five years. Use check marks in front of the name of each security for which you want pricing. The Mark All and Clear All buttons can help you make your selections. Click Update Now to use your Internet connection to download the data. The One Step

Update Summary dialog displays when the download is complete. Click Close to close the dialog and return to the Investing tab's Performance view.

Exploring Asset Allocation

The Allocation views of the Investing tab (see Figure 11-3) display a number of customizable graphs of your investment data, along with a few snapshots with links to other features. Each of the graphs that appears in the Asset Allocation view can be customized using commands on the graph's Options menu. Buttons beneath each chart enable you to go to a full-sized graph in a report window or view a related report. You can further customize the Asset Allocation view window by selecting one of the drop-down list options: All Accounts, Investing Only, Retirement Only, or one of your accounts. You can also select Customize to show just the data you prefer.

Reviewing Your Asset Allocation

Asset allocation, which is covered in detail later in this chapter, refers to the way in which your investment dollars are distributed among different types of investments. It's a measure of how well your portfolio is diversified.

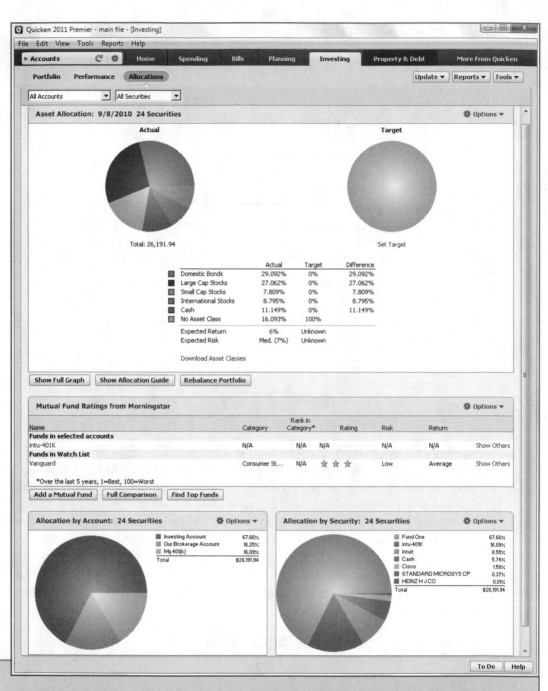

Figure 11-3 • The Allocation views of the Investing tab display analytical graphs of your investments.

The Asset Allocation graph displays two pie charts: Actual Allocation and Target Allocation. Actual Allocation indicates your portfolio's current diversification. Figure 11-3 shows that the majority of the securities in this account are invested in domestic bonds and large cap stocks. Target Allocation is the allocation you set up with Quicken's Portfolio Rebalancer, which is discussed later in this chapter, in the section titled "Using the Portfolio Rebalancer." If you have not yet used the Portfolio Rebalancer, the Target Allocation pie won't have any slices.

Mutual Fund Ratings from Morningstar

If you use Quicken Premier or a higher version, Quicken displays up-to-date ratings from Morningstar, an investment research organization that rates mutual funds based on a variety of criteria. Ratings for mutual funds you track in Quicken are automatically downloaded with asset class and related information. The more stars, the higher the rating.

Allocation By Account

The Allocation By Account chart indicates how your portfolio's market value is distributed among your Quicken investing accounts.

Allocation By Security

The Allocation By Security chart indicates how your portfolio's market value is distributed among the different securities.

Updating Your Investments

The Update button, at the right of the button bar, works with your Internet connection to keep your portfolio up to date.

- **Quotes** downloads the current quotations for your portfolio.
- **Historical Prices** opens the Get Historical Prices dialog discussed earlier in this chapter.
- **Update Portfolio On Quicken.com** opens the Preferences dialog for Quicken.com. Learn more about Quicken.com in Chapter 10, and learn more about Preferences in Appendix B.
- **One Step Update** opens the One Step Update Settings dialog from which you can tell Quicken which accounts you want to update.

Working with Reports

The Reports button's menu, shown here, offers a wide variety of reports, which can be customized to meet your needs. See Chapter 8 for customization options other than those included in each report.

Update ▼	Reports ▼
Capital Gains	
Investing Activity	
Investment Asset Allocation	
Investment Income	
Investment Performance	
Investment Transactions	
Maturity Dates for Bonds and CDs	
Portfolio Value	
Portfolio Value & Cost Basis	
All Reports	▶

- **Capital Gains** reports can be for any date range you choose and can be subtotaled by Short- vs. Long-Term, Month, Quarter, Year, Account, Security, Security Type, Investing Goal, and Asset Class.
- **Investing Activity** reports display the activity, income (or loss), and capital gains for your accounts, based on the date range you set.
- **Investment Asset Allocation** reports can be displayed both as graphs and reports, such as the one shown in Figure 11-4. You can tell Quicken the date range you want to display.
- **Investment Income** reports display the income and expenses related to your investments. These can be customized by date range and subtotals.
- **Investment Performance** reports show the return and average annual return on your accounts based on the date range and subtotal intervals you choose.
- **Investment Transactions** reports show complete data about your transactions for time periods you designate. You can subtotal in several different ways as well as customize the date range of the report to meet your needs.
- **Maturity Dates For Bonds And CDs**, a new report in Quicken 2011, creates a detailed report of when your instruments will mature.
- **Portfolio Value** displays the total value of your holdings in both a graph and a report. This report can be customized by date range and subtotal intervals to show your information in the way you want to see it.
- **Portfolio Value & Cost Basis** reports show the cost and value of each of your securities as of the date and subtotal interval you specify.
- **All Reports** opens the same menu you see when clicking Reports on the menu bar.

Investing Tab Tools

The Tools button's menu gives you access to the valuable estimators and guides provided by Quicken. See "Using the Asset Allocation Guide," "Previewing Your Buy/Sell Decisions," and "Estimating Capital Gains" later in this chapter.

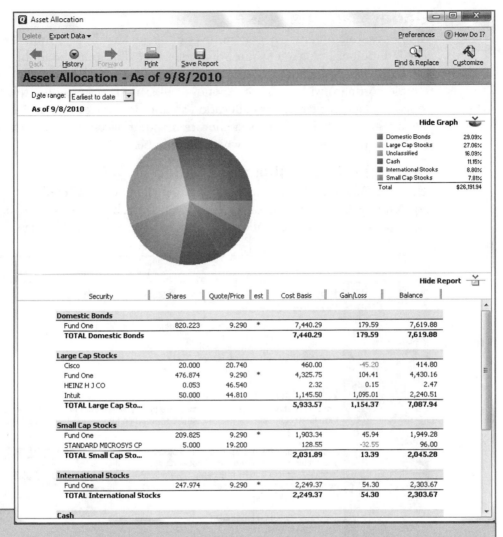

Figure 11-4 • Asset Allocation reports can be created easily in Quicken.

Using Investment Analysis Tools

In addition to the Quicken.com-based investment research tools discussed in Chapter 10, Quicken offers a number of built-in tools that can help you learn more about investing and analyze your investment portfolio.

This part of the chapter introduces these analysis tools so you can explore them more fully on your own.

Understanding Asset Allocation

Many investment gurus say that an investor's goals should determine his or her asset allocation. If you're not sure what your asset allocation should be, Quicken can help. It includes a wealth of information about asset allocation, including sample portfolios with their corresponding allocations. You can use this feature to learn what your target asset allocation should be to meet your investing goals. Then you can monitor your asset allocation and, if necessary, rebalance your portfolio to keep it in line with what it should be.

Using the Asset Allocation Guide

The Asset Allocation Guide explains what asset allocation is, why it's important, and how Quicken can help monitor it in your portfolio. Choose Investing | Tools | Asset Allocation Guide. The Asset Allocation Guide window appears (see Figure 11-5).

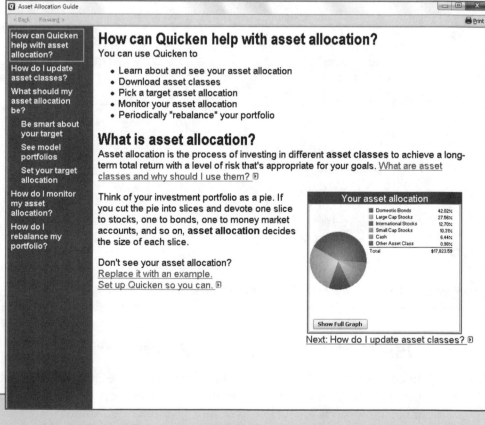

Figure 11-5 • The Asset Allocation Guide explains what asset allocation is and how it can help you meet your investment goals.

To take full advantage of this feature, read the information on the right side of the window. You can click links within the text or in the left column to learn more about specific topics. If you're new to asset allocation, you may find the See Model Portfolios link especially useful. It shows suggested asset allocations based on risk and returns for a number of portfolios. Click Close to return to the Investing tab.

Monitoring Your Asset Allocation

To monitor the asset allocation of your portfolio, you must enter asset class information for each of your investments. You can do this in two ways:

- **Manually enter asset class information**   Although this isn't difficult for stocks, it can be time-consuming for investments that have an asset class mixture, such as mutual funds.
- **Download asset class information**   If you have a connection to the Internet, this is the best way to enter this information. With a few clicks, Quicken does all of the work in seconds. The information is complete and accurate. Learn how to download asset class information in Chapter 10.

Viewing Your Asset Allocation

If you have chosen to display all of your accounts and all of your securities in the Asset Allocation graph in the Allocations button's Asset Allocation view, the pie chart that appears in the Asset Allocation Guide window (see Figure 11-5) is the same graph as seen in Figure 11-3. To get more information about a piece of the pie, point to that "pie slice" in either location. A yellow box appears, displaying the asset class, total market value, and percent of portfolio value.

Setting Your Target Asset Allocation

If you know what you want your asset allocation to be, you can set up a target asset allocation. Quicken then displays your target in the pie chart beside the current asset allocation chart on the Investing tab's Allocations button's Asset Allocation window so you can monitor how close you are to your target.

Display the Allocations button's view of the Investing tab window (refer to Figure 11-3). Then choose Change Target Allocations from the Options menu in the button bar of the Asset Allocation area. The Target Allocation dialog appears. Here's what it looks like with a sample allocation already entered (see next page).

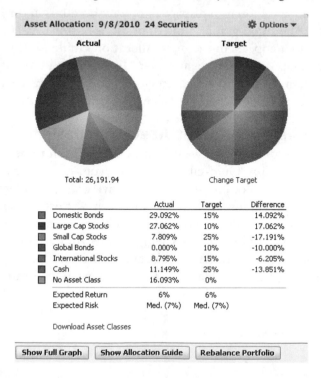

Enter the desired percentages for each asset class. When the total of all percentages equals 100, click OK to save your settings. The Target chart in the Asset Allocation area of the Investing tab window reflects your settings, as shown next.

Using the Portfolio Rebalancer

If your current asset allocation deviates from your target asset allocation, you may want to rebalance your portfolio. This means buying and selling investments to bring you closer to your target asset allocation.

Keep in mind that brokerage fees and capital gains impacts often are related to buying and selling securities. For this reason, you should carefully evaluate your investment situation to determine how you can minimize costs and capital gains while rebalancing your portfolio. If small adjustments are necessary to bring you to your target asset allocation, you may not find it worth the cost to make the changes. Use this information as a guideline only! As always, consult your tax professional for additional information about your specific situation.

Quicken can tell you exactly how you must change your current asset allocation to meet your target asset allocation. In the Asset Allocation snapshot of the Investing tab's Allocations button, click Options | Rebalance Portfolio. The Portfolio Rebalancer window, shown in Figure 11-6, appears. It provides instructions and shows you how much you must adjust each asset class to meet your targeted goals.

Here's an example. Figure 11-6 indicates that $3,691 less needs to be invested in domestic bonds and $2,619 more invested in global bonds to meet the target asset allocation. If $3,000 of the domestic bond investments were sold and reinvested in global bonds, the asset allocation would be closer to target, without changing the total value of the portfolio. Click Close to return to the Investing tab.

Understanding Your Portfolio Analyzer

Quicken's Portfolio Analyzer enables you to look at your portfolio in a number of ways. To display it, first turn on Classic menus by clicking View | Classic Menus. From the Classic menu, click Investing | Investing Tools | Portfolio Analyzer. You'll find these options on the left sidebar:

- **Performance** shows your portfolio's average annual rate of return. It also shows your five best and worst performers, so you can see how individual securities are doing.
- **Holdings** lists your investment accounts and then shows a pie chart of your top 10 holdings. Because most experts recommend that no single security take up more than 10 percent of your portfolio, you may find the percentage distribution helpful when considering diversification.
- **Asset Allocation** displays your current actual and target asset allocation so you can see how close you are to your target. How to set up a target allocation was explained earlier in this chapter.

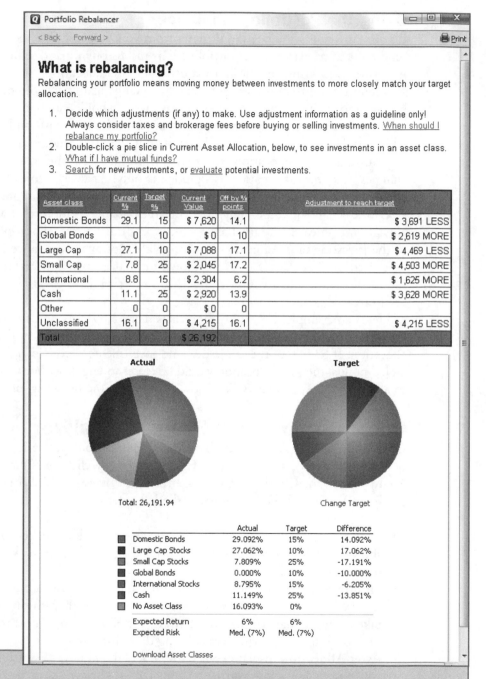

Figure 11-6 • The Portfolio Rebalancer window tells you what adjustments you need to make to bring your asset allocation closer to target.

- **Risk Profile** shows how "risky" your portfolio is when compared to the risk associated with specific classes of investments.
- **Tax Implications** summarizes your realized and unrealized year-to-date (YTD) capital gains or losses. Capital gains and losses are broken down into two categories: short term and long term. For additional information about tax implications, consult your tax professional.

What's great about the Portfolio Analyzer is that it provides tables and charts to show information about your portfolio, and then it explains everything in plain English so you know what the tables and charts mean. Using this feature regularly can really help you learn about the world of investing and how your portfolio measures up. To give it a try, choose Investing | Investing Tools | Portfolio Analyzer from the Classic menu. When you have finished reviewing the information, click Close to return to the Investing tab.

Previewing Your Buy/Sell Decisions

Quicken Premier includes a feature called Buy/Sell Preview, which offers a quick and easy way to see the impact of a securities purchase or sale on your finances—including your taxes.

From the Investing tab, choose Tools | Buy/Sell Preview. In the top half of the Buy/Sell Preview window that appears, enter information about the proposed purchase or sale. Quicken automatically enters the most recent price information for a security you own or watch, but you can override that amount if necessary. When you're finished setting options, click Calculate. Quicken displays its results in the bottom half of the window. On page 352 are two examples—one for a purchase and the other for a sale.

The Buy/Sell Preview feature works with Quicken's Tax Planner, which is discussed in Chapter 18, to calculate the net effect of a sale on your expected tax bill or refund. Check with your tax professional for additional information. Click Close to return to the Investing tab.

Estimating Capital Gains

Quicken's Capital Gains Estimator enables you to estimate capital gains or losses and their related tax implications *before* you sell a security. The information it provides can help you make an informed decision about which security to sell.

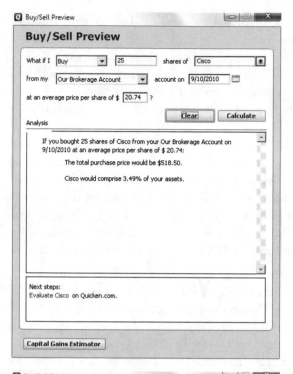

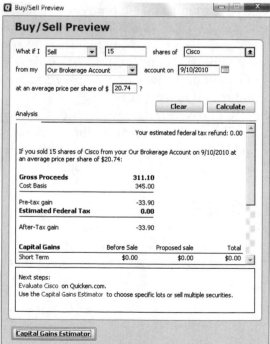

Getting Started

Choose the Investing tab and click Tools | Capital Gains Estimator. The Capital Gains Estimator's welcome window appears. If you have used the tool before, you may see an info message about previous proposed sales holdings changes.

Start by reading the information in the right side of the window. It explains what the Capital Gains Estimator does and offers links for learning more about specific terms and topics. Then click each of the links in the left side of the window, in turn, to step through the process of setting up the Capital Gains Estimator for your situation. You'll be prompted to name and choose a scenario, select taxable investment accounts to include, set your tax rate, and enter capital loss carryover information. When you enter complete and accurate information, Quicken can provide a more accurate indication of tax impacts.

Deciding What to Sell

Quicken Premier users can tap into a feature in the Capital Gains Estimator that enables Quicken to help you decide which securities to sell. Follow instructions in the What Should I Sell? screen to tell Quicken your goals for the sale, and click the Search button at the bottom of the window.

A dialog appears while Quicken makes complex calculations to meet your goals. When it's finished, you can click the View Results button in the dialog to display a scenario with Quicken's recommendation and the results (see Figure 11-7).

Manually Adding Proposed Sales

If you prefer, you can manually indicate proposed sales in the Scenario window (refer to Figure 11-7). The Step 1 area shows all the securities you hold in the accounts you selected during the setup process. You can add a proposed sale in two ways:

- Click the name of the security you want to sell. Then enter the number of shares and sales price in the Add To Scenario dialog that appears and click OK. If you have multiple purchase lots for the security, this automatically sells the oldest lots first.
- If necessary, click the plus sign (+) to the left of the security that you want to sell to display the purchase lots. Then click the lot you want to sell. This enables you to specify exactly which lots are to be sold in the Proposed Sales area.

No matter which method you use, the sale is added to the Step 2 area of the window, which lists all of the proposed sales (see Figure 11-7).

To adjust the number of shares to be sold, click in the Shares To Sell field for the proposed sale (in the Step 2 area) and enter a new value. The value you enter must be less than or equal to the number of shares purchased in that lot.

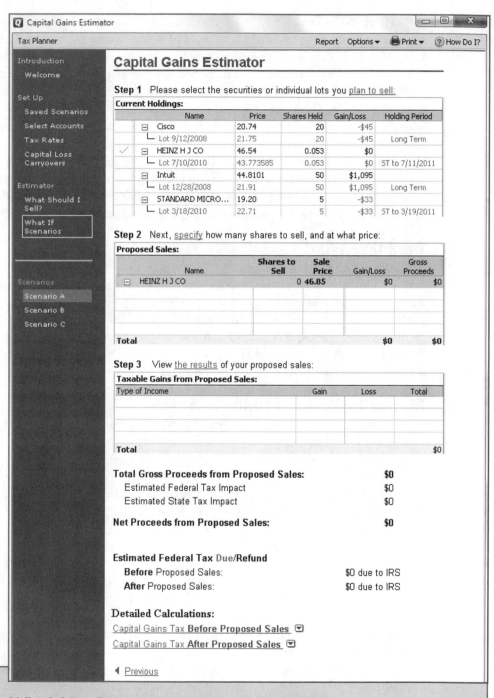

Figure 11-7 • Quicken displays its recommendations as a scenario.

You can set up proposed sales for up to three scenarios—just click the Scenario link on the left side of the window to see and set that scenario's options. You can mix and match any sales you like to reach your goal.

Reading the Results

When all information has been entered, you can see the true power of the Capital Gains Estimator. It tells you about the proceeds from the sales, as well as the gain or loss. If you scroll down in the What If Scenarios screen (refer to Figure 11-7), you'll find more information about the proposed sale and its tax implications in the Step 3 area, including the gross profit and net proceeds from proposed sales. You can click links to view the results of additional calculations, such as the tax situation before and after executing the proposed sales and gain or loss on the proposed sales. Do the same for each scenario to see how they compare—then make your selling decision. Click Close to return to the Investing tab.

Working with Investment Alerts

Investment alerts are downloaded automatically with quotes and news headlines, as discussed in Chapter 10. They appear in the Show All tab of the Alerts Center. There are 10 investment alerts:

- **Price And Volume** consists of three alerts. Price alerts notify you when a security's price rises above or falls below values you specify. Volume alerts notify you when the sales volume of a security exceeds a value you specify. News alerts give you the latest information about your securities, such as earnings announcements or analyst actions. The options for these are set on Quicken.com. Just click the link in the Preferences dialog and your Internet connection opens to http://investing.quicken.com/alerts.
- **Download Quotes Reminder** reminds you to download quotes from Quicken.com.
- **Maturity Date Reminder** reminds you when a CD or bond reaches its maturity date.
- **Stocks Ratings And Analysis** notifies you when ratings and analysis information becomes available for stocks you track.
- **Mutual Funds Ratings And Analysis** notifies you when ratings and analysis information becomes available for mutual funds you track.
- **Tax Implications On Sale** notifies you of your tax implications when you sell a security.
- **Cap. Gains For The Year** notifies you if you exceed your capital gains limit for the year.

- **Tax Efficient Investments** provides you with information about investments that are more tax-efficient than those you already have.
- **Mutual Fund Distributions** provides you with information about mutual fund distributions.
- **Securities Holding Period** provides you with information about holding periods for securities you own.

Many Quicken users report the most useful alerts are Price And Volume, Maturity Date Reminder, Stocks Ratings And Analysis, and Cap. Gains For The Year. These alerts give timely information without information overload.

Setting Up Alerts   To set up investment alerts, click Tools | Alerts Center | Setup. Quicken displays the Setup tab of the Alerts Center window, shown next, which Chapter 8 discusses in greater detail. On the left side of the window, click the name of an alert you want to set, and then set options for the alert in the right side of the window. (You must set some alerts, such as the Price And Volume alert, on Quicken.com.) You can disable an alert by removing the check mark beside its name. When you are finished making changes, click OK to save them.

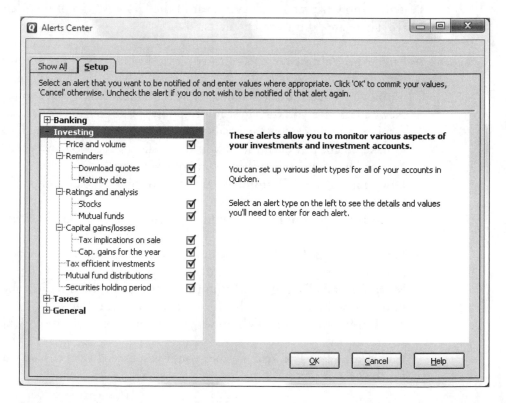

Deleting Alerts   To remove an alert, select Tools | Alerts Center, and click the Show All tab, as shown next. Then check the alerts you wish to delete and click Delete. A warning message appears telling you the alert will be deleted. Click OK to confirm your deletion, If you want the alert to continue, click Cancel. Either choice returns you to the Show All tab of the Alerts Center.

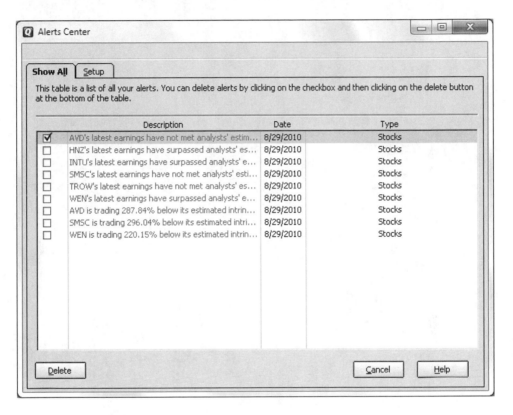

Net Worth

This part of the book explains how you can use Quicken Personal Finance Software's Property & Debt features to keep track of your property and loans. It starts by covering assets, such as a car and home, and the loans that you may have used to finance them. Then it moves on to tell you how you can use the Property & Debt tab and other Quicken features to monitor expenses related to your assets and debt. This part of the book has two chapters:

Chapter 12:   *Monitoring Assets and Loans*

Chapter 13:   *Keeping Tabs on Your Net Worth*

Monitoring Assets and Loans

In This Chapter:

- *Assets and debts defined*
- *Loan basics*
- *Setting up asset and loan accounts*
- *Tracking a loan*
- *Adjusting asset values*

Assets and debts (or liabilities) make up your net worth. Bank and investment accounts, which are covered in Chapters 4 and 9, are examples of assets. Credit card accounts, which are covered in Chapter 4, are examples of debts. But you may want to use Quicken Personal Finance Software to track other assets and debts, including a home, car, recreational vehicle, and related loans. By including these items in your Quicken data file, you can quickly and accurately calculate your net worth and financial fitness.

This chapter explains how to set up asset and debt accounts to track your possessions and any outstanding loans you used to purchase them.

The Basics

Before you begin, it's a good idea to have a clear understanding of what assets, debts, and loans are, and how they work together in your Quicken data file.

Assets and Debts

An asset is something you own. Common examples might be your house, car, camper, computer, television set, and patio furniture. Most assets have value—you can sell them for cash or trade them for another asset.

Although you can use Quicken to track every single asset you own in its own asset account, doing so would be cumbersome. Instead, you'll normally monitor high-value assets in individual accounts and lower-value assets in a group asset account. For example, you may create separate asset accounts for your home and your car, but group personal possessions, such as your computer, television, and stamp collection, in a single group asset account. This makes it easy to track all your assets, so you have accurate records for insurance and other purposes.

A *debt* is something you owe—often to buy one of your assets! For example, if you buy a house, chances are you'll use a mortgage to finance it. The mortgage, which is a loan that is secured by your home, is a debt. You can use Quicken to track all of your debts so you know exactly how much you owe at any given time.

Loans

A *loan* is a promise to pay money. Loans are commonly used to buy assets, although some folks often turn to debt consolidation loans to pay off other debts—this is discussed further in Chapter 16.

Here's how it works. The lender gives the borrower money in exchange for the borrower's promise to pay it back. (The promise is usually in writing, with lots of signatures and initials.) The borrower normally pays back the loan to the lender with periodic payments that include interest on the loan balance, or *principal.* The amount of the loan is reduced after each payment. The borrower incurs interest expense while the lender earns interest income.

While most people think of a loan as something you owe (a debt), a loan can also be something you own (an asset). For example, say you borrow money from your brother to buy a car. In your Quicken data file, the loan is related to a debt—money that you owe your brother. In your brother's Quicken data file, the loan is related to an asset—money that is due to him from you.

Types of Loans

There are several types of loans, some of which are designed for specific purposes. Here's a quick summary of some of what's available, along with their pros and cons.

This list is not exhaustive. Financial institutions are always coming up with new loan products, and it's impossible to keep up with them here. If you're interested in a loan product that isn't mentioned in this chapter, consult the financial institution that is offering it to learn more about how it works and what it can do for you.

Mortgage

A *mortgage* is a long-term loan secured by real estate. Most mortgages require a down payment on the property of 10 percent or higher. Monthly payments are based on the term of the loan and the interest rate applied to the principal. The interest you pay on a mortgage for a first or second home is tax-deductible. If you fail to make mortgage payments, your house could be sold to pay back the mortgage.

A *balloon mortgage* is a special type of short-term mortgage. Rather than make monthly payments over the full typical mortgage term, at the end of the fifth, seventh, or tenth year, you pay the balance of the mortgage in one big "balloon" payment. Some balloon mortgages offer the option of refinancing when the balloon payment is due.

Home Equity Loans or Lines of Credit

A *home equity loan* or *second mortgage* is a line of credit secured by the equity in your home—the difference between the home's market value and the amount of outstanding debt. Your equity rises when you make mortgage payments or property values increase. It declines when you borrow against your equity or property values decrease. A home equity loan lets you borrow against this equity.

A home equity loan has two benefits: Interest rates are sometimes lower than other credit, and interest may be tax-deductible. For these reasons, many people use home equity loans to pay off credit card debt; renovate their homes; or buy cars, boats, or other recreational vehicles. But, as with a mortgage, if you fail to make your home equity payments, your house could be sold to satisfy the debt.

Reverse Equity Loans

A *reverse equity loan* (sometimes called a *reverse mortgage*), provides people who own their homes in full with a regular monthly income. Instead of you paying the lender, the lender pays you. This type of loan is attractive to retirees who live on a fixed income. The loan is paid back when the home is sold—often after the death of the homeowner.

Auto Loans

An *auto loan* is a loan secured by a vehicle, such as a car, truck, or motor home. Normally, you make a down payment and use the loan to pay the balance of the vehicle's purchase price. Monthly payments are based on the term of the loan and the interest rate applied to the principal. Interest on car loans is not tax-deductible.

Personal Loans

A *personal loan* is an unsecured loan—a loan that requires no collateral. Monthly payments are based on the term of the loan and the interest rate applied to the principal. You can use a personal loan for just about anything. Some people use them to pay off multiple smaller debts so they have only one monthly payment. Interest on personal loans is not tax-deductible.

Loan Considerations

When applying for a loan, a number of variables have a direct impact on what the loan costs you, now and in the future. Ask about all of these things *before* applying for any loan.

Interest Rate

The *interest rate* is the annual percentage applied to the loan principal. Several factors affect the interest rate you may be offered.

- **Your credit record** affects the interest rate offered, because a borrower with a good credit record can usually get a better rate than one with a bad credit record. Of course, if your credit record is really bad, you might not be able to borrow money at any rate.
- **The type of loan** affects the interest rate offered because, generally speaking, personal loans have the highest interest rates, whereas mortgages have the lowest. From highest to lowest between these two types are a used car loan, a new car loan, and a home equity reserve or line of credit.
- **The loan term** affects the interest rate offered, because the length of a loan can vary the interest within a specific loan type. For example, for car loans, the longer the term, the lower the rate.
- **The amount of the down payment** affects the interest rate offered, because the more money you put down on the purchase, the lower the rate may be.
- **Your location** affects the interest rate offered, because rates vary from one area of the country to another.
- **The lender** affects the interest rate offered, because rates also vary from one lender to another. Certain types of lenders have lower rates than others.

Two kinds of interest rates can apply to a loan.

- **Fixed rate** applies the same rate to the principal throughout the loan term.
- **Variable rate** applies a different rate to the loan throughout the loan term. For example, the loan may start with one rate and, each year, switch to a different rate. The rate is usually established by adding a certain number of

percentage points to a national index, such as Treasury bill rates. A cap limits the amount the rate can change. Mortgages with this type of rate are referred to as *adjustable rate mortgages*, or *ARMs*.

Although ARMs usually offer a lower initial interest rate than fixed-rate mortgages, you should consider the overall economic conditions before deciding on one. For example, for a couple who purchased their first home in the mid-1980s when interest rates were high, they might have selected an ARM. When interest rates dropped, so did the rate on the mortgage. If they had selected a fixed-rate mortgage when they bought that home, they would have had to refinance to get the same savings. Rates were much lower in the late 1990s, so a fixed rate protected buyers from possible rate increases in the future.

You can use Quicken's Refinance Calculator to determine whether it's worthwhile to refinance your home. Quicken's calculators are discussed in Chapter 15.

Term

A loan's *term* is the period of time between the loan date and when the date payment is due in full. Loan terms vary depending on the type of loan.

- Mortgage loan and home equity reserve loan terms are typically 10, 15, 20, or 30 years.
- Balloon mortgage loan terms are typically 5, 7, or 10 years.
- Vehicle loan terms vary from 3 to 7 years.

Down Payment

A *down payment* is an up-front payment toward the purchase of a home or car. Most mortgages require at least 10 percent down; 20 percent is preferred.

Keep in mind that if you make only a 10 percent down payment on a home, you may be required to pay for the cost of private mortgage insurance (PMI). This protects the lender from loss if you fail to pay your mortgage, but it increases your monthly mortgage payments.

Application Fees

Most lenders require you to pay an application fee to process your loan application. This usually includes the cost of obtaining a property appraisal and credit report. These fees are usually not refundable—even if you are turned down.

Mortgage Closing Costs

In addition to the application fee and down payment, many other costs are involved in securing a mortgage and purchasing a home. These are known as *closing costs*. The Real Estate Settlement Procedures Act of 1974 requires that your lender provide a good faith estimate of closing costs. This document summarizes all of the costs of closing on a home based on the mortgage the lender is offering.

Here's a brief list of the types of costs you may encounter. Because they vary from lender to lender, they could be a deciding factor when shopping for a mortgage. Note that most of these fees are not negotiable.

- **Origination fee** covers the administrative costs of processing a loan.
- **Discount or "points"** is a fee based on a percentage rate applied to the loan amount. For example, 1 point on a $250,000 mortgage is $2,500.
- **Appraisal fee** covers the cost of a market-value appraisal of the property by a licensed, certified appraiser.
- **Credit report fee** covers the cost of obtaining a credit history of the prospective borrower(s) to determine creditworthiness.
- **Underwriting fee** covers the cost of underwriting the loan. This is the process of determining loan risks and establishing terms and conditions.
- **Document preparation fee** covers the cost of preparing legal and other documents required to process the loan.
- **Title insurance fee** covers the cost of title insurance, which protects the lender and buyer against loss due to disputes over ownership and possession of the property.
- **Recording fee** covers the cost of entering the sale of a property into public records.
- **Prepaid items** are taxes, insurance, and assessments paid in advance of their due dates. These expenses are not paid to the lender but are due at the closing date.

Tips for Minimizing Loan Expenses

Borrowing money costs money. It's as simple as that. But you can do some things to minimize the cost of a loan.

Shop for the Lowest Rate   This may seem like a no-brainer, but a surprising number of people simply go to a local bank and accept whatever terms they are offered. You don't have to use a local bank to borrow money for a home, car, or other major purchase. Check the financial pages of your local newspaper or go online to research what terms are available. And if you're shopping for a car, keep an eye out for low-interest financing deals. Sometimes, you can save a lot of money in interest by buying when the time is right. For example, suppose you have a choice of two five-year car loans for $20,000—one at 7 percent and the other at 7.75 percent. Over the course of five years, you'll pay $1,003 less if you go with the lower rate. That can buy a lot of gas—even at today's fuel prices.

Minimize the Loan Term   The shorter the loan term, the less interest you'll pay over the life of the loan. The savings can be quite substantial. For example, suppose you have a choice between two loan terms for a $200,000, 6.5 percent mortgage: 15 years or 30 years. If you choose the 15-year mortgage, you'll pay $113,599 in interest, but if you choose the 30-year mortgage, you'll pay a whopping $255,089 in interest—nearly $142,000 more! Neither option is appealing, but the shorter-term mortgage is certainly easier to swallow. The drawback? The monthly payment for the 15-year mortgage is $1,742, while the payment for the 30-year mortgage is just $1,264. Obviously, your monthly spending budget will weigh heavily into the decision.

Maximize the Down Payment   The less you borrow, the less you'll pay in interest—and the less your monthly payments will be. Take the loan term example just shown. Suppose your budget won't allow you to go with the shorter-term loan—you just can't make those monthly payments. But if you cashed in an individual retirement account (IRA) worth $30,000 and put that toward the down payment (talk to your tax advisor; you may be able to do this without penalty for the purchase of a first home), you could knock $261 per month off the 15-year loan's monthly payment, which might be enough to fit it into your budget—and save another $17,040 in interest!

Make Extra Loan Payments   If you can't go for a shorter-term loan, consider making extra payments toward the loan's principal. Take another look at the 30-year mortgage example just shown. If you pay an additional $100 per month (increasing your monthly payment to $1,364), you can save more than $55,950 in interest and pay off the loan almost six years early! Or perhaps you get a generous holiday bonus each year. If you put $1,000 of that bonus toward the mortgage each January as an extra payment, you can save $46,760 in interest and pay off the loan more than four years early!

Clean Up Your Credit Before Applying for a Loan   Loan terms vary based on credit history. To get the best deal, your credit should be as clean as possible. If you think there might be problems in your credit report, get a copy—you can learn how by choosing the More From Quicken tab and clicking Credit Score at the bottom of the page. Then do what you need to get things cleaned up, but be wary of services that promise to do this for you. Some may not help you.

When evaluating the dollar impact of different loan deals, use Quicken's Loan Calculator. It'll make complex loan payment calculations for you. Chapter 15 explains how to use Quicken's financial calculators, including the Loan Calculator and Refinance Calculator.

Setting Up Accounts

To track an asset or debt with Quicken, you must set up an appropriate account. All transactions related to the asset or debt will be recorded in the account's register.

In this section, you'll read about the types of accounts you can use to track your assets and debts, and how to set up each type of account.

Choosing the Right Account

Quicken offers the following Property & Debt account types for tracking assets and debts:

- **House** A house account is used for recording the value of a house, condominium, or other real estate. When you create a house account, Quicken asks whether there is a mortgage on the property. If so, you can have Quicken create a related debt account for you or associate the house account with an existing debt account. This makes it possible to set up both your house asset account and mortgage debt account at the same time.
- **Vehicle** A vehicle account is similar to a house account, but it's designed for vehicles, including cars, trucks, and recreational vehicles. Quicken asks if there is a loan on the vehicle; if so, it can create a related debt account or link to an existing debt account.
- **Other Asset** An asset account is for recording the value of other assets, such as personal property. For example, a Quicken data file might include asset accounts for horses and related equipment, art and antiques, or personal possessions.
- **Loan** A loan account is for recording money you owe to others. As mentioned earlier, when you create a house or vehicle account, Quicken can automatically create a corresponding loan account for you.
- **Other Liability (not a credit card)** You can create a debt account to record other debts that are not related to the purchase of a specific asset. Debt accounts are shown in the Account List as liabilities.

Creating Asset and Debt Accounts

You create asset and debt accounts with the Account Setup dialog, which walks you through the process of creating the account. Quicken offers a number of ways to open this dialog for an asset or debt account. The most straightforward way to open it for any type of account is to click Add An Account in the Account Bar, and then click what you want to add: either an asset, such as a house or vehicle, or a loan or other debt. Figure 12-1 shows what the initial dialog looks like. If you have not downloaded yet today, when you first open the Add Account dialog, Quicken downloads the latest list of financial institutions.

 A loan is actually a debt account that has special Quicken features attached to it. Use this option to set up a debt associated with a compounding interest loan, like a mortgage or standard car loan, which is explained later in this chapter.

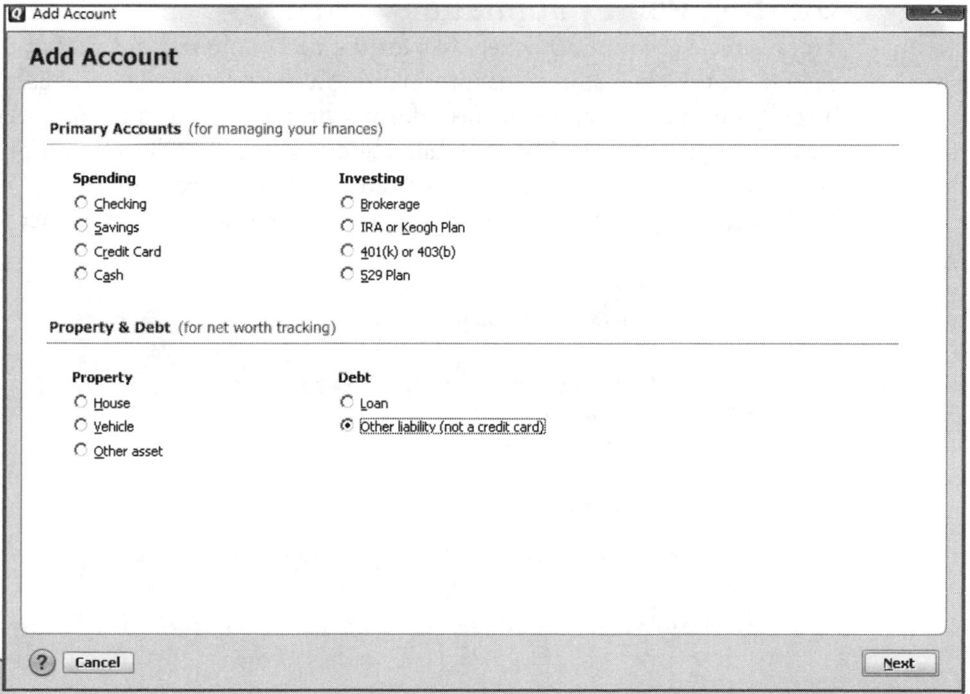

Add Account

Add Account

Primary Accounts (for managing your finances)

Spending
- ○ Checking
- ○ Savings
- ○ Credit Card
- ○ Cash

Investing
- ○ Brokerage
- ○ IRA or Keogh Plan
- ○ 401(k) or 403(b)
- ○ 529 Plan

Property & Debt (for net worth tracking)

Property
- ○ House
- ○ Vehicle
- ○ Other asset

Debt
- ○ Loan
- ● Other liability (not a credit card)

(?) Cancel   Next

Figure 12-1 • The Add Account dialog helps you set up asset and debt accounts.

Chapter 2 explains how to use the Quicken Account Setup dialog to create new Quicken banking accounts. This section provides information about the kinds of data you'll have to enter to create asset and debt accounts.

Account Type

The Add Account Setup dialog displays a list of asset types: House, Vehicle, or Other. You can see this in Figure 12-1.

Account Name

Give the account a name that clearly identifies the asset or debt. For example, if you have two cars and plan to track them in separate asset accounts, consider naming the account with the make and model of the car. *Ford Pickup* and *Chevy Volt* do a better job identifying the cars than *Car 1* and *Car 2*. When creating a debt account, you may want to include the word *mortgage, loan,* or *payable* in the account name so you don't confuse it with a related asset.

Starting Point Information

For a vehicle account, Quicken asks for the make, model, and year of the car, as seen here. Quicken stores this information in the Account Details dialog for the asset. (You can view and edit this information after the account has been created by opening the Property & Debt tab, choosing Account Overview, right-clicking the account, and clicking Edit This Account. Alternatively, right-click the account in the Property & Debt section of the Account Bar and click Edit Account.)

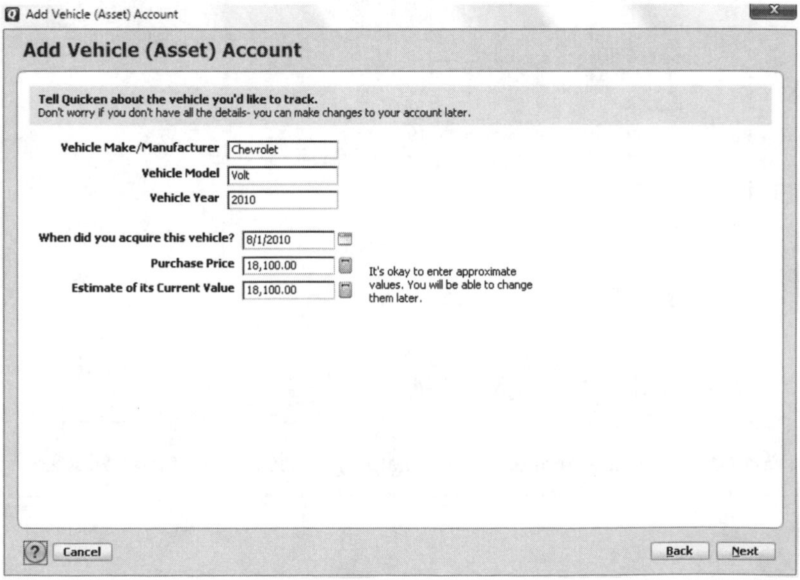

For house and vehicle accounts, Quicken prompts you to enter information about the asset's purchase, including the acquisition date and purchase price. You can find this information on your original purchase receipts. Quicken also asks for an estimate of the current value. For a house, this number will (hopefully) be higher than the purchase price; for a car, this number will probably be lower. This is the amount that will appear as the asset account balance. For other assets and debts, Quicken prompts you for a statement date and balance. If you don't know how much to enter now, you can leave it set to zero and enter a value when you know what to enter. You will see how to adjust asset values later in this chapter.

Optional Tax Information

For other asset and debt accounts, you can click the Tax Schedule button on the Account Details dialog to enter tax schedule information for transfers in and out of the account. This is completely optional and, in most cases, unnecessary. Chapter 17 explains how to set up Quicken accounts and categories to simplify tax preparation.

Related Mortgage or Loan

When creating a house or vehicle account, Quicken asks whether there is a related mortgage or loan. You have four options, as shown here:

- **Yes. I'd Like To Track This Mortgage/Loan In Quicken. Set Up A New Account For This** This option tells Quicken that there is a related loan and that Quicken should create a debt account.
- **Yes. I'm Already Tracking The Mortgage/Loan In Quicken** This option enables you to select an existing debt account to link to the asset.
- **Yes. I Do Not Want To Track the Mortgage/Loan In Quicken** This option tells Quicken that there is a loan but you don't want to include it in your Quicken data file.
- **No** This option tells Quicken that there is no loan, so no debt account is necessary. (Lucky you!)

As you've probably guessed or noticed, the use of the word *mortgage* or *loan* in this dialog depends on whether you're creating a house or vehicle asset account. To select any of the Yes options, you must select the first Yes option and then choose one of the options beneath it. Otherwise, choose the No option.

Loan Information

If you indicated that Quicken should track a loan for a house or vehicle, it automatically displays the Loan Setup dialog, which you can use to enter information about the loan. If you set up a debt account, Quicken asks if you want to set up an amortized loan to be associated with the debt. See how to set up a loan later in this chapter, in the section "Setting Up a Loan."

The Account Register

When you're finished setting up an asset or debt account (and related loans and loan payments, if applicable), Quicken automatically displays the account's register. Figure 12-2, shown later in the chapter in the section "Recording Other Asset Transactions," shows what a house account might look like. The first transaction, dated 4/27/2004, shows the opening balance, which was the amount paid for the house. The next transaction, dated 1/1/2006, shows an adjustment automatically made by Quicken to increase the account's balance based on an estimate of its worth on the day the account was created.

All transactions that affect an asset or debt account's balance appear in the account register. Learn more about using account registers for asset and debt accounts later in this chapter, in the section "Recording Other Asset Transactions."

Tracking a Loan

Quicken makes it easy to track the principal, interest, and payments for a loan. Once you set up a loan and corresponding debt or asset accounts, you can make payments with Quicken using QuickFill and Scheduled Transactions (see Chapter 6) or Online Payments (see Chapter 5). The Loan feature keeps track of all the details, so you don't have to.

Before you see how to use the Loan feature, let's make something clear: A loan is not the same as an asset or debt account. A loan in Quicken is information that Quicken uses to calculate the amount of interest and principal due for each payment of an amortized loan, such as a mortgage or car loan. A loan must be associated with an asset account (if you are a lender) or a debt account (if you are a borrower), as well as an income or expense category to record interest income or expense. Loan transactions are recorded in the associated asset or debt account—not in Quicken's loan records. It's possible to delete a loan without losing any transaction data, as explained later in this section. But you can't delete an asset or debt account that has a loan associated with it unless the loan is deleted first.

Setting Up a Loan

You can set up a loan in the following ways:

- Create a house, vehicle, or debt account with a related mortgage or loan, as discussed earlier in this chapter. Quicken automatically prompts you for loan information.
- From the Account Bar, click Add An Account and choose Loan in the Property & Debt | Debt section.

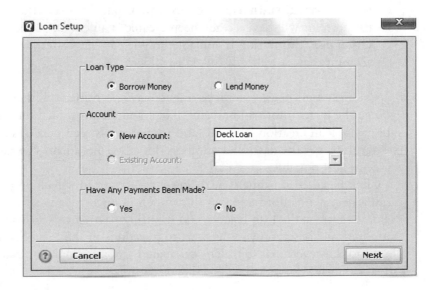

- From the Property & Debt tab, click Debt | Loan And Debt Options | Add A New Loan.
- Also from the Property & Debt tab, click Account Overview and, in the Loan Summary section, click Options and then Add A New Loan.

Quicken displays the Loan Setup dialog seen here. It doesn't matter what the loan is for; the information you need to enter is basically the same. Here's what you can expect.

Loan Account   The Loan Setup dialog starts by prompting you for a loan type. You have the following options:

- **Borrow Money** is for loans for which you're borrowing money from a lender, such as a car loan, mortgage, or personal loan. Quicken uses a debt account to record the loan.
- **Lend Money** is for loans for which you're the lender. Quicken uses an asset account to record the money owed from the borrower.

The Loan Setup dialog next prompts you to enter the account for the loan. Again, you have two options.

- **New Account** enables you to set up a brand-new account for the loan. Be sure to enter a name for the account.
- **Existing Account** enables you to select one of your existing debt accounts for the loan. If you're creating this loan as part of an asset creation process, the account will have already been created, named, and selected for you. Otherwise, this option is available only if you have already created a debt account that isn't already linked to a loan.

The next section asks you if payments have been made. Either option takes you to the Loan Information dialog. Here you are prompted for information about the loan creation, amount, and payments, as seen next. It's important to be accurate; get the dates and numbers directly from a loan statement or agreement if possible.

Click Next to continue. The dialog then asks you for balloon payment and regular payment information, as shown here. Quicken can calculate some of the values—such as the loan balance and monthly payments—for you. It does this automatically based on your answers to questions in the Loan Setup dialog. Keep in mind, however, that Quicken's calculated amounts may not exactly match those calculated by your bank or finance company.

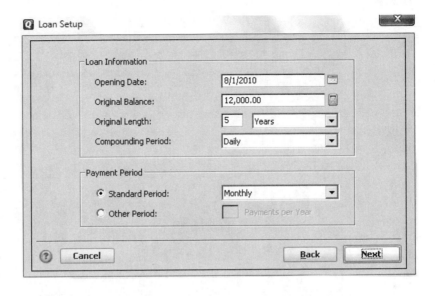

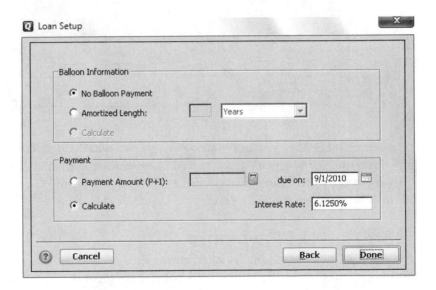

If you selected Calculate in the final Loan Setup dialog, click Done to have Quicken estimate the amount of your loan payment, as shown next. Click OK and you are returned to the Loan Setup dialog with the estimated payment amount and due date (based on the interest rate you entered) displayed, as shown on the next page. Click Done. The Set Up Loan Payment dialog appears, as discussed in the next section.

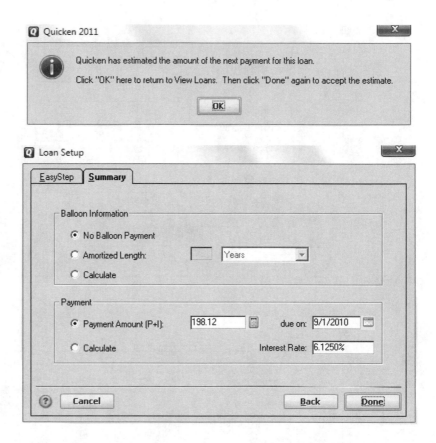

Remember, this may not match exactly with what your financial institution shows on the paperwork you received. Always use the financial institution's paperwork to enter information rather than relying on the Quicken calculations to ensure the amounts are exactly the same.

Setting Up Payments

When you set up a loan, Quicken automatically prompts you to set up payment information by displaying the Set Up Loan Payment dialog, which is shown at the top of the next page.

If you see this dialog after using the Loan Set Up dialog, the interest rate, principal and interest payment amount, payment type, next payment date, and interest category will be filled in for you. Otherwise, enter information in this dialog to set up the payment. If the total payment should include additional amounts for property taxes, insurance, or other escrow items, click the Edit

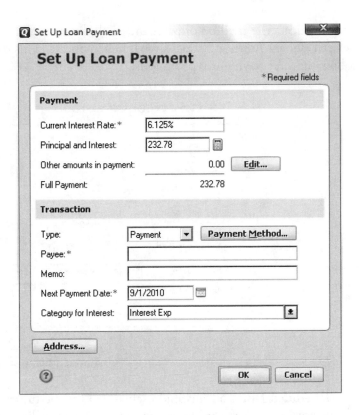

button. This displays the Split Transaction window, which you can use to enter categories, tags, memos, and amounts to be added to the payment.

In the Transaction area of the dialog, you can specify the type and method for the transaction. For type, three options appear on the drop-down list.

- **Payment** is a transaction recorded in your account register only. You must manually write and mail a check for payment. This is covered in Chapter 4.
- **Print Check** is a transaction recorded in the Write Checks dialog and account register. You can use the Print Check command to print the check, and then you can mail it for payment. This is also covered in Chapter 4.
- **Online Pmt** creates a payment instruction to be processed by your financial institution for use with online payment. This is covered in Chapter 5. This option appears only if at least one of your bank accounts is enabled for Quicken's Online Payment feature.

To indicate the method of payment, click the Payment Method button. The Select Payment Method dialog, shown here, appears. This dialog offers the following three payment type options:

- **Scheduled Bill** is a transaction scheduled for the future. If you select this option, you must also choose options and enter values to specify how Quicken should enter the transaction, which account should be used to pay, and how many days in advance it should be entered and paid. All this is covered in Chapter 6.
- **Memorized Payee** is a transaction memorized for use with QuickFill or Quicken's Calendar. This is also covered in Chapter 6.
- **Repeating Online Payment** is a recurring online payment instruction processed by your financial institution. If you select this option, you must also select a repeating online payment transaction from a drop-down list. If you have not already created a transaction to link to this loan payment, select one of the other options and return to this dialog after you have created the required transaction. Consult Chapter 5 for complete instructions.
    - **Register Entry** is available only if you have selected Scheduled Bill in the top section of the dialog. You have two choices.
        - **Prompt Before Entering** tells Quicken to remind you before actually entering this scheduled transaction into the appropriate account register.

- **Automatically Enter** tells Quicken to enter this transaction each time it becomes due without asking you.
- **Account To Pay From** lets you select the appropriate account from which this payment will be made.
- **Days In Advance** tells Quicken how many days before the due date to prompt you or to enter the transaction. The default is three days.

Click **OK** to return to the Set Up Loan Payment dialog.

- **Payee** is a required field into which you must enter the name of the entity to whom you will be making the payments.
- **Memo** is an optional field where you can enter additional information. Many users choose to put their payee's assigned account number in this field. However, if you print checks from Quicken and use window envelopes to mail your bills, make sure the account number does not show through the window.
- **Next Payment Date** is filled in automatically if you've used the Loan Setup dialog. Otherwise, enter the date the next payment is due.
- **Category For Interest** is filled in automatically from the Loan Setup dialog if you've used it. Otherwise, enter the category you wish to use for the interest portion of each payment.
- **Address** can be used if your payment type is "Print Check" or "Online Payment." Clicking the Address button opens the Address Book so you can enter the mailing information for this payee. See Chapter 6 for more information about the Address Book.

Creating an Associated Asset Account

At the conclusion of the payment setup process, Quicken may display a dialog asking if you want to create an asset to go with the loan, as shown here. This enables you to set up an asset account for the full purchase price of the item you used the loan to buy. Click Yes to create a new account; click No if you have already created one. See the section titled "Creating Asset and Debt Accounts" earlier in this chapter.

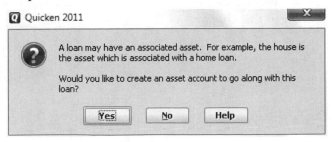

Reviewing Loan Information

All loans are associated with asset and/or debt accounts. However, you can use the View Loans dialog to edit information about your loans, as shown next. You can open this window from any part of Quicken by pressing CTRL-SHIFT-H.

You can also open the View Loans dialog from the Account Bar by clicking the loan account to open the register for the loan. Then click Account Actions | Loan Details.

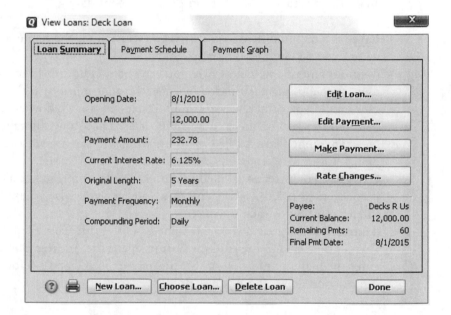

Button Bar Options

Most of Quicken's button bars are at the top of a dialog or window. In this case, there are several buttons at the bottom of the View Loans dialog offering options for working with loans.

- **New Loan** enables you to create a new loan. This option was explained earlier in this chapter.

- **Choose Loan** displays a menu of your current loans, as seen here. Use it to choose the loan you want to display in the window.
- **Delete Loan** removes the currently displayed loan. If you click this button, a dialog appears, asking if you want to save the associated account for your records. Click Yes to save the principal account information. For example, you might want this information for a net worth report. If you want to delete the entire loan account, click No.

- **Help** opens the Quicken Help dialog with the Managing Loans section displayed.
- **Print** prints a loan payment schedule for the currently displayed loan. The printout includes all of the information in the Payment Schedule tab of the View Loans window, which is shown and discussed next.

Window Tabs

The *tabs* along the top of the window's information area enable you to view various pieces of information about a loan.

Loan Summary   Loan Summary is the tab seen when you first open this dialog. As shown earlier, this tab's view summarizes the loan information.

Payment Schedule   Payment Schedule, shown on the next page, displays a schedule of past and future payments. You can turn on the Show Running Totals check box to display cumulative totals rather than individual payment information.

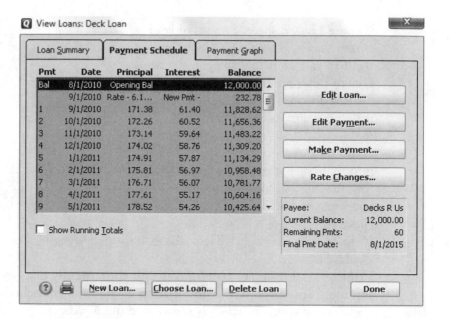

Payment Graph   Payment Graph, shown next, displays a graph of the loan payments. Where the two lines meet indicates the point at which you start paying more toward the loan principal than for interest. If you position your mouse cursor on a graph line, a magnifying glass tool appears displaying the dollar value at that point on the graph.

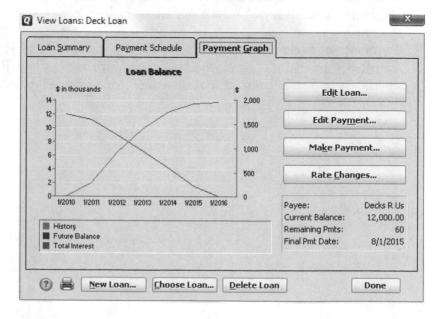

Modifying Loan Information

Once you've created a loan, you can modify it as necessary to record corrections, changes in the interest rate, or changes in payment methods. You can do all these things with buttons in the View Loans window.

Changing Loan Information

If you discover a discrepancy between the loan information in the View Loans window and information on statements or loan agreement papers, you can change the loan information in Quicken.

If necessary, choose the loan account's name from the Choose Loan menu in the button bar to display the information for the loan you want to modify. Then, click the Edit Loan button. A pair of Edit Loan windows enables you to change just about any information for the loan. Modify values and select different options as desired. Click Done in the last window to save your changes. Quicken automatically makes any necessary entries to update the account.

Changing Payment Information

Occasionally, you may want to make changes to a loan's payment information. For example, suppose the real estate taxes on your property are reduced (you can always hope!) and the resulting escrow amount, which is included in the payment, changes. Or suppose you decide to switch your payment method from a scheduled transaction to a repeating online payment.

If necessary, choose the loan account's name from the Choose Loan menu in the button bar to display the information for the loan payment you want to modify. Then click the Edit Payment button. The Edit Loan Payment dialog, shown here, appears. Make changes as desired and click OK. Quicken updates the payment information with your changes.

Changing the Interest Rate

If you have an adjustable rate mortgage, you'll periodically have to adjust the rate for the loan within Quicken to match the rate charged by the lender.

If necessary, choose the loan account's name from the Choose Loan menu in the button bar to display the information for the loan whose rate you want to change. Then click the Rate Changes button. The Loan Rate Changes window appears. It lists all the loan rates throughout the history of the loan.

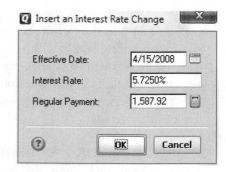

To insert a rate change, click New in the window's button bar. The Insert An Interest Rate Change dialog appears, as shown here.

Enter the effective date and new rate in the appropriate text boxes. Quicken automatically calculates the new loan payment. When you click OK, the rate appears in the Loan Rate Changes window. Click the Close button to dismiss the window. Quicken recalculates the loan payment schedule for you.

Making a Loan Payment

Although it's usually more convenient to set up a loan payment as a scheduled transaction or repeating online payment instruction, as discussed earlier, you can also use the View Loans window to make a loan payment. This method is especially useful for making extra loan payments—payments in addition to your normal periodic payments.

If necessary, choose the loan account's name from the Choose Loan menu in the button bar to display the information for the loan for which you want to make a payment. Then click the Make Payment button. A Loan Payment dialog appears, asking if you are making a regularly scheduled payment or an extra payment. Click the appropriate button.

Making a Regular Loan Payment

If you click Regularly Schedule Loan Payment, the Make Regular Payment dialog, which is shown next, appears. Set options to specify the bank account from which the payment should be made, the type of transaction, the payee information, the date, and a memo for the transaction. If the Type Of Transaction drop-down list is set to Payment, you can enter a check number in the Number box or use one of the options on the Number drop-down list to set a number option. The Category and Amount fields are already set using values calculated by Quicken—you shouldn't have to change them. Click OK to enter the transaction.

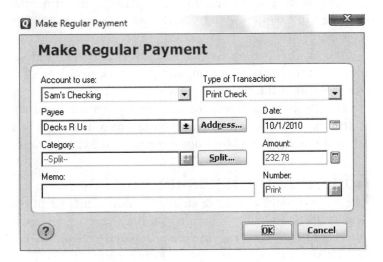

Making an Extra Loan Payment

If you click Extra Loan Payment, the Make Extra Payment dialog appears. As you can see in the following illustration, it's almost identical to the Make Regular Payment dialog, with two differences: The loan account is automatically set as the transfer account in the Category field, and the Amount field is left blank. Set options in the dialog to specify payment information, including the amount. Then click OK to enter the transaction.

Recording Other Asset Transactions

Part of tracking assets is keeping track of their current values and modifying account balances when necessary. Like bank or investment accounts, which are discussed in Chapters 4 and 9, activity for an asset account appears in its account register.

One way to open an asset's register is to click the Property & Debt tab, select the Account Overview button, and then click the name of the asset account from the list in the (Property) Assets account section to open that account's register. Figure 12-2 shows the account register for a house asset account.

In this section, you'll see how you can record changes in asset values due to acquisitions and disposals, improvements, market values, and depreciation.

Adding and Disposing of Assets

The most obvious change in an asset's value occurs when you add or remove all or part of the asset. For example, you may have a single asset account in which you record the value of all of your sports-related equipment. When you buy a new jet ski, it increases the value of the account. Similarly, if you sell one of your snowboards, it decreases the value of the account.

In many instances, when you add or dispose of an asset, money is exchanged. In that case, recording the transaction is easy: Simply use the appropriate bank account register to record the purchase or sale, and use the asset account as a transfer account in the Category field. Here's what the purchase of a new jet ski might look like being paid from the money market account:

7/15/2010	3412	Beaches And More		587	22
		[Sports Equipment]	new jet ski		

And here's the same transaction in the Sports Equipment asset account:

7/15/2010		Beaches And More		587	22
		[Money Market]	new jet ski		

If the asset was acquired without an exchange of cash, you can enter the transaction directly into the asset account using the Gift Received category (or a similar category of your choice) to categorize the income. Similarly, if the asset was disposed of without an exchange of cash, you can enter the transaction into the asset account register using the Gifts Given or Charity (or other appropriate category) to categorize the write-off.

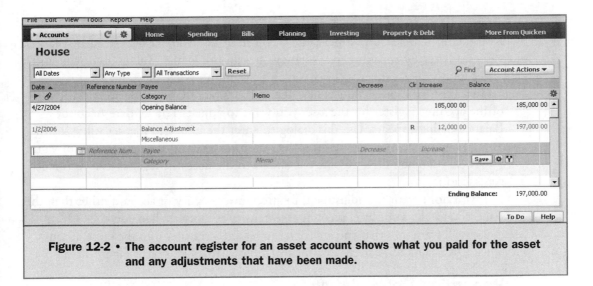

Figure 12-2 • The account register for an asset account shows what you paid for the asset and any adjustments that have been made.

If you have completely disposed of the asset and no longer need the account, don't delete the account! Doing so will remove all income and expense category transactions and uncategorize all transfer transactions related to the account. Instead, consider hiding the account to get it off account lists, as explained in Chapter 2.

Updating Asset Values

A variety of situations can change the value of a single asset. The type of situation will determine how the value is adjusted. Here are three common examples.

Recording Improvements

Certain home-related expenditures can be considered improvements that increase the value of your home. It's important that you keep track of improvements because they raise the property's tax basis, thus reducing the amount of capital gains you may have to record (and pay tax on) when you sell the house. Your tax advisor can help you determine which expenditures can be capitalized as home improvements.

Since most home improvements involve expenditures, use the appropriate cash flow account register to record the transaction. Be sure to enter the appropriate asset account (House, Condo, Land, and so on) as a transfer account in the Category field.

Adjusting for Market Value

Real estate, vehicles, and other large-ticket item assets are also affected by market values. Generally speaking, real estate values go up, vehicle values go down, and other item values can vary either way depending on what they are.

To adjust for market value, click Account Actions | Update Balance at the top of the account register for the asset you want to adjust. The Update Account Balance dialog appears. Use this dialog to enter the date and market value for the asset. Then select a category or transfer account to record the gain or loss of value.

When you click OK, the entry is added to the account register as a reconciled transaction.

If you don't want the adjustment to affect any category or account other than the asset, choose the same asset account as a transfer account. When you click OK, a dialog will warn you that you are trying to record a transfer into the same account. Click OK again. You can see examples of adjustments like this in Figure 12-3.

Recording Depreciation

Depreciation is a calculated reduction in the value of an asset. Depreciation expense can be calculated using a variety of acceptable methods, including straight line, sum of the year's digits, and declining balance. Normally, it reduces the asset's value regularly, with monthly, quarterly, or annual adjustments.

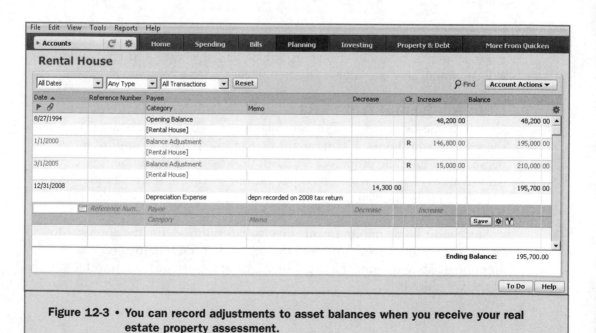

Figure 12-3 • You can record adjustments to asset balances when you receive your real estate property assessment.

Depreciation is commonly applied to property used for business purposes, since depreciation expense on those assets may be tax-deductible. If you think depreciation on an asset you own may be tax-deductible, use Quicken to track the depreciation expense. Otherwise, depreciation probably isn't worth the extra effort it requires to track.

To record depreciation, create an entry in the asset account that reduces the value by the amount of the depreciation. Use a Depreciation Expense category to record the expense. The transaction might look like this in the account's register:

12/31/2008				14,300 00
		Depreciation Expense	depn recorded on 2008 tax return	

Keep in mind that you can set up monthly, quarterly, or annual depreciation transactions as scheduled transactions. This automates the process of recording them when they are due. See more about scheduled transactions in Chapter 6.

Keeping Tabs on Your Net Worth

In This Chapter:

- *The Property & Debt tab*
- *Property and debt alerts*
- *Asset and debt account details*
- *Debt graphs*

When you create asset and debt accounts and enter related transactions into Quicken, as discussed in the previous chapters, Quicken summarizes your entries and calculates balances. It displays this information in a number of places: the Account Bar, the Property & Debt tab, account registers, and reports and graphs. You can consult Quicken's calculated balances and totals at any time to learn about your equity and the expenses associated with your debt and automobiles.

This chapter explains how to use Quicken's reporting features to keep tabs on your net worth. As you'll learn in these pages, a wealth of information about your net worth is just a mouse click away.

The Property & Debt Tab

Asset and debt account information, as well as an overview of your financial standing (net worth), are part of Quicken's Property & Debt tab. Open the Property & Debt section by clicking its tab near the top of Quicken's main window. The Property & Debt tab has three subtabs of information about your net worth: Net Worth, Account Overview, and Debt.

The Net Worth subtab displays graphs representing your net worth in a variety of ways, as well as a year-by-year look at your net worth as seen in Figure 13-1. The Account Overview subtab as seen in Figure 13-2, displays tables of numerical information about your net worth accounts. The Debt subtab shows more graphs, focusing on your credit cards and other debts. Together, these charts and tables paint a picture of your overall financial situation.

TIP   If the Property & Debt tab is not visible, open the View menu and click Tabs To Show | Property & Debt.

This part of the chapter takes a closer look at the snapshots in the Property & Debt tab's subtabs so you know what you can find there and how you can customize it for your own use.

Net Worth Subtab

The first snapshot in the Net Worth subtab is the Net Worth subtab (at the top of Figure 13-1). This graphs uses a stacked column to indicate your net worth for the

Figure 13-1 • The Net Worth subtab displays graphs and a table representing various components of your net worth.

Figure 13-2 • The Account Overview subtab summarizes property, debt, and loan account information.

past 13 months. The green bar represents your assets, the blue bar represents your debt, and the dark line represents the net of these two amounts. If you're looking for a trend, ideally, the green bars should get taller while the blue bars get shorter. The net effect would be a rise in the dark line. If the dark line is below the baseline, you're in some serious financial trouble because your debts exceed your assets.

Keep in mind that this graph represents all of your accounts in Quicken—including your banking and investment accounts. It's a true view of your net worth trend for the past year.

Figure 13-3 • See your debt load displayed graphically in the Debt subtab.

The Options menu and buttons within the window enable you to view a full-screen version of the graph, create a Net Worth report, or view the Account List.

Net Worth By Year

The Net Worth By Year snapshot uses a stacked column graph to show the value of your net worth for each year that Quicken has data, up to a maximum of three full years and year-to-date for the current year. If there's only partial data for a year, the graph isn't reliable for that period. Trend graphs like these are a good reason for using Quicken consistently—only with complete data can you get a complete and accurate picture!

Net Worth Allocation

The Net Worth Allocation chart (refer to Figure 13-1) graphically represents the allocation of your worth between cash or banking accounts, investments, and property and debt accounts as of the current date. The amount labeled "Total" is really your net worth.

Net Worth By Year Summary

The Net Worth By Year Summary (refer to Figure 13-1) summarizes the ending balances in each of your Quicken accounts for the previous three years and the current year to date. This is basically the same data shown in the Net Worth By Year graph, but it's displayed in tabular form with account-level detail. Again, having information like this readily available is a good reason to use Quicken consistently to manage your finances.

Any accounts you have hidden in Quicken are not included in the Net Worth by Year Summary.

Property and Debt Alerts

You can set up alerts in several areas for property and debts, as shown here, and have Quicken remind you when some action is due.

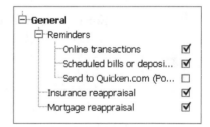

Setting Up Property and Debt Alerts

To set up an alert, begin by opening the Tools menu and clicking Alerts Center. Click the Setup tab, and click the name of the alert you want to set on the left side of the window to display its options on the right. Figure 13-4 shows what the Insurance Reappraisal alert settings might look like with two alerts already set.

Two alerts apply to Net Worth:

- **Insurance Reappraisal** (see Figure 13-4) notifies you before an insurance policy expires so you can either reevaluate coverage or shop for a new policy.
- **Mortgage Reappraisal** notifies you before a mortgage changes from variable to fixed (or fixed to variable) so you can consider refinancing. Even if your

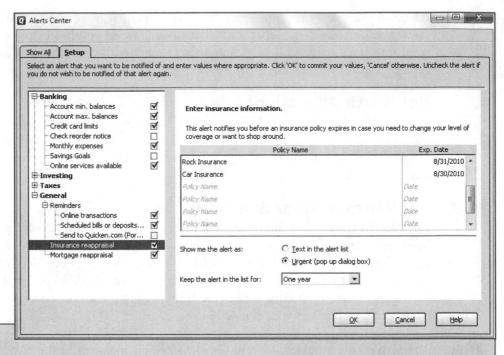

Figure 13-4 • Use the Setup tab of the Alerts Center window to set up alerts, such as the Insurance Reappraisal alert shown here.

mortgage doesn't convert, you can use this alert to remind you periodically to check for better mortgage deals.

Both alerts work pretty much the same way. For each alert, enter a name and date in the right side of the window. For example, to set insurance policy expiration dates, click in the Policy Name field. You'll see that your text appears on the right side of the box. Type the policy name and use your tab key to move to the Expiration Date field. Enter the expiration date.

Select one of the options at the bottom of the window to indicate how you want the alert to appear: as text in the alert list, shown in Figure 13-5, or as a pop-up dialog that appears when you start Quicken, shown here.

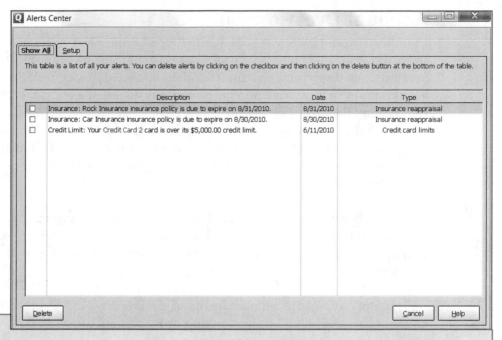

Figure 13-5 • In the Show All tab of the Alerts Center display those alerts you set to show as text as well as delete any alerts you no longer want to use.

Finally, use the drop-down list to specify the length of time the alert should remain in the list and click OK.

Repeat this process for each alert you want to set. When you're finished, click OK.

Working with Property and Debt Alerts

Once you have established property and debt alerts, you can manage them in several ways.

- In the Alerts Center's Show All tab (open from the Tools menu and shown in Figure 13-4), you can select the check box opposite an alert and click the Delete button to remove an alert.
- In the Alerts Center's Setup tab, you can uncheck an alert category to prevent all the alerts in that category from being displayed in any way.
- If you choose not to display the alert as a pop-up dialog when Quicken starts, you can click Don't Show This Type Of Alert As A Popup to stop the pop-up display.

Account Overview Subtab

From the Account Overview subtab, the Property And Debt Accounts section (refer to Figure 13-2) lists all of your property (asset), debt (liability), and credit accounts, and displays each account's ending balance. You can click the name of an account to view its account register, which is discussed later in this chapter, in the section titled "Account Details."

One of the nice things about the Property And Debt Accounts section is that it separates assets from debts and provides subtotals for each. The total at the bottom is the net of the two. If this is a negative number, your finances need attention.

The total shown in the Property And Debt Accounts section in the Account Overview subtab total does not match the Net Worth total shown at the bottom of the Account Bar. The difference between the two is the total of your cash accounts.

The Options pop-up menu at the top of the Property And Debt Accounts section offers several options for working with accounts:

- **Add An Account** option displays the Account Setup dialog, which you can use to create an asset or debt account. Chapter 2 discusses how to create accounts, and Chapter 12 provides details specific to asset and debt accounts.
- **Get Transactions Online** option is available if you have activated any of your accounts for online services. When you click this option, the One Step Update Settings dialog appears. See Chapter 6 for specific details on One Step Update.
- **View Account List** option displays the Account List which you can use to view and manage accounts. The Account List is covered in detail in Chapter 2.

Loan Summary

The Loan Summary section (refer to Figure 13-2) lists all of your amortized loans—the ones you set up in the View Loans dialog, as instructed in Chapter 12. It includes several columns of information for each loan:

- **Account** is the name of the account. You can click the account name to view its register, which is discussed later in this chapter.
- **Int. Rate** is the current interest rate.
- **Payments Left** is the number of payments left on the loan. This does not take into consideration any extra payments you may have made that will reduce the loan term.

- **Principal Paid** is the total of the payments made toward the loan balance.
- **Interest Paid** is the total of the interest paid for the loan.
- **Balance** is the ending balance for the account.

The Principal Paid, Interest Paid, and Balance columns contain information calculated by Quicken based on transactions entered in your Quicken data file. It's important to note that the Interest Paid column totals only the amount of interest entered in Quicken. If you set up an existing loan for which payments (including interest) had already been made, Quicken does not include principal or interest already paid on the loan in the totals.

The Options pop-up menu at the top of the Loan Summary section offers two loan-related options:

- **Add A New Loan** option displays the Loan Setup dialog, with which you can create a new loan. This dialog is explained in Chapter 12.
- **Make A Payment** option displays the Loan Summary tab of the View Loans window. To make a payment on a loan, choose the loan name from the Choose Loan pop-up menu, and then click the Make Payment button. The View Loans window and making payments is also explained in Chapter 12.

Debt Goals

If you have used Quicken's Debt Reduction Planner, which is discussed in detail in Chapter 16, you may also see the Debt Goals snapshot at the bottom of the Account Overview subtab. This snapshot lists the debts you set up in the Debt Reduction Planner, along with the current month's payment and target balance. The Options menu enables you to quickly open and view the Debt Reduction Planner to make changes or review settings in the planner.

Debt Subtab

The Debt subtab is new in Quicken 2011. It includes several graphs that can illustrate your current debt load, as seen in Figure 13-6. Each section lets you see your liability information in a slightly different format. At the top of the graphs are several drop-down lists that let you select what you want to see and the time period. A legend appears at the right of the section telling you the color used in the graph for each of your debts.

The first drop-down list, as seen here, lets you choose which accounts you want to use in the graph.

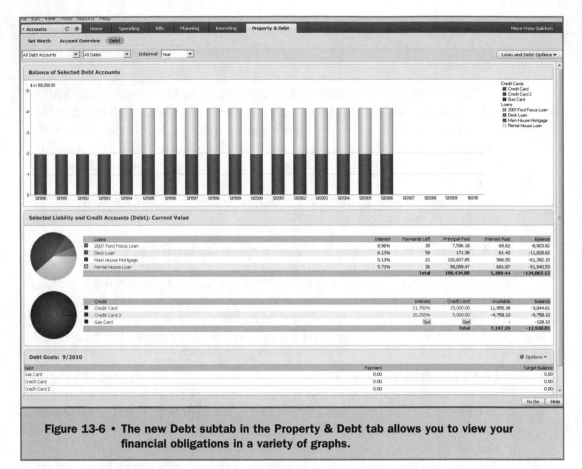

Figure 13-6 • The new Debt subtab in the Property & Debt tab allows you to view your financial obligations in a variety of graphs.

You have your choice of:

- **All Debt Accounts** sets the graph to display all of your debts as seen in Figure 13-6.
- **Credit Cards Only** will display just the amounts you owe to credit card companies.
- **Loans Only** shows all of your current loans, including any mortgages. If you move your mouse cursor over any total, a small magnifying glass will appear showing the balance of the loan at that point in time, as seen on the top of the next page.
- **Custom** opens a Customize dialog that lets you choose which accounts to display, as seen on the bottom of the next page. Click Select All to display all of your debts. Click Clear All and choose only the debts you want to display in your graph. Click the Show Hidden Accounts check box to include those

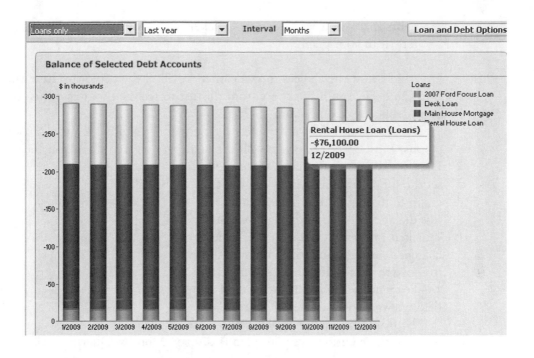

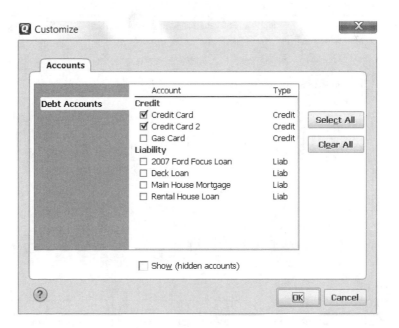

debts that you have hidden in Quicken. Click OK to close the dialog and return to your graph.

Listed below the choices shown earlier are all of the debts you have entered into Quicken. You may choose from this list to see the progress of just one of your debts, as seen in Figure 13-7.

The second drop-down list offers a variety of dates for which you can set your graphs. Most of the options are self-explanatory; however, when you click Custom Date, a dialog appears that you can use to set the time period for which you want the graph to display, as seen next. Be aware in this dialog, unlike most dialog boxes in Quicken, you have to click in the To field to change the date instead of using the TAB key to move to it. In this dialog, pressing the TAB key when you enter a date in the From field will move you to the OK button.

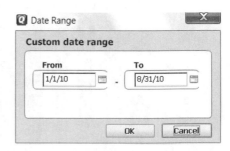

The third drop-down list lets you choose between three options for your graph's display: Months, Quarter, and Year.

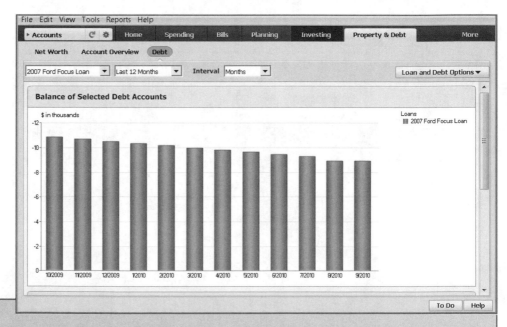

Figure 13-7 • You can view the progress you are making in paying down debt by customizing the graphs in the Debt section of the Property & Debt tab.

Graph Options

The choices that you make in the drop-down lists at the top of the Debt subtab section affect the graphs that are displayed in the Balance of Selected Debt Accounts as well as the Selected Liability and Credit Accounts (Debt): Current Value sections.

Selected Liability And Credit Accounts (Debt): Current Value

The graph in this section, as seen in Figure 13-8, displays several bits of information, depending on the choices you've made in the drop-down lists described earlier in this chapter.

Loans   If you have selected All Debt Accounts or Loans Only in the first drop-down list, you will see:

- **Interest**, which displays the rate of interest for each loan.
- **Payments Left** to show you how many more payments you have on this loan through the date you chose in the drop-down boxes.
- **Principal Paid** shows the amount of principal you have paid on this loan since its inception through the date you chose in the drop-down boxes.
- **Interest Paid** totals the interest you have paid through the date you chose in the drop-down boxes. Remember, interest is the amount you pay to rent someone else's money.
- **Balance** shows what you still owe on this debt. It shows as a minus because it subtracts from your net worth. The balance displayed is as of the date you chose in the drop-down boxes.

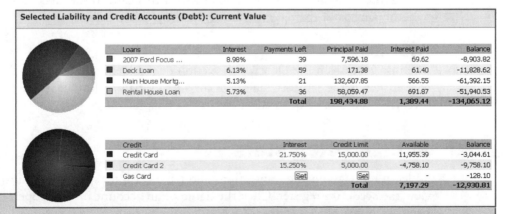

	Loans	Interest	Payments Left	Principal Paid	Interest Paid	Balance
■	2007 Ford Focus ...	8.98%	39	7,596.18	69.62	-8,903.82
■	Deck Loan	6.13%	59	171.38	61.40	-11,828.62
■	Main House Mortg...	5.13%	21	132,607.85	566.55	-61,392.15
☐	Rental House Loan	5.73%	36	58,059.47	691.87	-51,940.53
			Total	198,434.88	1,389.44	-134,065.12

	Credit	Interest	Credit Limit	Available	Balance
■	Credit Card	21.750%	15,000.00	11,955.39	-3,044.61
■	Credit Card 2	15.250%	5,000.00	-4,758.10	-9,758.10
■	Gas Card	Set	Set	-	-128.10
			Total	7,197.29	-12,930.81

Figure 13-8 • **Your debt load is displayed in a pie graph in the Current Value section in the Debt subtab of the Property & Debt tab.**

Credit   This section displays the credit cards or other loans you have entered into Quicken. As seen in Figure 13-8, the information is shown in pie chart form for the options you chose in the drop-down boxes. You see:

- **Interest**, which displays the interest rate being charged on each card. If it does not show, click the Set button to open the Interest Rate dialog shown here. Enter the interest rate for the card as shown on your monthly statement, and click OK to close the dialog. You may also use this dialog to change the interest rate for the credit card.

- **Credit Limit** displays the credit limit of the card. This is not available if you have not entered the limit. Click the Set button to open the Credit Limit dialog shown next. Type the amount of this card's credit limit and click OK to return to the graph.

- **Available** displays the amount you can still charge on this card. It is your credit limit minus the current balance.
- **Balance** displays the amount you owe on this card to the credit card company as of the date you set in the drop-down boxes.

Debt Goals

The information in the Debt Goals section of the Debt subtab of the Property & Debt tab is the same as you see in the Debt Goals section of the Account Overview subtab as explained earlier in this chapter.

Account Registers

To learn more about the transactions and balances for a specific account, you can view the account's register. Click the name of an account in the Property And Debt Accounts of the Account Overview subtab, or from the Selected Liability and Credit Accounts section of the Debt subtab to open the account you want to view. The account register will open, as seen in Figure 13-9.

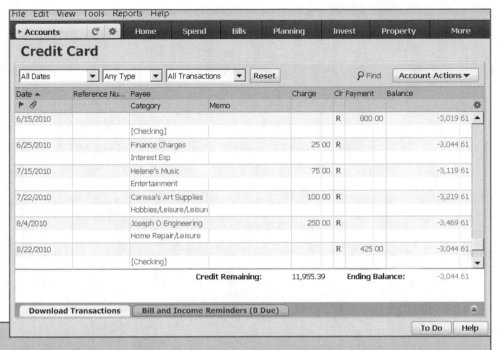

File Edit View Tools Reports Help								
▸ Accounts	C ✿	Home	Spend	Bills	Planning	Invest	Property	More

Credit Card

| All Dates ▾ | Any Type ▾ | All Transactions ▾ | Reset | | | 🔍 Find | Account Actions ▾ |

Date ▲	Reference Nu...	Payee		Charge	Clr	Payment	Balance	
▸ 🖉		Category	Memo					✿
6/15/2010					R	800 00	-3,019 61	▲
		[Checking]						
6/25/2010		Finance Charges		25 00	R		-3,044 61	
		Interest Exp						
7/15/2010		Helene's Music		75 00	R		-3,119 61	
		Entertainment						
7/22/2010		Carissa's Art Supplies		100 00	R		-3,219 61	
		Hobbies/Leisure/Leisure						
8/4/2010		Joseph O Engineering		250 00	R		-3,469 61	
		Home Repair/Leisure						
8/22/2010					R	425 00	-3,044 61	
		[Checking]						▼

	Credit Remaining:	11,955.39	Ending Balance:	-3,044.61

Download Transactions	Bill and Income Reminders (0 Due)	⌃

	To Do	Help

Figure 13-9 • This is an example of a credit account register that has been activated for onine services.

Register

An account's Register window (see Figure 13-9) lists all transactions entered into that account, as well as the ending balance. As covered in Chapter 12, you can enter transactions directly into the register. Other transactions—such as principal payments for a mortgage or other loans—are automatically calculated and entered by Quicken.

Planning

This part of the book tells you about Quicken Personal Finance Software's planning features, which you can use to plan for your retirement, major purchases, and other life events. It covers Quicken's built-in financial calculators, as well as features that can help you save money and make your dreams come true. Its three chapters are:

Chapter 14:   Planning for the Future

Chapter 15:   Using Financial Calculators

Chapter 16:   Reducing Debt and Saving Money

Part Five

Planning for the Future

Chapter 14

In This Chapter:

- *Quicken planning overview*
- *Playing "what if"*

To most of us, the future is an unknown, a mystery. After all, who can say what will happen tomorrow, next year, or ten years from now? But if you think about your future, you can usually come up with a few events that you can plan for: your marriage, the purchase of a new home, the birth of your children (and their education years later), and your retirement. (These are just examples—everyone's life runs a different course.) These events, as well as many unforeseen events, all have one thing in common: They affect your finances. This chapter tells you about planning for future events and how tools within Quicken Personal Finance Software can help.

Planning for Retirement

Throughout your life, you work and earn money to pay your bills, buy the things you and your family need or want, and help your kids get started with their own lives. But there comes a day when it's time to retire. Those regular paychecks stop coming, and you find yourself relying on the money you put away for retirement.

Retirement planning is one of the most important financial planning jobs facing individuals and couples. This section tells you about the importance of planning and offers some planning steps and suggestions.

The Importance of Planning

Retired people live on fixed incomes. That's not a problem—*if* the income is fixed high enough to support a comfortable lifestyle.

409

You can help ensure that there's enough money to finance your retirement years by planning and saving now.

Poor retirement planning can lead to catastrophic results—imagine running out of money when you turn 75. Or having to make a lifestyle change when you're 66 or 67 to accommodate a much lower income.

Planning is even more important these days as longevity increases. People are living longer than ever. Your retirement dollars may need to support you for 20 years or more, at a time when the cost of living will likely be much higher than it is today.

With proper planning, it's possible to finance your retirement years without putting a strain on your working years. By closely monitoring the status of your retirement funds, periodically adjusting your plan, and acting accordingly, your retirement years can be the golden years they're supposed to be.

Planning Steps

Retirement planning is much more than deciding to put $2,000 in an IRA every year. It requires careful consideration of what you have, what you'll need, and how you can make those two numbers the same.

Assess What You Have

Take a good look at your current financial situation. What tax-deferred retirement savings do you already have? A 401(k)? An IRA? Something else? What regular savings do you have? What taxable investments do you have? The numbers you come up with will form the basis of your final retirement funds.

Be sure to consider property that can be liquidated to contribute to retirement savings. For example, if you currently live in a large home to accommodate your family, you may eventually want to live in a smaller home. The proceeds from the sale of your current home may exceed the cost of your retirement home. Also consider any income-generating property that may continue to generate income in your retirement years or that can be liquidated to contribute to retirement savings.

Determine What You'll Need

What you'll need depends on many things. One simple calculation suggests you'll need 80 percent of your current gross income to maintain your current lifestyle in your retirement years. You may find a calculation like this handy if retirement is still many years in the future and you don't really know what things will cost.

Time is an important factor in calculating the total amount you should have saved by retirement day. Ask yourself two questions:

- **How long do you have to save?**   Take your current age and subtract it from the age at which you plan to retire. That's the number of years you have left to save.
- **How long will you be in retirement?**   Take the age at which you plan to retire and subtract it from the current life expectancy for someone of your age and gender. That's the number of years you have to save for.

Develop an Action Plan

Once you know how much you need, it's time to think seriously about how you can save it. This requires putting money away in one or more savings or investment accounts. There are several options here, which are covered a little later in this chapter.

Stick to the Plan!

The most important part of any plan is sticking to it. For example, if you plan to save $5,000 a year, don't think you can just save $2,000 this year and make up the $3,000 next year. There are two reasons: First, you can't "make up" the interest lost on the $3,000 you didn't save this year, and second, you're kidding yourself if you think you'll manage to put away $8,000 next year.

If you consider deviating from your plan, just think about the alternative: making ends meet with a job bagging groceries when you're 73 years old.

Don't Wait! Act Now!

Most of us don't think about retirement planning or savings in our twenties or even thirties. However, the earlier we begin, the more enjoyable our retirement can be.

See for yourself. Table 14-1 shows how $2,500, $5,000, and $7,500 per-year contributions to a tax-deferred retirement account earning 5 percent a year can grow. (These calculations do not take into consideration tax benefits or inflation.)

		Savings at Age 62		
Start Age	Years of Saving	$2,500/year	$5,000/year	$7,500/year
60	2	$5,125	$10,250	$15,375
50	12	$39,793	$79,586	$119,378
40	22	$96,263	$192,526	$288,789
30	32	$188,247	$376,494	$564,741
20	42	$338,079	$676,159	$1,014,238

Table 14-1 • Regular Savings Can Make Your Money Grow

Getting Started with the Quicken Lifetime Planner

From the Planning tab (refer to Figure 14-1), you have access to all of Quicken's built-in planning features, including the Quicken Lifetime Planner's main plan assumptions and individual financial planners. Once you have set up your plan, the Planning tab provides an up-to-date view of how well your plan is working.

Here's how it works. You start by entering plan assumptions, which include information about you, your current finances, and your tax rate. Quicken makes calculations based on what you entered to display plan results. As you continue working with Quicken, entering transactions that affect your finances, Quicken updates the result of the plan.

Setting up Quicken Lifetime Planner assumptions can be time-consuming. However, the benefits of using this feature far outweigh the cost (in time) of setting it up. This is especially true if you're raising a family—Quicken can help you plan for the major events of your life so you're prepared for them. If you don't have the time to set up the Quicken Planner now, make time in the near future.

This section explains how to set assumptions for the planners within the Quicken Lifetime Planner and how to view the results of your plan in the Planning tab.

Setting Plan Assumptions

The easiest way to see what plan assumptions need to be made is to view the Plan Assumptions area of the Lifetime Planner. Click Planning | Lifetime Planner. When you first start out, the Plan Assumptions area may look like the illustration on page 414.

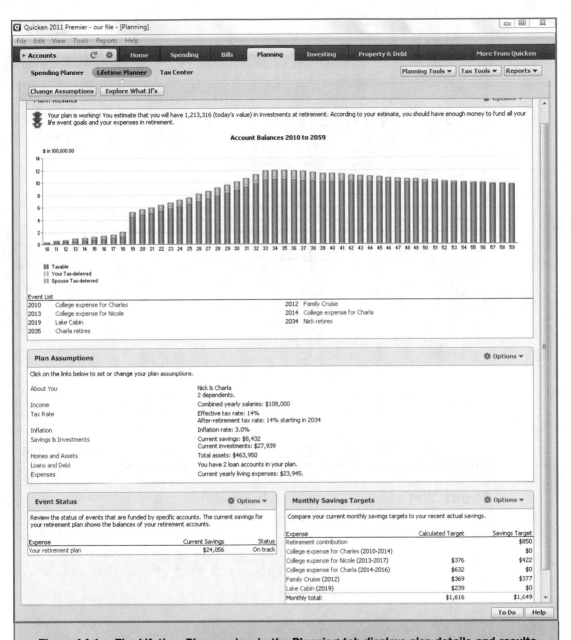

Figure 14-1 • The Lifetime Planner view in the Planning tab displays plan details and results.

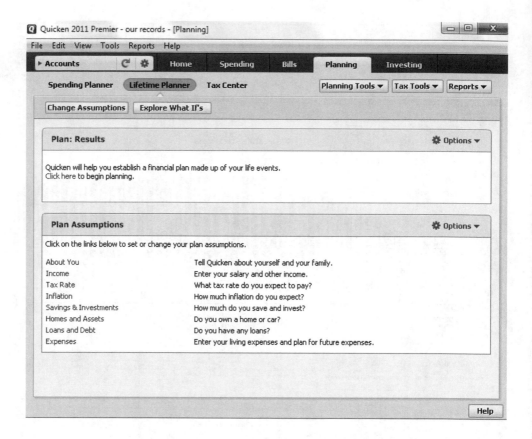

To set details for an assumption category, click its link. This displays a dialog you can use to enter information. Here's a look at each category.

About You

Clicking the About You link displays the About You dialog, which is shown on the next page. Its fields are pretty self-explanatory: your name and date of birth. When you're finished entering information in the dialog, click Done to save it.

Here are some less obvious things to consider when entering data into the About You dialog.

Include Spouse   If you turn on the Include Spouse check box, you can enter information into the Spouse column of the dialog. If you don't have a spouse or don't want to include him or her in your plan, leave that check box turned off.

Life Expectancy   You can either enter what you think might be your life expectancy or click the Calculate button to display the Calculate Life Expectancy

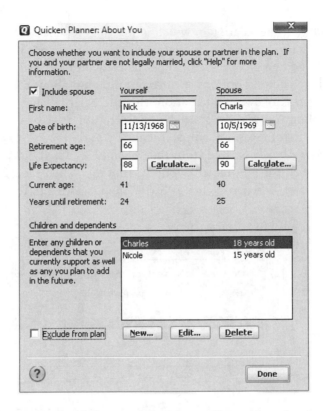

dialog. Set options in the dialog, and Quicken tells you how long you may live. Of course, this is an estimate based on current research into life expectancy; you may or may not live to reach the age Quicken suggests.

Children and Dependents   To enter information about children or other dependents, click the New button at the bottom of the dialog. This displays the Add Child/Dependent dialog, in which you can enter the name and date of birth for a dependent. When you click OK, the person's name and age are added to the list. Repeat this process for each child or dependent you need to add. Once a child or dependent has been added, you can select his or her name and click the Edit button to change information about him or her, or click the Delete button to remove him or her permanently from the plan, or turn on the Exclude From Plan check box so Quicken doesn't use him or her in its calculations.

Income

Clicking the Income link displays the Income dialog, which is organized into three separate tabs of information. This is where you enter salary, retirement benefits, and other income information for you and your spouse.

Salary   The Salary tab, which is shown here, enables you to record information about current and future salary and self-employment income.

To add an income item, click the New button to display the Add Salary dialog. Then set options to enter information about the income item. As you can see in the following illustration, the Add Salary dialog is extremely flexible, enabling you to enter start and end dates for a salary—which is useful for income from seasonal employment. If you don't need to enter specific dates, choose Already Started from the When Does This Salary Start drop-down list and one of the retirement options from the When Does This Salary End drop-down list. When you click OK, the item is added to the list.

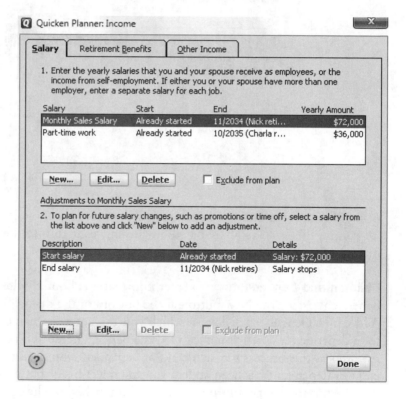

For each item you add, Quicken automatically includes adjustments that specify when the item begins and ends. But you can add other adjustments if you know about changes that will occur in the future. Select the item in the top half of the dialog, and then click the New button at the bottom of the dialog. Enter information in the Add Salary Adjustment dialog that appears and click OK. The information is added to the bottom half of the Salary tab of the Income dialog.

On the Salary tab, you can select any of the salary or adjustment items and click the Edit or Delete button to change or remove it. You can also select an item and turn on the Exclude From Plan check box to exclude its information from the Quicken Planner.

Retirement Benefits   The Retirement Benefits tab, which is shown here, enables you to enter information about Social Security or pension benefits you are currently receiving or to estimate future benefits.

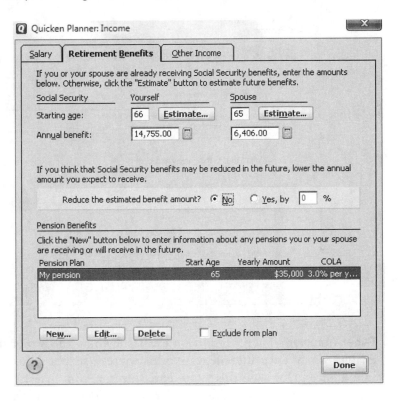

To estimate future Social Security benefits, enter the age at which you expect to begin collecting benefits and click the Estimate button. The Estimate Social Security Benefits dialog appears. You have two options:

- **Use Rough Estimate** enables you to select a salary range option to estimate benefits.
- **Use Mail-In Estimate From SS Administration** enables you to enter the amount provided by the Social Security Administration on your annual Social Security statement.

When you click OK, the amount is automatically entered in the Retirement Benefits tab.

To add a pension, click the New button at the bottom of the Retirement Benefits tab of the Income dialog. This displays the Add Pension dialog, which is shown here. Enter information about the pension and click OK to add it to the Retirement Benefits tab. In that tab, you can select the pension and click Edit or Delete to change or remove it, or select it and turn on the Exclude From Plan check box to exclude it from the Quicken Planner's calculations.

Other Income The Other Income tab, shown on the top of the next page, enables you to enter income from other sources, such as gifts, child support, and inheritances. Don't use this tab to enter income from investments or rental properties; the Quicken Lifetime Planner provides other places to enter this information.

To enter an income item, click the New button. Enter information in the Add Other Income dialog, which is shown on the bottom of the next page. An interesting option in this dialog is the ability to specify how the money will be used: either saved and invested or used to pay expenses. The option you select determines how this income is used in the plan. If you're not sure what to select, leave it set to the default option. When you click OK, the item is added to the Other Income tab's list. You can edit, delete, or exclude the item from the plan as desired.

Click Done to close the Quicken Planner: Other Income dialog.

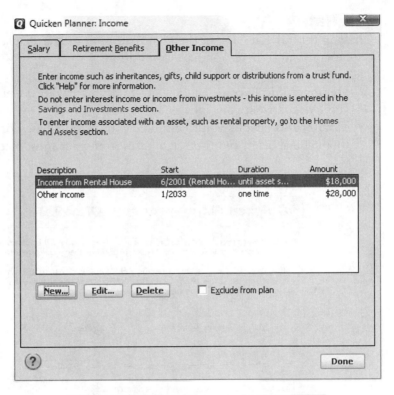

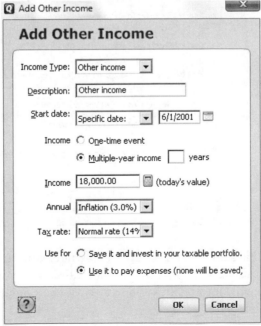

Tax Rate

Clicking the Tax Rate link in the Plan Assumptions area displays the Average Tax Rate dialog shown here. You have two options:

- **Demographic Average** enables you to estimate your tax rate based on where you live and what your income is.
- **Tax Returns** enables you to estimate your tax rate based on the total income, total federal taxes, and total state taxes from your most recent tax returns.

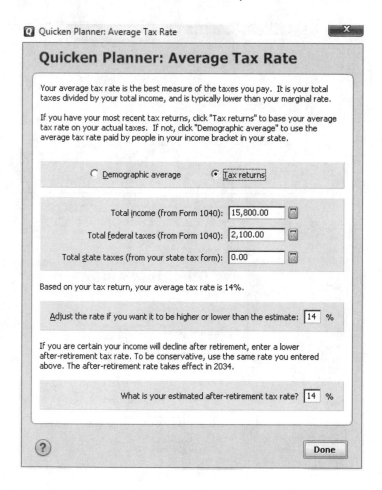

No matter how you estimate the tax rate, you can adjust it by entering a preferred value. You can also enter an estimate of your post-retirement tax rate, which may be lower. Click Done to close the Quicken Planner: Average Tax Rate dialog.

Inflation

Clicking the Inflation link displays the Estimated Inflation dialog, which includes a field you can use to enter the inflation rate you want to use for your plan. Quicken suggests an inflation rate of 3 percent, which is the average inflation rate since 1927, but you can enter any rate you think is correct in the text box. Click Done to save your estimate.

Savings & Investments

Clicking the Savings & Investments link displays the Savings And Investments dialog, which is organized into three tabs. Use these dialogs to enter information about current bank accounts, as well as contributions you make to investment accounts. Use the Return tab to enter the return you expect to earn on your investments.

Savings   Click the Savings tab to list all of the bank accounts you have set up in Quicken, along with their current balances.

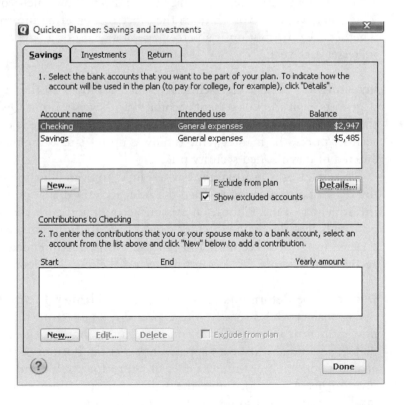

If you have omitted any accounts from Quicken, now is a good time to add them if you want them to be part of your plan. Click the New button to display the Add New Account dialog. Learn how to use this dialog to create new accounts in Chapter 2.

Quicken automatically assumes that each bank account will be used for general expenses. You can change this assumption by selecting an account and clicking the Details button. Choose a new purpose from the drop-down list in the Account Details dialog that appears and click OK. You may find that until you use Quicken's calculators and planners, general expenses is the only offered option. But if you have entered information into one of the Quicken Planners such as college expenses in the Expenses Planner, an option for that expense appears in the drop-down list.

If you or your spouse makes regular contributions to one of your bank accounts, you can enter information about that contribution in the Savings dialog. In the top half of the dialog, select the account that receives the contribution. Then click the New button at the bottom of the dialog. Use the Add Contribution dialog that appears to indicate how much you contribute. The dialog will walk you through the process of entering information based on whether the contribution is a percentage of a salary or a base amount that increases each year.

Investments   The Investments tab, which is shown on the top of the next page, lists all of the investment accounts you have set up in Quicken, along with their current market values. Remember, since market value is determined by security prices, the market value is only as up-to-date as the most recently entered or downloaded security prices.

This link works just like the Savings link. You can click the New button in the top half of the dialog to open the Add Account dialog to enter a new investment account. Choose an existing account and click the New button in the bottom half of the dialog to enter regular contribution information for any selected investment account. You can also specify the intended use for any account by selecting the account name and clicking the Details button.

Return   The Return link opens the Quicken Planner: Return tab dialog. This dialog enables you to specify your expected rates of return for pre-retirement and post-retirement investments. If you turn on the check box near the top of the dialog, additional text boxes appear, shown at the bottom of the next page, enabling you to enter different rates of return for taxable and tax-deferred investments. At the bottom of the dialog, you can enter the percentage of the taxable return that is subject to taxes. This is normally 100 percent, but for your

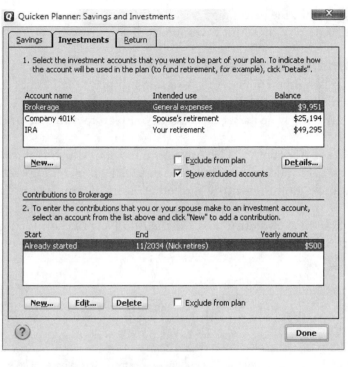

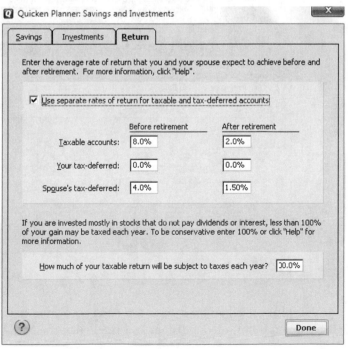

situation, the percentage may be different. Click Done to close the Quicken Planner: Savings And Investments dialog.

Homes And Assets

Clicking the Homes And Assets link displays the Homes And Assets dialog, which is organized into two tabs. This is where you can enter information about currently owned assets and assets you plan to purchase in the future.

Asset Accounts   The Asset Accounts tab, which is shown next, lists all of the asset accounts you have created in Quicken, including accounts for your home, vehicle, home inventory, and other assets. If you have additional assets that have not yet been entered in Quicken and you want to include them in your plan, click the New button and use the Add New Account dialog that appears to create the new account. See how to add a new asset account in Chapter 12.

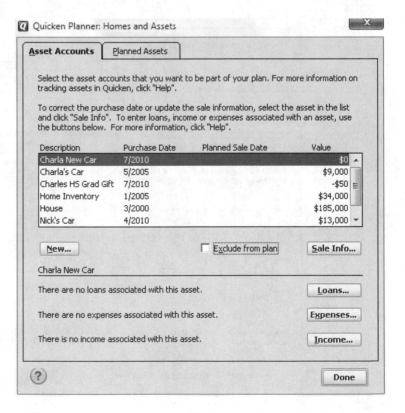

If you plan to sell an asset, you can enter information for that sale. Select the asset in the top half of the dialog, and then click the Sale Info button. A series of dialogs prompts you for information about the asset's purchase and sale date and price, as well as other information that affects how much money you can expect to receive and pay taxes on. This information is then added to your plan.

Three buttons at the bottom of the dialog enable you to associate loans, expenses, and income with a selected asset. This is especially important when working with assets you plan to sell, since the sale of the asset should also end associated debt, expenses, and income.

- **Loans** enables you to link existing loans to the asset or add new loans, including home equity loans. It also enables you to enter information about planned loans—for example, if you plan to use a home equity loan to build an addition on your house sometime next year. You can also enter information about planned payoffs—perhaps you're expecting a big trust fund check (lucky you!) and plan to use it to pay off your house.
- **Expenses** enables you to enter property tax information as well as other expenses related to the asset. For a home, this might include association fees, homeowner's insurance, and estimated maintenance and utility costs. For a car, this might include registration, fuel, service, and insurance. For each expense you add, Quicken prompts you for information about the expense, including how you expect to pay for it—with money in a specific bank account or with a loan. It even enables you to set up a monthly savings target to pay for the item.
- **Income** enables you to enter information about income you expect to earn from the asset. This is especially useful if you own rental property. The dialog that appears when you add an income item is almost the same as the Add Other Income dialog, shown earlier in this chapter. It even allows you to specify how you plan to use the income: for investment or to pay expenses.

Planned Assets   The Planned Assets tab (shown on the next page) enables you to enter information about any assets you plan to purchase in the future. For example, suppose you indicated in the Asset Accounts tab that you plan to sell your home or car on a specific date. If you plan to replace it with another home or car, this is where you'd enter information about the replacement. Quicken uses dialogs that walk you through the process of entering details about the future purchase. Once you've entered planned asset information, you can select the asset in the list and add loans, expenses, and income for it, as well as choose the accounts you plan to use to pay for it. Click Done to close the Quicken Planner: Homes And Assets dialog.

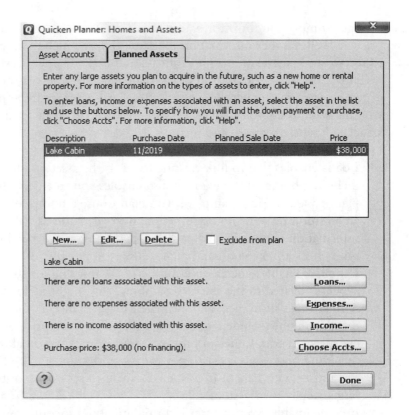

Loans And Debt

Clicking the Loans And Debt link in the Plan Assumptions area displays the Loans And Debt dialog, which is organized into three tabs. This is where you enter information about current and planned loans, as well as information from your debt reduction plan.

Loan Accounts   The Loan Accounts tab, which is shown next, displays information about current loans. This information comes from loans you have set up within Quicken. To add another loan that isn't already recorded in Quicken, click the New button to display the Loan Setup dialog, which is covered in Chapter 13. If you plan to pay off a loan before its last payment date, you can click the Payoff button to enter future payoff information.

Planned Loans   The Planned Loans tab enables you to enter information about loans you plan to make in the future. This does not include any loans you may have already planned in the Homes And Assets dialog discussed earlier in

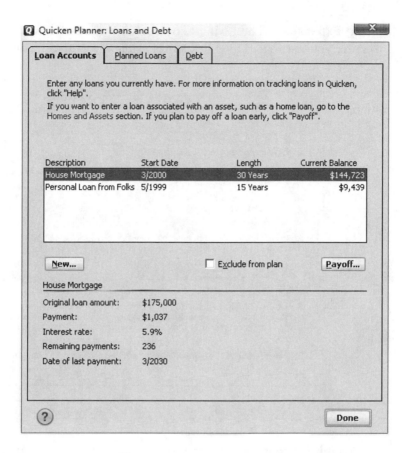

this chapter. Instead, this is for loans that are not associated with any particular asset, such as a personal loan you plan to pay for a really special vacation.

Debt   The Debt tab includes information from the Debt Reduction Planner, which is covered in Chapter 16. If you have credit card and other debt, it's a good idea to complete the Debt Reduction Planner as part of your overall planning strategy. Click Done to close the Quicken Planner: Loans And Debt dialog.

Expenses

Clicking the Expenses link displays the Expenses dialog, which is organized into four tabs. This is where you enter information about your living expenses, as well as any adjustments to expenses and the expenses for college or other special events.

Living Expenses   The Living Expenses tab, which is shown here, enables you to enter your estimated living expenses using one of two techniques:

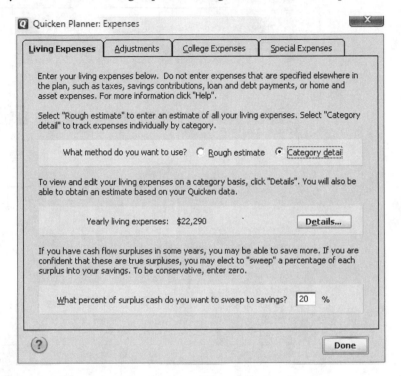

- **Rough Estimate** enables you to enter an estimate of your annual living expenses. Using this technique is quicker, but it may not be as accurate as using the Category Detail option.
- **Category Detail** enables you to have Quicken calculate an estimate of your annual living expenses based on transactions already entered in your Quicken data file. This technique is more accurate than Rough Estimate, especially if you have been using Quicken for a while and have a good history of transactions. If you select this method, you can click the Details button that appears in the middle of the dialog to display the Living Expenses Category Detail dialog. Toggle check marks in the list of categories to include or exclude specific categories and enter monthly amounts as desired. When you click OK, Quicken annualizes the amounts and enters them in the Living Expenses tab.

One thing to keep in mind here: Don't include expenses that you may have already included for an asset. For example, if you included car insurance expenses in the Homes And Assets dialog as an expense associated with an automobile, don't include them again here. Doing so would duplicate the expense and overstate your annual expenses.

At the bottom of the dialog, you can enter a percentage of surplus cash—cash left over after paying living expenses—that you want to put into savings.

Adjustments   The Adjustments tab enables you to enter any adjustments to your expenses that are related to planned changes in your life. For example, perhaps you plan to hire a nanny to take care of your child while you go back to work. You can add this planned expense as an adjustment for a predefined period. When you click the New button in the Adjustments tab, the Add Living Expense Adjustment dialog appears. The illustration shows how it might look if Nicole were to go to music camp next summer.

College Expenses   The College Expenses tab enables you to plan for the education of your children—or yourself! Clicking the New button in this tab displays the Add College Expense dialog, shown next, which walks you through the process of entering expected college expenses for a plan member. You'll have to do a little homework to come up with realistic estimates of college costs, including tuition, room, board, books, and supplies. Remember, if you underestimate expenses, your plan won't be accurate. The dialog also prompts you for information about expected financial aid, student loans, and student contributions to cover all sources of financing. If you have a college fund—such as an educational IRA—already set up for the college expense, you can associate it with the expense to indicate how it will be paid for.

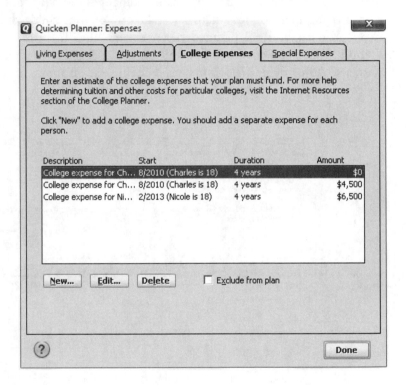

Special Expenses The Special Expenses tab, which is shown here, includes any expenses you may have already added in the Homes And Assets dialog and enables you to enter other one-time or annual expenses you expect to incur. Use this for items like a vacation, wedding, or large purchase. When you click the New button, Quicken prompts you for information about the expense, including the amount and how you expect to finance it. Click Done to close the Quicken Planner: Expenses dialog.

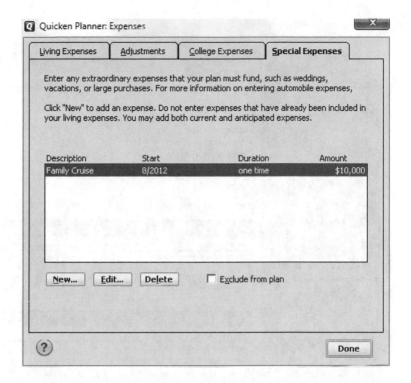

Reviewing and Changing Assumptions

You can review and modify your plan assumptions at any time. Quicken offers a number of ways to do this.

The Plan Assumptions Area

Once you enter assumptions into the Quicken Planners, a brief summary of the assumptions appears in the Plan Assumptions area in the Planning tab (see Figure 14-1). To open this window, choose Planning | Lifetime Planner.

You can click links in the Plan Assumptions area to open the same dialogs discussed earlier in this chapter. Review and change plan assumptions as desired, and click Done in the dialog to save them.

The Planning Assumptions Window

A better way to review plan assumptions is in the Planning Assumptions window, as seen on the next page. To open this window, choose Planning | Lifetime Planner. You can access the Planning Assumptions window from the Options button in any of the four sections of the Lifetime Planner. Click Options | Review Or Change Plan Assumptions.

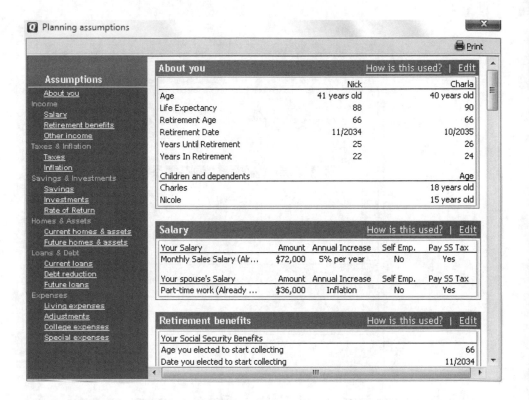

You can use links on the left side of the Planning Assumptions window to navigate quickly from one category of assumption to another. The details appear in the main part of the window. Each category of assumption offers two links:

- **How Is This Used?** explains how the information in that category of assumption is used in the plan.
- **Edit** enables you to edit the assumptions for that category, using the same dialogs discussed earlier in this chapter.

Saved Plans

Figure 14-1 shows the results of your saved plan, the plan assumptions, status of any planned events, and your monthly savings targets. You can use this screen to review your savings plans and change them if you need or want to. Click a link to open the associated planner and change data as desired.

Viewing Plan Results

When Quicken has enough data about your assumptions to calculate plan results, it displays them graphically in the Plan: Results area of the Planning tab (see Figure 14-1).

As with the information displayed in the other Quicken tabs, you can print the Plan Results, Assumptions, Event Status, and Monthly Savings Targets by clicking File | Print Lifetime Planner.

The top of the Plan: Results area tells you whether your plan is working and how much you should have in investments at retirement. Amounts are in today's dollars; to view them in future dollars, choose Show Amounts In Future Value from the Options pop-up menu at the top-right corner of the Plan: Results area.

The graph beneath this summary shows your taxable and tax-deferred savings. The ideal shape of this graph shows a steady increase until the year you retire and then a gradual decrease. Hover your mouse pointer over a column to show a yellow box with the amount for that year. Double-clicking the column opens a Plan Summary dialog for that year showing income and expenses, as shown here. You can use the <<Prev Year>> and <<Next Year>> buttons in the dialog to scroll through the years in the graph. This enables you to see the detailed numbers that make up the graph columns—very helpful! Plan results change automatically based on a variety of changes within your Quicken data file.

Income and Expenses Summary (2055)	
<< Prev Year Next Year >>	Print...

Plan Summary (2055)
(All amounts are reported in today's value.)

Income Summary

Income	
Salaries	
Monthly Sales Salary	$0
Part-time work	$0
Total Salaries	$0
Pension Benefits	
My pension	$35,000
My pension: Survivor's Benefit	$0
Total Pension Benefits	$35,000
Social Security Benefits	
Self	$14,755
Spouse	$6,588
Total Social Security Benefits	$21,343
Withdrawals	
Your Tax-deferred	$707
Spouse Tax-deferred	$2,932
Total Withdrawals	$3,639
College Incomes	
Student Contribution for Charles	$0

- When the account balances referred to in the plan change, the plan changes accordingly.
- When you change plan assumptions, the plan changes accordingly.
- When you use Quicken's planners to plan for major purchases, college, retirement, and other events that affect your finances, the plan changes to include these events.
- When you play "what if" with assumptions and save the changes as your plan, the plan changes accordingly. You'll see how to enter "what ifs" a little later in this chapter, in the section "Playing 'What If.'"

Viewing Event Status Items

Quicken also keeps track of your progress toward certain events and savings targets. It displays this information in the Planning tab of the Lifetime Planner window (refer to Figure 14-1).

The Event Status section displays information about events in your plan that are funded with specific accounts. From this section click Your Retirement Plan to open the My Retirement Plan window, seen in Figure 14-2, which looks a lot like the Plan Assumptions window.

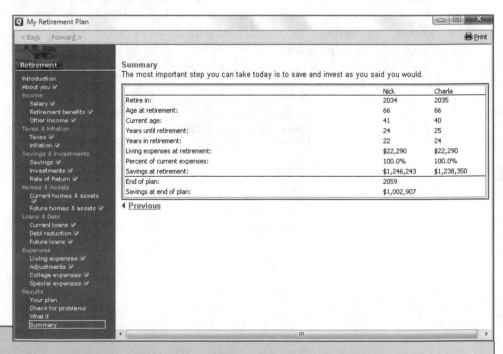

Figure 14-2 • The Summary section of the My Retirement Plan window shows the information you entered about your retirement plan.

Working with Your Future Expenses

The Monthly Savings Targets section of your Lifetime Planner displays information about your savings toward events in your plan.

Clicking a link for an expense displays the summary area for that expense in the Plan Assumptions window. You can review and modify event information in that window, as shown in Figure 14-3.

Playing "What If"

Once you've entered assumptions, created plans for specific events, and viewed your plan results, you might wonder how a change in one or more assumptions would affect the plan. You can use the "What If" Event Scenarios feature to see how the changes would affect the plan without changing the plan itself.

Here's an example. Say you've been offered a job in another state. The job pays about the same salary that you make now, but you can move to a town where your living expenses would be greatly reduced. You can see how the job change would affect your financial plans for the future by playing "what if" to modify existing assumptions, and then see the old and new plan results side by side.

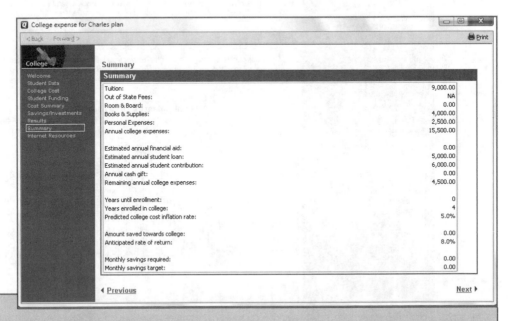

Figure 14-3 • A summary of major expenses is accessed from the Monthly Savings Targets section of the Quicken Lifetime Planner.

Setting "What If" Options

Each of the sections of the Lifetime Planner in the Planning tab has an Options button from which you can play What If. Click Options | What If I Did Something Different? to open the What If window seen in Figure 14-4. The first time you use it, the window displays the account balances shown in your plan results.

Choose a goal option from the drop-down list at the top left of the window. Then click appropriate links on the left side of the window to open dialogs to change assumptions.

In our example, you might use the following links:

- Click Current Homes & Assets to add proposed sale information about your current home.
- Click Current Loans to record the proposed payoff of your mortgage when you sell your current home.

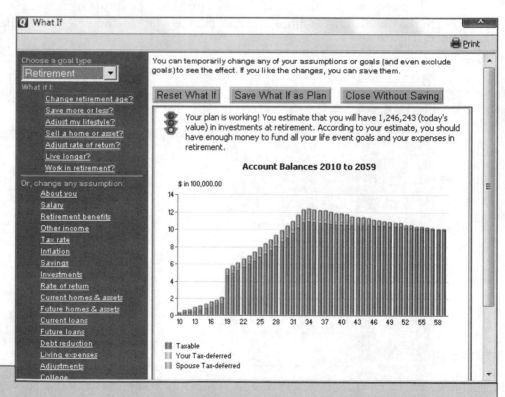

Figure 14-4 • You can use the What If window to play "what if" with your financial plans.

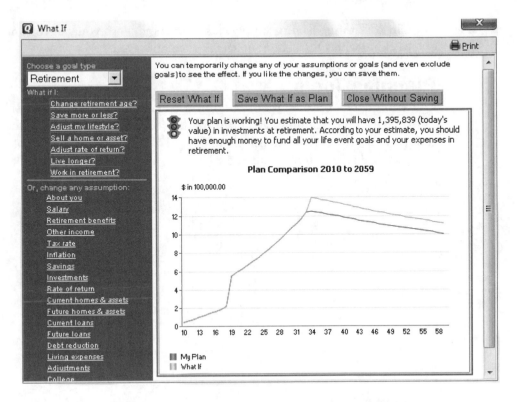

- Click Future Homes & Assets to add proposed purchase information about your new home and its associated mortgage.
- Click Adjustments to add a proposed adjustment for the reduced living expenses when you move to your new home.

See how that works? Each time you make a change, the Plan Comparison chart changes. The original plan is shown as an orange line and the change as a yellow line.

Using "What If" Results

When you've finished changing assumptions and viewing results, you can click one of the three buttons at the top of the What If window:

- **Reset What If** clears all the assumptions you changed while playing "what if." This enables you to start over.
- **Save What If As Plan** saves the assumptions you changed while playing "what if" as your actual financial plan. When the window closes, you'll see the results in the Planning tab change accordingly.

- **Close Without Saving** simply closes the window so you can continue working with Quicken. Your settings are not saved.

Planning Tools

Quicken offers additional tools found in the Planning Tools button on the button bar of the Planning tab. They are divided into two sections, budgeting tools, which are covered extensively in Chapter 16, and calculation tools, which are discussed at length in Chapter 15.

Using Financial Calculators

In This Chapter:

- *Financial calculators overview*
- *Retirement Calculator*
- *College Calculator*
- *Refinance Calculator*
- *Savings Calculator*
- *Loan Calculator*

Sometimes, the hardest part about financial planning is making the calculations you need quickly to determine the feasibility of a potential plan. For example, suppose you're thinking about refinancing your home because you can now get an interest rate that's lower than the rate you locked into six years ago. You know your monthly payment can decrease, but you're not sure if you'll save enough money to cover the fees involved in the refinancing. The calculations seem complex, and you're not sure what to do. That's where one of Quicken Personal Finance Software's financial calculators—the Refinance Calculator—can help. It can take raw data about your current mortgage and the one you're considering, and crunch the numbers in a flash to tell you whether it's worthwhile to take the next step.

This chapter tells you about each of Quicken's financial calculators. You'll find them handy tools for making the quick calculations you need to start the decision-making process with your financial plans.

A Look at Quicken's Financial Calculators

Quicken includes five financial calculators you can use to make quick financial calculations: the Retirement Calculator, the College Calculator, the Refinance Calculator, the Investment Savings Calculator, and the Loan Calculator. These calculators make complex calculations simple.

How the Calculators Work

All five of the financial calculators share the same basic interface. But although they are similar in appearance, each is designed for a specific purpose. It's important that you use the correct calculator to get the job done.

In most instances, you begin by telling the calculator what part of the formula you want to calculate. For example, when calculating a loan, you can calculate the loan amount or the periodic payment. Then you enter values and set other options in the calculator's dialog to give Quicken the information it needs to make its calculations. Clicking a Calculate button completes the process. Quicken is fast; the results appear as soon as you click Calculate—if not sooner.

Accessing the Financial Calculators

To view the financial calculators, click the Planning tab and choose Planning Tools. The five calculators appear at the bottom of the menu, as shown here.

If the Planning tab is not visible, click View | Tabs To Show | Planning on the menu bar. If you see Tools instead of Planning Tools, maximize your window to see Planning Tools.

Using the Financial Calculators

If you are ready to try Quicken's financial calculators, the rest of this chapter provides some detailed instructions for using each of them. All of the calculators open with one or more fields showing the text "CALCULATED" or "calculated." Click the Calculate button to change that text to the calculated number.

Retirement Calculator

The Retirement Calculator can help you calculate some of the numbers you need to plan for your retirement. To open it, choose Planning | Planning Tools | Retirement Calculator. The Retirement Calculator appears as seen in Figure 15-1.

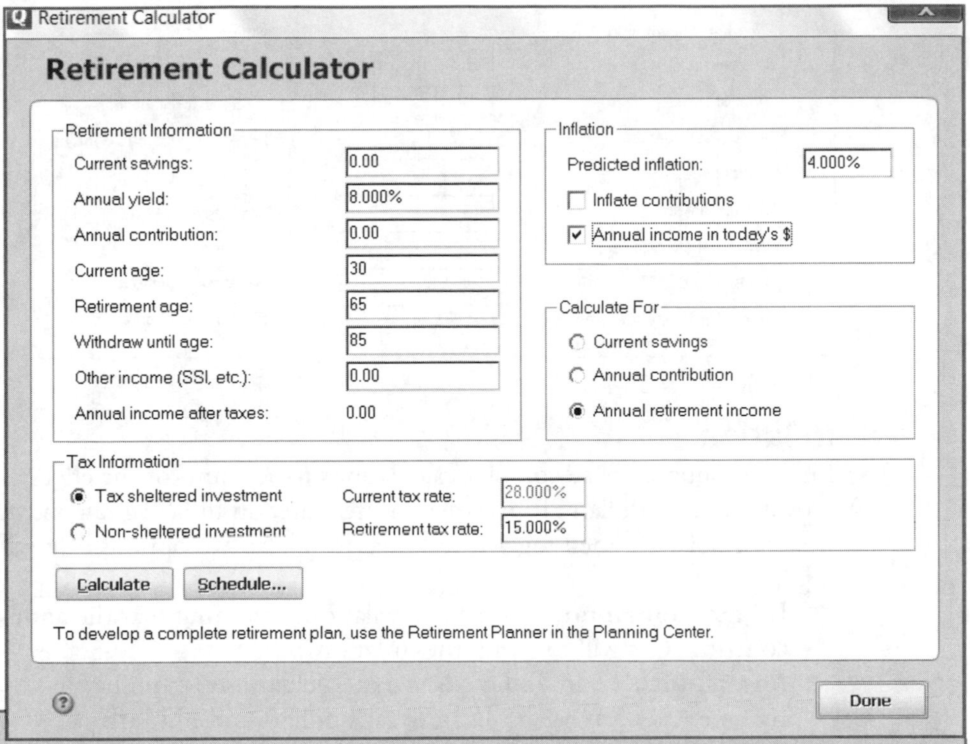

Figure 15-1 • Use the Retirement Calculator for a quick overview of your income when you retire.

Select a Calculate For option, and then enter or select values and options throughout the dialog. Most options are pretty straightforward and easy to understand. When you're finished, click the Calculate button to see the results. Click Done when you're finished.

Here's a closer look at the options in the Retirement Calculator.

Retirement Information

Retirement Information options enable you to enter the values Quicken should use in its calculations. The values you must enter vary depending on the Calculate For option you select. For example, if you are 37 years old and plan on retiring at age 70 and want to know how much to save each year to achieve an annual income at retirement of $30,000 in today's dollars, calculate for the annual contribution, as seen on the top of the next page.

Retirement Information		Inflation	
Current savings:	55,000.00	Predicted inflation:	4.000%
Annual yield:	4.000%	☐ Inflate contributions	
Annual contribution:	14,472.79	☑ Annual income in today's $	
Current age:	37		
Retirement age:	70	Calculate For	
Withdraw until age:	85	○ Current savings	
Other income (SSI, etc.):	12,000.00	● Annual contribution	
Annual income after taxes:	30,000.00	○ Annual retirement income	

Inflation

Inflation options make complex calculations to account for the effect of inflation on your savings dollars. To use this feature, enter an inflation rate in the Predicted Inflation box, and then toggle check marks for the two options below it.

- **Inflate Contributions** makes calculations assuming that the annual contributions will rise with the inflation rate.
- **Annual Income In Today's $** makes calculations assuming that the Annual Income After Taxes entry is in today's dollars and not inflated.

Calculate For

The Calculate For option affects which value is calculated by Quicken.

- **Current Savings** calculates the amount of money you should currently have saved to achieve the values you enter.
- **Annual Contribution** calculates the minimum amount you should contribute to a retirement account to achieve the values you enter.
- **Annual Retirement Income** calculates the annual amount of retirement income you'll have based on the values you enter.

Tax Information

Tax Information options enable you to indicate whether your retirement savings are in a tax-sheltered investment or a non-sheltered investment. If you select the Non-Sheltered Investment option, you can enter your current tax rate and Quicken will automatically calculate the effect of taxes on your investment income. By experimenting with this feature, you can clearly see why it's a good idea to use tax-sheltered or tax-deferred investments whenever possible.

Schedule

Clicking the Schedule button displays a printable list of deposits made and income withdrawn, with a running balance total. Here's what it looks like with the calculations shown earlier.

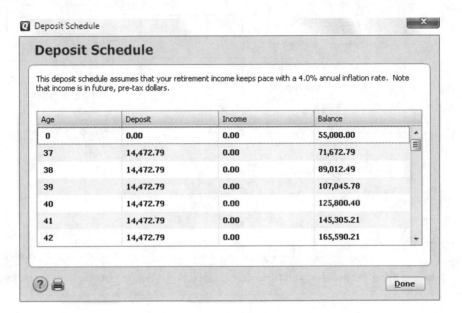

College Calculator

The College Calculator enables you to calculate savings for the cost of a college education. Choose Planning | Planning Tools | College Calculator. The College Calculator shown in Figure 15-2 appears.

Select a Calculate For option, and then enter or select values and options throughout the dialog. As with the other calculators, the available options are straightforward. When you click Calculate, Quicken calculates the results. When you are finished, click Done.

Here's a look at the options in the College Calculator.

College Information

The College Information area is where you enter the values Quicken should use in its calculations. The values you must enter vary, depending on the Calculate For option you select.

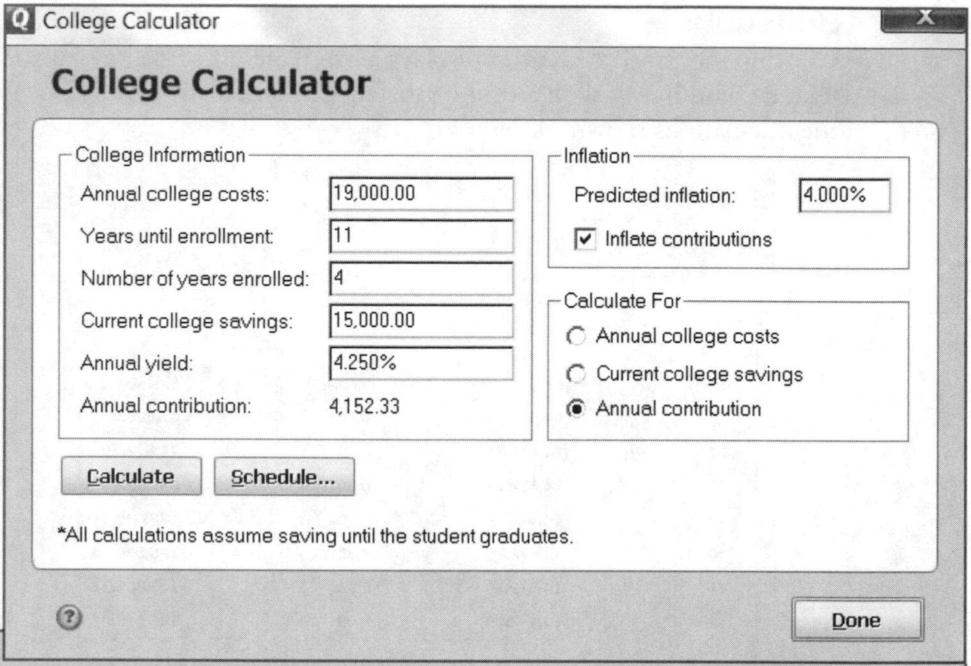

College Calculator

College Information

Annual college costs:	19,000.00
Years until enrollment:	11
Number of years enrolled:	4
Current college savings:	15,000.00
Annual yield:	4.250%
Annual contribution:	4,152.33

Inflation

Predicted inflation: 4.000%

☑ Inflate contributions

Calculate For

○ Annual college costs
○ Current college savings
◉ Annual contribution

[Calculate] [Schedule...]

*All calculations assume saving until the student graduates.

[Done]

Figure 15-2 • Planning ahead for college costs can eliminate stress for you and your student.

Inflation

Inflation options make complex calculations to account for the effect of inflation on your savings dollars. To use this feature, enter an inflation rate in the Predicted Inflation box. You can then toggle the Inflate Contributions check box, which makes calculations assuming that the annual contributions will rise with the inflation rate. Quicken automatically inflates the amount of tuition no matter how you set the Inflate Contributions check box.

Calculate For

The Calculate For option affects which value is calculated by Quicken.

- **Annual College Costs** calculates the annual tuition you'll be able to afford based on the values you enter.
- **Current College Savings** calculates the amount of money you should currently have saved based on the values you enter.
- **Annual Contribution** calculates the minimum amount you should contribute to college savings based on the values you enter.

Schedule

Clicking the Schedule button displays a printable list of deposits made and money withdrawn for tuition, with a running balance total. Here's what it looks like with the calculations shown earlier. Note the last four years of the schedule show the withdrawals.

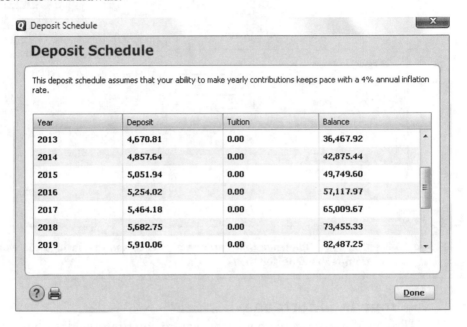

Refinance Calculator

If you own a home and are thinking about refinancing, you can try the Refinance Calculator to see whether refinancing will really save you money and, if so, how much. Choose Planning | Planning Tools | Refinance Calculator. The Refinance Calculator appears.

Enter values for your current mortgage and proposed mortgage in the text boxes to calculate your monthly savings with the new mortgage. When you are finished, click Done. Here's a closer look at the entries as seen in Figure 15-3.

Existing Mortgage

Existing Mortgage options enable you to enter your current total monthly mortgage payment and the amount of that payment that is applied to property taxes and other escrow items. Quicken automatically calculates the amount of principal and interest for each payment. If you already know the principal and interest amount, you can enter that in the Current Payment box and leave the Impound/Escrow Amount box empty. The result is the same.

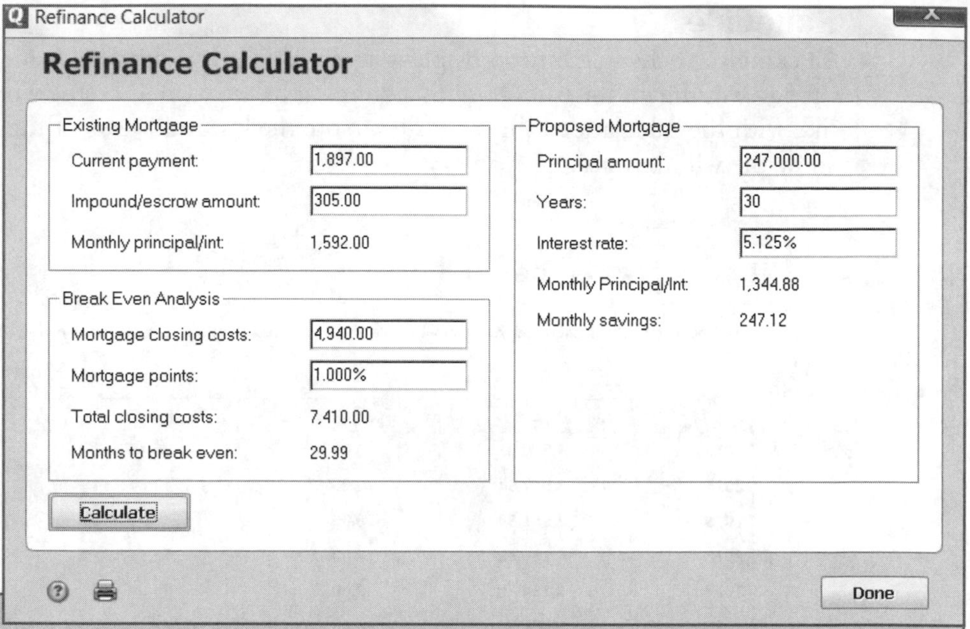

Figure 15-3 • Quicken's Refinance Calculator helps you to see the savings you would realize from refinancing your home.

Proposed Mortgage

Proposed Mortgage options enable you to enter information about the mortgage that you are considering to replace your current mortgage. The Principal Amount may be the balance on your current mortgage, but it could be more or less depending on whether you want to refinance for more or less money. (Refinancing often offers a good opportunity to exchange equity for cash.)

Break Even Analysis

Break Even Analysis options are optional. If you enter the closing costs and points for the proposed mortgage, Quicken will automatically calculate how long it will take to cover those costs based on your monthly savings. As you can see in Figure 15-3, after points and closing costs, the break-even point for this refinance is nearly two and a half years.

Print

Clicking the Print button displays the Print dialog, which you can use to print the results of your calculations.

Investment Savings Calculator

The Investment Savings Calculator enables you to calculate savings annuities—periodic payments to a savings account or investment. Choose Planning | Planning Tools | Savings Calculator. The Investment Savings Calculator appears, as shown in Figure 15-4.

Select a Calculate For option, and then enter or select values and options throughout the dialog. When you click Calculate, Quicken displays the results. When you are finished, click Done.

Here's a closer look at each of the entry options.

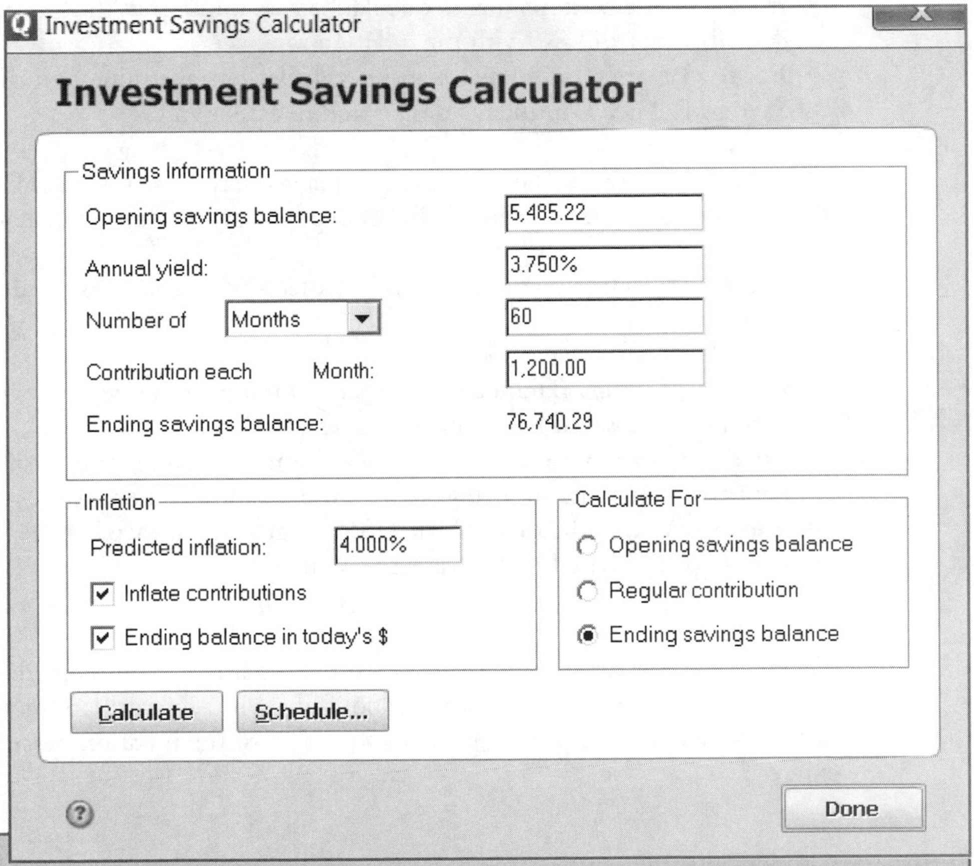

Figure 15-4 • Determining how contributing regularly to your savings can help you achieve your goals.

Savings Information

Savings Information options enable you to enter values for Quicken to use in its calculations. The option you choose from the Number Of drop-down list will determine how interest is compounded; in most cases, you'll probably set this to Months.

Inflation

Inflation options make complex calculations to account for the effect of inflation on your savings dollars. To use this feature, enter an inflation rate in the Predicted Inflation box, and then toggle check boxes for the two options below it:

- **Inflate Contributions** makes calculations assuming that the annual contributions will rise with the inflation rate.
- **Ending Balance In Today's $** makes calculations assuming that the Ending Savings Balance is in today's dollars and not inflated.

When you click Calculate, Quicken displays the results. You can click the Schedule button to see a printable list of deposits, with a running balance total.

Calculate For   The Calculate For option affects which value is calculated by Quicken.

- **Opening Savings Balance** calculates the amount of money you should currently have saved based on the values you enter.
- **Regular Contribution** calculates the minimum amount you should regularly contribute to savings based on the values you enter.
- **Ending Savings Balance** calculates the total amount saved at the end of the savings period based on the values you enter.

Schedule

Clicking the Schedule button displays a printable list of deposits made, with a running balance total. Here is what it looks like with the calculations shown earlier. Note that the schedule explains the effect of the inflation percentage you entered.

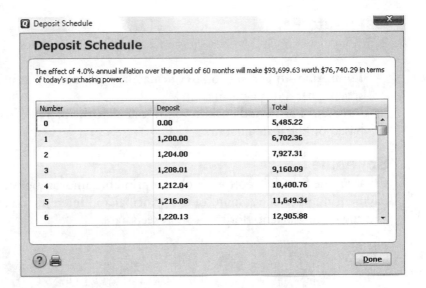

Loan Calculator

Quicken's Loan Calculator can quickly calculate the principal or periodic payment for a loan. Choose Planning | Planning Tools | Loan Calculator to open the Loan Calculator, as shown here.

Select one of the Calculate For options, enter information in the remainder of the dialog, and click Calculate. Getting the answer is a lot quicker and easier with the Loan Calculator than using one of those loan books or building an Excel spreadsheet to do the job. When you're finished, click Done.

Here's a look at the Loan Calculator options.

Loan Information

Loan Information options enable you to enter values for Quicken to use in its calculations. The information you must enter varies depending on the Calculate For option you select. Be sure to set the Periods Per Year and Compounding Period options correctly; an incorrect entry will misstate the results.

Calculate For

The Calculate For options determine what Quicken calculates.

- **Loan Amount** enables you to calculate the amount of a loan based on specific periodic payments.
- **Payment Per Period** enables you to calculate the periodic loan payment based on the loan amount.

Schedule

Clicking the Schedule button displays a printable amortization table that lists the payment number, the amount of the principal and interest paid at each payment, and the ending balance for the loan as seen here.

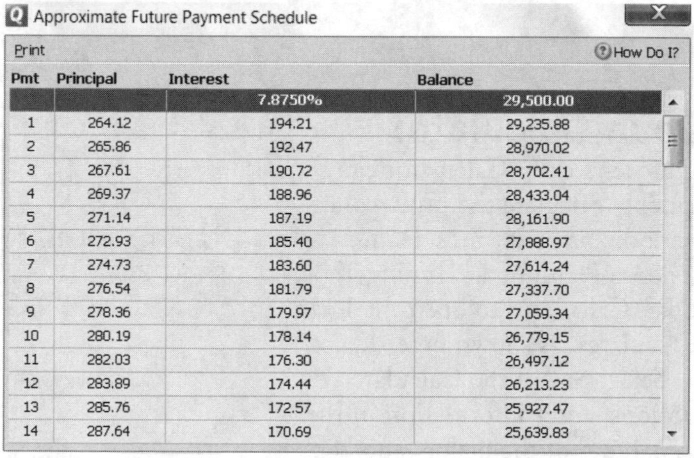

Pmt	Principal	Interest	Balance
		7.8750%	29,500.00
1	264.12	194.21	29,235.88
2	265.86	192.47	28,970.02
3	267.61	190.72	28,702.41
4	269.37	188.96	28,433.04
5	271.14	187.19	28,161.90
6	272.93	185.40	27,888.97
7	274.73	183.60	27,614.24
8	276.54	181.79	27,337.70
9	278.36	179.97	27,059.34
10	280.19	178.14	26,779.15
11	282.03	176.30	26,497.12
12	283.89	174.44	26,213.23
13	285.76	172.57	25,927.47
14	287.64	170.69	25,639.83

Approximate Future Payment Schedule

Print   How Do I?

Reducing Debt and Saving Money

In This Chapter:

- *Reducing debt*
- *Budgeting and forecasting*
- *Setting up savings goals*

The best way to prepare for life events is to build up your savings. Saving money is an important part of financial management. Savings enable you to take vacations and make major purchases without increasing debt, help your kids through college, handle emergencies, and have a comfortable retirement.

This chapter tells you about saving money and how tools within Quicken Personal Finance Software can help. If you're in debt and can't even think about saving until you dig your way out, this chapter can help you, too. It starts by covering Quicken tools for reducing your debt.

Reducing Your Debt

Consumer credit is a huge industry. It's still easy to get credit cards—even with the new regulations. And it's a lot easier to pay for something with a piece of plastic than with cold, hard cash. The "buy now, pay later" attitude has become an acceptable way of life. It's no wonder that many Americans are deeply in debt.

Those credit card bills can add up, however. And making just the minimum payment on each one only helps the credit card company keep you in debt—and paying interest—as long as possible. If you're in debt, don't skip this part of the chapter. It'll help you dig yourself out so you can build a solid financial future.

Chapter 16

Take Control

It's not easy to save money if most of your income is spent paying credit card bills and loan payments. If you're heavily in debt, you might even be having trouble keeping up with all your payments. But don't despair. There is hope! Here are a few simple things you can do to dig yourself out of debt.

Breaking the Pattern

Your first step to reducing debt must be to break the pattern of spending that got you where you are. For most people, that means cutting up credit cards. After all, it's tough to use a credit card if you can't hand it to a cashier at the checkout counter.

Before you take out the scissors, however, read this: You don't have to cut up *all* of your credit cards. Leave yourself one or two major credit cards for emergencies, such as car trouble or unexpected visits to the doctor. The cards that should go are the store and gas credit cards. They can increase your debt, but they can be used in only a few places.

Here's the logic behind this strategy. If you have 15 credit cards, each with a credit limit of $2,000, you can get yourself into $30,000 of debt. The minimum monthly payment for each card may be $50. That's $750 a month in minimum credit card payments. If you have only two credit cards, each with a credit limit of $2,000, you can get yourself into only $4,000 of debt. Your monthly minimum payment may be only $100. This reduces your monthly obligation, enabling you to pay more than the minimum so you can further reduce your debt.

Reducing Your Credit Limits

Sure, it's a real temptation to use your credit cards to spend just a little more every month—especially when you're not even close to your credit limit. But high credit limits are a trap. The credit card company or bank flatters you by offering to lend you more money. What they're really doing is setting you up so you'll owe them more—and pay them more in monthly finance and interest fees.

The next time your credit card company tells you they've raised your credit limit, do yourself a favor: Call them up and tell them to reduce it right back to where it was—or lower!

Shopping for Cards with Better Interest Rates

Yes, it's nice to have a credit card with your picture on it. Or one that's gold, platinum, or titanium. Or one with your college, team, club, or association name on it. A friend of mine who breeds horses showed off a new Visa card with a picture of a horse on it. She told me it was her favorite. I asked her what the interest rate was, and she didn't know.

The purpose of a credit card is to purchase things on credit. When you maintain a balance on the account, you pay interest on it. The balance and interest rate determine how much it costs you to have that special picture or name on a plastic card in your wallet. Is it worth 19.8 percent a year? Or 34 percent?

Here's a reality-check exercise: Gather together all of your credit card bills for the most recent month. Now add up all the monthly finance fees and interest charges. Multiply that number by 12. The result is an approximation of what you pay in credit card interest each year. Now imagine how nice it would be to have that money in your hands the next time you go on vacation or need a down payment on a new car or home.

Low-interest credit cards are still widely available; try a web search. But before you apply for a new card, read the terms carefully. Many offer the low rates for a short, introductory period—usually no longer than 6 or 12 months. Some offer the low rate only on new purchases, while others offer the low rate only on balance transfers or cash advances. Be sure to find out what the rate is after the introductory period.

Here are two strategies for using a low-interest card:

- Consolidate your debt by transferring the balances of other credit cards to the new card. For this strategy, select a card that offers a low rate on balance transfers. When you transfer the balances, be sure to cut up the old cards so you don't use them to add more to your debt.
- Make purchases with the low-interest card. Make the new card your emergency credit card. Be sure to cut up your old emergency card so you don't wind up using both of them.

And if you really like that special picture or name on the card in your wallet, call the credit card company and ask if they can give you a better interest rate. In many instances, they can—especially when you tell them you want to close your account.

Consolidating Your Debt

Consolidating your debt may be one way to dig yourself out. By combining balances into one debt, whether through balance transfers to a single credit card or a debt consolidation loan, you're better able to pay off the balances without causing financial hardship. This is sometimes the only option when things have gotten completely out of control and you can't meet your debt obligations. However, make sure you have cut up the old cards so you don't add new debt to the older, consolidated amount.

Although this can be a risky way to handle your debt, if you own a home, you might consider a home equity loan to consolidate your debt. The interest rate is usually lower than any credit card or debt consolidation loan, and the interest may be tax-deductible. There's more about home equity loans in Chapter 12.

Using Charge Cards, Not Credit Cards

There's a difference between a credit card and a charge card.

- **Credit cards** enable you to buy things on credit. If each month you pay less than what you owe, you are charged interest on your account balance. Most major "credit cards" are true credit cards. MasterCard, Visa, and Discover are three examples. Most store "charge cards" are also credit cards.
- **Charge cards** enable you to buy things on credit, too. But when the bill comes, you're expected to pay the entire balance. You don't have to pay any interest, but if you don't pay the entire balance on time, you may have to pay late fees and finance charges. American Express is an example of a charge card.

The benefit of charge cards is that they make it impossible to get into serious debt. How can you owe the charge card company money if you must pay the balance in full every month? Using these cards prevents you from overspending. Every time you use the card to make a purchase, a little accountant in the back of your head should be adding the charge to a running total. You should stop spending when that total reaches the limit of your ability to pay.

Chapters 4 and 5 explain how you can use Quicken to track credit and charge card balances either manually or online. If you use Quicken to keep track of expenditures, you won't need that little accountant in the back of your head.

If you don't want an American Express card (for whatever reason), use another major credit card as a charge card. Just pay the entire balance each time you get a bill. If you don't carry a balance, you won't be charged interest.

If You Can't Stop Spending, Get Help

Many people who are deeply in debt may have a spending problem. They can't resist buying that fifth pair of running shoes or that trendy new outdoor furniture. They don't *need* the things they buy, but they buy them anyway. There's nothing wrong with that if your income can support your spending habits, but if your net worth is less than $0, it's a real problem—one that might require counseling to resolve.

The next time you make a purchase, stop for a moment and think about what you're buying. Is it something you need? Something you can use? Something you can justify spending the money on? If you can't answer yes to any of these questions, don't buy it. If you have to buy it anyway, it's time to seek professional help.

Living Debt-Free

It is possible to live debt-free—and you don't have to be rich to do it. Just stop relying on credit to make your purchases and spend only what you can afford.

Imagine how great it would feel to be completely debt-free. It's worth a try, isn't it?

Using the Debt Reduction Planner

Quicken's Debt Reduction Planner is a tool for helping you reduce your debt. You enter information about your financial situation, and Quicken develops a debt reduction plan for you. The Debt Reduction Planner is thorough, easy to use, and an excellent tool for teaching people how they can get out of debt as quickly as possible, saving hundreds (if not thousands) of dollars in interest charges.

Note that the Debt Reduction Planner works best when you track all of your debt—including credit card debt—using Quicken accounts. That means setting

---

EXPERIENCED QUICKEN USERS AND NEW TO QUICKEN?

The Debt Reduction Planner

If you're in serious debt—actually having trouble making ends meet because you can't seem to get any of your debts paid down—a pair of scissors, a telephone, and the Debt Reduction Planner are probably your three best tools for getting things under control.

First, use the scissors to cut up most, if not all, of your credit cards. Next, use the telephone to call your credit card companies and try to get your interest rates reduced. (The worst they can do is say no.) Then use the Debt Reduction Planner to come up with a solid plan for reducing your debt.

Here's what the Debt Reduction Planner can do that you might not be able to do on your own:

- Objectively look at your debts and organize them by interest rate. The debts that cost you the most are the ones that are paid off first, thus saving you money.
- Show you the benefit of using some of your savings to reduce the balances on your most costly debt.
- Help you set up spending limits, with alerts, for the categories on which you spend too much money.
- Create an itemized plan based on real numbers that you can follow to reduce your debt.
- Show you, in dollars and cents, how much money you can save and how quickly you can become debt-free by following the plan.
- Don't dread the daily mail and its package of bills. Use the Debt Reduction Planner to get things under control.

up accounts for your credit cards rather than simply tracking monthly payments as bills paid. Chapters 2 and 4 discuss the two different ways to track credit cards in Quicken.

To get started, first turn on Classic menus. From the Quicken menu bar, click View | Classic Menus. From the Classic menu, choose Planning | Debt Reduction Planner. If you have explored this feature before, the Debt Reduction window appears with a chart showing the information you previously entered (refer to Figure 16-1, later in this chapter). If you have never used it before, the Debt Reduction dialog, with its Welcome screen as shown here, appears, enabling you to create a new debt reduction plan.

Entering Debt Information

To get started with the plan, click Next. The Debts tab opens as shown on the top of the next page.

This tab lists all of your current debts as they are recorded in Quicken. Use the buttons to the right of the list to modify it.

- If the debt list is not up to date or complete, click the Update Debts button to import current debt information from your Quicken data file.
- To add a debt that you do not track in Quicken, click the Add button. The Edit Debt Reduction dialog appears. Use it to enter information about the debt, and click OK to add it to the list.

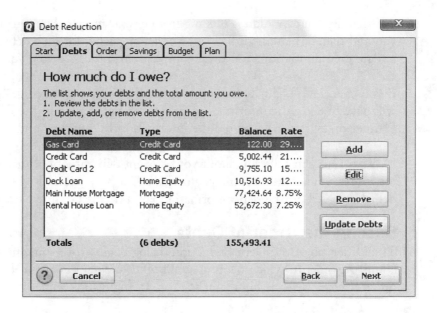

- To modify information about a debt, select it and click the Edit button to display the Edit Debt Reduction dialog shown here. Make changes as desired, and click OK to save them.
- To remove a debt from the list, select it and click the Remove button. In the confirmation dialog that appears, click Yes. This removes the debt from the Debt Reduction Planner but does not remove it from your Quicken data file. You may want to use this feature to remove a long-term debt, such as a mortgage, so you can concentrate on higher interest, short-term debt, such as credit cards and personal loans.

When the debt list shows all of the debts you want to include in your plan, click Next to continue.

If required information is missing from one or more debts, Quicken will tell you and then display the Edit Debt Reduction dialog for each debt so you can update the information. You must complete this process before you can continue.

If you cancel the Debt Reduction Planner at this point and come back later, you will have to enter the information again when you return to the Debt Reduction Planner unless you have edited the information in each account.

Next, Quicken tells you about your current debt situation, including your total debt, your total monthly payments, and a projection of when you will be debt-free based on the debt information you provided. Click Next to continue.

Setting the Order of Debts

The Order tab of the Debt Reduction dialog begins with some information about the order in which debts are paid off. Quicken puts your debts in the order of cost, with the highest at the top. It might look something like this:

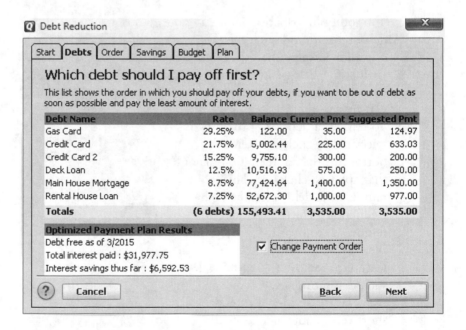

This tab sets the debt payoff order so that the most expensive debt (that is, the highest rate of interest) is paid off first, thus saving you interest charges. The Suggested Pmt column offers a suggested payment amount; following the suggestion makes it possible to pay off the debts faster without increasing your total monthly payments. If desired, you can turn on the Change Payment Order check box to change the order in which debts are paid off—this, however, will cost you more and increase the payoff time.

If you turn on the Change Payment Order check box and click the Next button, the dialog changes to enable you to change the order of debts. Click a debt to select it, and then click Move Up or Move Down to change its location in the list as seen here. When you've finished, click Next.

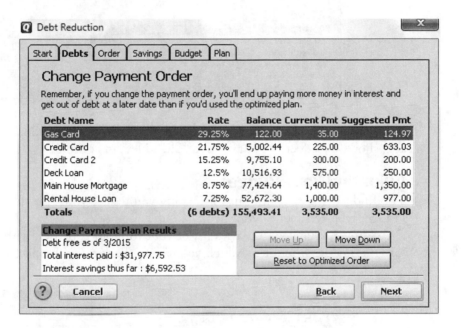

Using Savings to Pay Off Debt

The Savings tab summarizes your current savings and investments, and enables you to specify how much of your savings should be applied to your debt, as shown on the next page.

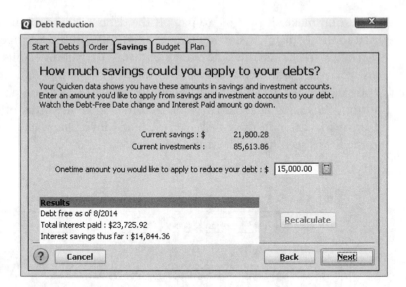

Enter a value in the text box, and click the Recalculate button. The Results area shows the effect of your change. Click Next to continue.

Adjusting Your Budget

The Budget tab offers options for helping you reduce your spending, which can, in turn, help you reduce your debt.

As shown, Quicken displays a list of your top four expenses, with text boxes for entering the amount by which you can cut back on each one every month.

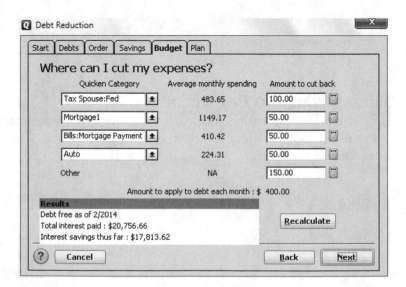

Enter the amounts by which you can cut back for the categories that appear or for different categories you select from the drop-down lists. Click Recalculate. Quicken automatically suggests that you apply the savings to the debt, thus adjusting the Results area for your entries. Click Next to continue.

Reviewing the Plan

The Plan tab, shown here, displays your custom debt reduction action plan.

Scroll through the debt reduction plan to see what it recommends. Better yet, click the Print This Action Plan button to print a copy you can refer to throughout the coming months. Click Next to continue.

Next, Quicken offers to track your debt reduction plan for you. You can toggle the settings for two different check boxes to enable this feature.

- **Alert Me If I Fall Behind** tells Quicken to alert you if you fall behind on debt reduction and to include your debt in budgeting and forecasting models. (Read about Planning Center alerts, budgeting, and forecasting later in this chapter.)
- **Set Up Scheduled Transactions For My Monthly Payments** tells Quicken to schedule transactions for the monthly payments included in your debt reduction plan. (Learn about scheduling payments in Chapter 6.)

Turn on the check box for each option that you want to enable, and then click Done.

Viewing the Debt Reduction Plan Results

When you click Done in the final screen of the Debt Reduction dialog, the Debt Reduction window appears (see Figure 16-1). It uses a graph to compare debt reduction using your current method (the right line) with that of your new debt reduction plan (the left line).

To see the results of your plan on a month-to-month basis, click the Payment Schedule button at the top of the Debt Reduction window. The Debt Reduction Payment Schedule dialog, shown on the top of the next page, appears. It lists the payments you should make for each month, according to the plan and your account balances at month-end.

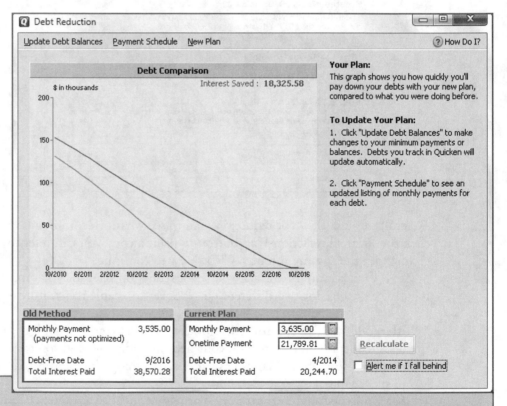

Figure 16-1 • The Debt Reduction Plan window clearly illustrates how quickly you can get out of debt and save interest costs.

Modifying the Plan

Once you have a debt reduction plan, you can modify it in a number of ways:

- Click the Update Debt Balances button on the button bar to import the current balances of your debt into the Debt Reduction Planner.
- Enter new values in the Current Plan area at the bottom of the Debt Reduction window. Click Recalculate to see how that new value will affect the plan.
- Click the New Plan button on the button bar to create a new plan from scratch. New data entered will replace the existing data for your plan.

No matter which method you choose, Quicken will automatically revise the graph and other information to reflect your changes.

Budgeting and Forecasting

When money is tight or you're interested in meeting financial goals, it's time to create a budget and monitor your spending. But if you're serious about managing your money, you might want to create a budget *before* you need one. Although Quicken's categories give you a clear understanding of where money comes from and where it goes, budgets enable you to set up predefined amounts for each category, thus helping you to control spending.

Budgets also make it easier to create forecasts of your future financial position. This makes it possible to see how much cash will be available at a future date—before the holidays, for summer vacation, or for the day you plan to put down a deposit on a new car.

In this part of the chapter, you'll learn how to create a budget and use it to monitor your spending habits. You'll also learn how to create a forecast so you can glimpse your financial future.

Budgeting

The idea behind a budget is to determine expected income amounts and specify maximum amounts for expenditures. This helps prevent you from spending more than you earn. It also enables you to control your spending in certain categories. For example, say you realize that you go out for dinner a lot more often than you should. You can set a budget for the Dining category and track your spending to make sure you don't exceed the budget. You'll eat at home more often and save money.

This section explains how to set up a budget and use it to keep track of your spending. Hopefully you'll see that budgeting is a great way to keep spending under control.

Organizing Categories into Groups

Budgets are based on transactions recorded for categories and subcategories. (That's why it's important to categorize all your transactions—and not to the Miscellaneous category!) Quicken also enables you to organize categories by customizable category groups. Although you don't have to use the Groups feature when creating your budget—it's entirely optional—grouping similar categories together can simplify your budget.

Choose Tools | Category List to display the window. You can also open the Category List by pressing SHIFT-CTRL-C. If the Group column does not appear in your list, choose Show Category Group from the Options menu at the bottom of the window to display it, as shown. By default, Quicken assigns nearly every category to either the Personal Income or Personal Expense group. Your bank and investment accounts have no groups assigned. How to assign groups is explained in "Assigning a Group to a Category," later in this chapter.

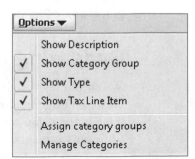

The Default Groups   By default, Quicken includes two category groups that it assigns to the categories it creates when you first set up your Quicken data file.

- **Personal Income** is for earned income, such as your salary, and miscellaneous income items, such as interest, dividends, and gifts received.
- **Personal Expenses** are all of your personal expenses, items you pay for and record in your account registers.

In addition, if your Quicken data file includes business-related categories, Quicken includes Business Income and Business Expenses groups to track the income and expenses from your business.

Creating a Custom Group   To create a custom group, in the Category List window, click Options and choose Assign Category Groups. The Assign Category Groups dialog appears, as seen in Figure 16-2.

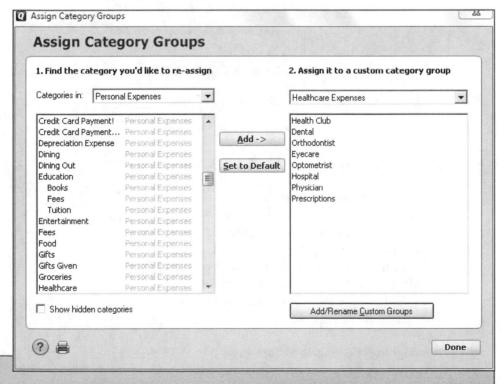

Figure 16-2 • You can assign category groups and create new groups to better organize your transactions.

Click the Add/Rename Custom Groups button to open the Custom Category Groups dialog. When it appears, click New to open the Create Custom Group dialog. Type the name of your custom group as shown, and click OK.

The new group appears in the Custom Category Groups dialog as seen here. Click Done to close the Custom Category Groups dialog and return to the Assign Category Groups dialog. Click Done once again to close the Assign Category Groups dialog and return to the Category List.

Assigning a Group to a Category

You can assign a standard or a custom group to a new category. In the Category List window, click New to

create a new category. The Set Up Category dialog appears. Click the arrow next to the Group box to display the drop-down list, which is shown here, and choose a group. You can create a new group in this dialog by clicking the New button, or edit an existing group by clicking Edit. (Chapter 2 discusses more about creating new categories.) After you have selected the group, click OK to include the group with this category and save your new category to the Category List.

If you have not yet created any custom category groups, you will not see the Group field in the Set Up Category dialog. Go back to the Category List and click Options | Assign Category Groups, and create at least one custom category group.

To add a group to an existing category, select the category, and, from the Action column, click Edit to open the Set Up Category dialog. Click the arrow next to the Group box to display the Group drop-down list. If the category is one of the default Quicken categories, the Personal Expenses group may appear in the group box, although it is not an option in the group list. Simply click the group to which you want this category assigned, and click OK. The custom group is now assigned to this existing category.

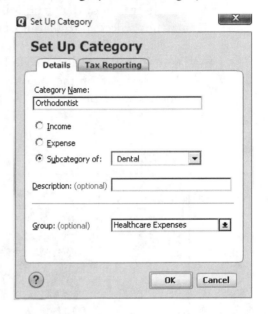

Modifying the Category Group List   You can modify or delete custom category group names. From the Category List, click Options | Assign Category Groups, and click Add/Rename Custom Groups. The Custom Category Groups dialog appears. Select a group name, and click Rename to rename an existing group. To delete a custom category group, select the group name and click Delete.

After you have made your changes, click Done to return to the Assign Category Groups dialog. Click Done one more time to close the Assign Category Groups dialog and return to the Category List.

Creating a Budget

Quicken can automatically generate a budget for you based on past transactions. You can edit the budget it creates to meet your needs, or you can create a budget from scratch.

To start creating a budget, choose Planning | Planning Tools | Budget. The Setup tab of the Budget window, which is shown in Figure 16-3, appears.

Creating a Budget Automatically The quickest and easiest way to create a budget is to let Quicken do it for you based on your income and expenditures. For Quicken to create an accurate budget, however, you must have several months' worth of transactions in your Quicken data file. Otherwise, the budget may not reflect all regular income and expenses.

Select the Automatic option in the Setup tab of the Budget window (refer to Figure 16-3), and click Create Budget. The Create Budget: Automatic dialog, which is shown on the top of the next page, appears. Use this dialog to set options for the budget.

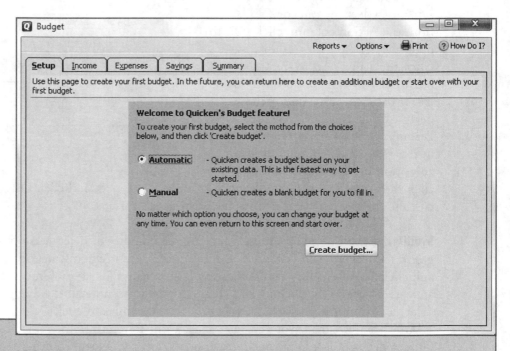

Figure 16-3 • The Setup tab of the Budget dialog helps you create a budget.

In the date range area, enter the starting and ending dates for the transactions on which you want to base the budget. Whenever possible, the date range should be the most recent 12-month period. But if you have less than 12 months' worth of data, enter the date range for the period for which you have data.

Next, select one of the following budget method options:

- **Average Amounts** enters monthly averages based on the period in the date range. If you select this option, choose a frequency from the drop-down list.
- **Monthly Detail** copies the total values for each month to the corresponding month in the budget.
- **Quarterly Detail** copies the total values for each quarter to the corresponding quarter in the budget.

If you're not sure which to select, consider this advice: Select Monthly Detail or Quarterly Detail if you have a full year of transactions (or close to it) and you have seasonal income (such as a teaching job) or expenses (such as a vacation home). Select Average Amounts if you have less than six months of transactions or don't have seasonal income or expenses.

Toggle the following check boxes in the Options area as desired:

- **Round Values To Nearest** enables you to round calculated values to the nearest $1, $10, or $100. If you enable this option, choose a value from the drop-down list beside it.
- **Exclude One-Time Transactions** tells Quicken not to consider one-time transactions when creating the budget. For example, suppose you made a single large payment to a furniture company to buy living room furniture. If that transaction is considered for budgeting purposes, Quicken will automatically assume that you make payments like that every year and include it in the budget. (Of course, you can always edit a budget to exclude such items after it has been created.)

Clicking the Categories button displays the Choose Categories dialog, shown here. You can use this dialog to select specific categories to budget. You may find

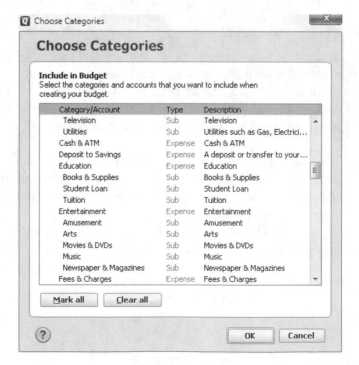

this useful if you want to budget only certain categories, such as dining, clothing, and entertainment. Initially, all the categories are selected. You can click Clear All to remove the selections for a fresh start. Click to toggle the check boxes beside each category name. The categories with check marks will be included in the budget when you click OK.

When you click OK in the Create Budget: Automatic dialog, Quicken displays a dialog telling you that the new budget has been created. Click OK to dismiss this dialog and return to the Create Budget: Automatic dialog. Click OK once more. A message appears asking you to click the Choose Categories button on the budget window. Click OK to close this message. The Income tab of the Budget window appears next.

Creating a Budget Manually   If you prefer, you can create a budget from scratch. This is more time-consuming, but it forces you to look at each category carefully to estimate future expenses.

Select the Manual option in the Setup tab of the Budget window (refer to Figure 16-3), and click Create Budget. The "Choose Categories" message appears. Click OK to dismiss the message. The Income tab of the Budget window appears next.

Completing a Budget

Once you have created a budget, you can fine-tune it to set the categories and amounts that should appear. If you created your budget automatically, this is a matter of reviewing budget income, expense, and savings items, and making changes you deem necessary. If you created a budget manually, however, you must manually add categories and set amounts for each one. You do this in the Income, Expenses, and Savings tabs of the Budget window. Because these windows all look and work pretty much the same way, only one is illustrated: the Expenses tab, which is shown in Figure 16-4.

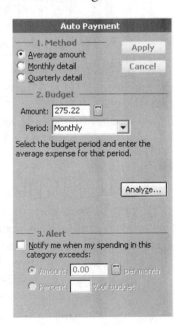

Depending on your monitor settings and the width of the budget window, you may see only the Edit and Analyze buttons, as shown in Figure 16-4, or you may see an expanded right pane. Increase the width of your screen or set your monitor resolution to a higher setting to see the expanded view, which is shown here.

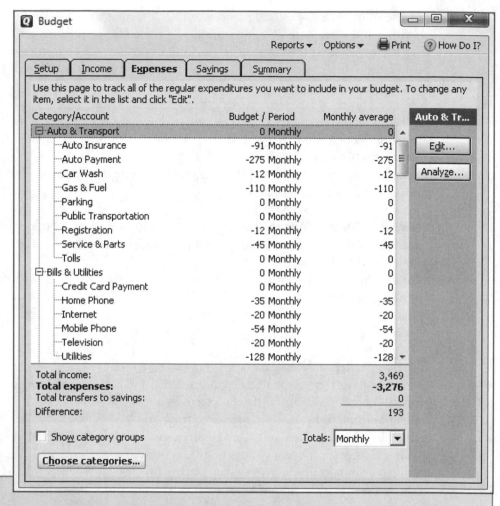

Figure 16-4 • Here's an example of the Expenses tab of the Budget window with several expense categories entered.

Adding or Removing Categories To add or remove a category from the budget, click the Choose Categories button at the bottom of the Budget window. This displays the Choose Categories dialog shown earlier. Click to place a check mark beside a category you want to include in the budget or to remove a check mark from beside a category you want to exclude from the budget.

By default, when you create a budget automatically, Quicken includes only the categories for which transactions exist. When you create a budget manually, Quicken does not include any categories at all; all categories must be added manually.

Setting a Budget Item's Options
You can modify the budget for a category or other item by modifying its settings using the buttons on the right side of the Budget window. Click the item name in the Budget window to select it, and then click Edit. The Edit Budget dialog, an example of which is shown here, will be displayed. Again, depending on your monitor settings, you may not see the Edit and Analyze buttons, but instead see the dialog shown in the Budget window. You have the following options:

- Change the budget method to enter budget amounts as averages, monthly details, or quarterly details. The budget options change depending on the method you select.
- Change the budget amount by entering values in each of the amount boxes in the Budget area. If you selected the Average Amount method, you can also choose a frequency from the Period drop-down list.
- Click Analyze to see a chart of your actual expenses for the category selected. This helps you visualize the actual pattern of income, expenses, or savings.
- Set up an alert for a category by turning on the Notify Me check box in the Alert area and entering an amount or percent in one of the two text boxes below it. (This option appears for Expense categories only.)

If your monthly spending exceeds the amount you specified, Quicken displays a dialog to tell you this.

Adding a Savings Transfer   The Savings tab of the Budget window enables you to add budgeted transfers to investment or savings accounts. Click the Choose Accounts button at the bottom of the window, and use the dialog that appears to select the accounts you want to transfer money to. Then set budget options for the account as instructed in the preceding section.

Viewing a Completed Budget

When you're finished setting options in the Income, Expenses, and Savings tabs of the Budget window, click the Summary tab. This displays the budget summary, which is shown in Figure 16-5.

You can change the graphic display content by clicking the drop-down arrow next to the graph and clicking the content you wish to see.

To view the details of a month's budget, first click the column month name, and then click Details, as shown for the month of April on the top of the next page. You see that month's budget entries listed. When you are done, click Done.

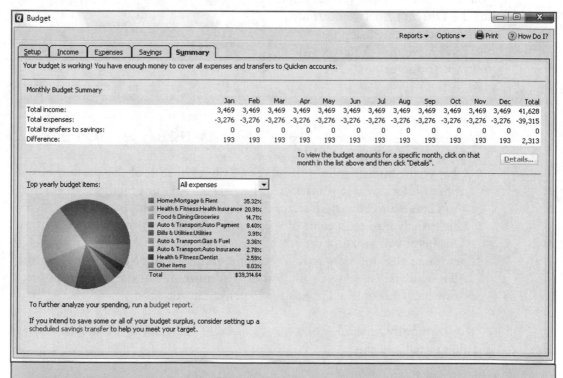

Figure 16-5 • The Summary tab of the Budget window summarizes your budget information.

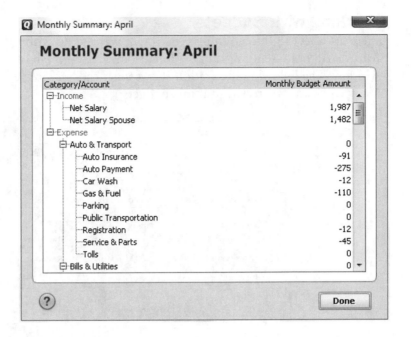

Saving the Budget

You need to save the budget so your work won't be lost. You can always revise it or create a new one from this data, as you'll see in "Working with Budgets."

To save your data, in the upper-right corner of the Budget dialog, click Options | Save Budget.

Changing the Budget View

The Budget dialog has alternative ways you can view your budget. These can be found in the Options menu in the upper-right area of the Budget dialog.

- Click Options | Separate View to show the Budget dialog as it is displayed in Figure 16-5. This shows all tabs for Setup, Income, Expenses, Savings, and Summary, allowing you to change data as you have been doing.
- Click Options | Income/Expense View to show only the Setup, Income, Expenses, and Summary tabs. You might use this if you have no desire to work with your savings data at this time.
- Click Options | Combined View to show only the Setup, Budget, and Summary tabs.

Working with Budgets

Here are a few additional things you might want to do with Quicken's budgeting feature. All of these things can be done from the Setup tab of the Budget window. The following illustration shows what the tab looks like in Combined View when you've created multiple budgets:

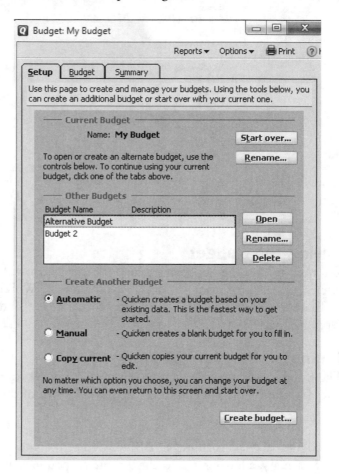

Creating Another Budget   Quicken enables you to create more than one budget. In the Setup tab, select the method you want to use to create the new budget, and click Create Budget. If you selected Automatic, the Create Budget: Automatic dialog that appears includes a place to enter a name for the budget. If you selected Manual or Copy Current, the Budget Name dialog appears so you can name the budget. Enter the requested information, and click OK. Then fine-tune your new budget as discussed earlier in this section.

Opening a Specific Budget   To open a specific budget, select the budget name in the middle part of the Setup tab and click Open.

Renaming a Budget   To rename the current budget, click the Rename button in the top part of the Setup tab. To rename another budget, select the budget name and click the Rename button in the middle part of the Setup tab. Enter a name and description in the Rename Budget dialog that appears, and click OK.

Deleting a Budget   To delete a budget, select the budget name and click the Delete button in the middle part of the Setup tab. You cannot delete the currently open budget.

Comparing a Budget to Actual Transactions

Once you have created a budget you can live with, it's a good idea to periodically compare your actual income and expenditures to budgeted amounts. Quicken lets you do this in a number of different ways.

There's one important thing to keep in mind when comparing budgeted amounts to actual results: Make sure your comparison is for the period for which you have recorded data. For example, don't view a year-to-date (YTD) budget report if you began entering data into Quicken in March. Instead, customize the report to show actual transactions beginning in March. Details about creating and customizing reports and graphs are in Chapter 8.

Budget Reports and Graphs   The Reports menu on the button bar in the Budget window offers two reports and one graph for comparing budgeted amounts to actual results.

- **Budget Report** displays actual and budgeted transactions. Figure 16-6 shows a budget report with YTD amounts.
- **Monthly Budget Report** displays the actual and budgeted transactions by month.

You can customize many of the reports or graphs by clicking the Options button and choosing Customize This [Report or Graph]. Some graphs and reports will also open the Customize This Report or Customize This Graph command from the context menu that appears when you right-click the report or graph. Chapter 8 explains how to customize reports and graphs.

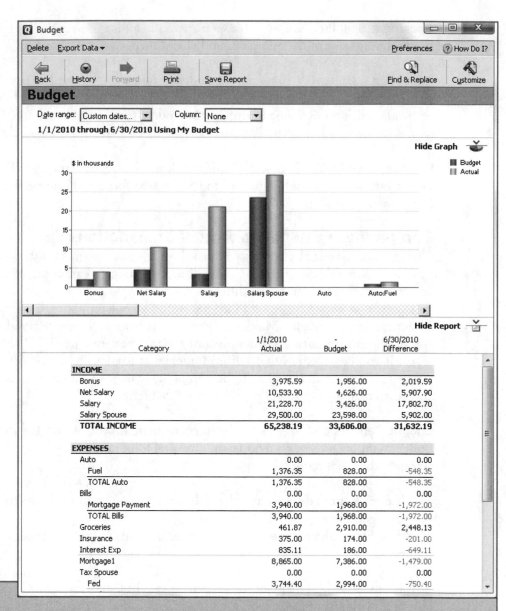

Figure 16-6 • A Budget Report compares actual and budgeted amounts.

Budget Comparison Graphs   You can display budget graphs in a custom view of the Quicken Home window. This feature enables you to keep an eye on the budget categories and groups that interest you most.

```
⊟·Planning
   ┊···Budget
   ┊···Budget Goal Progress
   ┊···Budgeted Categories
   ┊···Budgeted Net Income
   ┊···Category Group Budget
   ┊···Debt Goals
   ┊···Savings Analysis
   ┊···Savings Goal Progress
```

To use this feature, switch to the Home tab and click Customize. Use the Customize View dialog as instructed in Appendix B. The following items or snapshots found under Planning, as shown next, provide budget information:

- **Budget** displays a chart that compares your actual and budgeted income and expenses.
- **Budget Goal Progress** tracks spending for a single category's budget. This helps you monitor spending for a specific category that's important to you.
- **Budgeted Categories** compares actual category amounts with your budget.
- **Budgeted Net Income** displays a chart that compares your budgeted net income to what was actually received.
- **Category Group Budget** tracks progress against your budget by category group.
- **Debt Goals** includes a summary from your Debt Reduction Planner.
- **Savings Analysis** displays a summary of the money you are saving.
- **Savings Goal Progress** displays your progress toward a specific savings goal that you have established. See more information about savings goals later in this chapter.

Forecasting

Forecasting uses known and estimated transactions to provide a general overview of your future financial situation. This "crystal ball" can help you spot potential cash flow problems (or surpluses) so you can prepare for them. Quicken helps you to see your projected balances and can also help you create savings goals.

Projected Balances

Quicken helps you keep up with what your account balances will be in the future with the Projected Balances report. This report can be found in the Bills tab, as a link from the Stay On Top Of Monthly Bills section in the Main View of the Home tab, and by choosing the Planning tab and then Planning Tools | Projected Balances.

You can set the range for the Projected Balances report for the next 7 days; next 14 days; next 30, 60, or 90 days; or the next 12 months, or even customize a range that suits your requirements. See Figure 16-7 for an example of the Projected Balances report for the next 12 months.

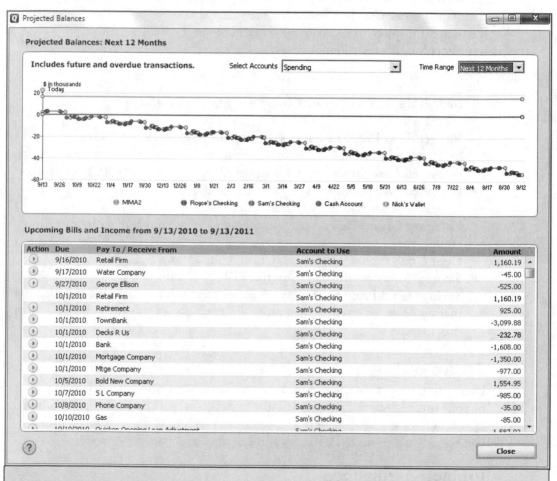

Figure 16-7 • The Projected Balances Report shows what the balance in your accounts may be for a selected time period.

Saving Money

Remember when you got your first piggy bank? It may not have looked like a pig, but it had a slot for slipping in coins and, if you were lucky, a removable rubber plug on the bottom that made it easy to get the coins out when you needed them. Whoever gave you the bank was trying to teach you your first financial management lesson: Save money.

As an adult, things are a little more complex. This section explains why you should save, provides some saving strategies, and tells you about the types of savings accounts that make your old piggy bank obsolete.

Why Save?

Most people save money so there's money to spend when they need it. Others save for a particular purpose. Still others save because they have so much they can't spend it all. Here's a closer look at why saving makes sense.

Saving for "Rainy Days"

When people say they are "saving for a rainy day," they probably aren't talking about the weather. They're talking about bad times or emergencies—situations when they'll need extra cash.

For example, suppose the family car needs a new transmission. Or your beloved dog needs eye surgery. Or your daughter manages to break her violin three days before the big recital. In the "rainy day" scheme of things, these might be light drizzles. But your savings can help keep you dry.

If your paychecks stop coming, do you have enough savings to support yourself or your family until you can get another source of income? On the "rainy day" scale, this could be a torrential downpour. Your savings can be a good umbrella.

Saving for a Goal

Planning for your future often includes planning for events that affect your life—and your wallet. Saving money for specific events can help make these events memorable for what they are, rather than what they cost.

For example, take a recently engaged couple, Sally and Joe. They plan to marry within a year and buy a house right away. Within five years, they plan to have their first child. That's when Sally will leave her job to start the more demanding job of mother and homemaker. They hope their children will go to college someday, and they want to help cover the expenses. They also want to be able to help pay for their children's weddings. Eventually, they'll retire. And throughout their lives, they want to be able to take annual family vacations, buy a new car every six years or so, and get season tickets for the Seattle Seahawks.

All of these things are major events in Sally's and Joe's lives. Saving in advance for each of these events will make them possible—without going into debt.

Saving for Peace of Mind

Some people save money because events in their lives showed them the importance of having savings. Children who lived through the Depression or bad financial times for their families grew up to be adults who understand the value of money and try hard to keep some available. They don't want to repeat the hard times they went through. Having healthy savings accounts gives them peace of mind.

Saving Strategies

There are two main ways to save: when you can or regularly.

Saving When You Can

When money is tight, saving can be difficult. People who are serious about saving, however, will force themselves to save as much as possible when they can. Saving when you can is better than not saving at all.

Saving Regularly

A better way to save money is to save a set amount periodically. For example, save $25 every week or $200 every month. Timing this with your paycheck makes sense; you can make a split deposit for the check. A savings like this is called an *annuity*, and you'd be surprised at how quickly the money can accumulate. Table 16-1 shows some examples based on a 4.5 percent annual interest rate.

Types of Savings Accounts

There are different types of savings accounts, each with its own benefits and drawbacks. Here's a quick look at them.

Keep in mind that all the accounts discussed in this chapter (except where noted) should be insured by the FDIC (Federal Deposit Insurance Corporation). This organization covers savings deposits up to $250,000 per entity (person or company) per bank, thus protecting you from loss in the event of a bank failure. (The $250,000 insured amount is true through December 31, 2013.)

	Weekly Contributions				Monthly Contributions				
Month	$25	$50	$75	$100	$50	$100	$200	$300	$400
1	$100	$200	$300	$401	$50	$100	$200	$300	$400
2	$226	$452	$677	$903	$100	$200	$401	$601	$801
3	$327	$653	$980	$1,307	$151	$301	$602	$903	$1,205
4	$428	$856	$1,284	$1,712	$201	$402	$805	$1,207	$1,609
5	$555	$1,110	$1,665	$2,220	$252	$504	$1,008	$1,511	$2,015
6	$657	$1,314	$1,971	$2,628	$303	$606	$1,211	$1,817	$2,423
7	$759	$1,519	$2,278	$3,038	$354	$708	$1,416	$2,124	$2,832
8	$888	$1,776	$2,664	$3,552	$405	$811	$1,621	$2,432	$3,242
9	$991	$1,982	$2,974	$3,965	$457	$914	$1,827	$2,741	$3,654
10	$1,095	$2,190	$3,284	$4,379	$509	$1,017	$2,034	$3,051	$4,068
11	$1,225	$2,449	$3,674	$4,899	$560	$1,121	$2,242	$3,363	$4,483
12	$1,329	$2,658	$3,987	$5,316	$613	$1,225	$2,450	$3,675	$4,900

Table 16-1 • **Your Savings Can Grow Over Time**

Standard Savings Accounts

All banks offer savings accounts, and most accommodate any balance. Savings accounts pay interest on your balance and allow you to deposit or withdraw funds at any time.

Holiday Clubs

A "holiday club" account is a savings account into which you make regular, equal deposits, usually on a weekly basis. Many banks offer these accounts, along with an option to withdraw the deposit funds automatically from your regular savings or checking account. The money stays in the account, earning interest until the club ends in October or November. The idea behind these accounts is to provide you with cash for the holidays, but there are variations on this theme, such as vacation club accounts that end in May or June.

Credit Union Payroll Savings

A bank isn't the only place where you can open a savings account. If your company has a credit union, it also offers a number of accounts. These accounts often offer the option of payroll savings deductions. This is a great feature for people who have trouble saving money, because the money comes out of their paychecks before they can see and spend it. It's as if the money never existed, when in reality, it's accumulating in an interest-bearing account. In case you're wondering, the withdrawn funds are included in your taxable income.

Certificates of Deposit

A certificate of deposit, or CD, is an account, normally with a bank, that requires you to keep the money on deposit for a specific length of time. Your earnings are based on a higher, fixed-interest rate than what is available for a regular savings account. The longer the term of the deposit and the more money deposited, the higher the rate. At the CD's maturity date, you can "roll over" the deposit to a new account that may have a different interest rate, or you can take back the cash. If you withdraw the money before the CD's maturity date, you pay a penalty, which can sometimes exceed the amount of the interest earned.

Money Market Accounts

There are two types of money market accounts. A money market deposit account held at a regularly chartered bank is insured up to $250,000 through December 31, 2013. (At this writing, the amount will revert to $100,000 as of January 1, 2014, but future legislation could change that again.) A money market mutual account is actually a form of investment, but it should be included here because some banks offer it. It has a higher rate of return than a regular savings account but is not insured by the FDIC. It is considered a conservative investment and can be treated just like a savings account for depositing money. There may, however, be restrictions on the number of withdrawals you can make each month.

Interest-Bearing Checking Accounts

Many banks offer interest-bearing checking accounts. They usually have minimum balance requirements, however, forcing you to keep a certain amount of money in the account at all times. Some banks are currently offering rewards or incentives of higher interest rates to encourage you to keep higher balances in your checking accounts.

Using Savings Goals

Quicken's Savings Goals feature helps you save money by "hiding" funds in an account. You set up a savings goal and make contributions to it using the Savings Goals window. Although the money never leaves the source bank account, it is deducted in the account register, thus reducing the account balance in Quicken. If you can't see the money in your account, you're less likely to spend it.

EXPERIENCED QUICKEN USERS AND NEW TO QUICKEN?

Why Create Savings Goals?

Kind of sounds silly, doesn't it? Using Quicken to transfer money from your checking account to another account that doesn't even exist.

But don't laugh—the Savings Goals feature really works. A friend used a similar technique. She simply deducted $10 or $20 from her checking account balance, thus giving the illusion that she had less money in the account than was really there. This helped her save money by making her think twice about writing a check for something they really didn't need. It prevented her from bouncing checks during the time when the needs of her growing family caused her to keep a dangerously low checking account balance. When her daughter graduated from high school, there was enough money in this "secret" account to pay for a new laptop as the girl went off to college!

Give it a try and see for yourself!

Getting Started

Open the Savings Goals window by choosing Planning | Planning Tools | Savings Goals. Here's what the window looks like with one savings goal already created:

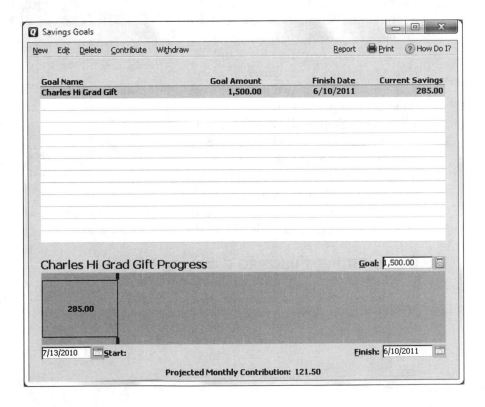

The top half of the Savings Goals window lists the savings goals you have created with Quicken. The bottom half shows the progress for the selected goal. You can use button bar options to work with window contents.

- **New** enables you to create a savings goal.
- **Edit** enables you to modify the selected savings goal.
- **Delete** removes the selected savings goal.
- **Contribute** enables you to contribute funds from a Quicken account to the selected savings goal.
- **Withdraw** enables you to remove funds from a savings goal and return them to a Quicken account.
- **Report** creates a report of the activity for savings goals.
- **Print** prints a report of savings goal details.
- **How Do I?** displays the Quicken Personal Finances Help window with instructions for using the Savings Goals feature.

Creating a Savings Goal

To create a savings goal, click New on the button bar in the Savings Goals window. The Create New Savings Goal dialog, which is shown here, appears.

Enter the information for your savings goal in the text boxes. The name of the savings goal cannot be the same as any Quicken category or account. In the Finish Date field, enter the date by which you want to have the money saved. For example, if you're using a savings goal to plan for a family cruise, the finish date should be shortly before the date you want to leave on the cruise. When you've finished, click OK to add the savings goal to the list in the Savings Goals window.

Contributing Funds to a Savings Goal

To contribute funds to a savings goal, select the savings goal in the Savings Goals window and click the Contribute button on the button bar. The Contribute To Goal dialog, shown on the top of the next page, appears.

Select the account from which you want to transfer the money from the drop-down list. The balance and name of that account appear in the bottom of the dialog. Then enter the amount of the transfer in the Amount box. By default, Quicken suggests the projected monthly contribution amount, but you can enter any amount you like. When you've finished, click OK.

As shown in the next illustration, Quicken creates an entry in the account register of the account from which the money was contributed. It also updates the progress bar and information in the Savings Goals dialog.

8/5/2010	Contribution towards goal		500 00
	[Cruise]		
8/19/2010	Contribution towards goal		135 00
	[Charles Hi Grad Gift]		

When you create a savings goal, Quicken creates an asset account to record the goal's transactions and balance. To automate contributions to the goal, you can create a scheduled transaction to transfer money periodically from one of your bank accounts to the savings goal asset account. Scheduled transactions are covered in Chapter 6.

Meeting Your Goal

Once you have met your savings goal, you can either withdraw the funds from the savings goal so they appear in a Quicken account or delete the savings goal to put the money back where it came from.

Withdrawing Money   In the Savings Goals window, select the savings goal from which you want to withdraw money. Click the Withdraw button on the button bar. The Withdraw From Goal dialog (shown here), which works much like the Contribute To Goal dialog, appears. Use it to remove funds from the savings goal and put them back into the account from which they were contributed.

Deleting a Savings Goal   In the Savings Goals window, select the savings goal you want to delete, and click the Delete button on the button bar. A dialog appears, explaining that this choice will return all funds to the source accounts.

- Click Remove It From Quicken Completely to eradicate any record of the savings goal.
- Click Keep It As A Zero Balance Asset Account For My Records to keep a record of the goal.

Tax

This part of the book explores the features of Quicken Personal Finance Software's Planning tab's Tax Center and Tax Tools, which can make tax preparation quicker and easier, enable you to plan for tax time, and even help you save money on your income taxes. Its two chapters are:

Part Six

Simplifying Tax Preparation

Chapter 17

In This Chapter:

- *Including tax information in accounts and categories*
- *Tax reports*
- *Online tax tools*
- *TurboTax*

Tax time is no fun. It can force you to spend hours sifting through financial records and filling out complex forms. When you're done with the hard part, you may be rewarded with the knowledge that you can expect a refund. But it is more likely that your reward will be the privilege of writing a check to the federal, state, or local government—or worse yet, all three.

Fortunately, Quicken Personal Finance Software can help. Its reporting features can save you time. By using the tax tools that are available through Quicken, the next tax season may be a little less stressful. This chapter will show you how.

Tax Information in Accounts and Categories

As discussed briefly in Chapter 2, Quicken accounts and categories can include information that will help you at tax time. This section explains how you can set tax information in accounts and categories.

Including Tax Information in Accounts

You enter an account's tax information in the Tax Schedule dialog for the account. Choose Tools | Account List or press CTRL-A to display the Account List window. Select the name of the account and click the Edit button that appears to the right of the account name. The Account Details dialog will appear. At the bottom of the Account Details dialog, click the Tax Schedule button. The Tax Schedule Information dialog, shown here, appears.

Use the Transfers In and Transfers Out drop-down lists to map account activity to specific lines on tax return forms and schedules. If the account has tax-deferred or tax-exempt status, be sure to turn on the Tax-Deferred Or Tax-Exempt Account check box. When you're finished, click OK. Repeat this process for all accounts for which you want to enter tax information.

Keep in mind that if you use the Paycheck Set Up feature to account for all payroll deductions, including retirement plan contributions, you shouldn't have to change the settings for any of your accounts. (That's another good reason to set up your regular paychecks in Quicken.) Chapter 6 explains how to set up a paycheck in Quicken.

Including Tax Information in Categories

Quicken automatically sets tax information for many of the categories it creates. You can see which categories are tax-related and which tax form lines have been assigned to them in the Category List window (refer to Figure 17-1). (If this information does not appear, choose Show Tax Line Item from the Options menu at the bottom of the window.) Concentrate on the categories without tax assignments; some of these may require tax information, depending on your situation.

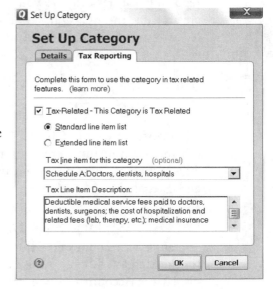

You can use the Set Up Category dialog, shown here, to enter or

Figure 17-1 • The Category List window shows the tax information provided for each category.

modify tax information for a category. Choose Tools | Category List to open the Category List window. Select the category for which you want to enter or edit tax information. Then click the Edit button in the Action column to display the Set Up Category dialog and choose the Tax Reporting tab.

You can also open the Category List by clicking SHIFT-CTRL-C.

If the category's transactions should be included on your tax return as either income or a deductible expense, select the Tax-Related – This Category Is Tax-Related check box. Then use the Tax Line Item For This Category drop-down list to choose the form or schedule and line for the item. (You can expand this list by selecting the Extended Line Item List option.) A description of the tax line item you chose appears at the bottom of the dialog. Click OK to return to the Category List. The Tax Line Item you chose appears on the same line as your category, as seen here. Repeat this process for all categories that should be included on your tax return. Keep in mind that you can also enter tax information when you first create a category, as explained in Chapter 2.

Category	Hide	Type	Tax Line Item	Action
✓ 🗋 Dentist & Orthodontist	☐	Personal Expense	Schedule A:Doctors, dentists, hospitals	Edit Delete Merge ▲

Auditing Your Tax Line Assignments

Quicken can "audit" the tax line information associated with categories and tell you where there may be problems with the assignments. This feature helps ensure that you have properly set up your categories to take advantage of Quicken's tax features.

Open the Planning tab and click Tax Center. Click Options in the Tax-Related Expenses YTD. Choose **Audit Tax Categories** from the menu as shown here. Quicken quickly reviews all your

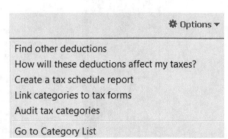

❖ Options ▼

Find other deductions
How will these deductions affect my taxes?
Create a tax schedule report
Link categories to tax forms
Audit tax categories

Go to Category List

categories. If it finds potential problems, Quicken displays them in the Tax Category Audit window (see Figure 17-2).

> If the Planning tab is not visible, open the View menu and click Tabs To Show | Planning to display the tab.

You have three choices for working with the items Quicken finds:

- To accept Quicken's suggested correction for the category, click the Change link in the Action column on the category's line. Then click OK in the Set Up Category dialog that appears. (This dialog looks and works just like the Set Up Category dialog shown earlier in this chapter.)
- To ignore the possible problem, click the Ignore link in the Action column on the category's line.
- To change the tax line assignment manually, click the category name link and make the desired changes in the Set Up Category dialog that appears,

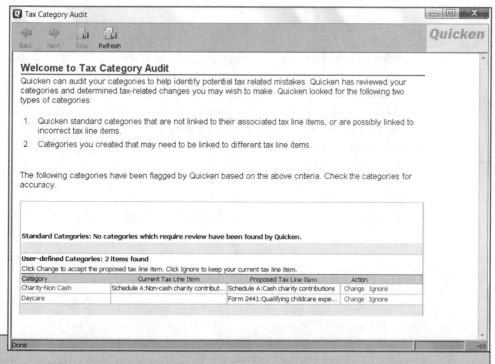

Figure 17-2 • The Tax Category Audit window lists categories that may have incorrect tax line assignments.

and then click OK. (This dialog looks and works just like the Set Up Category dialog shown earlier in this chapter.)

If Quicken doesn't find any problems with your categories, it displays a dialog that tells you so. Keep in mind, however, that this doesn't necessarily mean that your tax line assignments are error-free. You should review them the old-fashioned way—by looking them over yourself—before relying on them.

Tax Reports

Quicken offers several tax reports that can make tax time easier by providing the information you need to prepare your taxes. All of these reports are based on the tax information settings for the accounts and categories in your Quicken data file. You can learn more about Quicken's reporting feature in Chapter 8.

To create a report, select Reports | Tax from the menu bar. Choose the name of the report from the menu:

- **Capital Gains** summarizes gains and losses on the sales of investments, organized by the term of the investment (short or long) and the investment account.
- **Schedule A–Itemized Deductions** summarizes the itemized deductions that appear on Schedule A of a 1040 tax return.
- **Schedule B–Interest And Dividends** summarizes interest and dividends income that is reported on Schedule B of a 1040 tax return.
- **Schedule D–Capital Gains And Losses** summarizes the capital gains and losses from the sale of investments that are reported on Schedule D of a 1040 tax return.
- **Tax Schedule** summarizes tax-related transactions, organized by tax form or schedule and line item.
- **Tax Summary** summarizes tax-related transactions, organized by category and date.

Online Tax Tools

Click the Planning tab, and then click Tax Tools to access the Online Tax Tools submenu as shown here. This menu offers access to some tax-related features and information sources on the TurboTax.com website that can help you with your taxes. All you need to take advantage of these features is an Internet connection.

Here's a quick look at the online tax tools. The next time you're thinking about taxes, be sure to check these out.

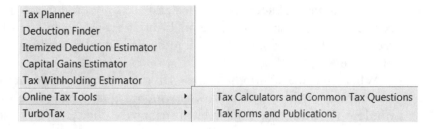

Tax Calculators and Common Tax Questions   The Tax Calculators option displays the TurboTax Free Tax Calculators And Money Saving Tax Guides page as seen in Figure 17-3. You can find links to various online tools for making tax and other financial calculations on this page. You can also follow links to get tax tips and learn more about TurboTax.

Figure 17-3 • You can find many money-saving tips and other information on the TurboTax page.

Tax Forms and Publications   The Tax Forms option displays the Tax Forms For Federal And State Taxes page on TurboTax.com, which offers links to various categories of tax forms. Click a link to display additional information and links to forms.

When you click a form link, the form is downloaded as an Acrobat PDF file that appears in either a Web browser window or an Adobe Acrobat Reader window. (You must have the freely distributed Adobe Acrobat Reader software to open and use these forms.) Print the form to fill it out manually.

Adobe Reader is often included with computers you purchase "off-the-shelf." Click Start | All Programs to see if it is already on your computer.

TurboTax Online

If you're tired of paying a tax preparer to fill out your tax return for you, but you're not quite confident enough about your tax knowledge to prepare your own return manually, it's time to check out TurboTax online tax-preparation software. It's a great way to simplify tax preparation.

TurboTax works almost seamlessly with Quicken to prepare your taxes. Just follow the instructions in this chapter to set up your accounts and categories with tax information. Then import your Quicken data into TurboTax. You can go through an easy interview process to make sure you haven't left anything out—much like the interview you might go through with a paid tax preparer. TurboTax calculates the bottom line and enables you to either print your returns or file them electronically.

Intuit offers several versions of TurboTax Online. You can learn more about them by opening the Planning tab and selecting Tax Tools | TurboTax | File Your Taxes With TurboTax. See Figure 17-4 as an example.

- **TurboTax Free Edition** is for taxpayers with basic tax preparation needs. It includes just the 1040EZ form.
- **TurboTax Deluxe** can perform tax calculations for taxpayers who own a home, make donations, or have childcare or medical expenses. In other words, most people.
- **TurboTax Premier** offers all of the functionality of TurboTax Deluxe and adds tax calculations for taxpayers who own stocks, bonds, mutual funds, or rental properties.
- **TurboTax Home & Business** offers all of the functionality of TurboTax Premier and adds tax calculations for small businesses, such as sole proprietorships or single-owner LLCs.

Figure 17-4 • You can order your copy of TurboTax from this Quicken link.

- **TurboTax Business** provides tax preparation for corporations, partnerships, and multimember LLCs while maximizing business tax deductions. It does not include the means to prepare your personal taxes.

Import TurboTax File   Click Import TurboTax File to import last year's TurboTax information and start this year's tax return. See Chapter 18 for more information on importing TurboTax data into this year's return.

Tax Center Overview

Open Quicken's Tax Center by clicking the Planning tab and choosing Tax Center. The Tax Center window, as seen in Figure 17-5, gives you an overview of the tax information you have entered into Quicken. Each section is explained in

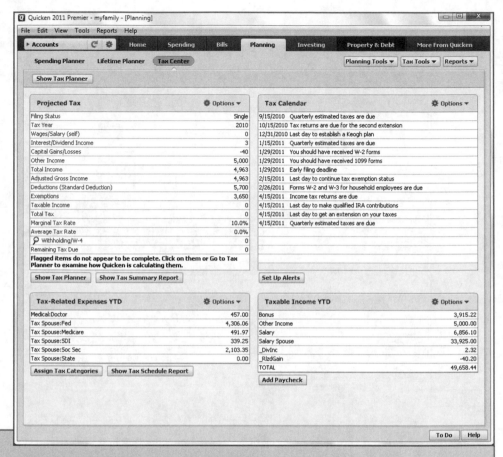

Figure 17-5 • The Tax Center in the Planning Tab displays tax information.

detail in Chapter 18; however, the following is an introduction to each section's options and buttons.

Viewing the Projected Tax Section

The Projected Tax section, as detailed in Chapter 18, offers several options. From this section of the Tax Center you can:

- Click Options to Open the Tax Planner or create a tax summary report.
- From the bottom of the section, click the Show Tax Planner button to open the Tax Planner or the Show Tax Summary Report to create a report of your current year's tax summary.

Using the Tax Calendar

The Tax Calendar section warns you of upcoming IRS tax deadlines. From here you can create Tax Alerts from either the Options menu or the Set Up Alerts button at the bottom of the section. See Chapter 18 for more information.

Understanding the Tax-Related Expenses YTD Section

This Options available from this section, shown here, are as follows:

- Find Other Deductions opens the Deduction Finder. This handy tool is explained in Chapter 18.
- How Will These Deductions Affect My Taxes? opens the Tax Planner, covered in Chapter 18.
- Create A Tax Schedule Report opens a report for the current tax year showing information for Form 1040 as well as Schedule A and B entries for categories you have indicated as described earlier in this chapter.

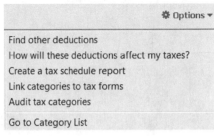

- Link Categories to Tax Forms opens the Category List so that you can associate categories with specific tax line items as explained in "Including Tax Information in Categories" earlier in this chapter.
- Audit Tax Categories opens the Audit Tax Categories dialog. See "Auditing Your Tax Line Assignments" earlier in this chapter.
- Go To Category List opens the Category List.

The Assign Tax Categories button at the bottom of this section opens the Category List. The Show Tax Schedule Report opens the report described above.

Reviewing the Taxable Income YTD Section

The Options menu of this section of the Tax Center, seen here, offers the following options:

- Report My Net Worth creates a net worth report as of the current date. See Chapter 13 for more information about net worth reports.

- How Does This Income Affect My Taxes? opens the Tax Planner.
- Audit Tax Categories opens the Tax Category Audit dialog as explained in "Auditing Your Tax Lines Assignments" earlier in this chapter.
- Go To Category List opens the Category List.

Click the Add Paycheck button at the bottom of the section to open the Paycheck Setup dialog. This process is explained in Chapter 6.

Planning for Tax Time

In This Chapter:

- *Tax planning basics*
- *Tax Planner*
- *Tax Withholding Estimator*
- *Minimizing Taxes by Maximizing Deductions*
- *Itemized Deduction Estimator*
- *Tax Center*

Surprises can make life interesting. But not all surprises are good ones. Consider the surprise you may get one April when your tax preparer announces that you'll have to write a rather large check to your Uncle Sam and another to his friends in your state revenue department.

Quicken Personal Finance Software's tax planning features, like the Tax Planner and Tax Withholding Estimator, can help you avoid nasty surprises. Other built-in tax tools, like the Deduction Finder and Itemized Deduction Estimator, can save you money and help you make smarter financial decisions. All of these features can be found in the Tax Tools menu in the Planning tab, which is full of options to help you plan and monitor your tax situation. In this chapter, you'll learn about Quicken's tax planning and monitoring features.

Planning to Avoid Surprises

One of the best reasons to think about taxes before tax time is to avoid surprises on April 15. Knowing what you'll owe before you owe it can help ensure that you pay just the right amount of taxes up front—through proper deductions or estimated tax payments—so you don't get hit with a big tax bill or tax refund.

You may think of a big tax refund as a gift from Uncle Sam. Well, it isn't. It's your money that Uncle Sam has been using, interest-free, for months. When you overpay your taxes, you're giving up money that you could be using to reduce interest-bearing debt or earn interest or investment income. Making sure you don't overpay taxes throughout the year helps you keep your money where it'll do *you* the most good.

Quicken offers built-in tax planning tools that you can use to keep track of your tax situation throughout the year. The Tax Planner helps you estimate your federal income tax bill for the 2010 and 2011 tax years. You can add up to three additional scenarios to your planner to help plan for possible changes in your life. In addition, Quicken provides several estimating tools to help you with your taxes. For example, the Tax Withholding Estimator helps you determine whether your withholding taxes are correctly calculated. Finally, the Tax Center in the Planning tab summarizes your tax situation with a number of useful snapshots. Here's a closer look at each of these features.

> **EXPERIENCED QUICKEN USER**
> **Finding the Tax Tools**
> If you have not yet turned on the Planning tab, you may not see the Tax Center or the other Planning tools. To see these useful tools, click View from the Quicken menu bar, and then click Tabs To Show. From that submenu, click Planning.

If it is still 2010 when you first open the Tax Planner to create your default Projected Value scenario, you may see a message stating that Quicken cannot display projected tax values for a future year. When your computer's calendar changes to 2011, you will be able to use both years for the Projected Value scenario. This does not apply to other scenarios that you can create.

Using the Tax Planner

Quicken's Tax Planner includes features from Intuit's TurboTax tax preparation software to help you estimate your federal income tax bill for the 2010 and 2011 tax years. While this can help you avoid surprises, it can also help you see how various changes to income and expenses can affect your estimated tax bill.

Opening the Quicken Tax Planner Window

To open the Tax Planner, open the Planning tab and choose Show Tax Planner. You can also click Tax Tools | Tax Planner. (If you don't see Tax Tools, expand your screen.) The first time you open the Tax Planner, it may display a dialog that offers to import TurboTax data into Quicken for tax planning purposes as seen here. If you click Yes, follow the instructions that appear onscreen to complete the import. If you click No, or when the import process is complete, the Tax Planner window appears. Read the introductory information to get a clear understanding of what the Tax Planner can do for you and how it works.

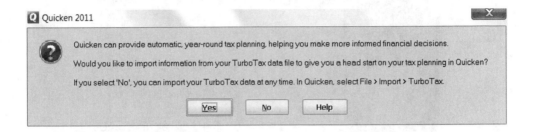

 You can also add the Tax Planner to the Quicken toolbar. Find out how in Appendix A.

Viewing the Tax Planner Summary

To see what data is already entered in the Tax Planner, click the Tax Planner Summary link in the navigation bar on the left side of the Tax Planner window. A summary of all data, as well as the calculated tax implications, appears as shown in Figure 18-1.

Entering Tax Planner Data

Data can be entered into the Tax Planner from three different sources:

- **TurboTax** data can be imported into Quicken. In the main Quicken application window, from the Planning tab, choose Tax Tools | TurboTax | Import TurboTax File. Then use the dialog that appears to locate and import your TurboTax data. This information can be used to project current-year amounts in the Tax Planner.

 You can also open the TurboTax import dialog by clicking File | File Import | TurboTax File.

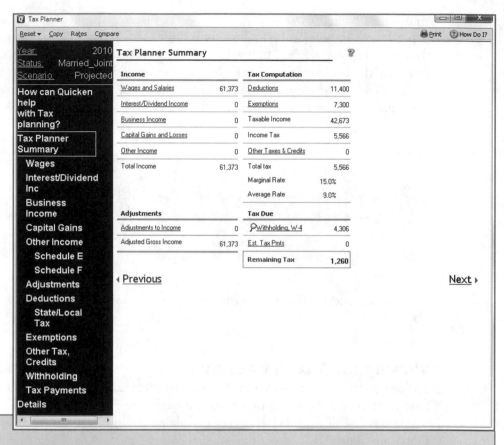

Figure 18-1 • The Tax Planner Summary screen displays a summary of all information stored in the Tax Planner.

- **User Entered** data can override any automatic entries. Use this to enter data that isn't entered any other way or that has not yet been entered into Quicken—such as the tax-deductible expense you paid with cash.
- **Quicken Data** is automatically entered into the Tax Planner if you have properly set up your tax-related Quicken categories with appropriate tax return line items, as discussed in Chapter 17.

Here's how it works. Click a link in the navigation bar on the left side of the Tax Planner window or in the Tax Planner Summary screen (refer to Figure 18-1) to view a specific type of income or expense. Then click a link within the window for a specific item. Details for the item appear in the bottom of the window, as shown in Figure 18-2. (You may have to click a Show Details link to

| Deductions | **Hide Details** ⊠ | | | | |

Medical and Dental Expense   View tax form line items used here

Data Source	Actual YTD	Projected Amount	Adjustment	Annual Total
○ TurboTax	0	0		0
○ User Entered				0
⦿ **Quicken Data (from 2010)**	457	0	4,988	5,445
Source for Projected Amount:				
○ Scheduled Bills and Deposits		None		
○ Estimate based on YTD daily average		262		
⦿ No Projected Amount		0		

Quicken YTD Transactions and   Scheduled Transactions

Date	Acct	Num	Payee	Category/Tag	Amount
1/16/2010	Checking		Dr. Feeney	Medical:Doctor	125.00
2/15/2010	Checking		Dr. Feeney	Medical:Doctor	332.00

Quicken YTD Total: 457.00

Sidebar menu:
- **Deductions**
  - State/Local Tax
- Exemptions
- Other Tax, Credits
- Withholding
- Tax Payments
- Details

Figure 18-2 • You can enter additional information directly into the Tax Planner.

expand the window and show the details.) If desired, change the source option and, if necessary, enter an amount.

The options you can choose from vary depending on whether TurboTax data is available or the item has transactions recorded in Quicken. For example, in Figure 18-2, TurboTax data is not available, but transactions have been entered in Quicken. You can either select the User Entered option and enter a value in the Annual Total column or select the Quicken Data option and enter an adjusting value in the Adjustment column, as shown. This makes it easy to manually override any automatic entries created by the data you have entered into Quicken.

Repeat this process for any Tax Planner items you want to check or change. The Tax Planner automatically recalculates the impact of your changes.

To reset values quickly to amounts automatically entered by Quicken, choose Reset on the Tax Planner's button bar and click Reset To Quicken Default Values as shown here.

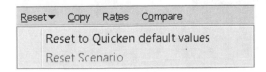

Reset ▾ Copy Rates Compare

Reset to Quicken default values
Reset Scenario

Using Scenarios

The Scenarios feature of the Tax Planner enables you to enter data for multiple scenarios—a "what if" capability that you can use to see tax impacts based on various changes in entry data. For example, suppose you're planning to get married and want to see the impact of the additional income and deductions related to your new spouse. You can use a scenario to see the tax impact without changing your Projected Value scenario.

To use this feature, click the Scenario link in the upper section of the navigation bar on the left side of the Tax Planner window (refer to Figure 18-1). The Tax Planner Options screen, which is shown here, appears. Click the Scenario's down arrow to choose a different scenario from the drop-down list. If Quicken asks whether you want to copy the current scenario to the scenario you chose, click Yes if that new scenario hasn't yet been created. Choose options from the Tax Year and Filing Status drop-down lists to set the scenario options. Then click the Next link at the bottom of the window to return to the Tax Planner Summary window. If necessary, change the values in the new scenario.

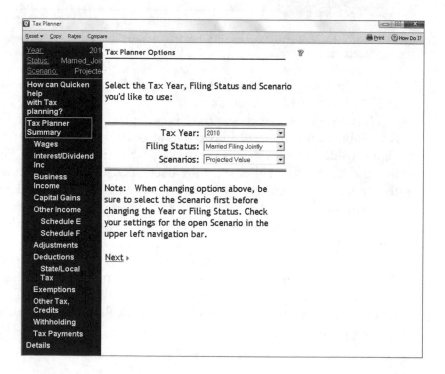

When creating or editing a scenario, you must choose the scenario first, before you change the tax year or filing status.

To compare one scenario to another, click the Compare button in the Tax Planner window's button bar. A Tax Scenario Comparisons dialog appears, showing the results of each scenario's calculations. When you're finished viewing the comparative information, click OK to dismiss the dialog.

Finishing Up

When you're finished using the Tax Planner, click the Close button above the button bar or switch to another window. This saves the information you entered and updates the Projected Tax calculations in the Tax Center. (Learn about the Tax Center later in this chapter, in the section "The Tax Center.")

Using the Estimators

Some of the most useful tips to aid your tax planning are found under the Tax Tools button in the Planning tab. From helping you determine your tax refund (or payment) to helping you find and itemize your tax deductions, each tool can help you make your tax situation clearer. The more you know about taxes that you must pay, the better you will be able to manage your money to ensure there are funds to pay them.

Tax Withholding Estimator

Quicken's Tax Withholding Estimator feature helps you determine whether your W-4 form has been correctly completed. It does this by comparing your estimated tax bill from the Tax Planner to the amount of withholding tax deducted from your paychecks.

Using the Tax Withholding Estimator Feature

To get started, in the Planning tab, choose Tax Tools | Tax Withholding Estimator. The Am I Under Or Over Withholding? window appears, as shown in Figure 18-3.

Read the information and follow the instructions in the middle column of the window. You'll be prompted to enter information related to withholding taxes. Since the instructions are clear and easy to follow, they're not repeated here. Each time you enter data, the Projected Refund Due or Projected Tax Due amount in the lower-right corner of the window changes. You can see in the two examples on the next page that by changing the amount of deductions or itemized deductions that the amount of your refund or tax payment displays in the Projected Tax field at the lower-right area of the Withholding Tax Estimator.

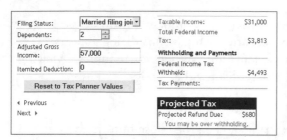
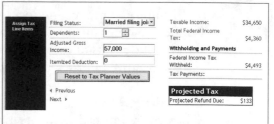

None of the entries you make in the Tax Withholding Estimator feature will affect your Quicken data or any other tax planning feature within Quicken, so don't be afraid to experiment.

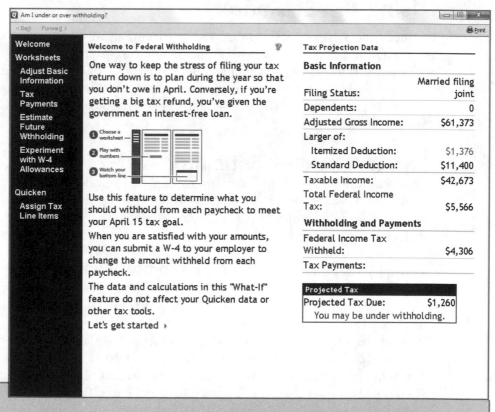

Figure 18-3 • Use the Tax Withholding Estimator to determine whether your federal withholding taxes are correct.

Acting on the Results of Tax Withholding Estimator Calculations

What do you do with this information once you have it? Well, suppose your work with the Tax Withholding Estimator feature tells you that you should change your W-4 allowances from 1 to 2 to avoid overpaying federal withholding taxes. You can act on this information by completing a new W-4 form at work. This will decrease the amount of withholding tax in each paycheck. The result is that you reduce your tax overpayment and potential refund.

Periodically Checking Withholding Calculations

It's a good idea to use the Tax Withholding Estimator feature every three months or so to make sure actual amounts are in line with projections throughout the year. Whenever possible, use actual values rather than estimates in your calculations. And be sure to act on the results of the calculations by filing a new W-4 form, especially if the amount of your projected refund due or projected tax due is greater than you anticipated.

Minimizing Taxes by Maximizing Deductions

One way to minimize taxes is to maximize your deductions. While Quicken can't help you spend money on tax-deductible items—that's up to you—it can help you identify expenses that may be tax-deductible so you don't forget to include them on your tax returns.

Quicken offers two features to help maximize your deductions. Deduction Finder asks you questions about expenditures to determine if they are tax-deductible. Itemized Deduction Estimator helps make sure you don't forget about commonly overlooked itemized deductions.

Deduction Finder

The Deduction Finder uses another TurboTax feature to help you learn which expenses are deductible. Its question-and-answer interface gathers information from you and then provides information about the deductibility of items based on your answers.

Working with the Deduction Finder Window

To open the Deduction Finder, open the Planning tab and choose Tax Tools | Deduction Finder. An Introduction dialog may appear. Read its contents to learn more about Deduction Finder and then click OK. Figure 18-4 shows what the Deductions tab of the Deduction Finder window says about the costs of operating your car if you are an employee.

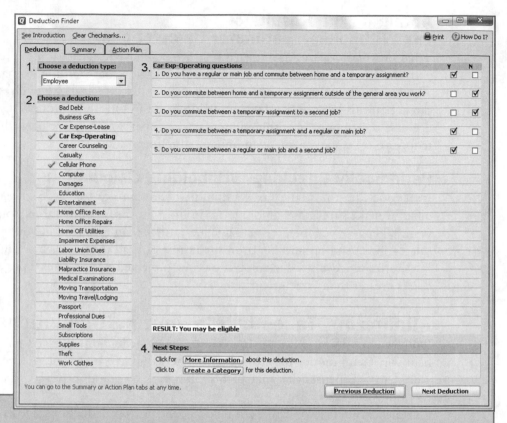

Figure 18-4 • The Deduction Finder helps you identify expenses that may be tax-deductible.

You can use button bar options to work with the Deduction Finder window:

- **See Introduction** displays the Introduction window so you can learn more about how Deduction Finder works.
- **Clear Checkmarks** removes the check marks from items for which you have already answered questions.
- **Print** prints a summary of deduction information about all the deductions for which you have answered questions.
- **How Do I?** opens the Quicken Personal Finances Help window, where you can find additional information about using the Deduction Finder.

Finding Deductions

As you can see in Figure 18-4, the Deductions tab of the Deduction Finder window uses clearly numbered steps to walk you through the process of selecting

deduction types and deductions, and then answering
questions. It's easy to use. You need only choose the type
of deduction from the drop-down list at number 1, as
shown here. As you see, Employee is the first option. You
don't have to answer questions about all the deductions—
only the deductions you think may apply to you. When
you've finished answering questions about a deduction,
the result appears near the bottom of the window. You can then move on to
another deduction.

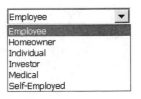

   The Summary tab of the window, shown here, summarizes the number of
deductions available in each category, the number for which you answered
questions, and the number for which you may be eligible to take deductions
based on your answers to the questions.

Deduction types	# Available	# Answered	# Eligible
Employee type	28	3	3
Homeowner type	5	1	1
Individual type	26	5	5
Investor type	7	3	2
Medical type	11	3	3
Self-Employed type	33	5	5

   When you've finished answering questions, you can click the Action Plan tab
to get more information about the deductions and the things you need to do to
claim them. Although you can read the Action Plan information on-screen, if
you answered many questions, you may want to use the Print button on the
button bar to print the information for reference.

Itemized Deduction Estimator

The Itemized Deduction Estimator feature helps make sure you don't overlook
any itemized deductions, specifically the deductions on Schedule A of your tax
return, for which you might qualify. It does this by guiding you through a review
of deduction ideas and providing the information you need to know whether
you may qualify.

To get started, open the Planning tab and choose Tax Tools | Itemized Deduction Estimator. The How Can I Maximize My Deductions? window appears, as shown in Figure 18-5.

Read the information and follow the instructions in the middle column of the window. You'll be prompted to enter information related to itemized deductions for medical expenses, taxes paid, interest paid, charitable contributions, and other items. The instructions are clear and easy to follow. Each time you enter information that can change your tax, the Projected Refund Due or Projected Tax Due amount in the lower-right corner of the window changes. Your goal is

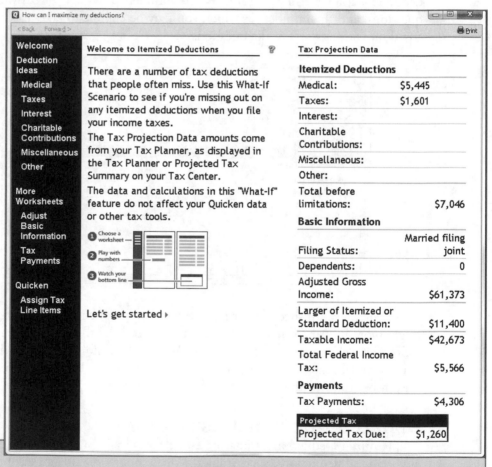

Figure 18-5 • Use the Itemized Deduction Estimator to ensure you find all of your Schedule A deductions.

to get a projected refund due amount as high as possible or a projected tax due amount as low as possible.

Again, none of the entries you make in the Itemized Deduction Estimator feature will affect your Quicken data or any other tax-planning feature within Quicken. Experiment as much as you like.

Other Tax Tools

The other items on the Tax Tools button—the Capital Gains Estimator, the Online Tax Tools, and TurboTax—are covered in other chapters in this book. However, here is a brief overview of each tool:

- **Capital Gains Estimator**   If you are tracking your investments in Quicken, the Capital Gains Estimator can help you calculate the taxable consequences of selling an investment. This tool is discussed in detail in Chapter 11.
- **Online Tax Tools and TurboTax**   These tools are detailed in Chapter 17.

The Tax Center

Quicken summarizes all information about your tax situation in the Tax Center (see Figure 18-6). Here's a quick look at what you can find in the Tax Center window.

Projected Tax

The Projected Tax snapshot provides a summary of your upcoming projected tax return, including the amount that you'll have to pay or get back as a refund. The information in this snapshot is based on the Tax Planner's Projected scenario, discussed earlier in this chapter.

Tax Calendar

The Tax Calendar lists recent and upcoming events on the IRS tax calendar. You can use the Options menu to set up alerts. See "Tax Alerts" later in this chapter.

Tax-Related Expenses YTD

The Tax-Related Expenses YTD snapshot summarizes all of your year-to-date tax-related expenses. Quicken automatically calculates this information based on the transactions you enter throughout the year. All expense categories that are marked "tax-related" and have transactions appear in this list.

Taxable Income YTD

The Taxable Income YTD snapshot summarizes all of your year-to-date tax-related income. Quicken calculates these totals based on the transactions you

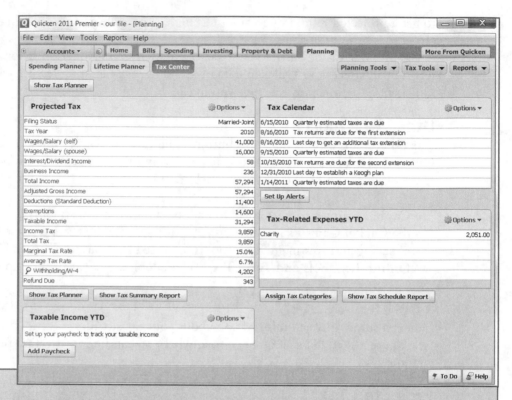

Figure 18-6 • The Tax Center window contains specific information about your tax situation.

enter throughout the year. All income categories that are marked "tax-related" and have transactions appear in this snapshot. If you have chosen to enter your net paycheck and have not told Quicken that this amount is tax related, nothing will appear in this list except a link to set up your paycheck.

Tax Alerts

Tax alerts, which in previous versions of Quicken were displayed at the top of what is now the Tax Center, are only visible in the Alerts Center, opened from the Tools menu, Alerts Center option. This is also where you go to set alerts related to your tax situation. You can access the Tax Alerts feature through the Options button in the Tax Calendar or from the menu bar by choosing Tools | Alerts Center | Setup. In the Setup dialog you have three options related to taxes:

- **Withholding Threshold** (next) enables you to set a value of dollars withheld from your paycheck to alert you if your payroll withholding is too much or not enough. This alert only works when you set up your paycheck in Quicken.

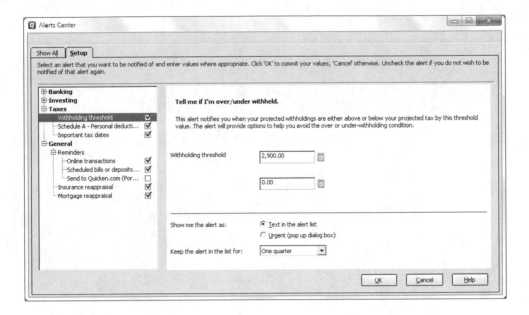

- **Schedule A – Personal Deductions** (Schedule A Reminder) displays information about the types of personal deductions you can claim on Schedule A of your tax return.
- **Important Tax Dates** notifies you in advance of tax calendar events, such as estimated tax due dates and extension deadlines.

Learn more about setting alerts in Chapters 8 and 17.

Appendixes

This part of the book provides some additional information you may find helpful when using Quicken Personal Finance Software. These three appendixes explain how to work with Quicken data files and how to customize Quicken.

Part Seven

Managing Quicken Files

In This Appendix:

- *Creating and opening data files*
- *Backing up and restoring data files*
- *Password-protecting Quicken data*
- *Performing other file management tasks*

All the information you enter in your Quicken Personal Finance Software is stored in a Quicken data file. This file includes all account and category setup information, transactions, and other records you have entered into Quicken.

Technically speaking, your Quicken data file consists of a single file with the QDF extension. Manipulating these files without using Quicken's built-in file management tools can cause errors.

Commands under Quicken's File menu enable you to perform a number of file management tasks, such as creating, opening, backing up, restoring, password-protecting, importing and exporting, and copying portions and years of data files, as well as validating and repairing your data files. This appendix discusses all of these tasks.

Working with Multiple Data Files

Chances are, you won't need more than one Quicken data file—the one that's created as part of the Quicken Setup process, covered in Chapter 2. But just in case you do, here's how you can create and open another one.

Creating a Data File

Start by choosing File | New Quicken File. A dialog appears, asking whether you want to create a new Quicken file or a new

Quicken account, as shown here. (Some users confuse the two and try to use the File menu's New command to create a new account. You learn how to create an account in Chapter 2.) Select New Quicken File and click OK.

A Create Quicken File dialog, like the one shown next, appears. Use it to enter a name for the data file. Although you can also change the default directory location, it's easier to find the data file if it's in the Quicken subdirectory of your Documents (or Documents And Settings) folder with other Quicken data files. It is also easier to find the Quicken file if it is renamed with no spaces or other special characters. Click OK.

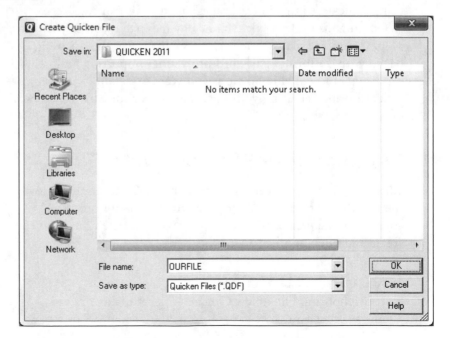

There are occasional issues if the filename is longer than eight characters.

Quicken's Setup appears next. You learn how to use Setup in Chapter 2; turn to that chapter if you need help.

Opening a Different Data File

If you have more than one Quicken data file, it's important that you enter transactions into the right one. You can see which data file is currently open by looking at the filename in the application window's title bar as shown here.

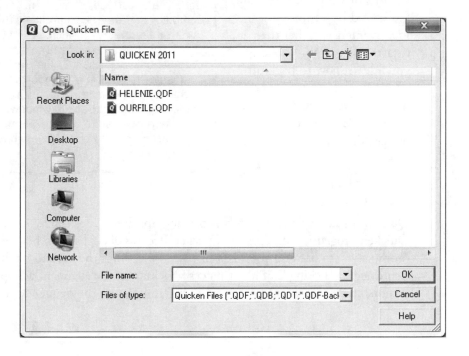

To open a different data file, choose File | Open Quicken File, or press CTRL-O, and use the Open Quicken File dialog that appears to select and open a different file. Only one Quicken data file can be open at a time.

Backing Up Your Quicken Data File

Imagine this: You set up Quicken to track all of your finances, and you record transactions regularly so the Quicken data file is always up-to-date. Then one evening, when you start your computer to check your e-mail or enter a cash transaction into Quicken, you find that your hard drive has died. Not only have your plans for the evening been ruined, but your Quicken data file is also a casualty of your hard drive's untimely death.

If you back up your Quicken data as regularly as you update its information, the loss of your Quicken data file would be a minor inconvenience, rather than a catastrophe. In this section, you'll learn how to back up your Quicken data file and how to restore it if the original file is lost or damaged.

EXPERIENCED QUICKEN USERS AND NEW TO QUICKEN?

Quicken Online Backup

By far, the most secure backup file is the one that resides someplace other than near your computer. Why? Well, if your computer is stolen or damaged in a fire or flood, don't you think your backup disks might be lost with it?

Quicken Online Backup can help protect your data by making it easy to back up your data to a secure server far from your computer and other backup files. This service is fully integrated with Quicken. Just use Quicken's Backup command to back up your data file using Quicken Online Backup.

If your Quicken data is important to you, check out this feature. Click the Learn More link in the Quicken Backup window to get the details on this useful service. Remember that your backup can be quite large, so it can take a long time.

Backing Up to Disk

Quicken makes it difficult to forget backing up. Every third time you exit the Quicken program, it displays the Quicken Backup dialog, shown here, which prompts you to back up your data file. You can change the backup reminder prompt frequency by clicking Edit | Preferences | Backup. In the Manual Backup Reminders section, change the number of times to be reminded to the frequency you want.

While you are using Quicken, you begin the backup process by choosing File | Backup And Restore | Backup Quicken File or by pressing CTRL-B at any time. This displays the Quicken Backup dialog for the currently open Quicken data file, as seen in Figure A-1.

Select one of the following backup location options:

- **Back Up On My Computer Or Hard Drive (CD, Hard Drive, Thumb Drive)** enables you to back up to another disk, either on your computer or on one that's accessible via a network. If you select this option, you can use the Change button to locate and select a backup disk and directory. It's a good idea to alternate between two disks for backup purposes. This means you'll always have two versions backed up, in case one version is corrupt. It's a good idea to choose a backup location other than your hard disk, such as a thumb drive (for small files) or an external hard disk. (Backing up to your hard disk defeats the purpose of backing up!) If you want to automatically append the current date to the backup filename, select the Add Date To Backup File Name check box.

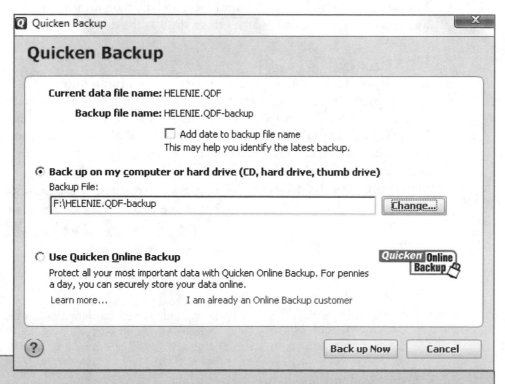

Figure A-1 • Use the Quicken Backup dialog to ensure you can recover your data in case of a hard disk failure.

(These instructions assume you have selected On My Computer.) Keep in mind that your computer may not be able to write directly to a CD-R or DVD-R. If you choose to back up to an optical disk, you might have to back up to your hard disk and then burn the resulting file to disk.

- **Use Quicken Online Backup** enables you to back up to a server on the Internet, using Quicken's Online Backup service, which is available for a nominal fee. You can learn more about this service by selecting Learn More in the Use Quicken Online Backup section to connect to the Quicken Online Backup website.
- If you have an online backup account, click the I Am Already An Online Backup Customer link to enter your account ID and password.

After selecting Back Up On My Computer or Hard Drive (CD, Hard Drive, Thumb Drive) and indicating a backup directory in the Quicken Backup dialog, click Backup Now. Your Quicken data file disappears momentarily and a small window tells you that Quicken is backing up your data. When the backup is complete, the data file's windows reappear and a dialog informs you that the file was backed up successfully. Click OK to dismiss the dialog.

Restoring

In the event of loss or damage to your data file, you can restore from a recent backup. Start Quicken and then choose a backup file from the Restore From Backup File submenu under the File | Backup And Restore menu. This submenu includes all backups that Quicken created automatically. It also includes a Browse command that you can use to browse for the file in your own computer. You can also select online backups to find the file you want to restore, as seen in Figure A-2.

When you choose the backup file, you have several options:

- If the file has the same name as the Quicken data file currently in use, a dialog appears, asking if you want to overwrite the file in use. You have two choices, as seen on page 528.

EXPERIENCED QUICKEN USERS AND NEW TO QUICKEN?

Warning Messages

The successful backup message has a check box you can select if you do not want to see the successful backup message in the future. Be cautious about checking the box as once you tell Quicken to stop showing the message, the message will not appear again. However, new in Quicken 2011, you can reset all warning messages you may have hidden by choosing Edit | Preferences | Alerts | Reset Quicken Warnings.

NEW TO QUICKEN?

Back Up vs. Copy

When should you back up and when should you copy? In today's computing world, that's a great question. When personal computers first came into general use, the storage devices, such as floppy disks, held much less information than today's spacious devices. Saving data was no less important in 1990, but the media held much less information. The 3-1/2" floppy disks that were often used held only 1.44MB of information. Today's flash (or thumb) drives, those small storage devices about 3" × 0.75", can store as much as 64GB. (When you remember that 1,024MB is 1 GB, you get an idea of the storage capacity of a flash drive.) In order to efficiently and safely save data, earlier backup programs compressed the information to fit on the small media. One had to use the same program to *restore* the information back to the hard disk.

The Quicken Backup And Restore utility, however, *encrypts* the data—that is, it puts the data into a special format that is unreadable unless you have the key. Quicken Backup encrypts data and Quicken Restore unencrypts the data so that it can be used once more.

With today's large external hard disks, saving space may not be as important as easy retrieval of your data. If that is the case, consider using one of the two Copy commands offered by Quicken. These Copy commands save the data bit by bit so that you can retrieve it quickly and get back to work.

Figure A-2 • You have several choices when restoring your Quicken files.

- To replace (or completely overwrite) the current file with the backup copy, choose Overwrite The Open File With Restored File and click Restore Backup. This will erase any information you have entered since this backup and replace all of the data in the currently open file.
- To create a second copy of this file, choose Create A Copy and click Restore Backup. Quicken prompts you for a location for this file copy. This option will *not* overwrite your currently open file, but will create a copy.

Quicken restores the file from the backup copy. It places a copy of the restored file on your hard disk, displaying a status window as it works. When it has finished, it displays a dialog telling you that the file has been restored successfully, as shown here. Click Yes to open the restored file, or click No to close the dialog and return to your current file.

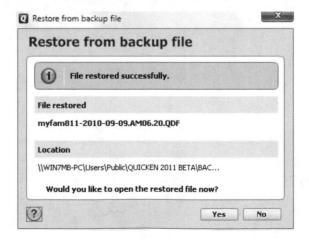

Moving a Quicken Data File Between Two Computers

Intuit's technical support staff is often asked how to move a Quicken data file from one computer to another. In fact, this question is so common that we are including it in this book.

The best way to move a data file from one computer to another is with the Backup and Restore Backup File commands. Begin by opening the file with Quicken on the computer on which it resides. Then follow the instructions in this appendix to back up the file to removable media, such as a thumb (or flash) drive, CD-R or external disk, or to a network drive (preferably one that the other computer is connected to). Then fire up Quicken on the other computer and follow the restoring instructions in this appendix to restore the backup copy. When you're finished, the Quicken data file is ready to use on the new computer.

It's important to remember that once you begin making changes to the file on the new computer, the file on the old computer will no longer be up-to-date. This means that if you want to use the file on the old computer again, you need to complete the backup and restore process to move the file back to that computer. As you can imagine, if you often move the file from one computer to another and back, it can be difficult to keep track of which version of the file is the most up-to-date.

Although you can make your Quicken data file "portable" by keeping it on removable media so you can access it from any computer, this is *not* the recommended method. Flash drives, CDs, and DVDs are all more susceptible to data loss and damage than an internal or networked hard disk. Quicken users have reported numerous problems using this technique; don't add your own problems to the list. A networked drive may not be a good place to store your file either, at least if you are going to keep it networked while you work on it.

Other File Management Tasks

Quicken's File menu enables you to perform a variety of tasks with Quicken data files. Figure A-3 shows the various tasks you can perform.

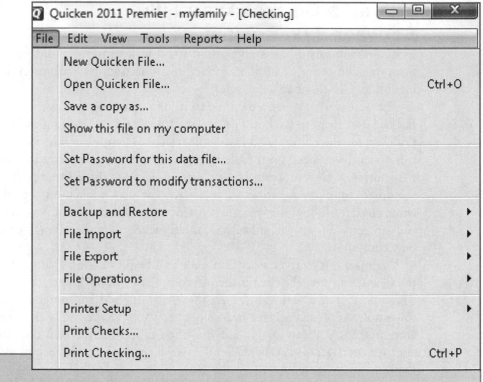

Figure A-3 • Use the Quicken File menu to perform many useful tasks.

Opening, Saving, and Copying Quicken Files

The first two options on the File menu help you access your Quicken files. Use these commands to create a new file, as discussed in Chapter 2, or open a Quicken file that already exists on your hard drive or a networked drive.

Save A Copy As

Click this menu command to open a dialog with which you can save an exact copy of your current file to another location. This other location can be a flash or thumb drive, another location on your network, or an external hard disk. This is different from the backup command covered earlier. See the sidebar "Back Up vs. Copy" elsewhere in this chapter for the difference between the two.

To copy your currently open file, click the down arrow by the Save In field at the top of the dialog box and choose a location other than the current folder. Create a new name for your copied file and click OK. Your file is now copied to the other location and you are returned to your currently open Quicken file.

Show This File On My Computer

You can immediately find where your current file is located by choosing File | Show This File On My Computer. When you click this command, Quicken opens a Windows Explorer window showing where the currently open file is located on your computer.

As you can see in the illustration, the file called myfamily.qdf is stored in the Quicken 2011 Official Guide folder on the local disk on this computer.

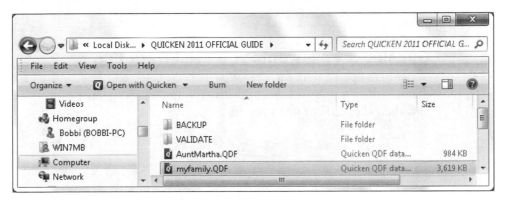

Password-Protecting Quicken Data

Quicken offers two types of password protection for your data: file passwords and transaction passwords. This section shows how these options work.

Protecting a Data File

When you password-protect a data file, the file cannot be opened without the password. This is the ultimate in protection—it prevents unauthorized users from even seeing your data.

Setting Up the Password

Choose File | Set Password For This Data File to display the Quicken File Password dialog, which is shown here. Enter the same password in each text box and click OK.

Read the suggestions from Quicken about secure passwords. And, one more thing, no password is secure if it is written on a sticky note and affixed to your monitor.

Opening a Password-Protected Data File

When you open a data file that is password-protected, the Quicken Password dialog, which is shown here, appears. You must enter your password correctly and then click OK to open the file.

Changing or Removing a Password

Choose File | Set Password For This Data File to display the Quicken File Password dialog. Enter the current password in the Old Password box, and then enter the same new password in the two boxes beneath it. (To remove a password, leave the two bottom boxes empty.) Click OK.

Protecting Existing Transactions

When you password-protect existing transactions, the transactions cannot be modified unless the password is properly entered. This prevents unauthorized or accidental alterations to data.

Setting Up the Password

Choose File | Set Password To Modify Transactions to display the Password To Modify Existing Transactions dialog, shown here. Enter the same password in the top two text boxes. Then enter a date through which the transactions are to be protected and click OK.

Modifying a Password-Protected Transaction

When you attempt to modify a transaction that is protected with a password, the Quicken Password dialog, shown here, appears. You must enter your password correctly and then click OK to modify the transaction.

Changing or Removing a Password

Choose File | Set Password To Modify Transactions to display the Change Transaction Password dialog. Enter the current password in the Old Password box, and then enter the same new password in the two boxes beneath it. (To remove a password, leave the two bottom boxes empty.) Click OK.

Password Tips

Here are a few things to keep in mind when working with passwords:

- Passwords can be up to 16 characters in length and can contain any character, including a space.
- Passwords are case-sensitive. That means, for example, that *PassWord* is not the same as *password*.
- If you forget your password, you will not be able to access the data file. Write your password down and keep it in a safe place.
- Your data file is only as secure as you make it. Quicken's password protection can help prevent unauthorized access to your Quicken data files.

File Operations

Click File Operations on Quicken's menu to open a submenu that allows you to further manage your data files. As shown in the next illustration, there are four options.

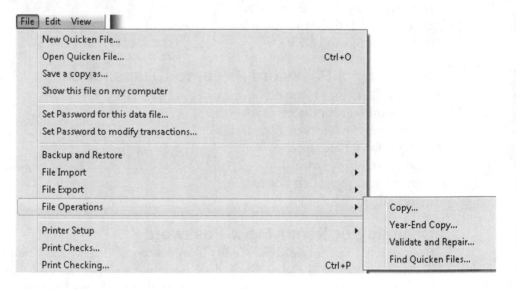

Copying the Current Data File

This Copy command enables you to copy all or portions of the current data file to a different disk or save a copy with a different name. While similar to the Save A Copy As command discussed earlier in this appendix, this command gives you choices regarding what time period to include in the copied file as well as a choice to include uncleared and investment transactions. It also may clear unused space in the Quicken file.

When you choose File | File Operations | Copy, the Copy File dialog, shown here, appears. Click Browse to choose a location for your file if you want the copied file stored in a location other than the current folder. The new filename will be the same as the current file but will have "Cpy" at the end of the filename. You can change the name if you choose. Select the date range that is to be included in the copy and clear either of the two check boxes should you not want to copy those transactions. Click OK to make the copy.

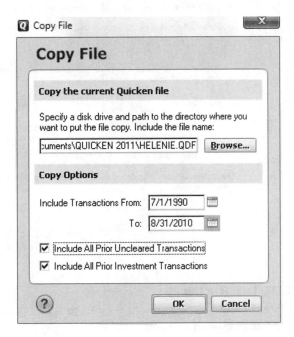

If there is already a Quicken file with the same name in your Quicken folder, you will receive a prompt for a new name for the file copy. If so, type a new name for this second file copy and click OK.

When the copy is finished, a dialog asks if you want to continue working with the original data file or the new copy. Select the appropriate option and click OK to continue working with Quicken.

Making a Year-End Copy of a Data File

The Year-End Copy command creates two special copies of your data file. Choose File | File Operations | Year-End Copy to display the Create A Year End Copy dialog, shown next, and set options for the two files.

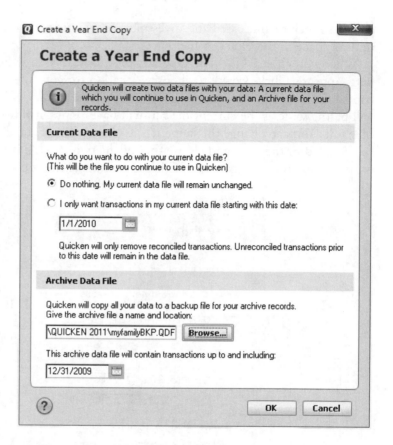

Current Data File

The Current Data File section allows you to set options for the file you will continue working with in Quicken.

Do Nothing. My Current Data File Will Remain Unchanged.   This option simply saves a copy of the current data file as is.

I Only Want Transactions In My Current Data File Starting With This Date.
This option enables you to enter a starting date for the files in the data file you will continue to use. For example, if you enter 1/1/2010, all transactions prior to that date will be removed from the data file. This option reduces the size of your data file, which makes it easier to back up and may help Quicken operate more efficiently.

Archive Data File

The Archive Data File section allows you to set options for creating an archive copy of the file. An *archive* is a copy of older transactions saved in a separate file. You can set two options:

- Enter a complete path (or use the Browse button to enter a path) for the archive file.
- Enter the date for the last transaction to be included in the file. For example, if you enter 12/31/2011, the archive file will include all transactions in the current file, up to and including those transactions dated 12/31/2011.

Creating the Files

When you click OK in the Create A Year End Copy dialog, Quicken creates the two files. It then displays a dialog that enables you to select the file you want to work with: the Current file or the Archive file. Select the appropriate option (normally Current File) and click OK to continue working with Quicken.

Archived files or copies with only some of the Quicken data cannot be recombined by any easy means.

Checking the Integrity of a Data File

The Validate And Repair command facilitates checking the integrity of a Quicken data file. This command is particularly useful if you believe that a file has been damaged. It is a good idea to copy your file to an external device, such as a CD or external hard drive, before you perform the Validate And Repair function.

When you choose File | File Operations | Validate And Repair, the Validate Quicken File dialog appears, as shown on the top of the next page. By default, the current file is selected, but you may use the dialog to select another file to check if you choose.

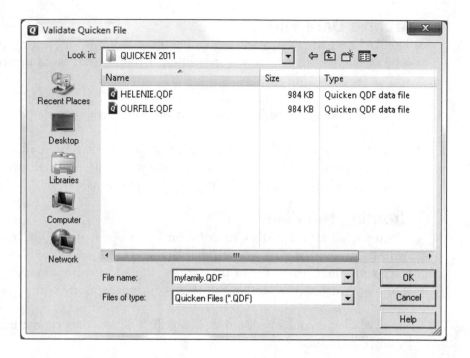

When you click OK, Quicken checks the data file's integrity. It then displays a text file that tells you whether the file has any problems, as seen here.

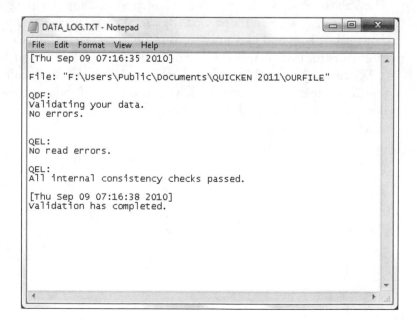

Sometimes you can repair a damaged file by simply opening it in Quicken. Use the Open command, as discussed near the beginning of this appendix. If Quicken can't open the file, it tells you. That's when it's time to reach for that backup file. You *did* make one recently, didn't you?

Importing Files into Quicken

Importing information into Quicken can make your financial life much easier. From downloading information from your financial institution, as discussed in Chapter 6, to converting from Microsoft Money, as discussed in Appendix C, importing data saves you time.

From within Quicken, click File | File Import to open the submenu that shows your options, as shown here. As you can see, four types of files can be imported.

| Web Connect File... |
| QIF File... |
| TurboTax File... |
| Microsoft Money® file... |

- **Web Connect Files** are those files created by financial institutions that do not have Direct Connect availability. You download these files onto your hard drive and then import them into your Quicken data file. See Chapter 6 for detailed information about Web Connect files.
- **QIF Files** are Quicken Interchange Format files that have been created in a third-party program for importing into Quicken. While not all programs support this format, many financial programs do.
- **TurboTax Files** can be imported into Quicken for tax planning.
- **Microsoft Money Files** are quickly converted into Quicken data files. See Appendix C for detailed instructions.

Exporting Quicken Files

There are two types of export files shown on the File Export menu. Both are used primarily for transferring Quicken data files from one version to another.

- **QIF Files** are used to export Quicken data from one Quicken account to another Quicken account or to another Quicken file. To export a file, click File | File Export | QIF File. The QIF Export dialog appears, as shown on the top of the next page.

- From the QIF File To Export field, choose the file you want to export and the account from the drop-down list. The default in this field is All Accounts. Set the date range for the transactions you wish to export. Select the check box for each item you want to include in the export and click OK. Your QIF file is saved in the same location as the file you chose to export.
- **Quicken Transfer Format (.QFX) Files** are used to transfer data files from Quicken for Windows to Quicken Essentials for Mac. Click File | File Export | Quicken Transfer Format to open the Export To Quicken Transfer Format dialog. By default, the file with which you are working is the filename you will export. Click Save. You will see this message box when the export file is created successfully. You will then need to import this .qfx file into your Quicken Essentials file.

Customizing Quicken

In This Appendix:

- *Creating custom Home tab views*
- *Customizing the Tool Bar*
- *Setting Quicken Preferences*

Once you've worked with Quicken Personal Finance Software for a while, you may want to fine-tune the way it looks and works to best suit your needs. Most of these options are discussed elsewhere in this book. Other customization options—like customizing the Tool Bar—are less commonly used. This appendix will explain many of the customization options available for Quicken and provide cross-references to other chapters in the book where you can learn more about the features they work with.

Customizing Quicken's Interface

Quicken offers a number of ways to customize its interface to best meet your needs. This part of the appendix explains how to customize the Home tab and the Quicken toolbar.

Creating Custom Home Tab Views

As discussed in Chapter 1, the Home tab offers customizable views of your Quicken data. You can use this tab to create multiple Home tab views, each of which shows the "snapshots" of summarized financial information that you want to display. Figure B-1 shows an example.

Figure B-1 • An example of the Main View of the Home tab, with some snapshots added

The Home tab was known as My Pages in some previous versions of Quicken. If you've upgraded to Quicken 2011 from a previous version, you may already have custom views of the Quicken Home page set up in your Quicken data file. You'll get access to these views on the Home tab, where you can switch from one to another, modify them, and delete them, as discussed in this section.

Displaying the Home Tab Views

To get started, click the Home tab near the top of the Quicken window. Quicken displays the Main View button. Before you customize this view, it displays three snapshots: See Where Your Money Goes, Stay On Top Of Monthly Bills, and Track Spending Goals To Save Money. Once you've customized the Home tab, it displays the snapshots you added to it (refer to Figure B-1).

Modifying the Current View

You can modify the current view with the Customize button. This button opens the Customize View dialog, which is shown next. Make changes as desired and click OK to save them.

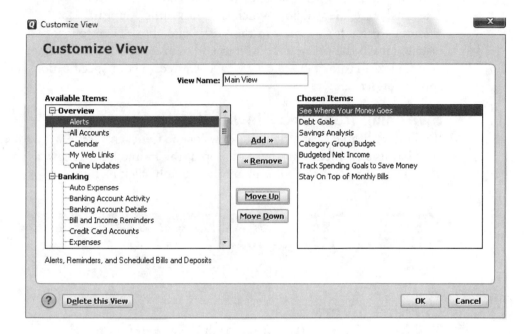

Adding an Item   Items are organized by type in the Available Items list, making it easy to find the one you want. To add an item to the view, select it in the Available Items list and click Add. Its name appears in the Chosen Items list. You can include up to 34 items in the view; however, rather than have a great number of items that crowd your window, it's better to create separate views with fewer items in each view.

Removing an Item   To remove an item from the view, select it in the Chosen Items list and click Remove.

Rearranging Items   To rearrange the order of items in the Chosen Items list, select an item and click Move Up or Move Down. Repeat this process until the items appear in the order you want.

Creating a New View

By creating multiple views, you can make several versions of the Home tab window, each with a specific set of information. You can then quickly switch from one view to another to see the information you want.

In the Home tab window, click the Add View button (refer to Figure B-1). The Customize View dialog, which is shown earlier, appears.

Enter a name for the view in the View Name box. Then follow the instructions in the previous section to add items to the view, and click OK. A new Quicken Home tab window view is created to your specifications and appears on-screen.

Switching from One View to Another

If you have created more than one view for the Quicken Home window, each view has its own menu button at the top of the Home tab window, as shown here. To switch from one view to another, simply click its button.

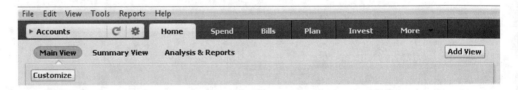

Deleting a View

To delete a view, select the button for the view you want to delete. Click Customize to open the Customize View dialog. Then choose Delete This View from the menu. Click Yes in the confirmation dialog that appears. The view is deleted. You cannot delete the Main View.

Customizing the Tool Bar

The Quicken Tool Bar is an optional row of buttons along the top of the screen, just beneath the menu bar. These buttons offer quick access to Quicken features.

You can customize the toolbar by adding, removing, or rearranging buttons, or by changing the display options for toolbar buttons. You can do all this with the Customize Toolbar dialog, which is shown on the top of the next page. To open this dialog, open the View menu and click Show Tool Bar. With the toolbar displayed, right-click it and choose Customize Tool Bar. (If you have already chosen to show the toolbar, you can click View | Customize Tool Bar as well.)

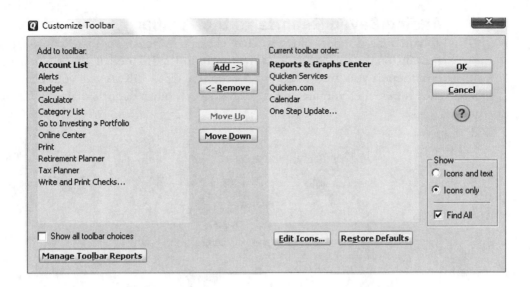

To customize the toolbar, make changes in this dialog and click OK. The toolbar is redrawn to your specifications.

Adding Buttons

To add a button, select it in the Add To Toolbar list and click Add. Its name appears in the Current Toolbar Order list. If you want more items to choose from, click the Show All Toolbar Choices check box to display all the possibilities. The list expands to show approximately three times as many items.

You can include as many buttons as you like on the toolbar. If the toolbar includes more buttons than can fit within the Quicken application window, a More button (a green down arrow) appears on the toolbar. Click this button to display a menu of buttons; choose the name of the button you want. The More button also appears on the toolbar when you make your Quicken window smaller, as shown here.

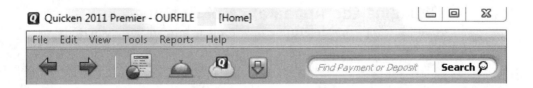

Adding Saved Reports to the Toolbar

To add a saved report to the toolbar, click the Manage Toolbar Reports button in the Customize Toolbar dialog. Then turn on the In Toolbar check box beside each saved report you want to add to the toolbar. Click OK to save your changes, as shown here. Learn more about the Manage Toolbar Reports dialog in Chapter 8.

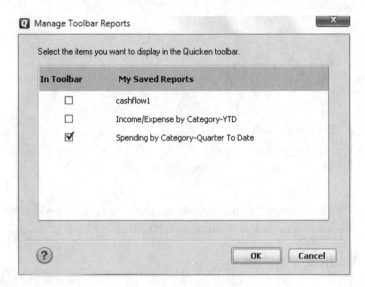

Removing Buttons

To remove a button, select it in the Current Toolbar Order list and click Remove. Its name is removed from the Current Toolbar Order list but is still available on the Add To Toolbar list should you want to include it another time.

Rearranging Buttons

You can rearrange the order of buttons in the toolbar by changing their order in the Current Toolbar Order list. Simply select a button that you want to move, and click Move Up or Move Down to change its position in the list.

Changing the Appearance of Buttons

Two Show options determine how toolbar buttons are displayed:

- **Icons And Text** displays both the toolbar button and its label, as shown here.

- **Icons Only** displays just the toolbar icon. When you point to an icon, its label appears.

Editing Buttons

You can also create custom keyboard shortcuts for the buttons on your toolbar. From the Customize Toolbar dialog, click Edit Icons to open the Edit Toolbar Button dialog, as shown next. Change the label or shortcut key combination, and click OK.

You can now open that item from your keyboard using the keystrokes shown in the Edit Toolbar Button dialog. However, if you remove the button from the toolbar, the keystroke combination no longer works for that item.

Also, the label change does not appear in the Current Toolbar Order list, but it does appear on the toolbar when you save your customized settings.

The Search Field

At the right of the toolbar is a search field you can use to search your entire Quicken data file for specific transactions, as discussed in Chapter 4. This feature is enabled by default. It can be deactivated by clearing the Find All check box in the Customize Toolbar dialog.

Restoring the Default Toolbar

To restore the toolbar back to its "factory settings," click the Restore Defaults button in the Customize Toolbar dialog. Then click OK in the confirmation dialog that appears. The buttons return to the way they appear when Quicken is first installed.

Setting Preferences

The Preferences menu gives you access to dialogs for changing Quicken Preferences settings. This section reviews all of the options you can change and tells you where you can learn more about the features they control.

Quicken Preferences

As the name suggests, Preferences control Quicken's general appearance and operations. To access these options, open the Edit menu and choose Preferences to open the Preferences dialog, as seen in Figure B-2. It lists a variety of categories, each of which is discussed next.

Startup

Startup preferences enable you to specify what should appear when you start Quicken. Use the drop-down list to select Home (the default setting), one of the tabs (Home, Bills, Planning, and so on), or one of the views within the tabs. You can choose what you want Quicken to do when it starts, such as download transactions or require a password, and also choose one of the predefined color schemes for the Quicken program: blue (the default), green, purple, or tan.

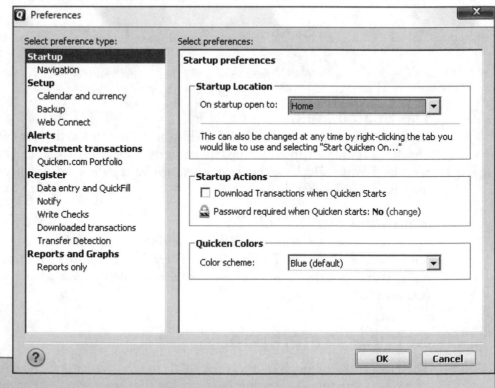

Figure B-2 • Use the Preferences dialog to make Quicken your own.

Depending on your monitor settings, sometimes changing the color scheme can make Quicken easier for you to read.

Navigation   Startup Navigation allows you to choose how you want to get around Quicken.

- **Main Navigation** lets you choose to use the Classic menus (those used prior to 2010) and what to show in those menus. If you choose Classic menus, you also have an option to turn off the display of the tabs.
- **Account Bar** lets you select where to place the Account Bar and whether to display cents in the Account Bar balances.
- **Other Options** lets you choose whether to show the Quicken Tool Bar. If you have a wide screen monitor, you may choose to dock the side bar permanently on the right side of your monitor.

Setup

Setup options, which are illustrated next, control basic Quicken operations, such as:

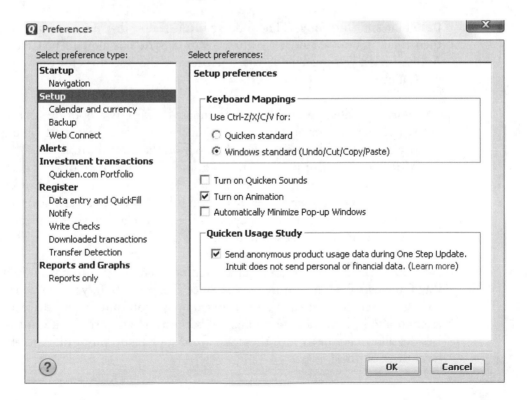

- **Keyboard Mappings** enables you to change what certain standard Windows keyboard shortcuts do. In most Windows programs, the CTRL-Z, CTRL-X, CTRL-C, and CTRL-V shortcut keys perform commands on the Edit menu. In Quicken 2011, these keyboard shortcuts are set to the Windows standard. See Chapter 1 for more information about keyboard shortcuts.
- **Turn On Quicken Sounds** turns on Quicken sound effects. You may want to leave this check box off if you use Quicken in an environment where sounds might annoy the people around you.
- **Turn On Animation**, which is turned on by default, activates the Quicken animation effects that appear when you complete certain actions.
- **Automatically Minimize Pop-up Windows** automatically minimizes a Quicken window—such as a report window or the Category List window— to the Quicken task bar when you click outside that window. (This is the window behavior in some older versions of Quicken.) With this option turned off, you can have multiple Quicken windows open at once and can manually minimize each one.
- **Quicken Usage Study** uses your Internet connection to send information anonymously about your use of the product.

Calendar and Currency   The folks at Intuit realize that not everyone manages their finances on a calendar year basis or in U.S. dollars alone. The Calendar And Currency options enable you to customize these settings for the way you use Quicken.

- **Working Calendar** enables you to choose between two options: Calendar Year is a 12-month year beginning with January, and Fiscal Year is a 12-month year beginning with the month you choose from the drop-down list.
- **Multicurrency Support** assigns a "home" currency to all of your current data, placing a currency symbol beside every amount. You can then enter amounts in other currencies by entering the appropriate currency symbol. It is not necessary to set this option unless you plan to work with multiple currencies in one Quicken data file.

Backup   The Backup options, illustrated next, enable you to customize the way Quicken's Backup feature works. Since Quicken 2010, you can choose to have Quicken automatically do backups on your computer's hard drive as well as choose to be reminded to do manual backups on any drive you want. Besides allowing you to turn these two forms of backup on or off, you also have these settings:

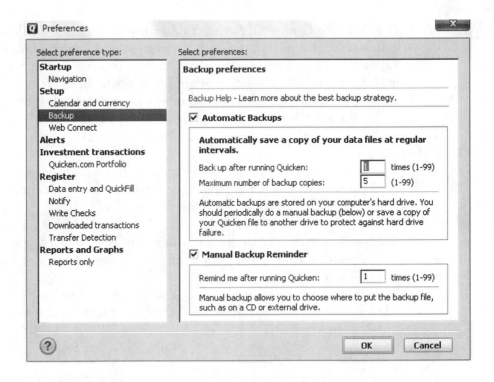

- **Back Up After Running Quicken** *NN* **Times** tells Quicken to automatically back up (make a copy of) your Quicken data on your normal hard drive after you have run Quicken the specified number of times.
- **Maximum Number Of Backup Copies** is the number of backup copies Quicken should automatically keep. The higher the value in this text box, the more backup copies of your Quicken data are saved. This enables you to go back further if you discover a problem with your current Quicken data file. You learn more about backing up data in Appendix A.
- **Remind Me After Running Quicken** *NN* **Times** enables you to specify when you want to be reminded to manually back up your Quicken data file. If you also have automatic backups turned on, this allows you to back up your data on another drive other than your normal drive. Learn how to back up your data in Appendix A.

Web Connect   The Web Connect options enable you to customize the way Quicken's Web Connect feature works. Web Connect, as discussed in Chapter 5, is a method for downloading transaction information from your financial institution into your Quicken data file.

- **Give Me The Option Of Saving To A File Whenever I Download Web Connect Data** displays a dialog that enables you to save the downloaded Web Connect information to a file. Normally, the data is imported directly into the appropriate account in your Quicken data file.
- **Keep Quicken Open After Web Connect Completes** tells Quicken to keep running after Web Connect completes a download from the Web.

Alerts

Alerts preferences enable you to set the lead time for calendar notes to appear in Alerts snapshots. Learn about alerts in Chapter 8. This does not affect the lead time for scheduled transactions or Billminder.

- **Billminder** is explained in detail in Chapter 6. You can select a lead time period from the drop-down list; timing options range from Last Month to Next Month.
- **Warnings** allow you to change all Quicken warnings back to their default. Click Reset Quicken Warnings, as seen here, and a message appears that all warnings are reset.

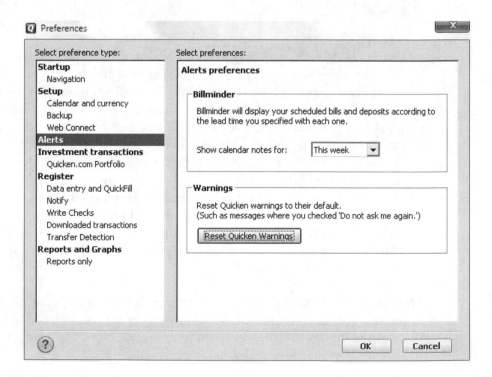

Investment Transactions

Investment Transactions options (shown here) let you customize the way the Investment Transaction list looks and works. Learn about the Investment Transaction list in Chapter 9.

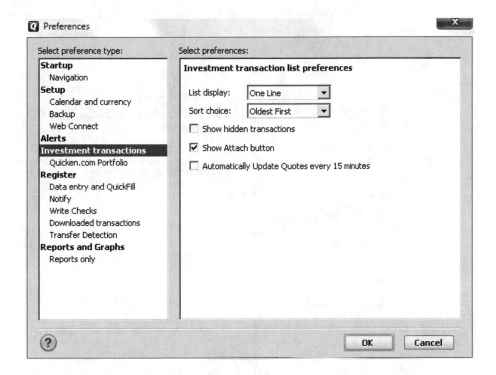

- **List Display** determines whether transactions should appear with one or two lines in the list.
- **Sort Choice** determines whether transactions should be sorted in ascending or descending order by date.
- **Show Hidden Transactions** displays hidden transactions in the list.
- **Show Attach Button** displays the Attach button beside the Edit and Delete buttons for the current transaction. You may want to turn off this check box if you do not use the Image Attachment feature. Chapter 4 explains how to attach images to transactions.
- **Automatically Update Quotes Every 15 Minutes** updates your stock portfolio with your Internet connection every 15 minutes. This feature comes with Quicken Premier edition and higher editions and is new in Quicken 2011.

Quicken.com Portfolio   As explained in Chapter 10, http://investing
.quicken.com is an online site where you can track your investment information
from any location with Internet access. This section tells Quicken what accounts
to view online at Quicken.com and how to send information. You may choose
to send your share information or only their symbols to your online portfolio.

Clear the Track My Watch List On Quicken.com check box to stop
Quicken.com from including that information.

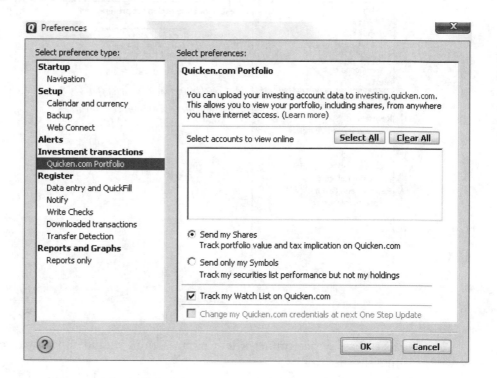

Register

Register preferences enable you to fine-tune the way the account register works.
Five groups of settings appear in addition to the Register preferences themselves.
Account register windows are discussed throughout this book, but details for
using them are provided in Chapter 4.

Register Preferences   Register options, shown next, affect the way the transactions you enter appear in the account register window.

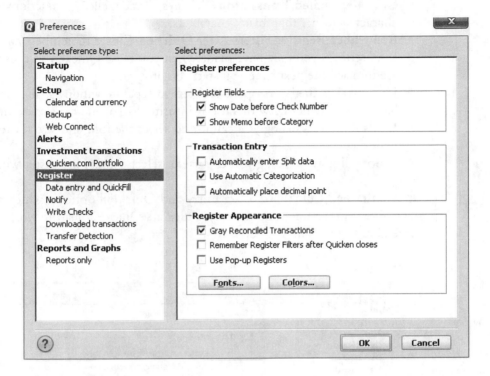

- **Show Date Before Check Number** is the default setting for your registers. Clear this check box to have the check number appear in the first column.
- **Show Memo Before Category** puts the Memo field before the Category field in your account register.

Transaction Entry

- **Automatically Enter Split Data** turns the OK button in the Split Transaction window into an Enter button for entering the transaction.
- **Use Automatic Categorization** uses the Automatic Categorization feature to "guess" which category should be assigned to a transaction based on a database of company names and keywords stored within Quicken. This applies both to transactions you enter and those that you download.
- **Automatically Place Decimal Point** automatically enters a decimal point two places to the left when using Quicken's built-in calculator. For example, if you enter **1543** in the calculator, Quicken enters 15.43.

Register Appearance

- **Gray Reconciled Transactions** displays all reconciled transactions with gray characters rather than black characters.
- **Remember Register Filters After Quicken Closes** remembers any register filter settings you may have made when you close Quicken so those settings are in place the next time you start the program.
- **Use Pop-Up Registers** opens registers in separate windows, allowing you to have several windows with various information open at the same time.
- **Fonts** displays a dialog you can use to select the font and size for register windows.
- **Colors** displays a dialog you can use to select colors for register windows.

Data Entry and QuickFill Data Entry and QuickFill options, which are shown next, allow you to fine-tune the way Quicken's QuickFill feature works. Learn more about QuickFill in Chapter 6.

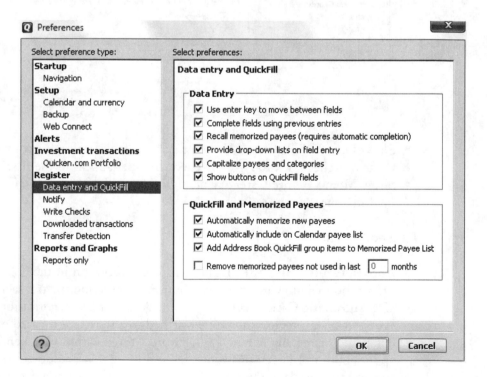

Data Entry

- **Use Enter Key To Move Between Fields** enables you to use both the ENTER and TAB keys to move from field to field when entering data.
- **Complete Fields Using Previous Entries** enters transaction information using the information from previous entries.
- **Recall Memorized Payees** uses memorized payees to fill in QuickFill entries. This option is not available if the Complete Fields Using Previous Entries option is disabled.
- **Provide Drop-Down Lists On Field Entry** automatically displays the drop-down list when you advance to a field with a list.
- **Capitalize Payees And Categories** automatically makes the first letter of each word in a payee name or category uppercase.
- **Show Buttons On QuickFill Fields** displays drop-down list buttons on fields for which you can use QuickFill.

QuickFill and Memorized Payees

- **Automatically Memorize New Payees** tells Quicken to automatically enter all transactions for a new payee to the Memorized Payee list.
- **Automatically Include On Calendar Payee List** tells Quicken to automatically add memorized payees to the Calendar window. This option is turned on by default. You can display the Memorized Payee list by choosing Show Memorized Payee List from the Options menu on the Calendar's button bar.
- **Add Address Book QuickFill Group Items To Memorized Payee List** tells Quicken to add entries from the Financial Address Book to the Memorized Payee list so they automatically fill in address fields when writing checks.
- **Remove Memorized Payees Not Used In Last *NN* Months** tells Quicken to remove memorized payees that have not been used within the number of months you specify. By default, this feature is turned off. By selecting this check box and entering a value of **6** (for example), Quicken memorizes only the payees you entered in the past six months, thus keeping the Memorized Payee list manageable. Using this feature with a lower value (for example, 3) can weed one-time transactions out of the Memorized Payee list. Changing this option does not affect transactions that have already been entered. Chapter 6 discusses memorized transactions.

Notify Notify options, shown next, affect the way you are notified about problems when you enter transactions in the register.

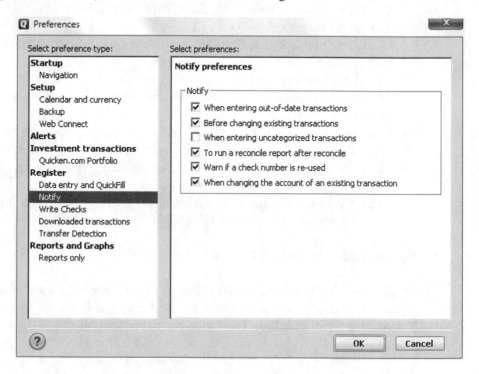

- **When Entering Out-Of-Date Transactions** warns you when you try to record a transaction for a date more than a year from the current date.
- **Before Changing Existing Transactions** warns you when you try to modify a previously entered transaction.
- **When Entering Uncategorized Transactions** warns you when you try to record a transaction without assigning a category to it.
- **To Run A Reconcile Report After Reconcile** asks if you want to display a Reconcile report when you complete an account reconciliation.
- **Warn If A Check Number Is Re-used** warns you if you assign a check number that was already assigned in another transaction.
- **When Changing The Account Of An Existing Transaction** notifies you when you change the account of a transaction you have already entered. This is new in Quicken 2011.

Write Checks Write Checks options affect the way the checks you enter with the Write Checks window appear when printed.

- **Printed Date Style** enables you to select a four-digit or two-digit date style.
- **Spell Currency Units** tells Quicken to spell out the currency amount in the second Amount field.
- **Allow Entry Of Extra Message On Check** displays an additional text box for a message in the Write Checks window. The message you enter is printed on the check in a place where it cannot be seen if the check is mailed in a window envelope.
- **Print Categories On Voucher Checks** prints category information, including splits and tags, on the voucher part of voucher checks. This option affects only voucher-style checks.
- **Change Date Of Checks To Date When Printed** automatically prints the print date, rather than the transaction date, on each check.

Downloaded Transactions   Downloaded Transactions options, which are shown next, control the way Quicken handles transactions downloaded into it from your financial institution. You learn more about downloading transactions into Quicken in Chapter 5.

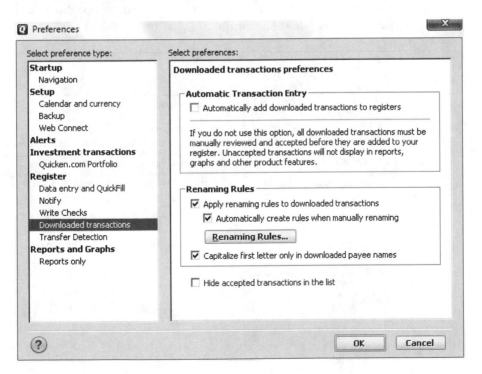

- **Automatically Add Downloaded Transactions To Registers** saves manually reviewing and accepting each transaction and possibly leaving an unaccepted transaction out of Quicken reports and graphs.
- **Apply Renaming Rules To Downloaded Transactions** turns on Quicken's renaming feature, which is discussed in Chapter 5.
- **Automatically Create Rules When Manually Renaming** tells Quicken to create renaming rules automatically based on transactions you rename manually.
- **Renaming Rules** displays the Renaming Rules dialog, which you can use to create, modify, and remove renaming rules.
- **Capitalize First Letter Only In Downloaded Payee Names** capitalizes just the first letter of a payee name for a downloaded transaction.
- **Hide Accepted Transactions In The List** does not display transactions that have already been accepted in the Downloaded Transactions list.

Transfer Detection   This option, new in Quicken 2011, tells Quicken to review each downloaded transaction to see if is matched with another transaction, as seen next. If you select this option, when Quicken finds matched transactions you have two options:

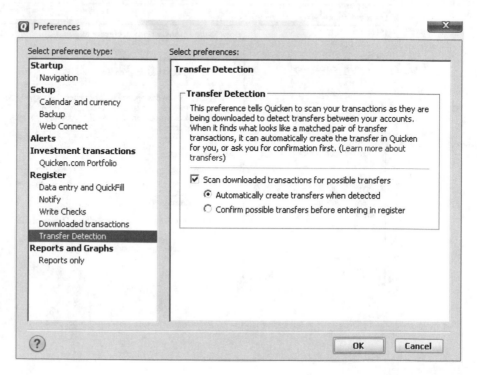

- **Automatically Create Transfer When Detected** makes the transfer from the one account to the other automatically and enters the transaction in both registers.
- **Confirm Possible Transfers Before Entering In Register** directs Quicken to ask you whether the transaction is, indeed, a transfer.

Reports and Graphs

Reports And Graphs preferences include two categories of options for creating reports and graphs. Creating reports and graphs is discussed in detail in Chapter 8.

Reports And Graphs Preferences   Reports And Graphs options, shown next, enable you to set default options for creating reports and graphs.

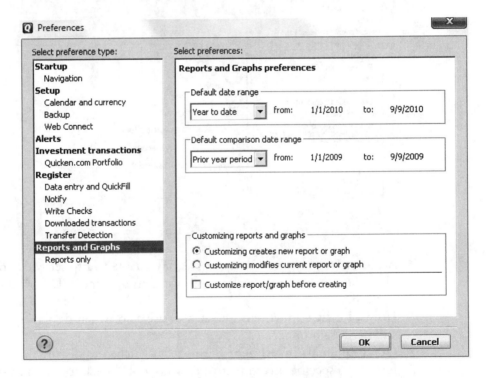

- **Default Date Range** and **Default Comparison Date Range** enable you to specify a default range for regular and comparison reports. Choose an option from each drop-down list. If you choose Custom, you can enter exact dates.
- **Customizing Reports And Graphs** options determine how reports and graphs are customized and what happens when they are. Customizing Creates New Report Or Graph, which is the default setting, creates a subreport based

on the report you customize. Customizing Modifies Current Report Or Graph changes the report you customize without creating a subreport.

- **Customize Report/Graph Before Creating** tells Quicken to offer to customize a report or graph when you choose one.

Reports Only   This group of options, which is shown next, applies only to reports.

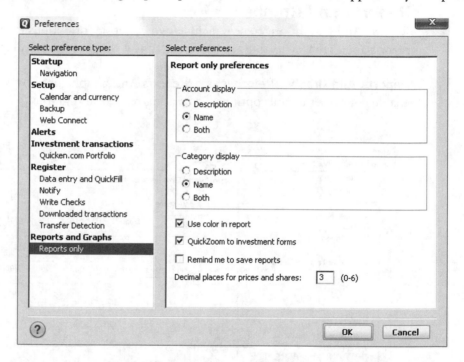

- **Account Display** and **Category Display** enable you to set what you want to display for each account or category listed in the report: Description, Name, or Both.
- **Use Color In Report** tells Quicken to use color when displaying report titles and negative numbers.
- **QuickZoom To Investment Forms** tells Quicken to display the investment form for a specific investment when you double-click it in an investment report. With this check box turned off, Quicken displays the investment register transaction entry instead.
- **Remind Me To Save Reports** tells Quicken to ask whether you want to save a customized report when you close the report window.
- **Decimal Places For Prices And Shares** enables you to specify the number of decimal places to display for per-share security prices and number of shares in investment reports.

Converting from Microsoft Money

Welcome to Quicken, Microsoft Money user! This document will help explain some of the similarities and a few differences as you start using Quicken. We'll talk about what you are used to seeing in Microsoft Money and what the same process looks like on your Quicken screen. Along the way, you'll see the many features that Quicken offers.

Converting Your Data Files from Money to Quicken

As you prepare to convert your Money data files to Quicken, there are a few things you can do in Money to make the conversion easier. Review your files as shown here, and ensure that all of your Money records are complete and up to date.

 If you are converting Money data files to versions of Quicken prior to Quicken 2010, see the information Intuit has available at http://quicken.intuit.com/support and type **Microsoft Money** into the Search box.

Before You Start Your Conversion

To ensure a smooth transition, first review your Money data files. Performing each of the following actions will improve the chances of a good conversion:

- Clean up your Payee list to ensure there are no duplicate names because of mistyping. It's a lot easier to do this *before* you convert than to take the time afterwards.
- Review your Category list and remove any that are unused.
- Review your online recurring payments and calendar to ensure you have stopped them. You'll be setting them up again in Quicken.
- Check that your financial institution can download into Quicken (most can) and how that download is accomplished.

To see what download types are provided by your financial institution, go to http://web.intuit.com/personal/ quicken/search.cfm.

- Reconcile all of your accounts prior to converting.
- Ensure that all of your downloaded transactions are complete and up to date.
- Review your account names in Money to ensure they are less than the Quicken maximum character length (40 characters), and change them if necessary.
- Consider running a repair on your Money file before you start the conversion to ensure that no problems exist in your file.

Your Money category names, payee names, and notes and memos do not have this same 40-character limit, and the Quicken file converter will truncate filenames if needed.

Both Quicken and Money are, by default, installed in the Program Files folder on your main hard drive (usually the "C" drive). However, you can keep your data files in whatever folder you choose, as discussed in Chapter 1. After you have installed Quicken, it is time to convert your files (those with the file extension .mny) from Microsoft Money to Quicken.

In order to convert your .mny files, you must have both Quicken and Microsoft Money installed on the same computer.

You should have no problem converting all of your bank transactions, your checking, savings, credit card, and investment accounts. Likewise, your category and other name information should also convert cleanly after you have made any necessary changes to the number of characters in each name. Remember that any recurring payments you have set up in Money, such as monthly insurance payments, will have to be canceled in Money and reset in Quicken.

Converting Your Money Files

Quicken 2011 can convert Microsoft Money Plus and Money 2008 files. If you have an earlier version, as of the date of this writing, you can download a trial version of Money Plus (2008) from their download website.

Microsoft has also made a Sunset version of the program available. As all online and support services end in January 2011, the Sunset version allows Money users to keep their data and enter new items manually. This link is to the Microsoft Download Center, where you can download this version: http://www.microsoft.com/downloads/en/confirmation.aspx?FamilyID= 60302e1e-207e-4710-ac80-d19c22e47488&displaylang=en.

Convert your old Money data files to Money 2008 files, and convert from the 2008 files into Quicken. Before you start your conversion, verify the balances in each of your Money accounts. Print a list of these balances to compare with your Quicken balances after the conversion. To print the list:

1. In Money, click Account List. Ensure that each of your accounts is displayed.
2. Click File | Print to print the report.

Then, check these account balances after the conversion to ensure the information has come across cleanly.

Begin the Conversion

To begin converting your .mny files:

1. Install and launch Quicken. The Welcome To Quicken window appears as seen in Figure C-1.

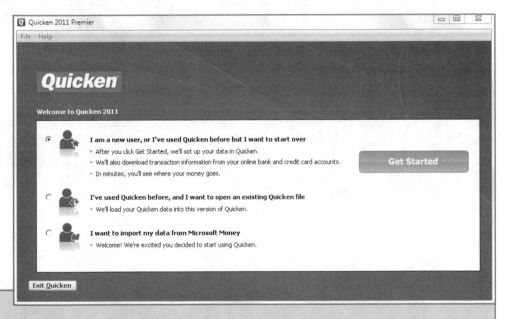

Figure C-1 • The Welcome To Quicken window lets you tell Quicken how you want to begin.

2. As seen in Figure C-1, from the three choices available, choose I Want To Import My Data From Microsoft Money, and then click the Get Started button.

3. A blank Quicken Home page opens as seen in Figure C-2.

4. Quicken will locate your .mny file and start the conversion automatically.

Figure C-2 • From a blank Quicken Home page, you can manually import your Microsoft Money data file.

5. Quicken starts to convert the .mny file on this computer. If the conversion does not start immediately, click File | File Import | Microsoft Money file as seen in Figure C-3.

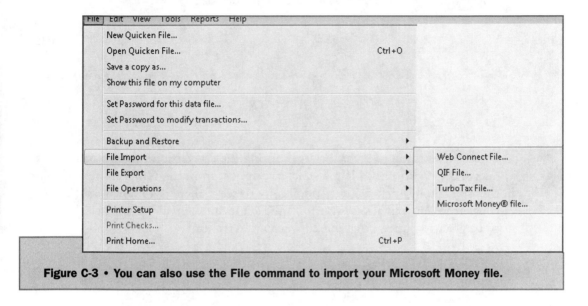

Figure C-3 • You can also use the File command to import your Microsoft Money file.

6. A message box appears showing the progress of the file being imported.

After the files have been converted, a message box appears telling you that your Microsoft Money data file has been imported, as seen earlier. Click Read Next Steps to see a list of steps you may take to ensure a smooth conversion. Click Close to close the Help dialog. Your converted file opens to the Home tab's Main View.

You import your Money data files into a new, empty Quicken file. Do *not* try to convert Money data files into an existing Quicken file with data in it. If you try to do this, you will see a message warning you that you'll have to create a new, empty file as seen next. Click Create File to do so.

 If you see warning or error messages during the conversion process, such as the ones shown here, click Help | Quicken Support from the Quicken menu bar or choose Help | Quicken Live Community to see if there is a known issue about your error. You can also visit http://quicken.intuit.com/support/articles/getting-started/upgrading-and-conversion/7416.html.

Warning Messages

During the conversion process, you may see the following warning messages:

- WARNING: One or more accounts in Money is in the middle of a reconciliation.
- WARNING: Account bank name truncated to: …
- WARNING: Transaction memo truncated to: …
- WARNING: Payee memo truncated to: …
- WARNING: Address notes truncated to: …

As you can see, some of these errors refer to issues that you fixed if you followed the "Before You Start Your Conversion" tips provided earlier in this chapter.

Using the View Log

After the conversion is complete, if there are some discrepancies, Quicken displays a message asking you to view a log file of the differences, as seen next. Click View Log to see the list and explanation, as seen in Figure C-4.

You can see this file at any time from within Quicken. From the Quicken menu bar, click Help | Log Files | Microsoft Money: File Import Results.

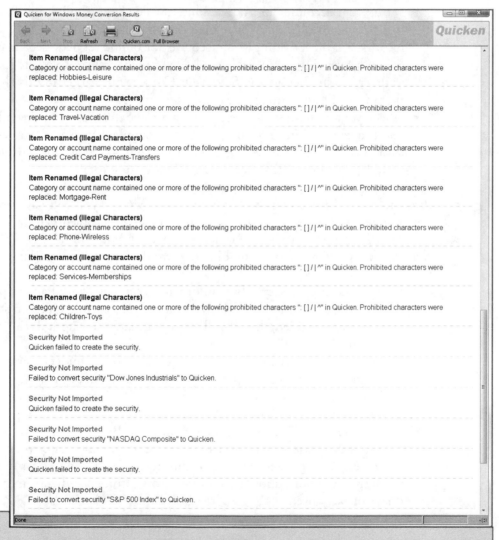

Figure C-4 • Quicken explains any discrepancies found after importing your Money data files.

First Steps in Quicken

After you have completed your successful conversion, there are a few steps you should complete before continuing.

- Review your account and payee names to ensure they converted properly. Because of the slight differences between the two programs in maximum character length and permitted characters, you may need to change the names of some of your payees or accounts.
- Set up your accounts for Transaction Download and Online Bill Pay. Any instructions you had in Money may need to be reset in Quicken. For more information on activating your accounts for online services, see Chapter 5.
- Set your recurring payments as described in Chapter 5. If you stopped them as described in "Before You Start Your Conversion" earlier in this chapter, there won't be any duplicate payments.
- Check your account's balances. There are some differences between how the two programs record information. As an example, Quicken separates the cash portion of your investing account into a banking account, while Money included this linked cash account in the investing total.

 Remember that if you had two separate files in Money, you will have two separate files in Quicken. For example, if you had a file called Family Business and another file named Home Accounts in Money, you will have two files in Quicken as well. You cannot combine the two during the conversion.

- Review, and if necessary, adjust information on loans with balloon payments. Money stores the amount of the balloon payment, while Quicken stores the balloon amortized length and will try to estimate the length during the conversion.
- Create a new retirement plan and, if necessary, a new budget using the tools found in Quicken. See Chapter 14 for information about planning with Quicken and Chapter 16 to create a budget. The information you created in Money does not transfer into Quicken.
- If you were using Microsoft Money Home and Business, all of your accounts, categories, transactions, payees, and scheduled bills will be quickly converted into Quicken Home and Business edition. However, some of the more specific information, such as inventory, project, and customer data, does not carry over.

Your Quicken accounts are shown on the Account Bar at the left of the Quicken window. You can also see them in the Account List. Open the Account List by pressing CTRL-A or click Tools | Account List from the Quicken menu bar.

 To show two lines in your register, from any account register, click Account Actions and click Two-line Display as shown here. To toggle between one- and two-line display for Investment Transaction lists, use Edit | Preferences and select Investment Transactions in the Select Preference Type pane. In the List Display drop-down menu, select One Line or Two Line.

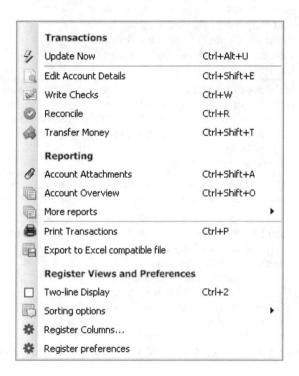

Bills Tab

The Bills tab in Quicken provides all of your bill information in one location. All of the bills you have scheduled appear on the list, and you can add new reminders with a simple click.

Table C-1 gives some comparisons to what you see in Microsoft Money.

Description	Quicken	Money
Calendar	Click Bills	View As	Calendar to see a colorful and complete calendar. Simply double-click or right-click a bill to enter the transaction.	Click Bills	Bills Summary	Show Calendar	Enter In Register to open the Record Payment window into an account.
Recurring Payments	In Quicken, recurring payments are called reminders. To set up a new reminder, simply right-click a transaction in an account's register. From the context menu that appears, click Schedule Bill Or Deposit to open the Add Transaction Reminder dialog, as discussed earlier in this book. You can also click the Add Reminder button in the Bills tab button bar.	Switch to Advanced Bills, and click the Bills tab. From the Bills Summary page, click New	*transaction type*. Complete the Create A Recurring Bill dialog, and click OK.
Printing Checks	From any account's register, select a transaction. From the Check Number drop-down list, select Print Check. Click File	Print Checks to open the Select Checks To Print dialog and print the check.	Click Banking	Account List *account name*. Right-click in the Num field and then choose Print This Transaction	Enter. Click File	Print Checks.
Online Payments	Activate online payments through your bank or Quicken Bill Pay service. From the Account Bar, right-click the account name. Choose Edit Account to open the Account Details dialog. Choose the Online Services tab. If your financial institution offers it, click Activate Bill Pay. See Chapter 5 for more information about setting up online payments.	Set up through your bank, MSN Bill Pay, or another bill-paying service. Click Banking	Account List	Common Tasks	Manage Online Services.

Table C-1 • Reviewing and Paying Bills in Quicken versus Microsoft Money

Projected Balances

Quicken can tell you what the projected balances of any (or all) of your accounts will be based on the transactions you have scheduled, as seen in Figure C-5. In the Bills tab, click Projected Balances, and select the account and time range you want to see. This is similar to the Forecast Cash Flow in Money.

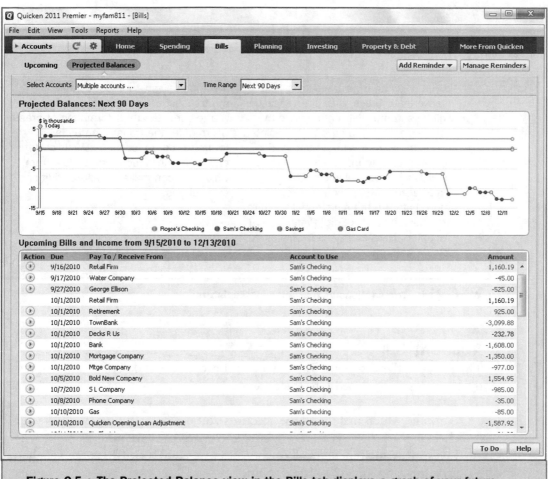

Figure C-5 • The Projected Balance view in the Bills tab displays a graph of your future account balances.

Account Registers

The Account Actions menu in each account register gives you the tools you need to update your transactions, write and print checks, transfer funds from one account to another, run reports, and change your register views, as described in Table C-2.

Description	Quicken	Money
Move through the account register	Press TAB.	Press TAB.
ENTER key	If you are entering a transaction and inadvertently press ENTER, the transaction will be automatically entered into the register, even if you have not completed the entry. To return to the transaction, simply click it to make any necessary changes. You can also set your Preferences to use the ENTER key to move between the register fields. From the menu bar, click Edit | Preferences | Register | Data Entry And Quickfill. Select Use Enter Key To Move Between Fields.	If you press ENTER without completing the transaction, a dialog appears asking you to complete the information or press OK to enter the transaction as is. To return to the transaction, double-click to open the transaction form dialog, from which you can make changes, additions, or deletions.

Table C-2 • Working with Transactions in Your Account Registers

Account Bar

The Account Bar displays a list of all of your accounts. As described in Chapter 1, the accounts are grouped into three areas:

- Banking, which includes those accounts you use for spending, such as your checking and cash accounts, savings, and credit card accounts
- Investing, which includes all of your brokerage, 401(k), IRAs and Keogh accounts, and any 529 Plan accounts
- Property & Debt, which includes all of your asset and liability accounts

Just as you would do in Microsoft Money, simply click any of the account names to open its register or, for investing accounts, its Transaction List.

Account Details

The Account Details dialog, shown next, shows the financial institution where the account is held, what you have set as the minimum balance (useful if your institution offers free checking if you maintain a minimum balance), the interest rate for the account if there is one, and other useful information.

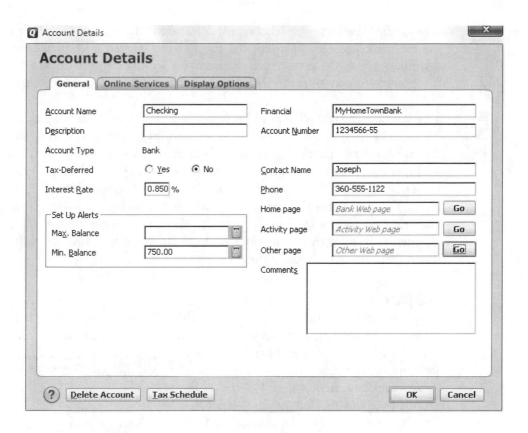

 If you set Money to automatically place a decimal point in all transactions, you can accomplish the same task in Quicken by choosing Edit | Preferences | Register | Transaction Entry | Automatically Place Decimal Point. For example, if you enter **12345**, Quicken will enter it as 123.45. Otherwise, Quicken will enter this transaction as 12,345.00.

Downloading Transactions

In Money, many users posted future transactions into account registers and then downloaded information from the bank and reconciled these entries. In Quicken, you may schedule recurring transactions in much the same way. However, you must tell Quicken to enter those transactions before you download. Otherwise, the scheduled transactions will show as past due and be duplicated by the download from your financial institution. After you have downloaded your transactions, carefully review the download to ensure that what the bank paid and the scheduled transaction you entered earlier are the same amount. Ensure as well that you have not told Quicken to automatically enter

downloaded transactions. To ensure this feature is turned off, click Edit |
Preferences | Register | Downloaded Transactions, and, if necessary, clear the
Automatically Add Downloaded Transactions To Registers check box. See
Chapters 5, 6, and 10 for more information about downloaded transactions.

You can move a transaction in Quicken in a similar way to moving one in
Money. Right-click any transaction in an account's register, and from the
resulting context menu, choose Move Transaction. You can also do this with
multiple transactions. Either hold down the SHIFT key and choose a group of
transactions, or hold down the CTRL key and choose transactions from several
dates. This highlights the transactions. Right-click to open the context menu,
and select Move Transaction(s). From the Move Transaction dialog that appears,
choose the account to which you want to move this transaction from the drop-
down list. Click OK to close the dialog.

Reports

Quicken includes robust reporting capabilities. You can create a report for any
period, using any information you choose. If you are accustomed to using
Advanced Reports in Microsoft Money, you'll
feel very comfortable with Quicken reports.

You can see a menu for all Quicken
reports by choosing Reports | Reports &
Graphs Center to open the Reports and
Graphs Center as seen in Figure C-6. In
addition, several of the tabs have a Reports
button that directs you to specific reports for
that section, as seen here. See Chapter 8 for a
complete discussion of reports in Quicken.

The Reports and Graphs Center gives you
options for colorful graphs that are
sometimes easier to read than a report full
of numbers, as seen in the example shown on
page 578.

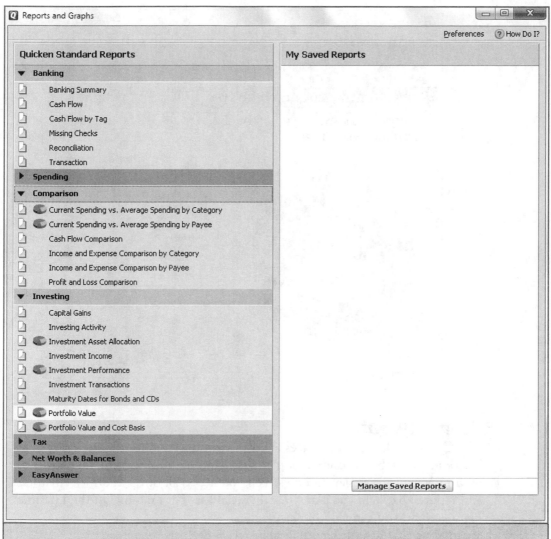

Figure C-6 • Quicken's graphs and charts make understanding your financial information easy.

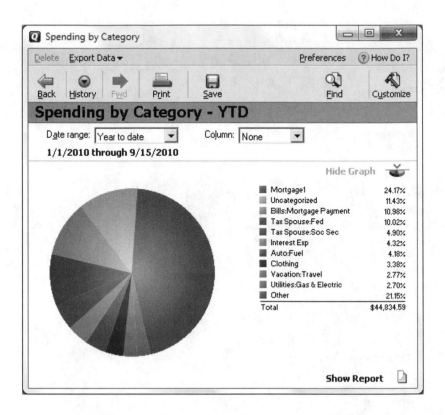

Planning Tab

The Quicken Planning tab places all of your budget and forecasting tools in one location. This tab is a combination of the Planning, Budget, and Tax tabs you used in Microsoft Money. In one screen you access all of the tools, calculators, and reports that help you plan your financial life. For example, in the Lifetime Planner view, you can tell Quicken facts about yourself and your family to plan for major expenses in your life, as seen in Figure C-7.

Along with your budget tools, the Planning tab includes a number of tax tools, as shown here. These include online tax calculators and links to common tax questions.

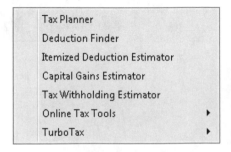

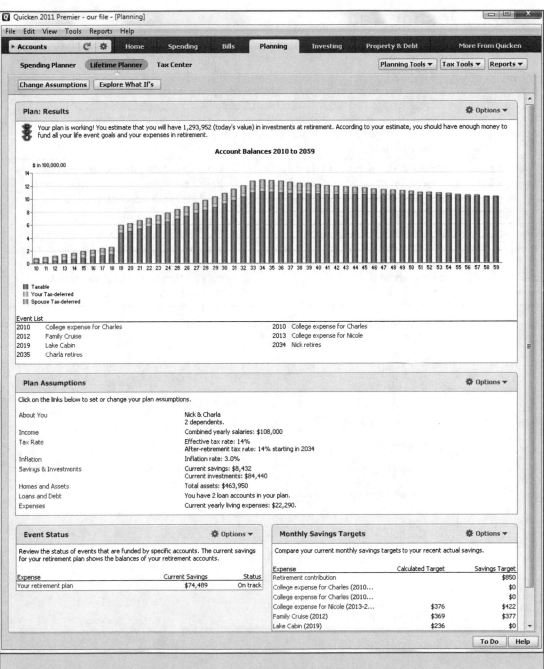

Figure C-7 • Quicken helps you plan with the Lifetime Planner.

Investing Tab

The Quicken Investing tab displays all of your investing information, as described in Table C-3.

Description	Quicken	Money
Retirement accounts	Does not allow cash accounts to be linked to retirement accounts. They are shown separately.	Allows linked cash accounts.
Investing information	Click the Investing tab and then choose Portfolio to see the current standing of your investing and retirement accounts.	Click Investing tab and then choose My Investing Tools | Portfolio Manager to view just your account information.
Investing tools	Choose View | Classic Menus. Then click Investing | Investing Tools from the menu bar to access several tools, as shown next.	The Investing tab opens a window with investing tips, the Investing Advisor, and several other tools. You see other information by clicking the Investing bar at the left of the window.

Table C-3 • The Different Activities on the Investing Tab

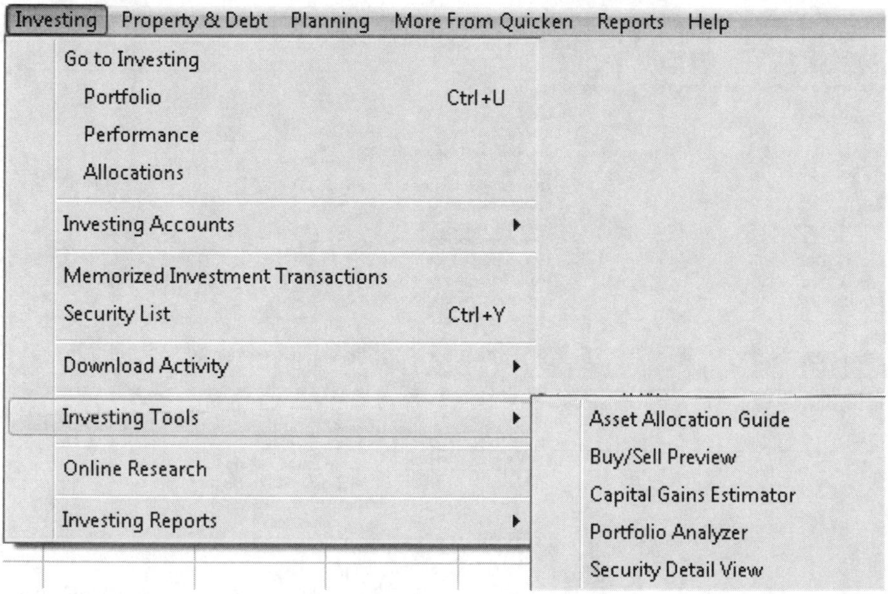

If you created reminders in Money to purchase investments on a regular schedule, you can do the same in Quicken.

1. From your investing account, memorize the transaction you want to schedule. To memorize a transaction, right-click the transaction and choose Memorize Investment Transaction. A dialog will appear letting you know this payee is about to be memorized. Click OK.
2. Press CTRL-J to open the Manage Bill & Income Reminder dialog. From the menu bar, click Create New | Scheduled Transaction Group. The Create Transaction Group dialog appears, as seen next.
3. Enter a name for your group, the account you want to use, the next due date, and the frequency. Choose Investment and check the items you want to remember.
4. Click OK to close the dialog.

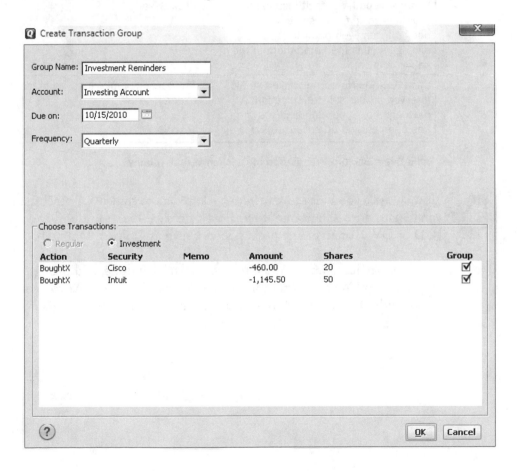

How Quicken Backup Procedures Differ from Money

As discussed in Appendix A, Table C-5 describes the backup procedures in Quicken compared to how you backed up in Microsoft Money.

Quicken	Money
From the menu bar, click File | Backup And Restore. Choose Back Up Quicken File, or from anyplace in Quicken hold down CTRL and press B.	From the menu bar, click File | Backup, and type a name for the backup file.
Either accept the default location for your backed-up file or select a new one. You can even enter today's date to distinguish this file from others in the same location.	Click Save.
Click Back Up Now. The backed-up file is saved in your selected location. A message box appears telling you the file has been backed up successfully.	The backed-up file is saved in the selected folder.

Table C-4 • Backup Procedures in Quicken versus Money

It is always a good idea to save your backup data to someplace other than your main hard drive. Choose an external hard drive, a flash (thumb) drive, a recordable CD or DVD, or an online backup service such as Quicken Online Backup.

These are just some of the Quicken screens, windows, and dialogs with which you'll be working as you transition from Microsoft Money. As you continue to work with Quicken, you'll find that it is intuitive and helpful. Again, welcome to Quicken!

Index

583

● **F**

● **G**

Y